History of Nebraska

UNIVERSITY OF NEBRASKA PRESS · LINCOLN

History of Nebraska

By James C. Olson

LINE DRAWINGS BY FRANZ ALTSCHULER

ADDITIONAL LINE DRAWINGS BY JACK BRODIE

Publishers on the Plains

UNP

Copyright 1955, © 1966 by the University of Nebraska Press

Library of Congress Catalog Card Number 54–8444
International Standard Book Number 0–8032–5790–2
International Standard Book Number 0–8032–0135–4 (cloth)

First Bison Book printing: January 1974

Most recent printing shown by first digit below:

2   3   4   5   6   7   8   9   10

The Bison Book edition is reproduced from the
second edition of *History of Nebraska*.

Manufactured in the United States of America

Dedicated TO THE PIONEERS OF NEBRASKA

Preface to the Second Edition

THE FIRST edition of this volume was published at the time of Nebraska's territorial centennial; this edition, at the time of the centennial of statehood. The general plan of the book remains the same, although the work has been brought up to date by including an account of the years, 1954–1965, and occasional changes, resulting from new research, have been made. The unicameral legislature, covered in but a section of a chapter in the first edition, has been given a separate chapter in this. Although much research still remains to be done on the history of Nebraska, a gratifying amount of solid work has been accomplished during the last ten years, much of it by graduate students in history at the University of Nebraska, and a rather considerable amount has been published. Partly to call attention to recent research, and partly to make this edition more useful to students, the "Suggested Readings" at the end of each chapter have been eliminated in favor of a more extended bibliographical essay. Two appendices list the governors and secretaries of the territory, and the governors of the state.

Again, in the preparation of this edition, members of the staff of the Nebraska State Historical Society, and particularly Marvin F. Kivett, Director, and Donald F. Danker, Historian, were most helpful.

JAMES C. OLSON

Preface

THERE HAS long been need for a one-volume general survey of the history of Nebraska which might serve as an introduction to the history of the state for both the college student and the general reader. This book represents an effort to meet that need.

No one can be more painfully aware than the author of the difficulties inherent in trying to encompass the history of one of our states within the covers of one brief volume. Necessarily, much of interest and value must be omitted, and it is easy to find fault with the author's judgment in this matter. In Nebraska, as in many other states, the problem of writing a general survey is further complicated by the fact that much of the basic research upon which sound synthesis must be based still remains to be done. Within these limitations, however, it is hoped that this survey will serve to introduce the student to the state's history and whet his appetite to study it further.

Sources have not been indicated except where it was felt that to do so might be of interest to the general reader. The "Suggested Readings" at the end of each chapter are not presented as a bibliography, but simply as suggestions for further reading in sources which, it is hoped, may be generally available in Nebraska.

I have drawn heavily upon many graduate theses prepared under the auspices of the Department of History at the University of Nebraska, most of which, unfortunately, remain unpublished. I should like at this time to acknowledge my indebtedness to the graduate students who prepared those theses. I should like also to acknowledge specific assistance received from a number of persons in the preparation of this book. Various members of the staff of the Nebraska State Historical Society have been particularly helpful. Marvin F. Kivett, director of the museum, read the chapter on "The Original Occupants" and made many useful suggestions. Dr. John B. White, librarian, Donald F. Danker, archivist, and Myrtle D. Berry, picture librarian, gave the entire manuscript the advantage of their specialized knowledge in various phases of Nebraska's history. Dr. White assisted in the preparation of the "Suggested Readings" and in many other ways rendered valuable reference assistance. Miss Berry assembled the photographs. Stanley D. Sohl, museum artist, prepared the maps. The manuscript has profited much from suggestions made by Professor Edward Everett Dale of the University of Oklahoma, and Professor James L. Sellers of the University of Nebraska. James E. Lawrence, president of the Nebraska State Historical Society, has given me the advantage of his profound understanding of the forces that have shaped Nebraska life. Miss Emily Schossberger and her staff at the University of Nebraska Press, particularly Mr. Stanley Moon, have rendered invaluable assistance in the preparation of the manuscript for publication.

For myself and the Nebraska State Historical Society, I wish to express appreciation to the Board of Regents of the University of Nebraska and the University of Nebraska Foundation for making this publication possible.

Finally, I should like to thank my wife and daughters for cheerfully accepting the schedule necessary for the completion of this work in the territorial centennial year.

JAMES C. OLSON

The quotation on pages 5–6 is reprinted from *The Great Plains,* by Walter Prescott Webb, by permission of Ginn and Company.

Table of Contents

Picture sections follow pp. 20, 148, 180, 276, 308.

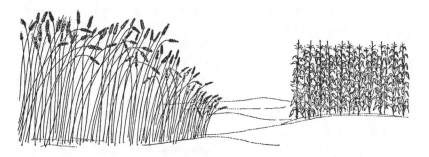

A Look at the Land

WHEN MAJOR STEPHEN H. LONG of the Army Engineers returned from his epochal expedition to the Rocky Mountains in 1820, he confirmed what many Americans had suspected all along—that most of the area between the Missouri River and the Rocky Mountains was a vast desert wasteland. "In regard to this extensive section of country," he wrote, "I do not hesitate in giving the opinion, that it is almost wholly unfit for cultivation, and of course uninhabitable by a people depending on agriculture for their subsistence." Dr. Edwin James, chronicler of the expedition, stated that he had "no fear of giving too unfavourable an account" of the region. It was "an unfit residence for any but a nomad population." He hoped it would remain forever, "the unmolested haunt of the native hunter, the bison, and the jackall."

Lewis and Clark, along the Missouri in 1804–06, had suspected the same thing. Lieutenant Zebulon M. Pike, who went out along the Republican in 1806 and then down to Santa Fe, had written of "barren soil, parched and dried up for eight months in the year," and had hazarded a guess that America's western Plains would "become in time equally celebrated as the sandy desarts [sic] of Africa." Even Thomas Jefferson—who, it must be admitted, had never visited the West—shared the popular misconception, referring to the "immense and trackless deserts" to be found in the region.

With Major Long's scientific stamp of approval, the idea became well

3

fixed, and by the end of the first quarter of the nineteenth century most Americans shared the notion that the region between the Missouri and the Rockies was a vast, uninhabitable desert. It is little wonder that in the late Twenties and early Thirties the suggestion that the area west of the Missouri be set aside as a permanent home for the Indians found ready acceptance. As the years wore on, others added their testimony to the cumulative condemnation of the Plains—Josiah Gregg, Francis Parkman, Maurice O'Connor Morris, Samuel Bowles, Horace Greeley, John H. Beadle, Ferdinand V. Hayden, and a host of lesser figures. Historians, geographers, and journalists now supplied with an abundance of apparently reliable source material, described in detail the Great American Desert.

There were a few who disagreed with the prevailing notion. As early as 1817, John Bradbury, the English naturalist, wrote that Americans were misled in their thinking about the Plains because they were accustomed to "a profusion of timber." To say that whites could not inhabit a timberless land simply because Americans had not yet pushed settlement beyond the region of the great timber was, in Bradbury's eyes, sheer nonsense. He expressed a definite opinion that the region could be cultivated "and that, in the process of time, it will not only be peopled and cultivated, but it will be one of the most beautiful countries in the world." Bayard Taylor, who went through the country in 1866, also disagreed with the common view. As a result of reflection on his trip to Colorado, via the Smoky-hill route, he was "fast inclining toward the notion that there is no American Desert on this [the eastern] side of the Rocky Mountains."

By the time Taylor's book appeared in 1867, a great many people had acquired a vested interest in the land west of the Missouri. Nebraska had been admitted to the Union and was in the process of claiming its landed endowment; millions of acres had been or shortly would be withdrawn for the benefit of the Union Pacific and the Burlington railroads; speculators were busy locating large tracts which they hoped to turn at a profit; settlement by homesteaders was well under way. These people were gambling that the desert concept was erroneous. Experience on the wet prairies east of the Missouri had demonstrated that one doesn't need trees to grow bountiful crops of corn, wheat, and oats. A brief experience west of the Missouri had shown that this area, too, would produce good crops. The Missouri then was not the dividing line between farm land and desert. But where was it? Even the most pessimistic of the early observers had admitted that some of the land just west of the Missouri was not bad—some, impressed by the rolling hills and tall, waving grass, had even praised its beauty and fertility. Almost all agreed, however, that as one got out on the flat land—well before reaching Fort Kearny—the country began to deteriorate: the grass became short and parched, streams failed and even the creek bottoms seemed unable to support anything more than low, sickly shrubs.

Nebraskans were a long time finding out where that line was. Indeed, a whole generation of them stoutly denied that it existed at all, and when in 1878 Major John Wesley Powell, chief of the Department of the Interior's Survey of the Rocky Mountain Region, stated that non-irrigable farming could not be carried on west of the one-hundredth meridian because the area had less than twenty inches of annual rainfall, a host—including Samuel Aughey, chairman of the Department of Natural Sciences at the University of Nebraska—denounced his findings as bureaucratic nonsense. Major Powell, of course, was not talking about a desert—he was talking about a region in which one would have to irrigate if he were going to farm safely and successfully over the years. There was a vast difference.

Indeed, Major Powell was much more optimistic regarding the prospects of western Nebraska and Kansas than Ferdinand V. Hayden, Chief of the United States Geological Survey, had been six years earlier. Hayden's report of 1872 had predicted that the occupation of the area would be indefinitely postponed because of insufficient rainfall, a lack of building material, the scarcity of fuel, and an insufficient number of running streams to provide water for livestock. Though he was much and unjustly abused by his own generation for his pessimism about the West, Major Powell was, if anything, too optimistic—there were many areas *east* of the one-hundredth meridian where farming needed the aid of irrigation. In general, however, Major Powell's appraisal was correct. It is a pity his contemporaries failed to appreciate it. If they had, some of the chapters in our history would have been vastly different.

The Plains *did* present a problem to the American pioneer. Perhaps nowhere has the nature of that problem been better stated than by Walter Prescott Webb in *The Great Plains:*

The Great Plains offered such a contrast to the region east of the ninety-eighth meridian, the region with which American civilization had been familiar until about 1840, as to bring about a marked change in the ways of pioneering and living. For two centuries American pioneers had been working out a technique for the utilization of the humid regions east of the Mississippi River. They had found solutions for their problems and were conquering the frontier at a steadily accelerating rate. Then in the early nineteenth century they crossed the Mississippi and came out on the great plains, an environment with which they had had no experience. The result was a complete though temporary breakdown of the machinery and ways of pioneering. . . . .

As one contrasts the civilization of the Great Plains with that of the eastern timberland, one sees what may be called an institutional *fault* (comparable to a geological fault) running from middle Texas to Illinois or Dakota, roughly following the ninety-eighth meridian. At this *fault* the ways of life and of living changed. Practically every institution that was carried across it was either broken and remade or else greatly altered. The ways of travel, the weapons, the method of tilling the soil, the plows and other agricultural implements, and even the laws themselves were modified. When people first crossed this line they did not immediately realize the imperceptible change that had taken place in their environment, nor, more is the tragedy, did they forsee the full consequences which that change was to bring in their own characters and in their modes of life. In the new region—level, timberless, and semi-arid—they were thrown by mother necessity into the clutch of new circumstances. Their plight has been stated in this way: east of the Mississippi civilization stood on three legs—land, water, and timber; west of the Mississippi not one but two of these legs were withdrawn,—water and timber,—and civilization was left on one leg—land. It is small wonder that it toppled over in temporary failure.

Whether you accept Webb's ninety-eighth meridian, which enters the state at Niobrara and leaves it at Superior, or Powell's one-hundredth, which runs down the main street of Cozad, it is clear that a rather considerable portion of Nebraska is in this "problem area" of the Plains, and that much of the history of the state must necessarily be a chronicle of man's adaptation to the Plains. The chronicle is complicated, however, by the fact that not all of Nebraska lies within the Plains —the state is indeed in the transitional area and for that reason, perhaps, its problems are more complicated.

In any event, I want to preface this survey of Nebraska with "a look at the land," a consideration of the environmental factors which have to a marked degree shaped the history of the people of this state.

THE LAND

On any generalized, small-scale map of the United States, Nebraska appears as part of the great prairie-plains flatlands comprising the central portion of the country. Within this general classification, however, there is considerable diversity. There is a gradual rise in altitude, at the rate of about nine to ten feet per mile, from 825 feet in Richardson County in the southeastern corner of the state to 5,330 feet in Banner and Kimball counties on the western border. There are considerable areas of flat land in the south-central portion of the state and on the high table around Alliance, but most of the state's surface has been roughened by glacial action, and by wind and water erosion.

All of the state lies within the drainage area of the Missouri River, which forms its eastern border. The Platte, most important of the Missouri's tributaries, sprawls like a huge snake across the state, its broad valley providing easy access to the mountains. The Platte's principal tributaries are the Loup and the Elkhorn, which drain the Sandhills. The swift Niobrara flows across the northern part of the state. The South Platte section is drained by the Republican and the Blue, tributaries of the Kansas River.

Topographically, Nebraska is divided into some nineteen regions, which embrace the following general topographic types: alluvial lowlands, loess, sandhills, high plains, and bad lands. The topography of the state can perhaps best be understood by a look at the accompanying map. The alluvial lowlands lie along the rivers, principally the Missouri, the Platte, and the Republican, with the broad, fertile Platte Valley being the most important. The loess region occupies about 42,000 of the state's 77,237 square miles and includes rich farming areas in the eastern, central, and southern parts of the state. There are both loess plains and loess hills. In the plains—generally south of the Platte and west of Saunders, Lancaster, and Gage counties—the land flows in gentle waves toward the southeast; along the Missouri and between the Platte and the Sandhills the waves converge into moderate hills. The Sandhills, the state's most distinctive topographic feature, occupy some 18,000 square miles west and northwest of the loess region, with outlyers extending to the southwest as far as Dundy County. The Sandhills, for the most part, consist of sloping hills twenty-five to a hundred feet higher than the valleys between but sometimes stretching into gentle plains as well as rising into sharp pinnacles. They are dotted with rich valleys, lakes, and fertile table lands. West and northwest of the Sandhills stretch the high plains, some 12,000 square miles of level table lands, broken occasionally by deep canyons. The general area includes two low groups of evergreen wooded mountains, the Wild Cat range in Scotts Bluff and Banner counties and the Pine Ridge in Sheridan, Dawes, and Sioux counties. Conspicuous on the plains are the rugged isolated buttes rising hundreds of feet above the surrounding tableland. The bad lands, or Pierre Hill region, occupy about 1,000 square miles, principally in Sioux County, with minor sections in Dawes

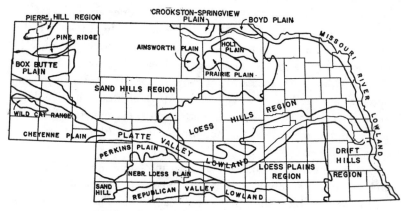

TOPOGRAPHIC REGIONS OF NEBRASKA

(Based on maps prepared under the direction of Dr. George E. Condra, Director, Division of Conservation and Survey, University of Nebraska.)

and Sheridan counties. Their weathered slopes and valleys, together with the Wild Cat range and the Pine Ridge, make northwestern Nebraska an area of rare scenic beauty. Their principal economic value is as range land.

Though topography is one of the most obvious physical phenomena —and during the period of settlement, along with such factors as vegetation, color of soil, and precipitation, it was about the only guide available for the selection of land—twentieth century research and soil surveys have added information about other, more important characteristics. We have come to appreciate that soil is the product of all the forces in the landscape. Since there are many combinations of biological, geological, and climatic conditions in the United States, there are correspondingly many types of soil. A detailed discussion of the nature of soil is outside the province of the historian—even a detailed description of all the various soil types existing in Nebraska is beyond the scope of this study. About all that can be attemped here is to indicate the principal soil associations of the United States—in which soils are grouped geographically rather than taxonomically—to be found in Nebraska. Again, a map is indispensable.

With the notable exception of the Sandhills and with certain other minor exceptions, the soils of Nebraska fall into three principal groups: Prairie soils, Chernozem soils, and Chestnut soils. Fortunately for a

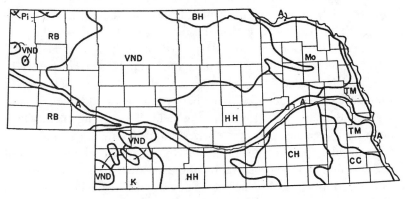

SOILS OF NEBRASKA

(From map, "Soil Associations of the United States," drafted by Robert F. Turnure and appearing as endpaper in *Soils & Men,* Yearbook of Agriculture, 1938 (Washington, Government Printing Office, n.d.)

KEY

A —Alluvial	CH —Crete-Hastings-Idana	RB —Rosebud-Bridgeport
BH —Boyd-Holt	K —Keith	TM —Tama-Marshall
CC —Carrington-Clyde	Mo —Moody	VND —Valentine-Nueces-
HH —Holdrege-Hall	Pi —Pierre	Dune Sand

state whose economy is almost entirely dependent upon the agricultural productivity of its soil, these are among the most productive soils in the world.

Prairie soils, found in southeastern Nebraska, are the soils of the great midwest corn belt. They have developed in cool, moderately humid climates under the influence of a grass vegetation. In Nebraska the principal series of Prairie soils are the Carrington-Clyde (CC) and the Tama-Marshall (TM). The Tama-Marshall soils are unexcelled for corn production, with oats ranking second, and clover, timothy hay, barley, and soybeans also appearing. Their only shortcoming is that their rolling surfaces erode easily under cultivation—and twentieth century farmers in southeastern Nebraska have become increasingly alert to the necessity for erosion control. The Carrington soils likewise are pre-eminently suited for cultivated crops, with corn again being the principal product. The Clyde soils find their best use as pastures and feed lots, although where drainage is adequate they, too, produce large yields of corn.

The dark brown to black Chernozem soils, which extend in a broad belt through the northern Plains, are the richest of all. In most years, however, they do not get sufficient rainfall to make them as productive as the slightly less fertile Prairie soils to the east. In Nebraska the principal series are the Boyd-Holt (BH), north of the Niobrara; the Moody (MO), in the northeastern part of the state; and the Holdrege-Hall (HH), in central Nebraska. The smooth areas of the Boyd-Holt soils are best suited for the production of oats, barley, and corn, although in most years inadequate rainfall reduces the yield. The rolling areas, which make up the greater part of the series, are primarily range lands. The basic problems throughout the Boyd-Holt region are the reduction of wind erosion and the conservation of the moisture supply. The Moody soils are corn-belt lands which compare favorably to the best corn lands of Iowa. Oats are the principal small grain and the soils are well adapted, too, for the production of legumes. Water erosion is a problem here also, and the more sandy types suffer from wind erosion in the dry years. The Holdrege-Hall soils constitute a general farming area, with corn the dominant crop, although their adaptability to winter wheat and alfalfa has in the twentieth century been steadily more successfully demonstrated.

Occupying the southwestern corner of the state and most of the panhandle west of the Sandhills are the Chestnut soils, which cover a vast area of the northern Plains from the Arkansas River to the Canadian border. The Keith (K) series, extending up into southwestern Nebraska from western Kansas, closely resembles the Holdrege-Hall soils to the east. The area is part of a high, smooth, treeless plain dissected at wide intervals by comparatively narrow valleys. In the twentieth century, Keith soils have been found pre-eminently suited to winter wheat, of which they produce good crops whenever moisture is adequate. The other series in Nebraska, Rosebud-Bridgeport (RB), extends northwestward from the Keith area through the panhandle. Wheat, corn, and oats have been the principal crops, with rye, barley, and potatoes also being grown. Relative acreage of each crop is apt to fluctuate with price levels. The non-arable lands provide range for cattle, and wild hay is cut on the meadows and smooth upper lands. Again, moisture is the principal problem.

The Sandhills, as distinctive in soil composition as they are topographically, occupy a larger area in Nebraska than any other single soil type. Classified by the soil survey as Valentine-Nueces-Dune sand, the soil is found only in Nebraska and in small areas in North Dakota, South Dakota, Colorado, and Texas. The Nebraska Sandhills are primarily Dune and Valentine sand, wind-blown sands released by disintegration of tertiary sandstones. They have accumulated considerable organic matter and with adequate moisture will support a relatively luxuriant grass cover. They are well adapted to livestock, providing range in summer and nutritious hay for winter use, but experience has shown that when broken with the plow they are apt to lose their grass cover with disastrous results.

Relatively important in south central Nebraska are the Crete-Hastings-Idana (CH) series of the Planosols, which extend in a belt from two to four counties wide through Nebraska and Kansas, between the Platte and the Arkansas rivers. Commonly referred to as claypan soils, they produce wheat, corn, oats and alfalfa as principal crops, although they are better suited to small grain than to corn because they lose their water supply over the claypan in dry weather. Alluvial soils, occurring along the river bottoms—principally the Platte, Republican, and Missouri—are much more important than their area would indicate. Those of the Platte Valley particularly provide some of Nebraska's richest farm land. Missouri River bottoms are equally fertile, but are subject to periodic flooding which greatly reduces their dependability. That region known topographically as the bad lands, or Pierre Hills, region consists primarily of the Pierre (Pi) series of the Lithosols, shallow stony soils on rough hilly terrain, of little use except as range land.

The soil map of Nebraska thus exhibits wide diversity, accounting in large measure for the highly diversified nature of the state's twentieth century agriculture. Except for the Sandhills, the dominant areas are extremely fertile and well suited to the production of cultivated crops.

The principal conditioning factor in the year-to-year productivity of the various soils is the amount of moisture available—as, indeed, the variation in the rainfall aspect of climate has been an important factor in the development of the soils themselves.

THE CLIMATE

There is an old saying in Nebraska, and in other states as well: "If you don't like the weather, just wait a minute and it'll change." Like many another old saying, this one contains just enough truth to keep it going. The climate in Nebraska, in common with that of the Plains region generally, is fickle, subject to violent and seemingly unpredictable fluctuations. There can be extremes of heat and cold, violent thunderstorms and hot dry winds, blizzards, tornadoes, and hail storms. The variation, particularly in rainfall, is long term as well as short term; the west differs markedly from the east. Although many residents are fond of complaining about the climate, there is nothing more glorious than a Nebraska autumn, and the air, as Professor E. A. Ross put it when he came to the University of Nebraska from Stanford, usually has "an almost intoxicating quality." More objectively considered, Nebraska's climate is typical of the interior of large continents in the middle latitudes, exhibiting light rainfall, low humidity, hot summers, severe winters, and wide variation, both short term and long term.

Nebraska's climate is controlled primarily by the state's latitude, its altitude, its inland position, and its position to the east of the Rocky Mountains. Mean annual temperature ranges from about 53° Fahrenheit in the southeast to about 45° in the northwest; summer temperatures get above 100° in most of the state, and winter readings as low as minus 45° have been recorded in the northwest. The average length of the growing season varies from 164 days in the southeast to 122 in the northwest.

The most important climatic feature, of course, is rainfall: it determines the type of agriculture, the prosperity, and the very way of life of the state's citizens. The mean rainfall is 22.84 inches, varying from 27.74 inches in the eastern division to 22.28 in the central and 17.93 in the western division. In Iowa, by way of comparison, the mean annual rainfall is 30.89 inches, and in Illinois, 36.61 inches. Fortunately, seventy-seven percent of Nebraska's yearly total falls in the six months from April to September, and forty-five percent in the three months of

May, June, and July. There is a great deal of fluctuation from month to month and from year to year. Precipitation records kept since 1876 show a succession of wet and dry periods as follows:

> 1876–1892: Wet period with one very dry year (1890); 1893–1901: Dry period with one rather wet year (1896); 1902–1909: Wet period with one rather dry year (1907); 1910–1920: Tendency irregular; most years dry but 1915 wettest year of record; 1921–1940: Dry period with only one wet year (1923); 1941–1965: Generally wet period, with four rather dry years (1943, 1954, 1955, 1956).

It goes without saying that the foregoing periodic variations in rainfall are reflected in the state's economic and political history. It should not be inferred, however, that man's difficulties with the climate of the Plains have been confined to the period of white occupation. An increasing body of evidence—largely from the work of archeologists—suggests that prehistoric man suffered from drouth, dust storms, and attendant evils long before the Plains felt the bite of the breaking plow.

MINERAL AND WATER RESOURCES

Though the early settlers occasionally got excited over the prospects of profit from exploiting coal and salt deposits believed to exist in the area, they soon learned that Nebraska, like much of the Plains, possessed relatively few mineral resources. To be sure, both coal and salt existed, but not in paying quantities. Likewise, there was neither iron nor precious metals. Such minerals as did exist in commercially significant quantities were stone, sand, gravel, clay, oil, and gas. There was enough potash in certain sections of the Sandhills to make government-financed production during World War I seem feasible, and for a time volcanic ash, known commercially as silica, was produced on a commercial basis.

Stone deposits include limestone, chalk rock, and sandstone; granite, rock salt, and gypsum also exist but at too great a depth to make their production commercially feasible. Though the sandstone generally is too soft for building purposes, the limestone and chalk are used in the manufacture of cement at Louisville and Superior. The limestone also was found to be useful in Missouri River stabilization work, and, to a degree, for liming soils. Large sand and gravel deposits existing in various parts of the state are useful for road building and the manufacture of concrete. Clay, occurring also at various places—principally around Hastings, Lincoln, and Nebraska City—has been used in the manufacture of brick tile, and terra cotta. Oil and gas wells brought in since World War II have added to the prosperity of southwest Nebraska.

Fortunately for an area characterized by uncertain rainfall, the state has vast ground-water resources which help to replenish the rivers and lakes, and provide water for irrigation. The Sandhills provide a particularly significant ground-water resource—the most important in the entire Plains region. Ground water in the Sandhills amounts to more than 500,000,000 acre feet—more than five hundred times the capacity of Pathfinder Reservoir—and is released to the rivers and lakes of the state in highly significant quantities. The Sandhills are dotted with hundreds of small lakes which play a major role in supporting the cattle industry of the region. The annual contribution of Sandhill ground water to the Platte Valley between Bridgeport and Gothenburg is more than the amount stored each year at Pathfinder, and the outflow to the Niobrara, Elkhorn, and Loup valleys is three times the capacity of the Pathfinder Reservoir.

PLANT AND ANIMAL LIFE

The most obvious characteristic of the landscape west of the Missouri was, of course, the absence of trees. Only about three percent of Nebraska was forested, and most of the trees that did exist were concentrated in the eastern part of the state, and along the streams. Characteristic trees found all over the state were the cottonwood, elm, ash, box elder, hackberry, various varieties of willow, and red cedar. Oak grew along the Missouri River, and the bur oak was found throughout the eastern half of the state. Western yellow pine was found in the valleys of the North Platte and Niobrara rivers, and quaking aspen in the northwest corner of the state. Many other varieties existed in small quantities. Among the fruit trees were wild plum and chokecherry.

Primarily, however, Nebraska, in common with other Plains states, was grass country. Professor Samuel Aughey, pioneer student of the state's natural resources, collected 149 species of grass native to the state, and 150 species of sedges; others, of course, have added to and redefined Professor Aughey's lists. Basically, the grass varied according to the rainfall. In the more humid eastern portion of the state tall prairie grasses—particularly the bluestem—abounded; the less humid western section was covered with short grasses, particularly grama and buffalo. Indeed, buffalo grass originally covered much of the state, and there was a legend among the old settlers that its disappearance was caused by the destruction of the buffalo.

Of the animals, the buffalo—or, more properly, bison—was the most characteristic, or at least the most plentiful. These shaggy beasts, admirably suited to conditions on the Plains, roamed the area by the millions and usually were encountered by travellers not far from Fort Kearny. Other animals found in great numbers by travellers and early occupants were the pronghorn antelope, the mule deer, and, along the streams, the beaver. Then, too, there were large numbers of coyotes, kit foxes, jackrabbits, ground squirrels, and prairie dogs. The prairie dog "towns" west of Fort Kearny frequently were commented upon by the early travellers. In the woodlands were found the porcupine, woodrat, and red squirrel. The ubiquitous skunk was common over the entire area.

Birds, too, were plentiful: prairie chicken, grouse, migrating waterfowl, and hundreds of species of songbirds. The ringnecked pheasant, which today constitutes the state's most important game bird, was not introduced until the second decade of the twentieth century.

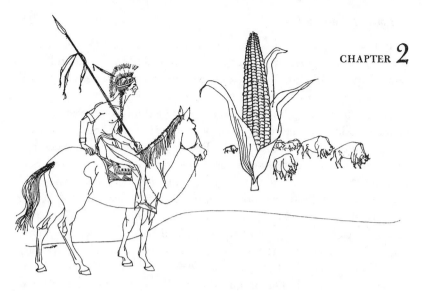

CHAPTER 2

The Original Occupants

WHEN WHITE MEN from the United States first began to venture out on the Plains in the early years of the nineteenth century, they found the region occupied by a variety of Indian tribes, speaking diverse languages and following various ways of life. They were particularly impressed by the superb horsemanship, expert marksmanship, picturesque costumes, and rugged fighting qualities of the nomadic Plains Indians—and these qualities became symbolic, in the minds of whites, for the red men of the West. While most of the trans-Missouri tribes possessed some of these attributes in varying degree, they were in full flower only among the nomads who roamed through the sub-humid and arid regions of the West, depending almost solely upon the hunt for their subsistence. The tribes dwelling in the river valleys of the more humid area lived semi-sedentary lives, based largely upon agriculture, and only occasionally ventured forth upon the extended hunt.

Whether semi-sedentary or nomadic, the center of the trans-Missouri Indian's culture was the horse. Without it, his extended wanderings, his methods of hunting, and his hit-and-run warfare would have been impossible. It is little wonder that he measured his wealth in horses. The Indians of the northern Plains acquired the horse from the Southwest sometime after 1700, through a series of raiding and trading operations—mostly raiding. Horse stealing was an honored occupation,

16

and no young man could count himself a warrior until he had returned from a successful thieving expedition.

Though the horse greatly modified the Indian's way of life, the full flower of horse culture as observed by whites in the early nineteenth century was the result of the adaptation of well-established traits and techniques to the demands and opportunities presented by the horse: traditional aspects of Plains culture—the tipi, the travois for transportation, the controlled buffalo hunt, and many ceremonies—were simply reorganized around the horse. There was greater emphasis on hunting, less on horticulture. Certain tribes—for example, the Cheyennes—abandoned the permanent village for the nomad's camp. Others, such as the Pawnees, retained their permanent villages but intensified their hunting activities. The horse, then, was the only new item in a centuries-old culture complex.

Moreover, the northern Plains had been occupied for an undetermined but exceedingly long period of time by a succession of peoples whose varied cultures reflect man's efforts to meet the challenge of his environment. This long and fascinating panorama is beyond the ken of the historian, who is largely dependent upon written materials for his sources. Yet a review of the findings of archeologists and others about the prehistory and ethno-history of the Plains is useful in any historical study of Nebraska and may give perspective to the historian's story of the relatively brief period of white occupation.

PREHISTORIC PEOPLES

So far as we now know, the earliest people on the Plains were those associated with the Folsom culture, so designated because the remains were first identified near Folsom, New Mexico. Folsom apparently was one of a number of paleo-Indian cultures existing on the Plains sometime prior to 8,000 B.C., and associated with large animals, now extinct —mastodon, ground sloth, giant beaver, giant cat, and others. Normally, their cultural materials are found under or are included within geological deposits laid down during or just after the last glacial retreat. They appear to have been nomadic hunters, but beyond that we know little about them. The Folsom people were skillful stone workers, and the culture is identified by the presence of a fine, fluted point apparently made only by this group and never subsequently produced on the plains. Folsom was succeeded by a number of distinct cultures whose projectile points are characterized by a high degree of workmanship. These points were at one time thought to represent a single culture—the Yuma, named for that county in Colorado—but excavations conducted near Scottsbluff, Nebraska, Eden, Wyoming, and elsewhere indicate that the points once lumped together as Yuma represent more than a single culture. Both Folsom and various points earlier referred to as Yuma have been found in southwest Nebraska.

We do not know what happened to these paleo-Indian peoples: they may have been forced by drouth and other difficulties to abandon the Plains altogether; they may have struggled for survival, and with reinforcements from Asia, become the ancestors of our modern American Indians. There is evidence of periodic—and perhaps, in certain areas, continuous—occupation of the Plains during the long period between about 10,000 B.C. and approximately 1,000 A.D. There is also evidence that conditions on the Plains were much less desirable during this period than they had been earlier: lakes, marshes, and streams were drying up; vegetation was by no means as lush, and trees were becoming scarcer; many animal forms had disappeared.

Though there is some disagreement regarding terminology, the period is generally designated as the lithic, and such evidence as is available suggests that lithic man was a nomadic hunter who lived in caves wherever they could be found. Several of the more important lithic sites are in western Nebraska: Signal Butte in Scotts Bluff County, Barn Butte in Garden County, and sites on Lime and Medicine Creeks in Frontier County. Three or more cultural layers have been identified at Signal Butte, two from the lithic period and one from relatively recent times. The earliest occupation, called Signal Butte I, appears to be 3,500 or more years old. Signal Butte I is particularly significant because it has yielded many artifacts—chipped flint scrapers and points, bone tools used for working flint, bone awls, gouges of split bison bone, incised bone fragments, and bone beads—and the points appear to resemble Folsom specimens found at the Lindenmeier site in Colorado. The second layer (Signal Butte II) appears to represent a relatively short occupation. The culture is different from that at Signal Butte I, and probably is from two to three thousand years younger.

Our knowledge of the lithic period is distressingly limited, but recent work by Marvin F. Kivett at Logan Creek in Burt County indicates the existence of four occupation levels ranging back to 6,471

B.C. This work, benefited by radiocarbon dating, has bridged some serious gaps and appears to provide the basis for defining an orderly succession of cultures between the Folsom people of more than 10,000 years ago and the pottery-makers who occupied the plains from about 400–600 A.D., and about whom much more is known.

The earliest of these pottery-making peoples to be identified from the Plains area are those designated as Woodland, a name which hints at the suspected origin of the culture in the forested regions of the East. They appear to have spread over much of the Plains during the years 400–600 A.D., and their remains have been found in virtually all parts of Nebraska. They lived primarily by hunting but may have practiced simple horticulture, and they appear to have been less nomadic than their predecessors on the Plains. Their dwellings were simple, semi-subterranean houses, equipped with a central fireplace (simply a depression in the ground) and probably covered with skins or mats supported by light poles. Recent work seems to suggest a longer occupancy than that indicated above and an increasing number of cultural variants.

The Woodland people appear to have been succeeded—at least in many areas of Kansas and Nebraska—by a more sedentary people who lived in relatively large unfortified villages and in addition to hunting and fishing practiced a fairly intensive corn and bean horticulture. They appear to have occupied the Plains between 1200 and 1500 A.D., and may represent the westernmost extension of the eastern maize culture complex. The two major variants found in Nebraska have been designated Nebraska and Upper Republican. The Nebraska culture is found all along the Missouri River, particularly between Omaha and Sioux City, and sites showing its influence have been excavated as far west as Howard County. The Upper Republican people—so named from the type site near Franklin—lived in the valleys of the Loup and the Republican and generally throughout southern and central Nebraska. They appear to have occupied at least seasonal hunting camps in the Sandhills. As a result of relative peace, agricultural advance, new influences and perhaps new people from the South, their arts were relatively more advanced than those of their predecessors: they produced high-grade pottery, and a wide variety of stone, bone, horn and shell tools and ornaments.

No one knows for sure what happened to these people. They may have been forced to abandon the Plains altogether in the late fifteenth century. There is evidence of a prolonged drouth during the latter part of the fifteenth century and fantastic dust storms—many of the village sites are buried under a heavy mantle of dust. There is evidence that by the early seventeenth century a culture related to the same Mississippian pattern as the Nebraska culture—Oneoto—appeared in western Iowa, eastern Nebraska, and eastern Kansas. More recent (1670-1705) is the Dismal River culture, remains of which have been found in western Nebraska and particularly in the Sandhills. They were more nomadic than the Upper Republican people, and placed a greater dependence upon hunting for their subsistence. Generally, their standard of living was lower than that of the Upper Republican people: their houses were not as substantial, their pottery was not as highly decorated, and their stone tools were considerably cruder. There is some evidence of white contact (a few metal objects and glass beads), but nothing to suggest that they had acquired horses. Archeologists believe that they were Plains Apache.

Contemporaneous with the Oneoto and Dismal River cultures was the Lower Loup or protohistoric Pawnee, which flourished in large villages on the Platte and Loup rivers. They appear to have been ancestors of the historic Pawnee and may have descended from the Upper Republican. They lived about as the Upper Republican people, but with a greater dependence upon horticulture. Their tools of stone and bone are similar to Upper Republican. Their pottery, in form, durability, and appearance, is some of the most advanced ever found on the Plains.

THE PAWNEES

Of the historic tribes, the Pawnees were the most closely associated with Nebraska. The name is of somewhat uncertain origin, although probably it derives from *Pa-rik-i,* a horn, an outgrowth of the typical Pawnee method of dressing the scalplock. Among themselves, they were known as *Chahiksi-cha-hiks,* "men of men." Tribal origins, like the name, are clouded in obscurity. According to one tradition, the Pawnees moved into the valleys of the Platte and Loup from the south and southwest; another points to a southeastern origin. In any event, they probably were in Nebraska by 1541, when Coronado explored the northern Plains, and certainly by 1673, when they appear on Marquette's map. Archeological evidence suggests that they may have been here much

Tipis of Southern Cheyennes, near Fort Laramie

Pawnee Earthlodges at Genoa, 1870 (*W. H. Jackson, Photo*)

INDIAN DWELLINGS

Meriwether Lewis

William Clark

Zebulon Pike

Stephen H. Long

FOUR EXPLORERS OF THE WEST

Manuel Lisa   Peter A. Sarpy

THE TRADERS

"Yoking Up" (*from a painting by W. H. Jackson*)

Handcart Pioneers (*from a painting by W. H. Jackson*)

ALONG THE TRAIL

John C. Fremont   Brigham Young

Robidoux's Post at Scotts Bluff (*from a sketch by Heinrich Balduin Mollhausen,*
photo courtesy Dr. Robert Taft, University of Kansas, and Kansas State Historical Society)

Stephen A. Douglas, Senator from Illinois   Augustus C. Dodge, Senator from Iowa

PROPONENTS OF NEBRASKA TERRITORY

Bellevue, 1858

Omaha, 1867

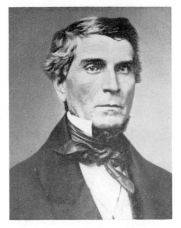

Francis Burt

Thomas B. Cuming

Fenner Ferguson

Mark W. Izard

Robert W. Furnas

Dr. George L. Miller

TERRITORIAL LEADERS

earlier—that the Upper Republican people of 1200–1500 A.D. may have been the ancestors of the historic Pawnee.

Throughout the eighteenth century, French explorers and traders came in contact with the Pawnees, and the detailed accounts of Lewis and Clark, Pike, Long, and other Americans in the early nineteenth century served primarily to corroborate and amplify earlier information. That information showed the Pawnees occupying large villages in an

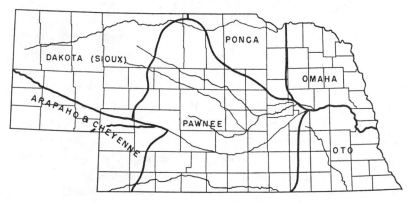

INDIAN TRIBES OF NEBRASKA, ABOUT 1800

area centering around the Platte, although hunting over a much wider area.

Linguistically, the Pawnees were part of the Caddoan family. They were divided into four bands, each of which earlier often occupied one or more separate earth-lodge villages: the *Chaui*, or Grand; the *Kitkehahki*, or Republican; the *Pitahauerat*, or Tappage; and the *Skidi*, or Wolf. Tribal organization was based on the village and each village had its name, its shrine containing sacred objects, and its priest, as well as its hereditary chiefs and leading men. The tribe was held together by ceremonies pertaining to a common cult in which each village had its place, and by the tribal council, composed of the chiefs of the various villages.

The Pawnees were essentially a farming people and in common with other such groups in the Missouri Valley lived in permanent villages. The characteristic dwelling was the communal earth lodge, a circular structure consisting of a framework of four or more center posts with rafters covered with brush and dirt. The floor was excavated slightly below the ground level, and an opening in the center of the roof served as a smoke hole for the fireplace directly below. The entrance was covered and usually faced the east or southeast. Periodically, usually twice a year, the entire community abandoned the village and went off on a buffalo hunt. While hunting, they lived in the skin tipis associated with the nomadic tribes. In the village and on the hunt, the women did most of the work and generally suffered a hard life. There were some compensations, however: the women owned the property and the chieftainship descended through the existing chief's sister.

The fact that the Pawnees lived both by agriculture and hunting accounts for the diverse elements in their culture. During part of the year they were sedentary farmers, living in permanent villages; during the remainder they were nomadic hunters, adopting dwellings and habits generally associated with the wandering tribes of the Plains. At heart, however, they were farmers, particularly corn growers, and this is reflected in their religion. To be sure, each dwelling had its sacred buffalo skull. But corn was their mother, figuring in their rituals and in their mythology even more prominently than did the buffalo. The sacred bundles of the tribe contained two ears of corn, renewed annually. Their most important ceremonies, including the sacrifice of a maiden to the Morning Star by the Skidi, were directed primarily toward securing a bountiful crop of corn.

The Pawnee cornfields were small, usually not more than an acre or so. The primitive tools—principally a hoe made from the scapula of a buffalo—were not suited to working heavy turf and the women located their fields at the mouths of ravines or in similar spots where the soil was loose and fertile. Sometimes they were compelled to go several miles from the village to find a suitable plot of ground. The corn was planted in hills and was usually hoed twice a year. The ears were small, generally not more than four inches long, although in one instance ears from sixteen to eighteen inches in length were reported as being not uncommon. Corn was gathered while it was still green, boiled, cut from the cob, dried, and placed in leather bags to be stored in caches for future use. In addition to corn, the Pawnees cultivated beans, pumpkins, and squash. They also seem to have been fond of the wild potato, which grew plentifully in the sand of the Platte and Loup valleys.

The buffalo, object of at least two great hunts each year, was an important source of food and was important also for its hide, hair, sinew, horns, and even its hooves. The summer hunt began immediately after the corn had been hoed the second time, usually about the middle of June, and occupied the tribe until September, when they returned to harvest the corn and other crops. Near the end of October, after the corn had been cached, the tribe set out on its winter hunt, remaining away until April, just in time for corn planting. A favorite hunting ground lay between the Republican and the Arkansas rivers, necessitating a trip of from four hundred to nine hundred miles on each hunt. The meat was eaten fresh whenever possible, and the hunt, if successful, was a time of great feasting. That which could not be eaten fresh was cut into strips and dried in the sun to form "jerky." In addition to buffalo, the Pawnees ate elk, deer, bear, beaver, otter, raccoon, badger, dogs, rabbits, and squirrels. They apparently used fish but little.

Prior to their contact with the white man, the Pawnees had developed to a rather high degree the art of making pottery and tools from stone and bone. After they secured metal containers from the whites they gave up the making of native pottery. Likewise, the arrow points, knives, scrapers, and other tools once chipped from hard native stone were abandoned in favor of substitutes furnished by white traders. At first the stone arrow points were replaced by metal ones and these in turn gave way to guns. The Pawnees did continue to carry on considerable work in wood, even after they had become heavily dependent upon metal goods furnished by the traders, making mortars, bowls, whip handles, platters, and cradle boards. Actually, the decline in traditional Pawnee culture seems to begin with the acquisition of the horse. This, too, was the result of white contact, even if indirect. We do not know exactly when the Pawnees acquired horses, but by 1800 every village possessed many animals and their use had become an integral part of Pawnee culture. Other evidence of Pawnee decline as a result of white contact is supplied by population figures. In 1838 the missionaries Dunbar and Allis estimated that there were ten thousand Pawnees. Increasing white contact, particularly as a result of the heavy overland emigration through the Pawnee country in the 1840's, introduced disease and dissipation and left the Pawnees in a weakened condition. In particular, they were left less able to defend themselves against the almost continuous attacks of the Sioux. In 1849 they were reported to have lost one-fourth of their number from cholera, leaving only about forty-five hundred. In 1856 they had increased to 4,686, but five years later they were reported at 3,416.

SEDENTARY SIOUAN TRIBES

Next in importance to the Pawnees in Nebraska were the sedentary Siouan tribes along the Missouri River: Omahas, Poncas, Otos, Iowas, and Missourias. The great Siouan linguistic family embraced many groups, tribes, and sub-tribes. The family included the Western Dakota (of whom more later), as well as the sedentary tribes. The Omahas and Poncas belonged to the Dhegiha group, along with the Quapaws, Osages, and Kanzas, who lived further south. The Iowas, Otos, and Missourias made up the Chiwere group, which, though similar, spoke a dialect that could not readily be understood by the Dhegihas.

At one time the Siouan peoples probably lived east of the Alleghenies, whence they pushed westward in search of food—spurred on, no doubt, by the pressure of enemies. Traditional evidence suggests that the sedentary tribes wandered up and down the Missouri River, through eastern Nebraska and western Iowa for many centuries prior to the dawn of history in the region. Historical evidence seems to indicate that their occupation of the area was rather late or at least that there was a re-occupation in the historical period. In any event, they were well ensconced along the west bank of the Missouri when the whites arrived in the region.

The Omahas (those going against the wind or current) probably moved up the Mississippi from the mouth of the Ohio, remaining for a while at the mouth of the Missouri, then going north into Iowa and southern Minnesota, and finally turning southwestward across the Missouri. They appear to have been in Nebraska from about 1650, settling on Bow Creek in the northeastern part of the state. The early nineteenth century saw them occupying the bluffs along the Missouri River from the mouth of the Platte to Sioux City. They were seriously hit by smallpox in 1802 but appear to have made a fairly rapid recovery: their population increased from 300 in 1802 to 600 in 1804; in 1829 it was estimated at 1,900, and in 1843, at 1,600. During the chieftainship of Black Bird in the late eighteenth century they appear to have been a strong, warlike tribe, striking fear into the hearts of their neighbors and occasional white traders who ventured into their country. During the early nineteenth century, however, pressure from the Dakotas and from the whites steadily reduced their will and their ability to defend themselves, and in 1854, under the leadership of Logan Fontenelle (himself a half-breed) they ceded all their land west of the Missouri, except 300,000 acres in northeastern Nebraska which they retained as a reservation.

The Poncas probably represent the same culture as the Omahas and appear to have lived with them at one time. The date of separation is uncertain, with estimates ranging from 1390 to the middle of the seventeenth century to "rather late." Traditional accounts of their migration up the Missouri are somewhat obscure, but there is evidence that they were in Nebraska at least by the beginning of the eighteenth century. Juan Baptiste Munier is said to have "discovered" the Poncas at the mouth of the Niobrara in 1789, but they appear on LeSeur's map of 1701. They suffered heavily from smallpox near the end of the eighteenth century and were estimated by Lewis and Clark in 1804 as having a population of only 200. They had increased to 600 in 1829, and 800 in 1842. In 1874, while the entire tribe was living on the Niobrara River, they numbered 733. Like the Omahas, the Poncas were under almost constant attack from the Sioux. They were abruptly removed to Indian Territory in 1877—an experience which almost destroyed the tribe.

Though many differences are apparent to the anthropologists, the Omahas and Poncas prior to the debasement of their cultures through white contact generally appear to have followed a way of life similar to that of other semi-sedentary tribes on the eastern Plains, depending upon both agriculture and hunting for their subsistence. They dwelt in earth lodges and skin tipis; they farmed a little and went on periodic buffalo hunts; they made pottery, tools, and weapons from native materials.

The Otos, Iowas, and Missourias, who comprised the Chiwere group, probably sprang from a common Winnebago stem, leaving the Winnebagoes at Green Bay to wander southwest, taking up positions west of the Missouri and south of the Platte. During historic times, at least, these tribes were never very large or important and when first observed by white travellers seem to have been much less highly developed than the Pawnees or the Omahas and Poncas. They lived semi-sedentary lives, farming a little, and hunting a little, but they appear never to have been able to achieve the degree of mastery over their environment accomplished by their neighbors. Lewis and Clark, for example, speak of Otos they saw near Council Bluffs as being almost naked, having no covering except a sort of breechcloth, with a loose blanket or painted buffalo robe thrown over the shoulder. Their permanent villages consisted of large earth lodges, and while travelling they lived in tipis.

The Otos (from Wat-ota, "lechers") were found by Lewis and Clark on the south side of the Platte, about thirty miles from the mouth of the river. Earlier they had lived about twenty miles north of the Platte on the Missouri. They, too, suffered from a siege of smallpox in the late eighteenth century, but unlike the Poncas they never seemed to have recovered. The Iowas (sleepy ones) were reported by Lewis and Clark as occupying a single village of 200 warriors (total population about 800) eighteen leagues up the Platte. The Missourias (named for the river) moved south of the Kansas River in the late eighteenth century but were driven out by the Sauk and Fox. When Lewis and Clark came along they were living in small villages south of the Platte. Smallpox forced them to abandon their village and they finally amalgamated with the Otos. By the middle Eighties all three tribes were on reservations in Indian Territory.

THE NOMADIC TRIBES

In addition to the Pawnees and the sedentary Siouan tribes who dwelt more or less permanently in Nebraska, various bands of Dakota, as well as Cheyennes, Arapahoes, Comanches, and possibly Kiowas, roamed over western Nebraska during the historic period. Most important of these, at least for the history of Nebraska, were the western Dakotas who, though quite unlike other members of the family, were part of the Siouan linguistic group. The Dakota-Assiniboin group contained many tribes. Those active in Nebraska were primarily Brules and Oglalas, sub-tribes of the Tetons.

The Dakotas were relative latecomers to the Plains. Hennepin placed them on the upper Mississippi as late as 1680. In general, they seem to have been driven out of their woodland habitat by the Chippewas, who were the first to get guns from the traders. LeSeur's map shows the Tetons and Yanktons just east of the Missouri River in western Iowa. Probably the first record of their being west of the Missouri is La-Verendrye's reference in 1743 to a band of prairie Sioux which he met somewhere west of the Missouri River in what is now South Dakota. In 1842 Fremont located the "Sioux" between the north and south forks of the Platte, near the Laramie plains.

Their early wanderings have never been satisfactorily documented, but it is safe to assume that they were a force in Nebraska at least by 1800. The early years of the nineteenth century saw them raiding and hunting through western and central Nebraska and even harassing the Pawnees and the sedentary Siouan peoples along the Missouri.

Dakota tribal structure was complex, the group consisting of a large number of local bands. Chieftainship was determined by personal fitness and popular appeal rather than by heredity. War parties were recruited by persons who had acquired reputations for prowess on the battle field, and with sufficient success a warrior could easily develop into a chief.

The Dakotas looked down on farming as an unfit occupation for a warrior. Nor would they coop themselves up in an earth lodge. They lived entirely on the fruits of the chase and upon such wild foods as the women could gather, roaming over the plains in fine disdain for any but the nomadic life. Physically, mentally, and probably morally, they were the highest type of Plains Indian. With the Cheyennes, and under the leadership of such men as Red Cloud and Crazy Horse, they provided significant resistance to the white occupation of the northern Plains.

CHAPTER 3

The White Man Comes to Nebraska

ALTHOUGH SETTLEMENT of the trans-Missouri country came about through the westward extension of the people of the United States, the earliest white explorers of the region came from the Southwest—and more than half a century before the English had established their first tentative settlement at Jamestown. When Lewis and Clark ventured up the Missouri in 1804, the Spanish had known the plains for more than two and a half centuries, had named the rivers as far north as the Platte —melodious names like *Rio de Jesus Maria* and *Rio de San Lorenzo*— and had designated the more important Indian tribes. The French, penetrating the region from the Northeast, were well established at St. Louis, knew intimately the Indians as far north as the Niobrara, and had entered the Mandan country in present North Dakota. Despite these long years, however, neither Spanish nor French had made much impression upon the area: the Spanish at Santa Fe could have penetrated the northern Plains no more easily in the early nineteenth century than they did in the early seventeenth; such influence as the French had among the people of the region was limited to that exercised by the itinerant trader. Both Spanish and French had been impelled onto the Plains by the age-old search for gold and by the hope—associated with virtually all of the early exploration of North America—that one of the beckoning rivers might lead to the Western Sea. They found no gold, and the rivers seemed to lead nowhere. They had to content themselves with trade and the exploitation of the native peoples. The peoples were widely scattered and the trade was difficult and not particularly profitable. Little wonder then that neither they nor the territory made much of an impression upon one another. Lewis and Clark, however, were in the vanguard of a colonizing people. Within half a century after they first set foot in Nebraska, the territory was opened for settlement. Within a century the entire state was peopled.

SPANISH AND FRENCH IN NEBRASKA

The first white men on the Plains were the Spanish soldiers under Francisco Vasquez Coronado, who marched north out of the valley of the Rio Grande in April, 1541, to search for the Kingdom of Quivira, a rich land where even the poorest people ate from dishes of wrought plate and bowls of gold. Many of Nebraska's earlier historians located Quivira within the bounds of the present state. Modern scholarship places it in central Kansas, but the traditional view is kept alive by the Knights of Ak-Sar-Ben, who crown each fall, in the state's most elaborate social function, the King and Queen of Quivira. And even for the purposes of history, the exact location of Quivira is of little moment. The importance of Coronado's search lies in the fact that for the first time it exposed white men to the central Plains. It was clear that those who came in search of gold were doomed to disappointment. Sadly, Coronado wrote the King of Spain: ". . . what I am sure of is there is not any gold nor any other metal in all that country, and the other things of which they had told me are nothing but little villages, and in many of these they do not plant anything and do not have any houses except of skins and sticks, and they wander around with the cows." For the colonist there might have been some hope. "The country itself," Coronado reported, "is the best I have ever seen for producing all the products of Spain, for besides the land itself being very fat and black and being very well watered by the rivulets and springs and rivers, I found prunes like those of Spain and nuts and very good sweet grapes and mulberries."

But the Spanish were not after farms. They wanted gold, and as Professor Webb suggests, Coronado's observations may help explain Spanish neglect of the Great Plains. In any event, after Coronado, Spanish interest in the Plains seems to have been confined to keeping others out. This they were unable to do—possibly they didn't work at it very

hard. As early as 1664 Juan de Archuleta, sent north to capture a group
of Pueblos who had fled from the Spanish at Taos, heard that the Pawnees were trading with the French. Similar news came frequently thereafter, and in 1699 a Navajo war party returning from a raid on the
Pawnees brought French carbines, powder flasks, clothing, and other
equipment. Finally, the Spanish stirred themselves to half-hearted efforts to check their rivals, and late in 1718, the viceroy at Mexico City
ordered countermoves against the French on both the Texas and New
Mexico frontiers. In the fall of 1719, Governor Valverde of New Mexico
led a faint-hearted expedition against the Comanches and Utes, and
the next year Lieutenant Colonel Pedro de Villasur was sent to recon-
noiter enemy positions on the northern Plains.

Accompanied by forty-five white soldiers, sixty Indians, a priest, and
an interpreter, Villasur set out from Santa Fe on June 16, 1720. Heading generally northeastward, the party crossed the Arkansas River and
then went on to the South Platte. Near the forks—or perhaps, the Loup
fork—they came upon a large, well-fortified village, probably Pawnee.
After being coldly rebuffed in his efforts to open a parley, Villasur fell
back to plan his next move. Despite the obvious hostility of the Indians, he encamped in an indefensible position in the tall grass beside
the river and apparently took no precautions for the safety of his men.
At daybreak on August 13, the Indians suddenly attacked. Villasur
was killed before he could reach his weapons. Most of the Indians apparently had scented the danger in time to get away, but only thirteen
of the Spaniards survived to make their bedraggled way back to Santa
Fe. When the news reached Mexico City, the troubled viceroy ordered
an investigation. Villasur, being dead, was a convenient scapegoat. Governor Valverde, for entrusting the expedition to an obvious incompetent,
was required to pay fifty pesos for charity masses for the souls of the
dead soldiers and one hundred and fifty pesos to purchase ornaments
for certain of the missions. Whoever was to blame, Spanish influence
on the upper Plains after 1720 was non-existent, and at Santa Fe and
Mexico City everyone was sure that the French were at the root of
their difficulty.

Whether the Villasur massacre had been led by Frenchmen, as the
survivors maintained, or whether it had been nothing more than a
simple Indian ambush, the French by 1720 were becoming well established in the trans-Missouri country. Louis Joliet and Father Jacques

Marquette passed the mouth of the Missouri in June, 1673. Impressed by its turbulent waters tumbling into the Mississippi, Father Marquette reported that several villages of savages were located along the river and surmised that it might lead to "the Vermillion Sea or California." Robert Cavelier, Sieur de La Salle, came along in February, 1682, and was able to gather from the Indians a fairly accurate description of the river and the peoples along it perhaps as far north as the Platte. Spurred on by La Salle's dream of empire and the obvious missionary opportunities, the French busied themselves with plans for extending their imperial embrace to the people of the Missouri. Missionaries in the Illinois country picked up a great deal of information about the Indians of the region and many legendary accounts grew up concerning traders who were supposed to have ventured up the river. Most, if not all, of these accounts have been discredited, however, and the first significant exploration of the Missouri River was that accomplished by Etienne Veniard de Bourgmont in 1714.

Bourgmont, a *coureur de bois* of adventuresome spirit and many talents, deserted his post as commandant of Fort Detroit to marry an Indian girl and live among the tribes of the Missouri. (He first became aware of them when unaccountably they showed up in 1712 to assist the French in a siege of Fort Detroit being levied by the Fox.) Bourgmont reported in considerable detail on his travels, noting in particular that the tributaries of the Missouri, as described to him by the Indians who had roamed the Southwest, might provide a route to the Spanish settlements. (Incidentally, Bourgmont's reports also contain the first recorded use of the word *Nebraska*: "Higher up the river, one finds the Large river, called'Nibraskier by the French and Indians.") French officials, who were learning that it would be difficult to reach the Spaniards by way of the Red or the Arkansas rivers, were much impressed by Bourgmont's reports, and Bienville asked the King to award him the Cross of St. Louis. The French in Louisiana, who, unlike the Spanish, were not content to let the trans-Missouri country remain a no-man's land, took steps to consolidate their position in the area. Villasur's defeat removed the threat of Spanish competition—all that was needed now was to cement the allegiance of the tribes and persuade them to live together in peace. To do this, the Company of the Indies commissioned Bourgmont—by now in Paris, where he was honored with the Cross of St. Louis—commandant of the Mis-

souri, with instructions to establish a fort on the Missouri, make an
alliance with the Padoucas, and then return to France with some
Indian chiefs.

All this Bourgmont accomplished: he established Fort Orleans on
the Missouri in 1723 (probably on an island in the river, long since

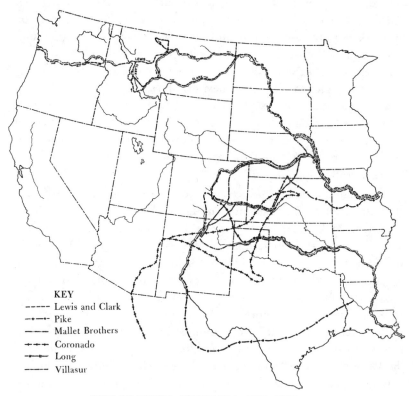

KEY
----- Lewis and Clark
-·-·- Pike
----- Mallet Brothers
+-+-+ Coronado
-■-■- Long
----- Villasur

EXPLORATION, NEBRASKA AND THE WEST

washed away, in the vicinity of Brunswick, Missouri); he visited the
Padoucas and various other tribes in the spring of 1724, holding long
and apparently successful powwows; and later in the year returned to
Paris with a delegation of Oto, Osage, and Missouri chiefs, the noted
Chicago, and "a young Indian woman." Had French officials in America
been as vigorous in carrying out their plans as they were in developing
them, Bourgmont might well have laid the foundations for a successful
imperial adventure in the Missouri Valley. Bienville, however, lost en-

thusiasm for adventures in upper Louisiana and failed to support the
Fort Orleans project; and two years after Bourgmont returned to France
(where, incidentally, he remained), the fort was abandoned. Bienville
even reduced the number of Indian delegates Bourgmont was allowed
to take with him to France. As it was, during the remainder of their
period of dominion in North America the French contented themselves
with relatively insignificant trading expeditions among the Indians and
somewhat more significant efforts to strike up a trade with the Spanish
in New Mexico.

The way to Santa Fe was opened in 1739 by Pierre and Paul Mallet.
Under the assumption that the Missouri would lead to New Mexico,
the two brothers ascended that river to the mouth of the Niobrara,
where they concluded they were travelling in the wrong direction. They
retraced their steps by land, almost parallel to the Missouri, striking a
river which they called the Platte (probably between South Bend and
Fremont), they followed it to a point about twenty-five miles beyond
the Loup fork, where they crossed the Platte and turned southward.
They probably crossed the Republican between Superior and Red
Cloud, continuing their southwestward course until they reached the
Arkansas. In due time they found an Indian who was able to guide
them to the Spanish settlements.

The Spanish tried to prohibit the French from trading with their
New Mexican settlements, but after the Mallet brothers had opened
the way, numerous pack trains crossed the wilderness each year to the
Spanish settlements, and during the Forties and Fifties the contraband
trade took on rather large proportions. Meanwhile, the French continued to trade with the Indians of the lower Missouri, and from Canada
French traders had opened traffic with the tribes of the upper river—
when the La Verendryes went across the Dakotas to the Rocky Mountains in 1742, they were told by the Indians that three days from the
Arikaras they would find a Frenchman who had lived in the area for
several years.

By the late 1750's, however, the French were losing their hold on
North America, and in the Treaty of Paris, 1763, all the land west of
the Mississippi River became Spanish.

The Spanish were slow to exploit the upper Missouri. For the most
part, they seem to have been content to trade with the tribes adjacent
to St. Louis, and as late as 1785 appear to have had little definite knowl-

edge of the river beyond the mouth of the Niobrara, the upper limit of the French advance from the Illinois country. Following the close of the American Revolution, however, the Spanish began to press their claim to the upper Missouri. The Americans, who had succeeded the British as masters of the Illinois country, were aggressive and ambitious and were looked upon as a definite threat to Spanish influence over the Indians. More important, the British, who remained in economic control of the upper Mississippi Valley after the Revolution, were pushing into Spanish territory from the north and east, taking over the trade of the Sioux and competing seriously for that of the Pawnees, Omahas, and Iowas. Finally, traders in St. Louis were becoming so numerous that ruinous competition was developing in the trade with the nearby tribes.

In 1789, Juan Munier "discovered" the Poncas living near the mouth of the Niobrara and in return was given exclusive trading privileges with them. The next year, Jacques D'Eglise obtained a license to hunt on the Missouri and wandered as far north as the Mandans. In 1793, D'Eglise and an apparent rogue named Garreau set off up the river with goods advanced by Bentura Collell and Joseph Robidoux. According to D'Eglise, this venture failed because of Garreau's perfidy and the hostility of the Sioux and the Arikaras, and as reimbursement for his efforts D'Eglise requested a monopoly on the trade of the Mandans similar to that which had been granted Munier among the Poncas. Already, however, Spanish officials in St. Louis had granted a monopoly on the trade of all the tribes above the Poncas to the "Company of Explorers of the Upper Missouri."

This company, which represents the first and only large-scale Spanish effort to extend their trade to the upper Missouri, was organized in St. Louis on October 15, 1793, under the leadership of Jacques Clamorgan. Spanish officials were enthusiastic, and Governor-General Carondelet, in addition to giving the company the monopolistic privileges it demanded, offered a prize of $2,000—later raised to $3,000— to the first Spanish subject who should reach the South Sea by way of the Missouri River. Though the company included, in addition to Clamorgan, such well-known and experienced traders as Bentura Collell, Joseph Robidoux, Gregoire Sarpy, and Antoine Roy, they chose Jean Baptiste Truteau, a schoolmaster, to lead their first expedition. Accompanied by eight men in a pirogue, Truteau left St. Louis for the

Mandan villages, June 7, 1794. He spent a miserable winter near Fort Randall, trading a little with the Sioux, the Omahas, and the Poncas. The next spring he headed north but got no further than the Arikaras. He appears to have got along well with the Arikaras and apparently was in contact with the Cheyennes. He was back in St. Louis by the early part of 1796 with little to show for his efforts.

Meanwhile, in April, 1795, the company dispatched a second expedition under the leadership of a man named Lecuyer. It was much better equipped than Truteau's (costing 96,779 pesos, twice as much as the first expedition), but it never got beyond the Poncas. Lecuyer is reported to have taken two wives among the Poncas and wasted much of the company's goods. Near the end of August, 1795, the company sent out a third expedition. This, the best equipped of all, was led by Jacques Mackay, a Scot who had traded among the Mandans for the British and who had changed his allegiance to Spain. The party stopped for a few days at the Oto village near the mouth of the Platte, building a cabin nearby for those who were left to trade with the Otos. Mackay himself spent the winter at the Omaha village in present Dakota County, building Fort Charles (the exact site of which is unknown) and forming an alliance with the celebrated chief, Black Bird. From Fort Charles, Mackay sent his trusted lieutenant, Juan Evans, on a mission to the Arickaras. Stopped by the Sioux, Evans returned to Fort Charles, to be sent out again—this time to discover a passage across the continent to the Pacific.

Evans, it goes without saying, did not find a passage to the Pacific. Both he and Mackay were back in St. Louis in 1797, and though the Company retained the hope that it would find a route to the Western Sea, its activities after Evans' abortive effort were confined to developing trade with the tribes along the Platte and, as its resources permitted, extending its influence up the Missouri. The Company underwent numerous reorganizations, but it remained under the domination of Jacques Clamorgan, and for a time operated under the name of Clamorgan, Loisel and Company. By the turn of the century the Spanish were trading as far north as the Mandans and knew the river as far as its confluence with the Yellowstone. Given time, they might have made their way to the Pacific.

But Spanish days on the Missouri were numbered, and the destiny of the valley was being determined not by the traders on the river but

by the diplomats in Paris and Madrid. In the secret Treaty of San Ilde-
fonso, signed on October 1, 1800, the Spanish agreed to turn Louisiana
back to France, thus paving the way for the rebuilding, under Napoleon,
of the French empire in North America. Before Napoleon could get on
with his plan, however, he concluded that it was impracticable, and on
April 11, 1803, Talleyrand, the French foreign minister, asked Robert
Livingston, resident United States minister in Paris, what he would give
for all of Louisiana. Livingston, who had been trying unsuccessfully to
buy New Orleans—and who was a little deaf besides—could hardly
believe his ears. He was not so overwhelmed, however, but that he was
able to seize his opportunity, and on April 30 he and James Monroe
signed a treaty transferring Louisiana to the United States for 80,000,000
francs—about $15,000,000, or four cents an acre. Little men in and
out of Congress doubted both the wisdom and constitutionality of adding the vast territory to the United States, but President Jefferson in an
act of enduring statesmanship pushed it through, thus setting his country on the road to greatness.

LEWIS AND CLARK

More immediately, the Louisiana Purchase enabled Jefferson to realize an ambition of twenty years' standing—the exploration of the Far
West: as early as 1783 he had tried to interest George Rogers Clark
in exploring the country from the Mississippi to California; in 1786,
while minister to France, he had persuaded John Ledyard to try to explore the country from west to east—an effort which failed when the
Russians objected to Ledyard's transit across Siberia; in 1792 he had
been the leading spirit in the American Philosophical Society's ill-fated
attempt to send André Michaux across the continent. The presidency
brought new opportunities, and on January 18, 1803, Jefferson sent
a secret message to Congress urging that efforts be made to establish
trade with the Indians of the Missouri River. Congress responded by
appropriating $2,500, "for purposes of extending the external com-
merce of the United States," and Jefferson chose young Meriwether
Lewis, age twenty-eight, son of an Albemarle County neighbor and his
private secretary, to head the expedition. With his usual prescience,
Jefferson instructed Lewis: to ascend the Missouri, cross the mountains,
and descend by the most practicable river to the Pacific; to make
geographic and scientific observations; to ascertain the routes of Cana-

dian traders in their traffic with the Indians; to determine the feasibility of collecting furs at the source of the Missouri and transporting them downstream; and to cultivate friendship and trade with the native tribes.

Lewis selected as his companion and co-leader William Clark, a younger brother of the famed Revolutionary War hero, George Rogers Clark. On Jefferson's authority, Lewis, a captain of Infantry, had offered Clark a captaincy also; when the commission came through, however, it was a second lieutenancy. Nevertheless, to their men and to history they were Captain Lewis and Captain Clark, and shared equally the leadership of the expedition. They were fortunate choices. Both were seasoned campaigners with vast frontier experience: Lewis had served in the army from the Whiskey Rebellion to his detachment as Jefferson's secretary; Clark, member of a famous military family, had served four years with Anthony Wayne in the Indian wars of the Northwest.[1] Both had the ability to control their men, the Indians, and virtually every situation in which they found themselves. They worked as an incomparable team to accomplish the most fruitful expedition in the history of American exploration.

Lewis bade President Jefferson goodbye on July 5, 1803. He embarked at Pittsburgh, August 31. The trip down the Ohio was slow and tiresome, and it was October 26 before he left Louisville with Clark, the latter's Negro slave, York (an exceedingly useful member of the party, whose amatory and terpsichorean accomplishments were soon to become part of the folklore of the West), and a group of young Kentucky hunters. They reached the River DuBois, just across the Mississippi from St. Louis, in mid-December, and there went into winter camp. The winter months were spent drilling the men and making preparations for the trip up the Missouri. Lewis spent a great deal of time in St. Louis talking to traders who knew the river and otherwise perfecting arrangements. On March 9 and 10, 1804, he was the chief official witness to the formal transfer of Upper Louisiana from Spain to France and from France to the United States.

On May 14 the party, numbering forty-five in all, broke camp at the

[1]As Bernard DeVoto suggests: "They were remarkable men. And in the end, allowing as much as need be for unusual leadership, resourcefulness, boldness, and skill, the quality that must be insisted on is intelligence." (*The Course of Empire* [Boston: Houghton Mifflin Company, 1953], p. 437.)

River DuBois "in the presence of many of the neighboring inhabitants and proceeded on under a jentle breese up the Missouri."[2] Their equipment consisted of a fifty-five foot keelboat with twenty-two oars, an open pirogue with seven oars, and another with six. All three were equipped with sails, push poles, and tow lines—the latter items being much more frequently used than the first. The boats were loaded with arms, ammunition, extra clothing, scientific instruments, food, and presents for the Indians. Two horses were taken along for the use of the hunters.

On July 15, they made camp near the mouth of the Little Nemaha, their first in Nebraska. Clark reported: "I saw Great quantities of Grapes, Plums of 2 kinds, Wild Cherries of 2 Kinds, Hazelnuts, and Goosberries." They were along the Nebraska shore until September 7. On July 21 they reached the Platte, as important to the early rivermen as the equator is to those who sail the seas. The next day they went ten miles up the river, concluding to remain for a few days at what they called "Camp White Catfish" to explore the country and try to persuade chiefs of the neighboring tribes, particularly the Otos, to come in for a conference. After some difficulty—including the desertion of Liberté, a French hireling sent after the Otos, and Private Reed, who was later recaptured—the explorers met with a group of Otos and Missourias at a point they called the Council Bluff (near the present town of Fort Calhoun) fifty miles up the river, on August 3. Clark's account of this first parley west of the Missouri between representatives of the United States and the Indians shows that he and Lewis were no novices at the art of handling the natives:

Mad up a Small present for those people in perpotion to their Consiquence, also a package with a Meadle to accompany a Speech for the Grand Cheif after Brackfast we collected those Indians under an owning of our Main Sail, in presence or our Party paraded & Delivered a long Speech to them expressive of our journey the wishes of our Government, Some advice to them and Directions how they were to conduct themselves. The principal Chief for the Nation being absent, we Sent him the Speech flag Meadel & Some Cloathes. after hering what they had to say Delivered a Medal of Second Grade to one for the Ottos & one for the Missourie and present 4 medals of a third Grade to the inferior chiefs two for each tribe. . . .

Those Chiefs all Delivered a Speech, acknowledgeing their approbation

[2]Clark, who kept the journal during much of the trip, was an acute observer and an ingenious speller.

to the Speech and promising two prosue the advice & Derections given them that they wer happy to find that they had fathers which might be depended on &c.

We gave them a Cannister of Powder and a Bottle of Whiskey and delivered a few presents to the whole, after giveing a Br. Cth. some Pain guartering & a Meadell to those we *made* Chiefs, after Capt. Lewis's Shooting the air gun a fiew Shots (which astonished those nativs) we Set out. . . .

Clark's comment on the region—which was to become the cradle of white culture in Nebraska—is also of interest: "The Situation of our last Camp *Councile Bluff* or Handsome Prarie, (25 Days from this to *Santafee*) appears to be a verry proper place for a Tradeing establishment & fortification."

A few days later the party suffered its only fatality—that there was only one is perhaps one of the most remarkable aspects of the whole trip. On August 19, Sergeant Charles Floyd was "taken verry bad all at once with a Biliose Chorlick." The next day he died and was buried on top of a bluff one-half mile below the mouth of a small river. To both bluff and river the captains gave his name.

Without further adventure the party proceeded into South Dakota. By late October they had put the Sioux and the Arikaras behind them and were at the Mandan villages near present Bismarck, North Dakota. There they built winter quarters. On April 7, 1805, they set out again. After a season of almost unbearable hardship and harrrowing adventure, they came in view of the Pacific on November 7. They had found a route to the Western Sea.

It was not a good route, and the explorers knew it. Hence, during a miserable winter at Fort Clatsop, which they built on Young's Bay, the leaders decided that on the return trip they would divide the party —there were other routes through that tangled mountain wilderness, they were sure, and they must try to find them. They parted at Travellers' Rest Creek, July 3, Lewis to go directly to the falls of the Missouri and then explore the Marias River region, Clark to go to the head of navigation of the year before and then cross over to the Yellowstone. When they came together on August 12, a few days below the mouth of the Yellowstone, their earlier optimism was gone: any route to the Pacific would involve a long and difficult land carry.

They were back in St. Louis on September 23. Others would find a better route to the Western Sea, but Meriwether Lewis and William

Clark had pointed the way. The significance of their achievement can hardly be overestimated.

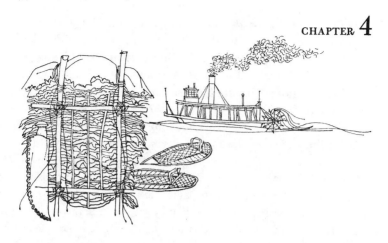

Fur Trader and Missionary

ALONG WITH PRESIDENT JEFFERSON, Americans in the West moved quickly to exploit the Louisiana Purchase. In 1805, General James Wilkinson, Governor of Louisiana territory, sent twenty-six year old Lieutenant Zebulon M. Pike to find the headwaters of the Mississippi. No sooner had the young lieutenant returned to St. Louis—after having dealt successfully with the Indians of the region, even though mistaking Leech Lake for the source of the Mississippi—than General Wilkinson sent him into the Southwest to explore the headwaters of the Arkansas and the Red, and conclude a treaty with the Comanches. His first duty, however, was to escort a group of Osages and Pawnees back to their homeland and arrange peace between the two tribes. When he left St. Louis, July 15, 1806, with his party of twenty-two, he had with him half a hundred Indians. By September 25 he was at the Pawnee villages on the Republican.[1]

The Kansas and Osage were willing to smoke the pipe of peace, but the Pawnees were not so tractable: they had recently been visited by a

[1] In the 1920's an interesting controversy over the exact location of these villages developed between Kansas and Nebraska. The Kansas State Historical Society erected a monument to Pike in Republic County, Kansas, on the presumed site of the village. Later, archeological research by A. T. Hill demonstrated conclusively that the villages were located in Webster County, Nebraska. See *Nebraska History*, X (July-September, 1927), pp. 157–261.

large party of Spaniards under Don Facundo Melgares (sent out, incidentally, to turn back the Americans); Characterish, the Pawnee chief, had a commission from the Governor of New Mexico; several of the chiefs had medals from Melgares; and the Spanish flag flew at the head chief's door. Despite his small force, however, Pike was able to persuade Characterish to haul down the Spanish flag and raise the Stars and Stripes in its stead. This accomplished, he headed southwest—against the advice of the Pawnees, who warned him that the Spanish force was very large and powerful—following the homeward trail of Melgares. The remainder of Pike's journey, which was to include imprisonment by the Spanish in Santa Fe, is of little direct interest to us here—except, perhaps, to recall that he was most unfavorably impressed with the Plains, predicting that they "may become in time as celebrated as the sandy deserts of Africa."

While Pike was penetrating the Southwest, St. Louis traders continued to move up the Missouri. Indeed, on their outbound journey in 1804, Lewis and Clark met no less than eight parties of traders coming downstream before they reached the Platte; on their homeward journey in 1806, they encountered eleven separate parties heading up the river. After Lewis and Clark returned to St. Louis with glowing reports of the profits that could be made in furs, the trade increased rapidly, continuing unchecked as the most important activity in the trans-Missouri region until about 1843, when the high tide of western emigration set in. The traders and trappers roamed everywhere, involving themselves and their government with the Indians and even with foreign powers, drinking, gambling, squawing and carousing, making huge fortunes almost overnight and losing them even more rapidly. Through it all, however, they were exploring this vast, wild country—both plain and mountain—seeking the sources of its rivers and finding new roads to the West. The map of the West was indeed first drawn on a beaver skin.

THE FUR TRADE

The fur trade of the Far West had its headquarters at St. Louis, whose warehouses bulged alternately with trade goods and furs and whose port became the center of a commerce almost as widespread as that of New York. Nebraska's role was primarily that of providing a highway. To be sure, the Nebraska tribes—particularly in the early years—were the source of a fairly profitable trade, but once the traders had penetrated to the tribes dwelling in the rich beaver grounds of the upper Missouri and the Rocky Mountains, the relative significance of the Nebraska trade steadily declined. The Missouri River, however, and later the Platte, were the highways to the rich grounds farther on, and the traffic to and from the Far West played an important role in Nebraska's pre-territorial history. Trading posts flourished along the Missouri, particularly near the mouth of the Platte, and in the Scotts Bluff region. Fort Atkinson provided protection for the early up-river trade and was the point from which the first Rocky Mountain expedition was launched.

First of the large-scale operators to penetrate the upper Missouri after Lewis and Clark was Manuel Lisa, who left St. Louis in the spring of 1807 with a keelboat full of trade goods. At the mouth of the Platte he met John Colter—who had been with Lewis and Clark—and persuaded him to go back up the river. After encounters with various hostile tribes, especially the Dakotas and Assiniboines, he halted at the mouth of the Bighorn River in the heart of the Crow country. Here he built a post, variously known as Fort Lisa, Fort Manuel, and Manuel's Fort. His activities during the winter are somewhat obscure, but the next spring he was back in St. Louis, elated with his success and anxious to expand the trade. To accomplish this, the St. Louis Missouri Fur Company was organized on March 7, 1809, as a co-partnership. Lisa's partners in this venture included some of the best-known men in St. Louis—Pierre and Auguste Chouteau, William Clark, Andrew Henry, Sylvestre Labadie, Reuben Lewis, Pierre Menard, William Morrison, and Benjamin Wilkinson. Even so, the company's early efforts were not notably successful. The first expedition left St. Louis in June, 1809, with 172 men and nine barges loaded with goods worth $4,269, including whiskey valued at $165. By the time they reached Fort Osage, sickness and desertion had reduced the crew to 153 men, and though trade on the Big Horn was fairly successful, they lost most of their goods and many men to the Blackfeet. After much difficulty and some dissension the company was reorganized in 1812. Also in that year pressure from the British and Indians forced Lisa—who continued to be the company's principal agent in the field—to abandon the upper river. He retreated to a point near the Council Bluff and there built a new post (Fort Lisa), which soon came to be the most important on the Missouri River. Fort Lisa controlled the trade of the Omahas, Pawnees, and Otos, and after the war served as a base for the revival of trade on the upper river. Its proprietor exercised dominion over the Nebraska country. Hot-tempered, erratic—but always forceful—Manuel Lisa was one of the most controversial figures in the fur trade. Though hated by his competitors and some of his employees, he seems to have got on well with the Indians. After the custom of most fur traders, he took an Indian wife, a beautiful Omaha girl who bore him two children and who helped solidify his position with the tribe—but the source of much embarrassment when Mrs. Lisa accompanied her husband to the post in 1819. He served as agent for the tribes on the Missouri above the Kansas, and appears to have been instrumental in preventing the British from winning these tribes as allies. Through all this he was successful financially, and business had so far revived by 1818 that he was considering the possibility of re-establishing trade at the headwaters of the Missouri and even beyond the Rocky Mountains. He died in 1820, however, before he had had an opportunity to carry out his plans.

After Lisa's death, Joshua Pilcher took over the management of the company. He tried to carry out Lisa's plans for re-establishing trade on the upper Missouri, but was no more successful than Lisa at first had been. He withdrew altogether from trade above the Omahas, retiring to the main establishment at Fort Lisa. The company continued to do business for several years and may have operated in the Rockies, but its activities were of little importance in comparison with the growing power of the Western Department of John Jacob Astor's American Fur Company.

Lisa himself had had a brush with this colossus, which would soon largely dominate the fur trade of the Far West. In 1811, on his last trip to the upper river, Lisa got involved in a desperate keelboat race and even more desperate maneuvering for the favor of the up-river tribes with Wilson Price Hunt, who was making his way to Astoria, the American Fur Company's projected post at the mouth of the Columbia River.[2] Though Astoria, like Lisa's upper Missouri enterprises, was a casualty of the War of 1812, failure there did not dull Astor's ambition to con-

---

[2]Lisa was accompanied by Henry M. Brackenridge, well-known author and traveller; accompanying Hunt was John Bradbury, naturalist and traveller. Each kept a journal from which much of interest regarding the two expeditions and the Missouri Valley can be learned. They were reprinted in Reuben Gold Thwaites, ed., *Early Western Travels* (Cleveland: Arthur H. Clark Company, 1904), Vols. V and VI.

trol the trade of the Far West. Following the war he moved seriously to achieve his monopolistic goal.

Meanwhile, the War Department, under the leadership of Secretary John C. Calhoun, was moving aggressively to exploit the advantage won in the war. A succession of treaties at Portages des Sioux in 1815 had provided a basis for peace with thirteen of the western tribes, including the Omahas, Poncas, Iowas, and Sioux. To preserve the peace and counteract remaining British influence, Calhoun proposed to build a series of self-sustaining military posts at strategic points along the Mississippi and Missouri rivers and their tributaries, and to connect them with adequate roads. Fort Snelling was to be the principal post on the upper Mississippi. On the Missouri, posts were to be constructed at the Council Bluff, the Mandan villages, and possibly at the great bend and at some point above the Mandan villages, perhaps the mouth of the Yellowstone.

The Missouri enterprise—commonly referred to as the Yellowstone Expedition—consisted of a military force under Colonel Henry M. Atkinson and a scientific party under Major Stephen H. Long of the Army Engineers. Atkinson had 1,126 men—the Sixth Infantry and the United States Rifle Regiment. Abandoning keelboats in favor of steamboats—hitherto untried on the Missouri—Atkinson found himself in trouble from the beginning. Of the five steamboats provided by the contractor —a particularly corrupt and inefficient operator—two never entered the river at all, a third was abandoned thirty miles below Franklin, Missouri, and the other two stopped below the mouth of the Kansas. Atkinson's men were lucky to reach the Council Bluff before winter set in. Major Long was more fortunate. His steamboat, the *Western Engineer,* despite its fantastic design, was much better suited to the Missouri than were the others: it was of lighter draft and was a stern-wheeler, probably the first ever built. The *Western Engineer* made it all the way to the Council Bluff, the first steamboat to ascend the Missouri to that point.

Atkinson's troops spent a scurvy-ridden winter at "Camp Missouri," in the bottoms below the Council Bluff; Long's fared little better at "Engineer Cantonment," five miles down the river. With spring, news came that Congress, weary of the expense and dubious of the whole Northwest project, had clipped the War Department's wings. Long, who had spent the winter in Washington, returned to lead a small ex-

ploring party up the Platte; Atkinson's troops were to go no farther.
The Council Bluff was to be the outpost of the nation's Northwest de-
fenses. There was another small expedition; Captain Matthew J. Magee
of the Rifle Regiment was sent to open a route from the Council Bluff
to Fort Anthony, later Fort Snelling.

Long's force, consisting of twenty men, left Engineer Cantonment
on June 6, 1820. The most notable result of the expedition was the
unfavorable impression it fostered regarding the country west of the
Missouri.[3] At the Loup fork, the party came upon the Pawnee villages.
Long estimated their population at something less than the 6,223 found by
Pike in 1806, but they were "still numerous, and . . . said to be increasing."
Around the villages were six to eight thousand horses, grazing on the
plains during the day but confined in corrals at night. Picking up two
French guides at the villages, Long followed the north side of the Platte
to the forks, and then crossed over to the south side. The party reached
the Rocky Mountains, and Dr. Edwin James, scientist for the expedition, scaled Pikes Peak, the first white man to do so. They continued
south to the Arkansas River, and in an unsuccessful effort to find the
headwaters of the Red, Long divided his party. Finally, in mid-Sep-
tember they were reunited at Fort Smith, having suffered much but accomplished little.

Meanwhile, the Sixth Infantry, thwarted in its plan to go further up
the Missouri, was occupied in transforming Camp Missouri from a temporary cantonment into a permanent post, to be designated Fort Atkinson. The camp was moved to higher ground, and new barracks, covered with shingles and furnished with brick chimneys, were erected.
The soldiers raised good crops of corn, turnips, and potatoes, and large
herds of cattle and hogs. A saw mill was built and a brickyard established. Colonel Atkinson was promoted to the command of the western
wing of the Western Department, and Colonel Henry Leavenworth arrived to take command of the Sixth Infantry. As Calhoun had written
the chairman of the House Committee on Indian Affairs, "the position
at Council Bluffs is a very important one. . . . It is believed to be the
best position on the Missouri to cover our flourishing settlements in
that quarter and ought, if it were wholly unconnected with other objects,
to be established for that purpose alone."[4]

[3]See pp. 3–4.
[4]*American State Papers, Military Affairs*, II, 33.

But there were "other objects." The fur trade, in a decline since the war, was showing marked signs of revival. The *Missouri Intelligencer,* September 17, 1822, estimated that a thousand men were employed on the waters of the Missouri.[5] The American Fur Company had established its Western Department at St. Louis. The Columbia Fur Company had entered the field the year before. The Missouri Fur Company was carrying on Lisa's business. Others new in the business or with increased capital were Stone, Bostwick and Company, Bernard Pratte and Company, and Ashley and Henry. They all had designs on the dangerous upper Missouri country. They would all need protection.

Trouble was not long in coming. Men from the Missouri Fur Company, floating down-river with a load of furs, were attacked by the Blackfeet on the Yellowstone, May 31, 1823. The leaders of the party and five men were killed, and all their furs and equipment lost. On June 2, General William H. Ashley, returning up-river from St. Louis (his partner, Andrew Henry, had wintered on the Yellowstone) was attacked by the Arickaras near the mouth of the Grand. He retreated down the river to a fortified point near the present town of Chamberlain, South Dakota, and sent calls for help to Colonel Leavenworth at Fort Atkinson and Major Henry on the Yellowstone. Henry promptly came down the river with most of his party, and by early August Colonel Leavenworth had arrived with 220 regulars from Fort Atkinson. Also on hand were Joshua Pilcher with a party of men from the Missouri Fur Company, and a sizable band of Dakotas. These forces were at cross purposes from the beginning. The Dakotas were interested only in plunder, and when they saw no prospect of that, they left in disgust. The traders wanted the Arickaras exterminated, to get them out of the way and to serve as an example to other tribes. Colonel Leavenworth, however, wanted only to punish the offenders. As a result, the so-called "Arickara War" settled nothing. Leavenworth got a peace treaty with the Arickaras, but it was by no means satisfactory to the traders. Ashley and Henry decided to transfer their activities to other fields. In so doing, they opened the fur trade of the rich Rocky Mountain area and blazed the Platte Valley trail, soon to become the West's great emigrant road.

Robert Stuart had come down the Platte in 1812–13 when returning

[5]H. C. Dale, ed., *The Ashley-Smith Explorations and the Discovery of a Central Route to the Pacific* (Cleveland: Arthur H. Clark Company, 1918), p. 64.

from Astoria with word for John Jacob Astor about the plight of that post. In the spring of 1824, Thomas Fitzpatrick and James Clyman also followed the Platte River route from the mountains to the Missouri, reporting to Ashley—who had returned to St. Louis after the Arickara trouble—the rich beaver grounds in the Green River country and the practicable road to them.[6] Ashley, who had spent the summer unsuccessfully campaigning for governor of Missouri, immediately organized an expedition to the Rocky Mountains. He set out from Fort Atkinson with a party of twenty-five men, fifty pack horses, and a wagon, on November 3, 1824—very late in the season for such a venture. He followed the Platte to its forks, then went up the South Fork because it seemed to promise more wood. Mid-April, 1825, found him at the Green River. Here he divided his men into four groups with instructions to trap the region and rendezvous on the Green, near Henry's Fork, in July. Thus Ashley, in addition to pioneering a new route and opening a new trade region, inaugurated the fur trade's lustiest institution—the summer rendezvous which annually brought together traders, trappers, and Indians for a period of dealing, double-dealing, and carousing.

Meanwhile, Fort Atkinson continued to flourish. The agricultural experiment of 1820 was repeated annually on an ever-increasing scale; the post was improved and became the center of white activity on the Missouri. It was not very effective, however, in fulfilling its original mission, the protection of the fur trade. The War Department began to question the need for its continuance. General Atkinson and Major Benjamin O'Fallon had gone up the river in 1825 and concluded treaties with seventeen of the tribes. The success of this expedition made it appear that a post on the upper Missouri was unnecessary. Perhaps there was little need for Fort Atkinson, too. Inspector George Croghan, who visited Fort Atkinson in 1826, denounced it as the weakest fort with the worst trained garrison he had ever seen. The fact that the sol-

[6]Fitzpatrick and Clyman were but two of the men sent by Ashley after the Arickara War to explore the mountain region south of the Missouri. The party, as H. C. Dale suggests, "was the most significant group of continental explorers ever brought together." Their wanderings during the next ten to fifteen years covered the entire West. The group included, in addition to Henry, Fitzpatrick, and Clyman: Edward Rose, Louis Vasquez, Jim Bridger, David E. Jackson, Hugh Glass, Seth Grant, and Jedediah Smith. See Dale, *op. cit.*, pp. 86–87.

diers had so much time for agriculture was, to him, the key to its use-lessness. With great irritation, he wrote:

. The men say there is no danger—well than as well argue that there should be no army and I would as soon argue there be none. The present system is destroying military spirit and making officers the base overseers of a troop of awkward ploughmen. Let the soldier be one. Let him no longer boast of his skill as a tiller of the soil, but as a soldier . . . Look at Fort Atkinson and you will see barnyards that would not disgrace a Pennsylvania farmer, herds of cattle that would do credit to a Potomac grazier, yet where is the gain in this, either to the soldier or to the Government? Why all the corn and hay? To feed to cattle. Why the cattle? to eat the corn and hay.

Shortly thereafter, in June, 1827, Fort Atkinson was abandoned, and the Sixth Infantry was transferred to Jefferson Barracks, near St. Louis. Later in the year, a new post, Cantonment Leavenworth, was established farther south near the jumping-off place for the growing Santa Fe trade and for an ever-increasing number of expeditions to the Rocky Mountains. Though Fort Atkinson was too far north to protect this trade and too far south to protect the trade of the upper river—and though it was generally vilified as an unfortunate and expensive aftermath of the abortive Yellowstone Expedition—the post at the Council Bluff played an important, if brief and neglected, role in frontier history. Nationally, it gave protection to the fur trade when the need was greatest, and it represented a significant extension of the military frontier line. Locally, it was the site of initial farming operations by whites in a state that in less than a century was to become noted for its agriculture.

Though Fort Atkinson was abandoned and the area completely deserted,[7] the position at Bellevue, a few miles down the river, continued to flourish. In 1823 Andrew Drips was operating a post there for the Missouri Fur Company, and in that same year John Dougherty moved the agency for the Omahas, Otos, Missourias, and Pawnees to Bellevue from Fort Atkinson. When Drips went west, Lucien Fontenelle took over the post and in 1831 sold it to the Government as headquarters for the Indian Agency. This left the American Fur Company, whose post was operated by Peter Sarpy, in complete control of the fur trade at Bellevue; and from the early 1830's on, Peter Sarpy was the dominant

[7]Prince Maxmilian, who visited the site in 1833, reported: "everything of value had been carried away by the Indians. We were told that numerous rattlesnakes are found among the ruins." (Thwaites, ed., *Early Western Travels*, XXII, 275.)

figure in the Nebraska country. His post at Bellevue was a rendezvous
for Indians, traders, and travellers.

The Missionary

The fur trade had a profound effect upon the Indians, resulting in
the substitution of so many features of white culture for native traits—
weapons, implements, clothing, and vices—as to bring about an almost
complete breakdown of the native way of life. Particularly disastrous
to the Indian was the white man's "fire water." The red man found it
irresistible and under its influence was a menace both to himself and
all those around him, as well as an easily defrauded customer. No West-
erner believed that an Indian could be trusted with liquor. There may
be something to this persistent legend, but trade whiskey was a con-
coction so vile that its deleterious effect was not limited to Indians.
The trader's recipe called for one gallon raw alcohol, three gallons
water, a pound of chewing tobacco. As Montana's cowboy artist, Charles
M. Russell, wrote: "I never knowed what made an Injun so crazy when
he drunk till I tried this booze. . . . It was sure a brave-maker."[8] The
Indian Intercourse Act of 1834 prohibited the importation of liquor
into the Indian country, and inspectors were stationed at Leavenworth,
Bellevue, and other points to enforce the prohibition. All efforts at enforcement, however, were ineffectual. Liquor was the one indispensable article in the fur trade, and the St. Louis traders argued that they
needed it to meet competition from Hudson's Bay Company representatives who had free use of it. Hence, in spite of the best efforts of federal authorities—or with their connivance—vast quantities of liquor
were smuggled into the Indian country each year.

Striving hard but rather ineffectually to counteract the traders' influence among the Indians was a small band of missionaries. Widespread
interest in western missionary activity dates from a celebrated visit of a
delegation of Flatheads, or Nez Perces, to St. Louis in 1831, request-
ing General William Clark to send them a "Bible and a Black Robe."
Here was really a call to action. Here were fields "white unto harvest."
The religious press of the country circulated the news excitedly, calling for volunteers and funds. Despite the obvious reference to a Catholic priest, the Methodists were first to respond, sending Jason Lee to

[8]Charles M. Russell, *Trails Plowed Under* (Garden City: Doubleday, Page and Company, 1927), p. 32.

Oregon with the trapper caravan of 1834. The next year, the Presbyterians sent out Samuel Parker and Marcus Whitman. Dr. Whitman went only as far as the Green River, then returned to the States, to go back in 1836 with his bride, Narcissa, and the Reverend and Mrs. Henry H. Spalding. Narcissa Whitman and Eliza Spalding thus became the first white women to go over the overland trail.[9] In the 1830's, Father Pierre Jean DeSmet, the noted Jesuit, came into the region to begin his life of service among the Indians of the plains and mountains.

Meanwhile, as early as November, 1830, the Baptist Missionary Union had made preliminary arrangements with the Government to establish a mission among a number of the Nebraska tribes. Early in 1833, Reverend Johnston Lykins was sent to visit the tribes along the Missouri. He found a fallow field, the Indians in the vicinity of American Fur Company posts being particularly debased. That same year the Baptists selected Moses P. Merrill to establish a mission at the Bellevue Agency. Accompanied by Mrs. Merrill, Miss Cynthia Brown, and Ira D. Blanchard, the Reverend Mr. Merrill arrived at Bellevue, November 8. Mrs. Merrill opened a school on the seventh day after their arrival. In 1835, Merrill was appointed a government teacher, thus making it possible for him to augment the meager support provided by the Missionary Union. Merrill was particularly active in providing literature in the native tongues—a spelling book, reader, and a small collection of hymns. He worked diligently, but he was only partially successful. This he attributed to the evil influence of the traders. In 1839 he accompanied the Pawnees on their autumn hunt. He returned ill, and died in 1840.

Most adventuresome of the early missionaries in Nebraska were John Dunbar and Samuel Allis, sent by the Presbyterians to the Pawnees in 1834. They arrived at Bellevue in October, hoping to make arrangements to spend the winter with the Pawnees. When the Pawnees came in for their annuities later in the month and learned of the desires of the two men, they welcomed them with open arms. There was only one difficulty. Each tribe wanted one of them. The missionaries had assumed that they would spend the winter together, and the prospect

[9]For accounts of their experience, see Narcissa Whitman, "A Journey Across the Plains in 1836," *Transactions,* Oregon Pioneer Association, 19th Annual Reunion, 1891, pp. 40–68; and Eliza Spalding Warren, *Memoirs of the West; the Spaldings* (Portland: privately printed, n.d.).

of living alone with a heathen tribe in the wilderness was not something to be relished. Nevertheless, "after prayerful and mature deliberation on the subject, and advising with the agent," they decided to separate, Dunbar going with the Grand Pawnees and Allis with the Loups. Both men were treated with the utmost consideration by their savage hosts, who, in turn, felt that the missionaries had brought them good fortune. The buffalo were lower down the Platte in 1834–35 than they had been for twenty years. The Pawnees told Dunbar that it was because he had come to live with them: "They say the buffalo have been gone a long time, but now a man has come to live with them who loves *Te-rah-wah,* and he has sent back the buffalo."[10]

Though Allis was to spend one and Dunbar two more years wandering with the tribes, both men were anxious to have the Pawnees permanently located. In the spring of 1841 they established a mission among the Tappages on Plum Creek, not far from the present town of Fullerton. Dunbar thought this "fine corn country," and believed wheat could "be cultivated to advantage." By the autumn of 1842, the Tappages, together with many Grands and Republicans, had a village of forty-one lodges near the mission. The mission at Plum Creek failed to prosper. Dunbar and Allis became estranged, and much of their time seems to have been occupied in fruitless controversy over both temporal and spiritual matters. Moreover, the Sioux were a constant threat, and finally in 1846 forced an abandonment of the mission.

That same year the Presbyterians established a mission for the Omahas at Bellevue, with Mr. and Mrs. Edward McKinney in charge. They opened a school in 1847, and despite much opposition and many difficulties, the mission prospered. Reverend William Hamilton took charge in 1853, continuing with the Omahas—except for the decade 1857–67 —until 1870, when the tribe was assigned to the Society of Friends. "Father Hamilton," as he was called, was much beloved by both Indians and whites and was to play an important role in early territorial history.

It is difficult to assess the work of the missionaries. They had the welfare of the Indians at heart and, according to their lights, worked

[10]"Letters Concerning the Presbyterian Mission in the Pawnee Country, near Bellevue, Neb., 1831–1849," *Collections,* Kansas State Historical Society, XIV (1915–18), 608. This valuable series of letters provides much useful information on both the missionaries and the Pawnees.

to promote it, particularly against the influence of the traders—an influence which, all the missionaries agreed, was particularly baneful. Moreover, while the trader was merely indifferent to the Indian's culture, the missionary saw in it something that must be changed. Both contributed to its ultimate dissolution. Of greatest immediate—and perhaps permanent—significance was the fact that in the Oregon country the missionaries were able to win ground in the region where the traders had failed. They may not have been successful in converting the heathen, but their efforts were a major force in calling the country's attention to Oregon and inducing emigration thither—emigration that in less than a generation would almost completely transform the face of the West.

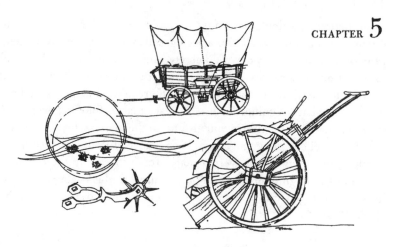

CHAPTER 5

The Great Road West

BY THE TIME any substantial American interest had developed in the Oregon country, the Platte River trail had replaced the Missouri River as the way to the Pacific Northwest. It was shorter and, with the use of South Pass, much easier. The broad, flat valley of the Platte with its easy ascent to the foothills of the Rockies provided westward-moving Americans with one of the world's great natural highways, and the Platte Valley became the funnel through which America literally spilled over into the West.

The Platte Valley's significance resulted from the incomparable road-bed it provided for wagons—the river itself was not navigable, as all who tried to use it as a means of water transport learned to their sorrow. Robert Stuart, the first white man through the valley, had reported its potentiality as a wagon route in 1813. Ashley's party of 1824 had a wagon along when it set out from Fort Atkinson. There is no record, however, as to how far that wagon went, and even if it got all the way to the mountains, Ashley followed the South Platte rather than the North Platte, which led to the Sweetwater and South Pass. The first wagons to leave their tracks on what was to become the Oregon Trail were those taken west by Jedediah Smith, David Jackson, and William Sublette in 1830. Successors to Ashley, the firm of Smith, Jackson and Sublette set out from St. Louis with ten wagons drawn by five mules each and two Dearborns—four-wheeled carriages with curtained sides

—drawn by one mule each. Leaving the Santa Fe Trail about forty miles west of Independence, Missouri, they angled northwestward across the Kansas and the Blue to the Platte, arriving ultimately at the head of Wind River. Here they stopped to gather furs, but, they observed, "the wagons could easily have crossed the Rocky mountains, it being what is called the Southern Pass."[1] In 1832 Benjamin E. Bonneville took wagons through South Pass and as far as the Green River. In 1836 Dr. Marcus Whitman tried to take a two-wheeled cart all the way to Oregon but was forced to abandon it at Fort Boise. Finally, in 1838, Reverend W. H. Gray and party managed to get a two-wheeled cart all the way.

THE OREGON TRAIL

Meanwhile, interest in Oregon was growing apace. By the early 1820's a young Boston school teacher, Hall J. Kelley, was writing letters, newspaper articles, and pamphlets urging the United States to assert her right to Oregon. In 1838 Jason Lee returned East to preach the glories of Oregon from pulpits all over the country. Dr. Marcus Whitman, whose greatest ambition was to settle Oregon with Protestant Americans, wrote and talked extensively on the subject. An Oregon Emigration Society was organized in Lynn, Massachusetts, in 1838, and others developed elsewhere. To patriotic and missionary motives were added the pressures of the panic of 1837, the desire to escape the seemingly unhealthful climate of the Mississippi Valley, the lure of opportunity in a new land, and just plain adventure. The Oregon agitation was soon to bear fruit.

Early in May, 1841, the first band of settlers—about eighty in all, including a few missionaries—set out from the Missouri frontier. Their guide was the veteran mountain man, Thomas Fitzpatrick. Near Soda Springs, in present Idaho, the group divided, with half heading for California and the remainder pushing on to Oregon. The next year more than one hundred persons—men, women, and children—were in the emigrant party. Their leader, Dr. Elijah White, who had gone to Oregon as a missionary with Jason Lee, was now returning as an Indian

[1]Letter, Jedediah Smith, David E. Jackson, and W. L. Sublette, St. Louis, to J. H. Eaton, Secretary of War, 29 October 1833, in Archer B. Hulbert, ed., *The Documentary Background of the Days of the First Wagon Train on the Road to Oregon* (Missoula: University of Montana, 1930), pp. 20–21.

agent. Also in 1842 Lieutenant John C. Fremont led an exploring expedition through the Platte Valley to South Pass. Fremont was to go down in history as the "Great Pathfinder," but he was travelling a trail over which hundreds of traders, missionaries, and emigrants had gone before. Though he found no new trails, Fremont's report—written in part by his beautiful and talented wife, Jessie, daughter of Missouri's noted expansionist senator, Thomas Hart Benton—greatly stimulated interest in Oregon and definitely established the Platte Valley-South Pass route as the best way west.

By 1843 the full tide of emigration had set in, and in that year more than a thousand persons went over the trail, taking with them about 120 wagons drawn by six-ox teams, and several thousand loose horses and cattle. This "great migration" was not the result of an organized movement, but was simply the coming together of restless and adventurous souls from all parts of the country, who assembled at Independence because they had heard that a wagon train would start from there for Oregon as soon as the weather permitted. In the beginning, some effort was made to travel in one body, but this proved so unwieldy that at the crossing of the Big Blue the group divided into two columns to proceed separately but within supporting distance of each other. At Independence Rock on the Sweetwater—the danger from the Indians being deemed over—they divided further into small parties and proceeded on their individual ways.

Eighteen-forty-three was only the beginning. Reliable statistics are not available, but it is safe to say that almost each succeeding year through the 1850's additional thousands headed for Oregon. The Oregon Trail became the highroad of American expansion.

The two-thousand mile trail began at Independence, Missouri, also the jumping-off place for Santa Fe. From Independence, the emigrants followed the old Santa Fe Trail for about forty miles (generally a two days' journey) to where a crude sign marked the "Road to Oregon." Here they angled northwest to the Platte, crossing the Kansas and the Blue. They followed the Platte to the forks and beyond, crossed the South Platte, and went over to the North Fork, following that past Scotts Bluff and Fort Laramie. They crossed the North Platte and went on to the Sweetwater and South Pass. Though the journey across the Plains and up the east slope of the mountains had been unbelievably wearisome and beset with danger from the Indians—both real and imagined

—it was the easier part of the trip. The Pacific side was much more difficult: the narrow valleys and high passes were almost impassable, and only the most determined could prod their footsore oxen into dragging the worn-out wagons past Fort Bridger, Soda Springs, and Fort Hall, along the Snake and down the Columbia to the Willamette Valley.

The trail entered present-day Nebraska at about the line between Gage and Jefferson counties, followed the Blue Valley across Jefferson, Thayer, Nuckolls, and Adams counties, and joined the Platte near the head of the "Grand Island" in Hall County. It went along the south side of the Platte to a point in Keith County, about seven miles east of Big Springs. There the South Platte was crossed, and the emigrants went northwest through Ash Hollow to the North Platte, then past Court House and Jail rocks, Chimney Rock, and Scotts Bluff to Fort Laramie. Initially, the trail swung south of Scotts Bluff—named for Hiram Scott, a fur trader who lost his life there—through Robidoux Pass, rejoining the river to the west of the bluffs. Beginning about 1850, Mitchell Pass, nearer the river, was used. In many places, of course, there was no "one" trail. Whenever the ruts became too deep for the wagons, the emigrants simply broke out a parallel trail; during dry years certain trails were used which became impassable in wet years, when the streams were full and the lowlands swampy.

THE MORMON TRAIL

Beginning in 1847, the Mormons, writing an additional chapter in the history of American expansion, broke a new trail through the Platte Valley. Driven out of Nauvoo, Illinois, they made their way across Iowa to the Missouri River in the spring of 1846. Here Brigham Young, their gifted leader, made an agreement with the Government to furnish five hundred "volunteers" for the Mexican War in return for the privilege of stopping for the winter in the Indian country just across the river. Selecting a beautiful tract of land a few miles above Bellevue—the site is now Florence, Omaha's northern suburb—the Mormons busied themselves during the summer and fall in constructing "Winter Quarters." More than three thousand of the faithful moved across the Missouri to take up temporary residence at Winter Quarters. Others remained along the way in Iowa, and a small detachment spent a miserable winter among the Poncas on the Niobrara, finally abandoning the faith altogether. But those at Winter Quarters had a miserable time of it, too. Some of them built log houses, but most clung to life in their wagons or in caves dug in the hillsides. Poorly housed and inadequately fed, the pitiful residents of Winter Quarters fell before scurvy, malaria, and just plain cold and starvation. More than six hundred died that winter. Many of them lie in nameless graves in the little Mormon cemetery overlooking Florence. Winter Quarters, however, was more than just a wayside camp. It was the administrative center of a great movement, and through all the suffering and starvation Brigham Young worked relentlessly to organize his followers for the push next year to some point well beyond the States where they might create a new Zion. As Bernard DeVoto put it: "Nothing in American history . . . is like Winter Quarters," and few leaders can compare with Brigham Young—"a great leader, a great diplomat, a great administrator, and at need a great liar and a great scoundrel . . . one of the finders and one of the makers of the West."[2]

By early spring, Young's plans were firm. He would lead a small, picked band to point the way and select the site; the others would follow. The "pioneer band" left their appointed rendezvous on the Elkhorn on April 16. The party numbered 143 men and boys, three women, and two children; they had 72 wagons, 93 horses, 52 mules, 66 oxen, 19 cows, 17 dogs, and a few coops of chickens. To keep as far away from the Gentiles as possible, Young chose the north side of the Platte. They crossed the Loup Fork—the most substantial barrier along the Platte—on April 23, building two light rafts to carry their supplies and equipment, and fording the empty wagons. June 1 saw them at Fort Laramie, where they halted to rest the animals and build ferry boats. Finding they had to recross the North Platte 124 miles further on, subsequent emigrations were instructed to keep to the north side of the river. By July 24 they had arrived at the valley of the Great Salt Lake and decided that here they would build their new Zion. The "pioneer band" was followed by some two thousand of the faithful during 1847. (In addition, more than six thousand Gentiles went through the Platte Valley that year to Oregon and California.) The Mormons generally were less well equipped than those who travelled the south side of the Platte—as DeVoto puts it, "they were migrating on a frayed shoe string"[3]—but generally they made better time and suffered less hardship.

[2]Bernard DeVoto, *The Year of Decision: 1846* (Boston: Little, Brown and Company, 1943), pp. 435, 439.

Having established his followers at Salt Lake, Young returned to Winter Quarters, arriving October 31, to organize the next year's emigration. In what probably was the first example of printing in Nebraska, he issued a call to the Saints, "abroad, dispersed throughout the earth," to gather at Winter Quarters "and, if possible, be ready to start from hence by the first of May next, or as soon as grass is sufficiently grown, and go to the Great Salt Lake City, with bread stuff sufficient to sustain you until you can raise grain the following season." Those who could not afford to make the trip to Salt Lake he advised to work the Pottawatomie lands: "In a year or two their young cattle will grow into teams; by interchange of labor they can raise their own grain and provisions, and build their own wagons; and by sale of their improvements, to citizens who will gladly come and occupy, they can replenish their clothing, and thus speedily and comfortably procure an outfit."[4]

Young led some 2,500 emigrants to Salt Lake in 1848, more than doubling its population. If Zion was to succeed, however, still more people would be needed. Missionaries were sent throughout the United States and to Europe to convert people to the faith and to persuade them to journey to the promised land. To assist the indigent, a perpetual emigration fund was formed. The lure was great, especially among the impoverished of Europe, and converts continued to come. Winter Quarters was abandoned, but the north bank of the Platte still was recognized as the official trail. Many, however, used the South Platte trail, starting from old Fort Kearny, and after 1856 from Wyoming in Otoe County, which flourished briefly as an outfitting point. Unfortunately, most of the emigrants were so poor that they needed almost total assistance, and it took all of Young's ingenuity to keep the perpetual emigration fund alive. Finally, in 1855, Young, in desperation, announced that no longer could the Church provide wagons for the emigrants: he would "make hand-carts, and let the emigration foot it." And so he did, setting in motion the most bizarre phase of the entire westward emigration.

The new town of Florence, located on the site of old Winter Quarters, was selected as the starting place. The first company, comprising about five hundred persons, set out on July 17, 1856. A traveller, coming down the Platte from Oregon, described them:

[4]Douglas C. McMurtrie, ed., *The General Epistle of the Latter Day Saints Dated: Winter Quarters, Nebraska, December 23, 1847* . . . (Chicago: Black Cat Press, 1935).

. . . The carts were generally drawn by one man and three women each, though some carts were drawn by women alone. There were about three women to one man, and two-thirds of the women were single. It was the most motley crew I ever beheld. Most of them were Danes, with a sprinkling of Welsh, Swedes, and English, and were generally from the lower classes of their countries. Most could not understand what we said to them. The road was lined for a mile behind the train with the lame, halt, sick, and needy. Many were quite aged, and would be going slowly along, supported by a son or daughter. Some were on crutches; now and then a mother with a child in her arms and two or three hanging hold of her, with a forlorn appearance, would pass slowly along; others, whose condition entitled them to a seat in the carriage, were wending their way through the sand. A few seemed in good spirits.[5]

On September 26, the handcarts rolled down Emigration Canyon to the edge of Salt Lake City to be met by Brigham Young, a military escort, hundreds of Saints, and a brass band. Said Young, "I count the hand-cart operation a successful one." He wrote to his missionaries in England: "It is worthy of notice, that almost all the sisters who have this season crossed the Plains in the handcarts, have got husbands; they are esteemed for their perseverance."

Altogether, five handcart companies set out from Florence in 1856. The last two got caught in the snows, and 150 of 500 in the fifth company perished, a greater loss than that suffered by the Donner party. Though Young had counted the operation a successful one, the handcarts were little used after 1856—two expeditions in 1857, one in 1859, and two in 1860 (the last). Altogether, however, three thousand persons walked across the Plains to Salt Lake City. After 1860, Young sent "church teams" to meet emigrants at the railroad terminal. With the completion of the transcontinental railroad, of course, the Saints could make the entire trip by rail.

THE CALIFORNIA GOLD RUSH

The pioneer Mormons were hardly settled at Salt Lake City before gold was discovered in the tail race of Captain John A. Sutter's mill

[5]William A. Linn, *The Story of the Mormons* (New York: The Macmillan Company, 1902), pp. 422–423, quoted in Jay Monaghan, "Handcarts on the Overland Trail," *Nebraska History*, XXX (March, 1949), 3–18, which contains an excellent account of the Mormon handcart experiment.

on the South Fork of the American River in California. Sutter tried to keep the discovery secret, but news such as this could not be kept. By May, 1848, diggings were being worked for thirty miles along the river; during the summer rich placers were found on other streams; by autumn the whole world was alive with excitement. As the New Year dawned hundreds of excited gold seekers already were on the high seas in ships bound for California. Thousands more were making plans to go overland as soon as the grass was green in the spring.

There were various overland routes to California, but the one most heavily used was the Platte Valley-South Pass trail. By early spring more than twenty thousand persons were congregated at Independence, Fort Leavenworth, St. Joseph, and Council Bluffs eagerly awaiting the day when they could begin their trek across the Plains. And a motley crew they were. Gamblers, pickpockets, prostitutes and the off-scouring of a frontier society rubbed shoulders with men of high purpose and serious design. As one emigrant wrote his wife from Westport: "It would astonish you to see the number of people going to California. It would be the greatest sight you ever saw. The people are of all kinds, some of the first people in the United States are a-going and some of the meanest are also along."[6]

Though thousands had been over the trail before them, many of the Forty-Niners were unable or unwilling to make use of the information that had accumulated over the years. As a result, many started west preposterously overloaded; many others tried to walk, carrying their worldly goods on their backs. By the time they reached Fort Kearny, both classes were aware of their folly, and the trail near that post was literally strewn with abandoned equipment, foodstuffs, and even wagons. Some sold their excess baggage; others left it along the trail for whoever wanted it; still others burned their wagons, mixed turpentine with their sugar, and dirt with their flour. Those who started out with too little had to call on the commandant at Fort Kearny for relief, and had not the Army come to their rescue, many would not have been able to go farther.[7]

[6]"Diary of the Overland Trail, 1849, and Letters 1849–50 of Captain David De-Wolf," *Transactions of the Illinois Historical Society*, No. 32 (1925), p. 186.

[7]For an excellent account of this aspect of the gold rush, see Lyle E. Mantor, "Fort Kearny and the Westward Movement," *Nebraska History*, XXIX (September, 1948), 175–207.

There were other problems, even more serious. The grass of the Platte Valley was ground and eaten away by the vast throng of animals. Buffalo and other wild game—upon which many planned to depend for food—became scarce, and hunters had to range far from the trail. Most serious of all, the dread cholera struck in 1849 as never before. Whether it was an epidemic or the result of contaminated water—no one knew for sure—the heterogeneous mass of humanity on the trail provided an ideal medium for its spread. The disease struck quickly and without warning, and the victims often died within twenty-four hours. New graves appeared almost every day.[8]

Despite cholera and other hardships, the eager Argonauts pushed on to California. Reliable statistics are not available, but the best estimates place the number who went over the trail in '49 at about 40,000. The emigration of 1850 was even greater. By August 14, the official register at Fort Laramie had recorded 39,506. Altogether, probably 55,000 went through the Platte Valley that year, most of them headed for California. Again cholera ravaged the trail across the Plains. One emigrant wrote: "I had intended to notice in my journal every grave and burying-place that we passed, but I have abandoned this part of my plan. . . . Graves are so numerous, that to notice them all would make my narrative tedious."[9] Another, in sight of Court House Rock, noted: "It is supposed that one-fifth are dying here now with cholera and diarrhoea. Thus far one-tenth of our company have died."[10] There was virtually no letup in 1852, and 40,000 probably crossed the Plains that year. By 1853 the gold fever had diminished, and the emigrants who went over the trail in decreasing numbers during the Fifties were primarily home-seekers.

The gold-seekers generally followed the Oregon Trail across the Plains, which after '49 might more properly be called the California Trail. Each year, however, an increasing number used the north side of the Platte, coming up the Missouri or across Iowa to Kanesville,

[8]One of the best-recorded cholera deaths was that of George Winslow of Massachusetts, whose grave is in Jefferson County, near Fairbury. See George W. Hansen, "A Tragedy of the Oregon Trail," *Collections,* Nebraska State Historical Society, XVII (1913), 110–126.

[9]Franklin Langworthy, *Scenery of the Plains, Mountains, and Mines,* ed. by Paul C Phillips (Princeton: Princeton University Press, 1932), pp. 37–38.

[10]John Wood, *Journal* . . . (Columbus, Ohio: Nevins and Meyers, 1871), p. 31.

whose enterprising merchants advertised the merits of their crossing
and the North Platte route so effectively that the inadequate ferry service they provided usually was loaded beyond capacity.

LIFE ALONG THE TRAIL

Though no two years and no two trips were quite alike, life on the
trail was about the same for all the overland emigrants, whether they
were bound for Oregon, California, or Utah, whether they went along
the north side of the Platte or the south. Some were better equipped

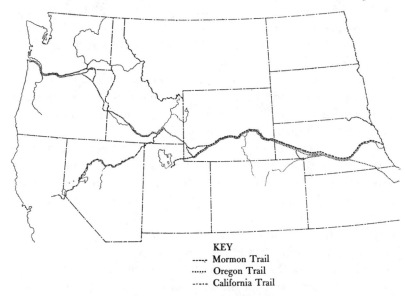

KEY
----- Mormon Trail
·········· Oregon Trail
----- California Trail

PLATTE VALLEY ROUTES WEST

than others, some were wiser, some were simply luckier. All suffered
weariness, hardship, and danger, and it should be remembered that
even though their experiences, seen in retrospect, followed a similar
pattern, the experience for each traveller was new, exciting, and at times
awesome. Little wonder that many of them kept diaries and wrote long
letters home to their friends and the hometown newspaper. The Plains
portion of the trail, except perhaps in the cholera years, was the easiest
part of the journey. In prospect, however, that long stretch of "desert"
between the Missouri and the mountains was a fearful thing to con-
template. In actuality, the emigrants learned the lessons of overland

travel—the hard way—on the Plains, and this made that leg of the journey more difficult than it might have been for experienced travellers. But even had they been experienced, nothing could have alleviated the effect of the sudden and violent storms, the dust, and the oppressive monotony of travel across the Plains. Those harbingers of the mountains—Chimney Rock and Scotts Bluff—were eagerly watched for and always reached with rejoicing.

By early spring in the peak years thousands of emigrants had congregated at the principal jumping-off places—Independence, Fort Leavenworth, St. Joseph, and Kanesville (later Council Bluffs)—eagerly awaiting the day when the grass was green enough to make it safe to start. Occasionally, those who could afford it, having an advantage over the generality of the emigration, carried enough grain to feed their animals during the first hundred miles. While waiting, the emigrants bought provisions and equipment, perfected their organizations, and eagerly discussed conditions on the trail with any who seemed to have information. Guidebooks of various sorts made their appearance, but many of the emigrants apparently did not have access to these, and some of those used were unreliable. Mountain men who could no longer make a living in the declining fur trade occasionally hired out as guides, but anyone who had been over the trail qualified as a veteran and found his services much in demand. The jumping-off places exhibited all the characteristics of frontier boom towns: supplies and equipment were scarce, prices were high, and everything was overcrowded. Particularly overcrowded were the ferries, and human nature exhibited itself at its worst as the emigrants fought for places in line. Occasionally, small parties wearied of the struggle and left the towns to get across the river where they could; in the late Forties a rather considerable ferry business developed at old Fort Kearny, largely as overflow from St. Joseph.

By late April or early May the emigration was on the move, and the trails west of the Missouri were lined as far as eye could see with the swaying, white-topped wagons—not the Conestoga, which carried an earlier emigration into the eastern Mississippi Valley, but the Murphy, manufactured in St. Louis. For mutual protection and assistance, the emigrants generally organized into companies. The importance of order and discipline was generally accepted, and once a leader was chosen he was given comprehensive powers. If he became overzealous in the exercise of those powers, however, he was apt to be deposed. The rate of travel varied considerably with the size of the company, the obstacles encountered, and the ability of the leadership; sixteen miles a day with oxen was considered fairly good on the Plains. The travelling day was from sunup to sundown, with a long period of rest at noon. At the end of the day, the wagons would be formed into a circle, the evening meal cooked, and guards posted.

The emigrants brought to the trail all their strength and weakness, their hopes, fears, and foibles. If the environment wrought any change, it was generally to intensify characteristics already present: the cowardly had opportunity to show their cowardice, the excitable went to pieces, the calm and brave managed somehow to get along. The strain of the trail frayed tempers and brought on an unusual amount of bickering. A particularly aggravating problem was posed by the loose cattle: the well-to-do might have hundreds along; those who had few or none thought them a great nuisance and complained bitterly of the trouble they caused.

Uppermost in the minds of virtually all emigrants was the danger from the Indians. Though the Indians were alarmed and frightened at the long lines of wagons rolling through their country, they generally kept the peace during the period of heavy overland emigration prior to the organization of Nebraska territory. To be sure, they occasionally attacked a wagon train, but even then they were primarily interested in plunder, and the attacks were not part of any organized effort to drive the white man from the Plains—as later efforts were. They were persistent beggars, however, and when begging failed they turned to thievery. In any event, emigrants and western congressmen insisted upon military protection along the trail. The troops at Fort Leavenworth covered the trail in Kansas. To provide additional protection the Army established Fort Kearny on the Missouri at the mouth of Table Creek (on the site of present-day Nebraska City). The Army soon found, however, that this position was outside the general stream of overland travel, and in 1848 a new Fort Kearny was established at the southernmost point of the big bend in the Platte. The next year, the Army purchased Fort Laramie, which had served as a fur trading post since 1834, from the American Fur Company. (The American Fur Company then moved down to the Scotts Bluff region, where one of the St. Louis Robidoux already was well ensconced, operating a blacksmith shop and trading establishment and generally profiteering at the expense of the emigrants.)[11] Though troops from Fort Kearny later were to provide protection for freighting trains and stage coaches and Fort Laramie was to be the Army's headquarters during the Indian wars of the northern Plains, during this period they functioned primarily as relief and rest stations. At both places the emigrants usually stopped for a day or two to rest, repair wagons and equipment, write letters, and (if possible) secure additional supplies.

And so, summer after summer the wagons rolled west, their heavy wheels grinding deep ruts in the Platte Valley—ruts that in places are still visible. Within a decade after those first home-seeking emigrants had pushed west to California and Oregon in 1841, the United States— fulfilling its "manifest destiny"—had extended its boundaries to the Pacific, from the forty-ninth parallel on the north to the Rio Grande on the south. Texas and California had been admitted to the Union; Oregon, New Mexico, and Utah had achieved territorial status. The only remaining unorganized territory was "the great American desert" between the Missouri and the Rockies, and pressures from both East and West would soon bring territorial status to most of this area.

[11]For excellent accounts of the activity at Scotts Bluff, see T. L. Green, "A Forgotten Fur Trading Post in Scotts Bluff County," *Nebraska History*, XV (January, 1934), 38–46; Green, "Scotts Bluffs, Fort John," *ibid.*, XIX (July, 1938), 175–190; Merrill J. Mattes, "Robidoux's Trading Post at 'Scott's Bluffs,' and the California Gold Rush," *ibid.*, XXX (June, 1949), 95–138.

CHAPTER 6

The Kansas-Nebraska Act

THE REPORTS OF Pike, Long and other explorers, describing the Plains as an uninhabitable desert, provided Congress with a seemingly easy solution to the knotty problem of what to do with the Indians standing athwart the early nineteenth-century American advance into the eastern Mississippi Valley: remove them to the Plains, thus opening the land east of the Mississippi to white settlement and at the same time providing a haven for the Indians where they would be free from further white encroachment. The process was begun in the South in the 1820's. In 1830 Congress passed a general Indian removal act, and in 1834, the Indian Intercourse Act, which forbade whites without license from the government to trespass on Indian lands, and provided for the administration of the Indian country. Though the line of demarcation was thought of as a "permanent Indian frontier," the process of shifting it westward began almost as soon as it was established. By the early 1830's, federal officials were thinking of the Indian country—i.e., the area set aside for the tribes removed from east of the Mississippi—as occupying the land between the Platte and Red rivers, and in furtherance of this policy the Pawnees in 1833 were persuaded to cede their lands south of the Platte.

The shifting frontier and the changing policy presaged what was evident almost from the beginning: the "permanent Indian frontier" was doomed to failure. In the first place, the eastern semi-sedentary

tribes and the western nomads found it almost impossible to live peace-
ably together. Secondly, and more important, the American pioneer
was not to be stopped at the Mississippi, the Missouri, or any other
point short of the Pacific coast. By 1850, the Indian country was not
outside the United States; it was right in the middle, a barrier that had
to be removed.

The Kansas-Nebraska Act, which signalled the abandonment of the
concept of a "permanent Indian frontier" so hopefully set forth less
than a generation earlier, fanned into flame all the embers of controversy that had been smoldering in the hearth of expansionist politics
for almost half a century. It was one of the most controversial and far-
reaching measures to come before Congress in the nineteenth century.
Almost as great has been the controversy among historians over the
nature of the real controversy, its causes, and its significance. Here an
effort will be made to discuss briefly the principal elements entering
into the Act—the Pacific railroad, the controversy over the extension
of slavery, and the western demand for the organization of the territory
—together with a short legislative history.

THE PACIFIC RAILROAD

Some Americans were agitating for a railroad to the Pacific even before the coast region had become part of the national domain. Chief
among them perhaps was Asa Whitney, a New York merchant interested in the China trade, who as early as January, 1845, submitted a
plan to Congress providing for a transcontinental railroad from the
Great Lakes to Oregon, and did much to arouse public opinion in favor of his project. Most Americans in and out of Congress looked on
Whitney's early proposals as impracticable and visionary, but as railroads began to demonstrate their practicability and as settlements developed in the Pacific coast region, interest in the transcontinental railroad grew apace. By the early Fifties, the stumbling block was not
apathy but rivalry over the route. This was a sectional rivalry between
North and South, and within the sections a local rivalry among cities
which scrambled for selection as the eastern terminus. The rivalry was
made all the more intense by the fact that not even the wildest visionary
believed that there would ever be more than one transcontinental railroad.

Initially, the South possessed a distinct advantage: it could provide an all-weather route; with the annexation of Texas and the organization of New Mexico territory, a southern route could skirt the Indian country. The Gadsden Purchase of 1853, adding suitable right-of-way south of the Gila River, further strengthened the southern position. Meanwhile, northern routes were not without their proponents. Whitney advocated his Lake Superior-Oregon route as the shortest and most practicable. The thousands who by the early 1850's had gone over the Platte Valley trail had demonstrated the practicability of that way west. So much interest and such great rivalry had developed by 1853 that the Army Appropriation Bill of that year contained a rider authorizing the Secretary of War to survey such routes as seemed advisable to ascertain the most practicable. Secretary Jefferson Davis immediately dispatched engineers to survey four routes: (1) the northern, or Whitney, route, between the forty-seventh and forty-ninth parallels; (2) what was known as Senator Benton's route, between the thirty-eighth and thirty-ninth parallels; (3) a route along the thirty-fifth parallel recommended by Senator Gwin of California; and (4) the Gila River route along the thirty-second parallel. Oddly enough, the Platte Valley route, deemed by many Northerners as the most practicable—and the one ultimately selected—was not included in the Davis surveys. The surveys themselves demonstrated that several routes were feasible, thus throwing the question back to Congress.

Meanwhile, Northerners were aware that an overriding obstacle in the way of any northern route was the fact that it would have to traverse the Indian country. Territorial organization of the country west of the Missouri was a necessary prerequisite to any northern railroad. Many voices were raised in favor of the organization of Nebraska territory, as it was then being called,[1] but the most persistent and effective was that of Stephen A. Douglas of Illinois. Vitally interested in developing Chicago as a great national railroad center, he saw clearly that a transcontinental railroad running west from Chicago through the Platte Valley

---

[1] In the report of his exploring trip of 1842, Lieutenant John C. Fremont had written: "The names given by the Indians are always remarkably appropriate; and certain none was ever more so than that which they have given to this stream—'the Nebraska, or Shallow River.'" In his report for 1844, urging that the territory be organized, Secretary of War William Wilkins stated: "The Platte or Nebraska, being the central stream leading into and from the Great South Pass would very properly furnish a name for the territory."

was an important factor in that development. As early as 1844, while a member of the House of Representatives, he had introduced a bill to organize Nebraska territory. His bill did not come up for consideration, but he introduced a similar measure in the next session of Congress. The primary purpose of these early bills, Douglas explained, was to serve notice on the Secretary of War not to locate any more Indians in the territory. For the next decade Douglas worked actively to promote the organization of Nebraska territory to provide a route for the Pacific railroad, and to forestall commitments to any route other than

NEBRASKA TERRITORY, 1854

that through the Platte Valley. His election to the Senate in 1847, where he immediately became a member of the Committee on Territories, widened the scope of his activities and increased his influence. In 1849 he presided over a great railroad convention in St. Louis, and while that body declared in favor of St. Louis as the eastern terminus of the Pacific railroad, it also favored the South Pass route, which could lead only to a direct connection with Chicago.

The organization of New Mexico territory in 1850 gave proponents of a southern route a great advantage, causing Douglas to intensify his efforts for Nebraska. The Davis surveys and the Gadsden Purchase in 1853 further emphasized the importance of immediate action if the

Southerners were to be forestalled. By early 1854, therefore, Douglas was willing to make any reasonable compromise to get a Nebraska bill through, and as chairman of the Senate Committee on Territories he was in a position to exercise great influence. In other words, Douglas' primary concern was the Pacific railroad, and he was willing to shape other issues around that. Unfortunately for Douglas, and for the country, one of those "other issues"—the extension of slavery—became the overriding, central issue of the whole Nebraska discussion.

THE SLAVERY CONTROVERSY

From the founding of the Republic the slavery question had been a growing divisive force in American politics. Possessing strong moral and economic implications, it was particularly important in connection with territorial expansion which envisioned the creation of new states and the consequent readjustment of representation in Congress. Throughout the first half of the nineteenth century, a majority in Congress and in the country, primarily concerned with working out the nation's "manifest destiny," sought to compromise the slavery question whenever it impinged upon the central issue; a growing intransigency among extremists both North and South, however, made compromise progressively more difficult. When the issue came to a head in 1820 in connection with the admission of Missouri, it was compromised by providing that while Missouri could be admitted as a slave state in accordance with its constitution, Maine would be brought in as a free state, and slavery would be prohibited "forever" in all the rest of Louisiana territory north of 36°30'. This concession from the South by no means indicated that Southerners had resigned themselves to setting limits on the expansion of slavery: the admission of Missouri as a slave state was a significant immediate victory; for those who thought beyond short-term goals there was the belief that the area would never be settled; should that prove unsound, there was always the possibility of reinterpreting the word "forever."

The controversy flared into the open again over the organization of the territory acquired from Mexico. Northern extremists generally rallied behind the proviso submitted in August, 1846, by Congressman David Wilmot, a Pennsylvania Democrat, to the effect that slavery be forever prohibited in the lands obtained from Mexico. Southern extremists insisted that Congress had no power whatever to ban slavery in the territories, though they had agreed to its doing so a few years earlier; more moderate spirits in the South wanted the Missouri Compromise line extended to the Pacific, which would have given most of the new territory to slavery. Douglas and other westerners suggested that the good western principle of "squatter sovereignty" be applied to the question—let the people of the territories decide for themselves whether or not they would have slavery. Facts came to the aid of compromise: California already had organized a state government and was clamoring for admission as a free state—the South could hardly ignore this; the sandy deserts and rocky hills of Utah and New Mexico would never support slavery—the North could surely bend sufficiently to allow the people of the territories to decide for themselves whether they would have slavery or not when they applied for admission to the Union as states. And so it was. California was admitted as a free state in 1850 and the territories of Utah and New Mexico were organized with the understanding that they would be admitted as states with or without slavery as their constitutions provided.

Then came Nebraska. Southerners, unenthusiastic about the organization of a territory to make possible a northern route for the Pacific railroad, were downright hostile to setting in motion the machinery that ultimately would grind out more free states. It was clear that to gain Southern support for a bill organizing Nebraska territory, the Missouri Compromise would have to be greatly modified or repealed altogether.

THE WESTERN DEMAND

Almost lost—at least on many historians—in the flaming controversy over slavery was the growing insistence in Missouri, Iowa, and even the Indian country itself that Nebraska be organized: to provide a route for the Pacific railroad, to legalize settlement already existing in defiance of the law, and to open the way for a further general extension of settlement westward. "Nebraska Boomers" perambulated the area and wrote glowing accounts of the fertility of the soil, the salubrity of the climate, and the general excellence of the region—no desert this![2] Mass meetings were held in Iowa and Missouri demanding the organization

[2]For an excellent account of the activities of one of these "boomers," see James C. Malin, "Thomas Jefferson Sutherland, Nebraska Boomer," *Nebraska History*, XXXIV (September, 1953), 181–214.

of Nebraska territory. Led by the Wyandots, the inhabitants of the territory organized a provisional government whose officers worked for territorial organization.

In Iowa, Senators Augustus Caesar Dodge and George W. Jones held meetings throughout the western part of the state from 1850 onwards urging the organization of Nebraska. Missourians were even more active, and the Nebraska question became embroiled in Missouri politics. Senator Thomas Hart Benton, Missouri's old expansionist, had long advocated the organization of Nebraska territory to make possible a "Central National Highway to the Pacific" along what he liked to call "the old buffalo trail." When his moderate course on slavery cost him his seat in the Senate in 1851, he tried to make a comeback based on a campaign for a Pacific railroad with St. Louis as its eastern terminus and the organization of Nebraska territory for both railroad and settlement purposes. Though he won election to the House of Representatives, he was unable to unseat Senator David R. Atchison, strongly pro-slave. Atchison had opposed the organization of Nebraska because of the Missouri Compromise. When it became evident that the Missouri Compromise might be repealed and when mounting pressure from home made an anti-Nebraska position untenable for a Missouri politician, Atchison shifted his course to become ardently pro-Nebraska—and, indeed, in later years was willing to take credit for the whole thing. More significant than the pulling and hauling of Missouri's politicians was the generation of pro-Nebraska pressure, particularly in northwestern Missouri. A series of mass meetings in northwestern Missouri and southwestern Iowa culminated in a Nebraska Delegate Convention at St. Joseph, January 9 and 10, 1854, at which strong resolutions were adopted protesting further delay in the organization of Nebraska territory.[3]

Meanwhile, residents of the Indian country were doing what they could to promote the Nebraska movement. There was some activity at Florence, on the site of the old Mormon Winter Quarters; a growing number of traders and others were congregating around Peter Sarpy's establishment at Bellevue; Hiram P. Downs (a delegate to the St. Joseph convention) operated a ferry at old Fort Kearny; further south, civilians gathered around Fort Leavenworth, Fort Riley, and the Shawnee mis-

[3]A detailed discussion of this convention will be found in James C. Malin, *The Nebraska Question, 1852–1854* (Lawrence, Kansas: privately printed, 1954), pp. 207–287.

sion. Leadership for the movement, however, seems to have been provided by the Wyandot Indians, who had been removed from Ohio in
1843 and settled on the west bank of the Missouri at the mouth of the
Kansas. The Wyandots had much white blood and many white customs.
Somehow, they appeared to believe that territorial organization would
improve their position against the pressures they were sure would be
brought against them. In the fall of 1852, they elected Abelard Guthrie
delegate from the provisional territory of Nebraska and sent him to
Washington to urge organization. The next August a convention was
held at "Wyandot City," nominating Guthrie for re-election as delegate. In September a second convention convened at Kickapoo and
nominated the Reverend Thomas Johnson of the Shawnee mission for
the same post. Johnson, supported by the missionaries and Commissioner of Indian Affairs William C. Manypenny, defeated Guthrie for
the empty honor. Meanwhile, in October a group from Council Bluffs
and vicinity appear to have gone over to Bellevue and participated in
an altogether independent movement to organize a provisional government. They elected Hadley D. Johnson as delegate to Congress.

Both Hadley D. and the Reverend Thomas Johnson journeyed to
Washington to represent the provisional government of Nebraska territory. Both sat in the House of Representatives for a while, and both
were removed. The two men worked for the organization of Nebraska
territory, but whether they and the movement they represented had any
effect on organization cannot be determined. In any event, they had an
opportunity to watch the smooth-functioning Democratic machine
push the Nebraska bill through.

LEGISLATIVE HISTORY

It was against a backdrop of violently conflicting cross-purposes, expansionist politics, and local ambition that the Kansas-Nebraska Act
became law. Senator Douglas' original bills have been mentioned.
Though he did not introduce a Nebraska bill after 1848, Douglas
worked actively for the Nebraska cause, both in Congress and out.[4] As
the years wore on, the urgency of the situation increased, insofar as
northern railroad ambitions were concerned. So, too, did the acrimony
of the debate over the slavery question. The presidential election of

[4]See James C. Malin, "The Nebraska Question: A Ten-Year Record," *Nebraska
History*, XXXV (March, 1954), 1–15.

1852 found the leaders of both parties committed to compromise and willing to do anything to prevent sectional discord. After a campaign in which both candidates praised the Compromise of 1850 and urged sectional unity, the Democrats, augmented by the return of many Southern Whigs, returned to power with a sweeping victory. The Whigs, having enjoyed a term of power based on the magic of an old-soldier candidate and dissatisfaction with the long-entrenched Democrats, were no longer effective. If the Democrats had returned to power, however, they were by no means united, and any action affecting slavery—and that meant any action relating to territorial organization—would call for the most delicate sort of compromise. Yet the division was within the party, and with the proper leadership the compromise might be effected. That leadership was provided in the person of Senator Douglas of Illinois, chairman of the critical Committee on Territories, and easily one of the strongest men in the country.

On February 2, 1853, Representative William A. Richardson of Illinois, chairman of the House Committee on Territories, introduced a bill to organize Nebraska territory. It passed the House, 98 to 43, but despite Douglas' efforts, failed to get through the Senate, largely because of opposition from Southern Democrats. The bill made no mention of slavery; presumably the provisions of the Missouri Compromise would apply. Senator Sam Houston of Texas, the hero of San Jacinto, orated against it; Senator Atchison violently opposed it. The South, in short, would have none of it.

On December 5, 1853, the opening day of the First Session of the Thirty-third Congress, Senator Dodge of Iowa gave notice that he would introduce "a bill to organize a territorial government for the Territory of Nebraska." Dodge introduced his bill on December 14. It provided that all the territory between the states of Iowa and Missouri on the east and the summit of the Rocky Mountains on the west, the parallel 36°30′ on the south and 43°30′ on the north should be organized as Nebraska territory. The bill contained no reference to slavery; presumably the Missouri Compromise would apply. Douglas' Committee on Territories reported the bill January 4, as a substitute, vastly altered. Instead of one territory, two were created: Kansas (after a later boundary adjustment), to occupy the area between the thirty-seventh and fortieth parallels from Missouri to the crest of the Rockies; Nebraska, that between the fortieth and forty-ninth parallels from the Mis-

souri River and Minnesota territory to the crest of the Rockies.[5] Where
the Dodge bill had made no mention of slavery the Committee substitute provided: "That all questions pertaining to slavery in the Territories, and in the new States to be formed therefrom, are to be left to
the decision of the people residing therein, through their appropriate
representatives"; and further, "the eighth section of the act preparatory
to the admission of Missouri into the Union, approved March 6, 1820,
which was superseded by the principles of the legislation of 1850, commonly called the compromise measures . . . is declared inoperative."

The gauntlet was now down. The Abolitionists' swords flashed out
against the repeal of the Missouri Compromise—almost as inviolate as
the Constitution itself—at the behest of Southern slaveholders. Seward,
Chase, and Sumner led the opposition, but against Douglas, who in
the "popular sovereignty" formula had found a means of holding the
Democratic majority together, they hadn't a chance. The bill passed
the Senate on March 3, 37 to 14. The only Democrats Douglas couldn't
hold in line were Dodge and Walker of Wisconsin and Houston of
Texas. There was a closer vote in the House, but the bill was passed
on the evening of May 21, by a vote of 113 to 100. The bill was finally
passed May 25, and President Pierce signed it on May 30.

The fires of controversy, kindled by the congressional debate, soon
spread over the country. Fanned by disgraceful events in Kansas, as
abolitionist and pro-slave forces tried to pervert the doctrine of popular sovereignty to their own ends, the flames by the end of the year
had all but engulfed the nation. "Anti-Nebraska" meetings were held
throughout the North, particularly in the Northwest, and out of them
developed new organized opposition to the Democrats in the form of
the Republican party, a militant substitution for defunct and decaying
Whiggery. In the center of the holocaust was Stephen A. Douglas,
architect of the territories of Nebraska and Kansas. Anti-Nebraska orators charged that he sold freedom out to slavery solely to further his
own political and financial ambitions, that he not only repealed the

[5]The bill creating the two territories has for almost a century been known as "The
Kansas-Nebraska Act," and the centennial of 1954 was so celebrated. Thus, Nebraska,
which prior to 1854 had been the only territory mentioned, was relegated to second
place, not in the act, which is "an act to organize the territories of Nebraska and Kansas," but in popular parlance, probably, as Albert Watkins suggests, because "it is
more easily spoken in that form." (J. Sterling Morton and Albert Watkins, *Illustrated*
History of Nebraska [Lincoln: Jacob North and Company, 1904]. I, 155)

Missouri Compromise but created two territories instead of one to make sure that his nefarious purpose would succeed. Historians for a century have repeated these charges, with the result that the name of Stephen A. Douglas has been one of the most maligned in American history.

The canard that Douglas divided the territory to further the interests of slavery in the West is easily dealt with. The two delegates claiming to represent the provisional government (Hadley D. and the Reverend Thomas Johnson) agreed that division of the territory so that the people would have two delegates instead of one would be desirable. Senator Dodge supported division because he believed that the railroad interests of Iowa demanded it. Likewise, Douglas' support of division was based on the fact that it would protect Chicago's railroad interests, a natural and perfectly legitimate interest for a senator from Illinois. That Douglas was ambitious, no one can gainsay, but that the Kansas-Nebraska bill was designed solely to further his ambition cannot be supported. The compromises were simply those he had to make as the leader of a divided majority party to pass legislation he believed to be vitally important. Finally, the doctrine of popular sovereignty—local self-government—is good American doctrine, even though extremists in Kansas sought with terrible consequences for themselves and the nation to pervert it to their own ends.

Without ignoring the profound ramifications of the sectional strife stirred up by the Kansas-Nebraska Act, the important consideration for the history of Nebraska—and for that of the nation—is that it set in motion the machinery that would open to settlement all that remained of Louisiana territory acquired only a half century before. The United States had gone far toward working out its "manifest destiny" in that half century.

CHAPTER 7

Territorial Beginnings

THERE HAD BEEN persistent objection to the organization of Nebraska territory on the grounds that the area had been permanently set aside for the Indians and guaranteed to them in perpetuity by treaty. An amendment which provided that no lands could be settled in the territory until the Indian title had been extinguished had been attached to the Richardson bill of 1853 to organize Nebraska territory. That bill, of course, did not pass; but Congress in 1853 did authorize the President to negotiate with the tribes west of Missouri and Iowa with a view to extinguishing Indian titles in as much of the area as possible. In Nebraska, the only area specifically guaranteed to the Indians by treaty was a small tract between the Little Nemaha and the Nemaha set aside for the half-breeds in the Treaty of Prairie du Chien, July 15, 1830. The Kansas lands southwest of the Nemaha, ceded to the Government in 1825, and the Pawnee lands south of the Platte, ceded in 1833, had not been further assigned. North of the Pawnee cession from the Missouri River to a little beyond the hundredth meridian various tribes held original titles, but without perpetual treaty guarantees. To the west were the lands roamed over by the nomadic tribes; in the Treaty of Fort Laramie (1851) those tribes had agreed to certain boundaries and to the construction of roads and military and other posts.

During the winter of 1853–54, while the politicians debated the Nebraska bill in Congress, the Commissioner of Indian Affairs busied himself with the negotiation of treaties to extinguish Indian titles in the area. The Otos and Missourias had ceded their rather indefinite claim to land lying between the Nemahas in 1833. On March 15, 1854, in a treaty concluded in Washington, they ceded all claims to lands west of the Missouri except a reservation ten miles wide and twenty-five miles long on the Big Blue. The next day the Omahas ceded all their lands west of the Missouri, except 300,000 acres to be set aside as a reserve (and ultimately located in what later became Thurston County). The Omahas had claimed the country bounded by the Missouri River on the north and east, Shell Creek on the west, and the Platte River on the south. Thus, by the time the Kansas-Nebraska Act was passed, the Indian title, except for reservations, had been extinguished north of the Platte as far west as Shell Creek (roughly on a line running along Shell Creek to its source and then north roughly through present-day Neligh), and south of the Platte as far west as a line running roughly from the forks of the Republican to the forks of the Platte. An additional large tract was opened on September 24, 1857, when the Pawnees, in a treaty negotiated at Table Creek, north of Nebraska City, ceded all remaining lands claimed by them in Nebraska (as far west as a line running north from the forks of the Platte)—except 450 square miles on the Loup set aside as a reservation.

THE EARLIEST SETTLEMENTS

Though there were a few squatters' cabins scattered along the Missouri, and ferries at what were soon to become St. Stephen, Nebraska City, Plattsmouth, and Omaha, the only point which could be described as a settlement prior to May 30, 1854—aside perhaps from the vagrant civilian community clustered about Fort Kearny on the Platte—was Bellevue. Here possibly as many as fifty persons were gathered about the Indian agency, the Reverend William Hamilton's Presbyterian mission, and Peter A. Sarpy's trading post. Sarpy maintained a ferry across the Missouri and conducted most of his trading activities at St. Mary on the Iowa side.

Anticipating the Kansas-Nebraska Act, Sarpy and his friends had organized the Bellevue Town Company, February 9, 1854. Once Congress gave the signal for legal settlement, the town company feverishly set to work to transform Bellevue into a city. On July 15, it began publication of a newspaper, *The Nebraska Palladium*. Though printed across the river in Iowa, that paper greeted its readers with a triumphant review of progress already made: "Within the last month a large city upon a grand scale has been laid out, with a view of the location of the capital of Nebraska, at this point, and with a view to making it the center of commerce, and the half-way house between the Atlantic and Pacific Oceans. . . ." Prospective settlers could have the word of Colonel Sarpy, who had traveled "through all parts of the plains and mountains," and who had "come to the final conclusion that the great line of communication between ocean and ocean must cross the Missouri River at Belleview . . ."

Others disagreed, and all along the river promoters and land jobbers from western Iowa were busy pre-empting townsites and laying out cities—each of which, its promoters confidently proclaimed, was destined to become the gateway to the West. Hiram P. Downs, custodian of the government's property at old Fort Kearny and a long-time Nebraska boomer, joined with men from Sidney, Iowa, in laying out Nebraska City. Samuel Martin of Glenwood, who had been operating a ferry across the Missouri below the mouth of the Platte since 1852, established a log trading post on the Nebraska side in the winter of 1853 and shortly after the territory was opened began booming the town of Plattsmouth. James C. Mitchell and others from Council Bluffs had taken over the old Mormon Winter Quarters and as early as 1853 were planning to develop the new town of Florence. Altogether, the first legislature granted charters to seventeen of these would-be cities.

By far the most successful of the early towns was "Omaha City," promoted into being by ambitious residents of Council Bluffs, and specifically by the Council Bluffs and Nebraska Ferry Company. There had been a settlement at Council Bluffs (first Miller's Hollow, then Kanesville) since the Mormon activity of 1846–47. The California Gold Rush boomed the town into an important emigrant outfitting point, and as the Nebraska agitation developed, the more enterprising of the town's citizens began to take a keen interest in the prospects of a town immediately across the river. Specifically, they reasoned that if this town could be developed into the territorial capital, Council Bluffs might yet draw a transcontinental railway. In 1853, William D. Brown, who since 1850 had been operating a leaky scow called the "Lone Tree Ferry," staked out a claim to a townsite across the river. That same year a group of Council Bluffs promoters organized the Council Bluffs and Nebraska Ferry Company, purchasing Brown's ferry business and his interest in the townsite. Though the company acquired a steam ferry boat —the *General Marion*—and thus greatly improved the service, almost from the beginning it was a town company first and a ferry company second. Claims were staked out on the townsite as early as November; the company adopted the name Omaha and in the spring, through the influence of western Iowa's Congressman Bernhart Henn (an ardent advocate of the Kansas-Nebraska Act), got a postmaster appointed.

Immediately after the territory was organized, the company set out to develop its site. Postmaster A. D. Jones, employed to survey the site, laid out the town in 320 blocks, with streets one-hundred feet wide, except "Capitol Avenue," which was 120 feet wide. On July 4, the ferry company organized a picnic on the townsite, and a log cabin was partly erected that day. A newspaper, the *Omaha Arrow*, printed in Council Bluffs, made its appearance on July 28. By autumn, Omaha gave promise of being more than a paper town. A. D. Jones still used his hat for a post office, but Omaha City had some twenty houses, two shacks with dirt floors serving as hotels, saloons, stores, and, to quote the *Arrow*, "an extensive brickyard."

Omaha, the progeny of Council Bluffs, would soon be greater than the parent. Its "growing pains," however, were felt all over the territory and threw Nebraska into a controversy whose ramifications were felt even after statehood had been achieved.

Political Chaos

President Pierce appointed Francis Burt, forty-seven year old Pendleton, South Carolina, editor, as governor of Nebraska territory. (Earlier he had offered the job to William O. Butler of Kentucky, who had declined.) Burt, son of a South Carolina planter, had been active in politics since early youth. He served almost twenty years in the South Carolina legislature, as a member of the constitutional convention, and as a member of the famous nullification convention of 1832. At the time of his appointment to the Nebraska post he was serving as Third Auditor of the United States Treasury.

A trip from South Carolina to Nebraska was no easy journey in 1854, and by the time Governor Burt arrived at Bellevue, October 7, he had travelled by private conveyance, railroad, stagecoach, steamboat, and wagon. He might have made the journey all the way from St. Louis to

Bellevue by steamboat, but the river was so low in the fall of 1854 that boats were not going above St. Joseph. At St. Joseph he hired a hack to Nebraska City, then went by wagon to Bellevue. He had been sick when he arrived at St. Louis and had had to spend several days there in the care of a physician. He was so weak when he got to Bellevue that he went to bed immediately in the Reverend William Hamilton's mission house. He never got up. The oath of office was administered at his bedside on October 16, and two days later he died.

Governor Burt's untimely death lowered a cloud of uncertainty on the territory's political horizon, particularly in regard to the most hotly-contested local issue, the location of the territorial capital. Always a bitterly-fought question in new territories, the capital issue in Nebraska was intensified by the assumption that the transcontinental railroad would probably go through the territorial capital. Although every town in the territory looked covetously at the plum, the leading contenders were Omaha and Bellevue. Burt appears to have had no fixed notions regarding the permanent territorial capital, although apparently he planned to convene the first session of the territorial legislature at Bellevue.[1] Whatever Burt's intention, it soon became apparent that Secretary Thomas B. Cuming, who took over the reins of government as Acting Governor, was open to suggestion on the capital question.

Cuming, the son of a Protestant Episcopal minister and a graduate of the University of Michigan, was only twenty-five years old when President Pierce appointed him Secretary of Nebraska territory. At the time of his appointment he was editing a Democratic weekly in Keokuk, Iowa. In common with all the rest of the politicians descending upon Nebraska, he was deeply concerned with his own political advancement; and now that the hand of fortune had placed him in control of organizing the territory he did not intend to be bound by any commitments of the dead Governor, expressed or implied. Moreover, Cuming owed his appointment to Iowa influence, and insofar as Ne-

[1] Residents of Bellevue stoutly maintained that he intended to locate the territorial capital there permanently. Armistead Burt, the Governor's son, who accompanied him to Bellevue, later recalled: "The governor's intention was to convene the first legislature at Bellevue; I think the Rev. Mr. Hamilton had offered the mission house for the purpose. As to locating the capital I remember hearing him say he intended to choose a place that would, he hoped, be permanently the capital of the state. He intended to make Nebraska his home." (Morton and Watkins, *op. cit.*, I, 163n.)

braska was concerned, that influence was primarily interested in using the territory to further the ambitions of Council Bluffs.

As a step toward the establishment of civil government, Cuming ordered that a territorial census be taken by November 20. The population was counted with much difficulty: the line between Kansas and Nebraska had not yet been surveyed; the "permanence" of almost every settler was open to question. As finally compiled, the returns showed a total of 2,732 inhabitants, 1,818 living south of the Platte, and 914 north of the river. Despite the fact that almost twice as many persons were living south of the river, Cuming assigned the four counties he had created in the North Platte section a total of seven councilmen and fourteen representatives, while giving only six councilmen and twelve representatives to the four counties south of the river:

	NORTH				SOUTH		
County	*Population*	*Council*	*House*	*County*	*Population*	*Council*	*House*
Burt	} 163	1	2	Pierce }	614	3	5
Washington		1	2	Forney		1	2
Dodge	106	1	2	Cass	353	1	3
Douglas	645	4	8	Richardson	851	1	2

This flagrant favoring of the North Platte section caused great alarm and indignation south of the river. Bellevue, though north of the Platte, objected strenuously to being included in the same county with Omaha and joined the South Platte in suspecting the Governor's motives. On December 9 the citizens of Bellevue held a mass meeting as part of their effort to secure the capital and invited Cuming to attend. The meeting developed into an indignation session, with the Acting Governor charged with not only accepting but exacting bribes from the Omaha town company. On December 20, Bellevue's worst fears were realized as Governor Cuming announced that the first session of the territorial legislature would convene at Omaha.

With the gauntlet thus thrown down, Bellevue's politicians joined those from south of the Platte in a protracted program of vilification. Leading the attack on Cuming was twenty-two year old J. Sterling Morton, who had arrived from Michigan less than a month earlier. Mass meetings were held at many places in the South Platte region. A delegate convention at Nebraska City adopted resolutions (written by Morton) denouncing Cuming as "an unprincipled knave" and demanding his removal from the secretaryship as well as from the post of acting governor. The controversy was carried to the legislature, where, as will be seen, most of the first session was devoted to an investigation of Cuming and an effort to undo his work in locating the capital at Omaha.

The capital question continued to agitate territorial politicians for many months to the detriment of more serious legislative business. The struggle was sectional as well as local. The Platte River naturally splits Nebraska into two sections. It was too wide and shallow for ferries, the sandy bottom made it unsuitable for fording, and during territorial times the people were too poor to build bridges. Governor Cuming, by apportioning the territory to favor the North Platte region, intensified a natural sectional division.

The struggle reached comic-opera proportions during the fourth legislature when a majority of the members, after a turbulent frontier row during which both fists and guns flashed, adjourned to Florence to hold a rump session. Though the Florence secession accomplished nothing, it did awaken a slumbering sentiment in the South Platte region for annexation to Kansas. J. Sterling Morton, who had removed to Nebraska City following Bellevue's initial defeat and who had promptly got himself elected to the legislature from Otoe County, had introduced a resolution in the second session memorializing Congress to move the boundary of Kansas north to the Platte River. The resolution was not considered and the project seems to have been dropped. After the Florence fiasco, however, South Platte politicians renewed the idea with vigor. Mass meetings were held all over the region, and delegates were elected to represent the South Platte section at the free-state constitutional convention being held in Wyandot, Kansas. There was some sentiment among the anti-slavery element in Kansas for annexation—it would help strengthen them in the bloody struggle for control of that unfortunate territory—but when they soon came to see that southern Nebraska would not be needed to carry the day for abolition, most of them lost interest. Kansas, moreover, had its own sectional problems: those living south of the Kansas River had no interest in increasing the strength of those living north of the river.

The failure of the annexation movement by no means put an end to the sectional controversy. Though somewhat quiescent during the Civil War when party lines began to replace sectional divisions, it remained a divisive factor in Nebraska's politics throughout the territorial period and played an important part in the ultimate location of the state capital.

THE FIRST LEGISLATURE

In accordance with Cuming's call, the first legislature assembled in Omaha on January 16, 1855. The capitol, a two-story brick building, thirty-three by seventy-five feet, fronting east on Ninth Street between Farnam and Douglas, had been provided by the Council Bluffs and Nebraska Ferry Company—"without a cost of one single dollar to the government." The House of Representatives met on the first floor, and the Council, or upper house, on the second. Both chambers were fitted out with school desks, and each desk was shared by two members. The windows were curtained with red and green calico. Despite such lack of pretension, however, that first capitol was in a sense as distinct in the landscape of its day as the present monumental structure is to-day—it was the only brick building in Omaha.

J. W. Pattison, local correspondent for the New York *Times* described the legislature in action:

It is a decidedly rich treat to visit the General Assembly of Nebraska. You see a motley crowd inside of a railing in a small room crowded to over-flowing, some behind their little schoolboy desks, some seated on the top of desks, some with their feet perched on the top of their neighbor's chair or desk, some whittling—half a dozen walking about in what little space there is left. The fireman, doorkeeper, sergeant-at-arms, last year's members [he was describing the second session], and almost anyone else become principal characters inside the bar, selecting good seats and making themselves generally at home, no matter how much they may discommode the members. The clerk, if he chooses, jumps up to explain the whys and hows of his journal. A lobby member stalks inside the bar, and from one to the other he goes talking about the advantages of his bill. A row starts up in the secretary's room, or somewhere about the building, and away goes the honorable body to see the fun ... then a thirsty member moves an adjournment and in a few minutes the drinking saloons are well patronized. ...

The early days of the session were devoted to an acrimonious struggle over seats and procedure. Bellevue sent three men whom it had elected to represent Douglas County. Though they had received virtually all of Bellevue's votes, Omaha's candidates had received a larger number and were, of course, certified by Governor Cuming. Denied admission, the Bellevue men served notice of contest. Others also tried to contest seats of members certified by the Governor. All such contests were referred to a committee dominated by Omaha men and in due course the committee reported that it was "inexpedient" to investigate further the subject of contested seats. Governor Cuming and Omaha had the situation well in hand.

The principal reason advanced in the notices of contest was that the certified member was not a resident of the territory. With a population as shifting and impermanent as that of early Nebraska, such a charge was almost meaningless. Out of a total membership of thirty-nine, at least five were never residents of the territory and many of the rest were transients at best. Joseph L. Sharp, elected president of the Council, represented Richardson County but actually lived in Glenwood, Iowa, and never became a resident of Nebraska. Indeed, so unsettled were both the population and the geographical divisions of the territory that many of the members were referred to as "from Iowa," "from Michigan," or from some other place outside the territory.

Most of the legislature's time was consumed with investigating and trying to undo Cuming's action in locating the capital at Omaha. Though this was of great concern to the promoters, it merely prevented consideration of much other important business. Omaha was too well entrenched and the opposition was badly divided, with the result that Omaha retained the prize. Thomas Cuming, who had been appointed to the relatively perfunctory post of secretary, had been given control of the territorial government at a critical juncture, and he used that control to advance the interests of his Iowa constituents who were promoting Omaha to assist in the development of Council Bluffs. His actions were bitterly assailed by Bellevue and South Platte partisans, in the press and in the legislature. Much of this criticism has been reflected in our historical literature, with the result that his achievements have been submerged in an avalanche of vituperation. He gave great promise, however, and had not his career been cut short by death in 1858, he might have exercised even greater influence in the development of the territory and state.

On February 20, Mark W. Izard, Burt's successor, arrived in Omaha. Originally from Arkansas, he had been United States marshal for Nebraska. He had taken the oath as governor on December 23, 1854, in Washington—where he had gone to further his appointment—and hence was not on hand to participate in the initial organization of territorial government. Born in Lexington, Kentucky, on December 25,

1799, Izard was somewhat older than most of the territorial politicos, and he provided a certain badly-needed stability in territorial affairs, although his short term was distinguished more by good intentions than by accomplishment. He felt constrained to address the legislature upon his arrival, and while regretting that he was not "sufficiently familiar with the progress already made to indicate a course of policy for the government of your future action," he did recommend that the laws of Iowa be adopted for temporary purposes, "as a large portion of our citizens at present are from that state, and are more or less familiar with its system."

To legislators preoccupied with partisan political squabbles this seemed like a good suggestion, and the problem of providing laws for the new territory was solved by the simple expedient of adopting *in toto* the civil and criminal code of Iowa. In addition, the first legislature located and established ten territorial roads; defined the boundaries and established the seats of the eight original counties—none of which retained its original form—and of sixteen additional ones; incorporated industrial companies, bridge and ferry companies, and towns; and enacted a series of general laws. Among the general laws were acts legalizing the activities of claims clubs, the territory's *de facto* local governments;[2] providing for the organization of courts; establishing a free public school system; and, curiously for a frontier legislature, prohibiting the manufacture, sale, and consumption of intoxicating beverages. This incongruous law remained on the books until 1858, when it was replaced by a license law, but there is no evidence of any attempt to enforce it. Indeed, saloons flourished adjacent to the capitol and enjoyed steady patronage from members of the legislature and territorial officials.

Thus, when the legislature adjourned on March 16 it had provided the framework of civil government in Nebraska territory. Considering the fact that it was in session only two months and that much of its time was occupied with political pulling and hauling, the achievement was not a small one.

[2]See pp. 90–91.

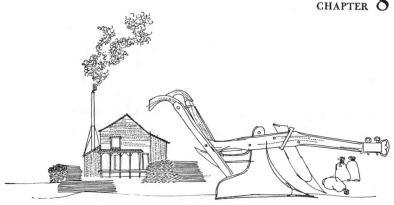

CHAPTER 8

Territorial Economic and Social Development

ON MARCH 3, 1854, western Iowa's Congressman Bernhart Henn, addressing his colleagues on behalf of the Kansas-Nebraska bill, prophesied that within three days after passage there would be not less than three thousand people in Nebraska. Like many another hope for Nebraska expressed by the territory's ebullient Iowa promoters, this prophecy fell far short of fulfillment. The census of November, 1854—which included some who, after the boundary was surveyed, were found to be living in Kansas—returned a population of only 2,732, many of them transients. Though in virtually every instance territorial development fell far short of advertised expectations, there was a steady growth. Indeed, when one considers that the territory had been untried by the pioneer farmer, ever the backbone of westward expansion, that much of it was believed unsuited to agriculture, and that thousands of vacant acres remained in Iowa whose agricultural possibilities had been demonstrated. Nebraska's territorial growth might be considered remarkable. A territorial census taken in October, 1855, showed a population of 4,494. This had increased to 10,716 by 1856, 28,841 by 1860, and an estimated 50,000 by 1867, the year the territory was admitted as a state. Where the population of 1854 had been scattered in small clusters along the Missouri River, that of 1867 stretched westward one hundred miles in the South Platte region, forming an irregular but almost continuous line running south from Columbus to a point near Fairbury; and north of the Platte, the valley was settled from its mouth to Grand Island, with a few homesteaders on the Elkhorn as far north as Norfolk and a fringe of settlement along the Missouri from Sioux City to the mouth of the Niobrara.

More than three-fourths of the territorial population (as of the census of 1860) was native-born, and for the most part they represented a stream of migration which had moved out across the Old Northwest from New England and the Middle Atlantic states. The leading native states of the population were, in this order, Ohio, New York, Pennsylvania, Illinois, Iowa, Indiana, and Missouri. Of the foreign-born, the Germans comprised the largest group, more than one-fourth of the total, to be followed by the English and the Irish, each of which accounted for nearly one-fourth. Many of the foreign-born concentrated in Omaha, accounting for sixty percent of Douglas County's population, although they comprised fifty-one percent of the population of Platte and Madison counties, forty-nine percent of that of Kearney County, thirty-three percent in Dakota, and twenty-five percent in Otoe. Hall County, with a population of only 116, was predominantly German. Native or foreign, however, the Nebraska territorial pioneer was apt to be a young man, and young men dominated the territory's affairs.

LAND AND LAND POLITICS

As soon as the Indian title to a tract of Nebraska land was extinguished, it became part of the public domain and was available for acquisition by private persons. Prior to the Homestead Act of 1862, title to the public domain in Nebraska territory could be acquired by: (1) purchase under the Pre-Emption Law of 1841, by which a settler could file a claim upon 160 acres of the public domain and acquire title by paying $1.25 per acre at the time the land was put up for sale; (2) purchase with military bounty land warrants; and (3) direct purchase, on or after the date on which the land was put up for public auction. Had procedures in force since 1785 been followed, the settlers would not have been able to take up legal residence on the land until it was surveyed. From the beginning, however, the American pioneer

had moved far ahead of the surveys, squatting on desirable tracts of
land in sublime defiance of federal law; and in March, 1854, Congress,
recognizing the futility of trying to hold back the squatter, provided
that in certain areas, including the proposed Nebraska territory, individuals could make settlement on unsurveyed land and be permitted,
as soon as the surveys were completed, to select the quarter section
whose lines corresponded most closely with the land on which they
had settled.

In Nebraska, as elsewhere, the early settlers moved far ahead of the
surveys. The first surveying contract, dated November 2, 1854, provided that by January 20, 1855, the base line, or Kansas boundary,
was to be established along the fortieth parallel for a distance of 108
miles or to the sixth principal meridian, the western border of the Omaha
cession (the west boundary of present Jefferson County). A second
contract, dated April 26, 1855, provided for establishing the guide
meridian between ranges eight and nine, and the first, second, third,
fourth, fifth, sixth, and seventh parallel lines. A third contract provided for the subdivision of the east tier of townships in Pawnee County,
the southeast corner of Johnson, and the southwest corner of Nemaha
by December 1, 1855. Initial subdivisions in Douglas County were to
be completed by June, 1856. The surveys continued to be pushed
rapidly, and by September 30, 1857, 2,420,062.88 acres had been subdivided and staked. By then, however, there were more than 10,000
people in the territory, and virtually all the heads of families had staked
out claims on their own.

To protect these pre-survey claims, the settlers fell back upon an
old frontier device, the claim club. One of the first public meetings in
the territory was that under the famous "Lone Tree" near the ferry
landing on Omaha's river front, July 22, 1854, which in the name of
the "Omaha Township Claim Association" promulgated a set of "laws"
and announced that "the jurisdiction of the Association shall extend
north and south of the grade section line in Omaha City three miles
and west from the Missouri River six miles." The "Belleview Settlers
Club" promulgated similar laws and defined the area of its jurisdiction
on October 28. Numerous other claim clubs were organized, so that
by the time the first townships were subdivided, claim law was in force
for about one hundred miles along the Missouri River and as far back
as the settlers thought the land to be of any value. Anyone who dared

disregard the land system thus established was visited by a committee from the local club, headed by the "sheriff," and under the persuasion of rifles and a coil of stout rope was convinced of the error of his ways. Though wholly in defiance of federal law, the claim clubs provided order where there could easily have been chaos, and with the sanction of a vast majority of the settlers served for all practical purposes as the most effective agency of local government during the early years of settlement. The first session of the territorial legislature, supremely indifferent to the constitutional niceties of the situation, passed an act recognizing and defining the authority of the claim clubs. As surveys were completed, making possible the filing of valid claims in the federal land offices, the need for the claim clubs ceased, and they quietly passed out of existence.[1]

From the beginning, land policies were an important factor in territorial politics. By the 1850's westerners were committed to the free homestead as the only satisfactory solution to the problem of disposing of the public domain. The claim clubs had sought to achieve that goal by establishing 320 acres as a valid claim on the theory that after the survey the settler could sell 160 acres to obtain the money with which to purchase the other quarter-section. Though this principle was affirmed by the first legislature, it collapsed, of course, with the opening of the land offices. The settlers then turned their attention to the possibility of acquiring at least a temporary free homestead through the postponement of land sales. In this they found themselves sorely at odds with the Buchanan Administration, and in the midst of the depression of 1857[2] word came from Washington that lands in Nebraska would go on sale beginning September 6, 1858. The howl of protest was instantaneous and almost unanimous. Governor Izard attempted to mollify the settlers, but his words were drowned in the chorus of denunciation that poured from mass meetings and newspaper offices in all parts of the territory. If necessary, the settlers would resist the order by force, and "Mutual Protection Associations" were formed in many communities. Finally, Buchanan was persuaded to postpone the evil day until the summer of 1859: July 5 and 25 at Omaha, July 10 at

[1]The Omaha land office, while nominally established in 1854, was not opened until 1856. In 1857, additional land offices were established at Brownville, Nebraska City, and Dakota City.

[2]See pp. 94–95.

Dakota City, August 1 and 29 at Nebraska City, August 8 at Brownville.

The protests against the land sales had been based on the contention that they would throw the settlers into the hands of speculators and money lenders. That contention was not unfounded. Settlers, frantically trying to salvage their claims, borrowed money at usurious rates—as high as sixty percent in some cases—to pay for their land. Military land warrants were as good as cash, and speculators bought them from needy soldiers and their widows for as low as fifty cents per acre and advanced them to settlers at the full price and at high rates of interest. For those who wanted to speculate in land directly by buying large tracts, the situation was equally favorable. By July 1, 1862, 912,898.86 acres had been entered with land warrants in Nebraska, and only 139,898.01 with cash. Looking back, in 1872, Robert W. Furnas, who had spearheaded the fight against land sales, wrote:

> In '59 the land from the Missouri river for sixty or seventy miles west was offered for sale and immediately after the sale nearly all of the land in Nemaha county was entered by speculators with their land warrants and tens of thousands of acres are to this day unimproved in consequence.
>
> Numbers entered land on credit, with trust deeds for security, and after struggling for several years and paying hundreds of dollars of interest money, walked off and left their farms to the speculator that had sucked the life blood from him for several years in the shape of forty percent interest.[3]

BOOM AND BUST

The frenzied speculation in farm land into which the territory was plunged in 1859—and which continued into the Seventies and Eighties —came on the heels of frantic speculation and subsequent demoralizing panic in many other lines: town lots, banks, business and industrial enterprises.

The Iowa boomers who poured across the Missouri in the summer of 1854 were interested first and foremost in founding towns in the hope that they could get a personal stake in the future "gateway of the West." The procedure was simple: a group of enterprising promoters would organize a town company, stake out the 320 acres allowed under the Federal Townsites Act, and then, to enlarge the site, individually

[3]Brownville *Advertiser*, May 2, 1872, as quoted in Addison E. Sheldon, *Land Systems and Land Policies in Nebraska*, Nebraska State Historical Society, *Publications*, XXII (Lincoln, 1936), 58.

pre-empt adjacent quarter-sections; the site was cut up into lots, 125 by 25 feet, and shares were sold usually on the basis of ten lots per share; then at the first opportunity the legislature was petitioned for a special act of incorporation. The first session incorporated seventeen towns, all but three with the word "city" in the name. Once the organization was set up and the site located, the town company began booming its property. Important in this was the newspaper, and most of the early territorial newspapers were little more than advertising sheets for their various town companies, with the larger part of each edition being sent east to attract prospective settlers. Locally, the editor played politics for the benefit of his employers, and in particular advertised his community as the ideal location for the territorial capital. As J. Sterling Morton, himself the hired editorial hand of the Nebraska City Town Company, later said, the greater part of their time was spent "talking and meditating upon the prospective value of city property. Young Chicagos, increscent New Yorks, precocious Philadelphias, and infant Londons were duly staked out, lithographed, divided into shares, and puffed with becoming unction and complaisance."[4]

All this had its effect. In 1857, individual lots on the river landings of some of the towns were valued at $10,000. Three or four blocks back they sold for $2,000, and even those as far distant as half a mile brought $1,200. Actually, of course, few, if any, of the early towns developed as their promoters hoped, and the map of eastern Nebraska is dotted with the ghosts of once-to-be-great cities long since given over to farming. Even Omaha, which soon worked itself into a position of political and commercial dominance, was characterized by uncertainty and instability. But the optimism continued. In his annual message to the legislature, January, 1857, Governor Izard boasted of the "unexampled degree of prosperity which has crowned the efforts of our infancy . . . of flourishing towns and prosperous cities, with their handsome church edifices, well regulated schools, and busy streets." The Governor should have looked out the window at the Omaha sprawled about him, but, undoubtedly, with his fellow men his eyes were on the future. To quote Morton again:

We all felt, as they used to print in large letters on every new town plat, that we were "located adjacent to the very finest groves of timber, surrounded

[4] James C. Olson, *J. Sterling Morton* (Lincoln: University of Nebraska Press, 1942), pp. 52–53.

by a very rich agricultural country, in prospective, abundantly supplied with building rock of the finest description, beautifully watered, and possessing very fine indications of lead, iron, coal and salt in great abundance." In my opinion we felt richer, better and more millionarish than any poor deluded mortals ever did on the same amount of moonshine and pluck.[5]

Such prosperity as was not based on hope was supported by an inflated currency. Hard money was even scarcer in Nebraska territory than in the country at large. All over the nation irresponsible legislatures were creating banks of issue to increase the amount of money in circulation, and Nebraska's lawmakers, working hard to strengthen the "prosperity of their infancy," opened the gates to a flood of paper money. The second territorial legislature created five banks of issue, each capitalized at from $50,000 to $500,000, with the provision that they could begin operations—including the issue of paper money—as soon as $50,000 was subscribed. In other words, they didn't need a cent of cash on hand. The third legislature passed six more bank bills. Governor Izard vetoed them all, but two were passed over his veto, amid charges of bribery, fraud, and corruption. Some of the disappointed applicants set up in business without the benefit of a legislative charter. After all, they argued, the soundness of any bank was dependent upon the responsibility and integrity of the banker and not upon a legislative charter.

The boom persisted throughout the spring and early summer of 1857. The wildcat notes issued from the new Nebraska banks were not good in the states and were viewed with some suspicion in the territory. They did provide a medium of exchange, however, and as such they passed around, keeping prices up and appearances prosperous. Had anyone bothered to look, he would have found plenty of evidence that the appearances were misleading—the territorial auditor's report to the second legislature, for example, showed a total assessed valuation of only $617,822, and not a cent of tax had been collected on the meager two mills levied against that. Late in the summer the territory began to get news of general financial panic in the East, involving the failure of many well-established firms. At first the territorial financiers thought themselves safe from trouble, but by fall the panic had spread to Nebraska. Almost as fast as they had been established the territorial banks came tumbling down, and as they closed their doors, their utter worth-

[5]*Ibid.*

lessness was brought into full light. The sheriff of Burt County, trying to collect an execution against the Bank of Tekamah—which had $90,000 in paper money oustanding—reported that he could find as assets only a shanty used as the banking house, and furniture consisting of an old table and a broken stove. One of two banks in De Soto had an office, safe, and cashier, but all the other had to show for its existence was its name engraved upon its bills. Again, a sheriff's writ of execution against the closed Bank of Nebraska at Omaha showed as assets: "Thirteen sacks of flour, one large iron safe, one counter, one desk, one stove drum and pipe, three arm chairs, and one map of Douglas County."[6]

The territory's whole financial structure collapsed with the banks. Town lots tumbled in value, businesses failed, money became practically nonexistent. For a time, interest rates soared as high as ten percent per month. In some places, merchants issued scrip simply to facilitate exchange; actually, this was much better than the paper money it replaced inasmuch as it was based on stocks of merchandise rather than on nothing more than "faith and credit." In any event, one need not wonder why the settlers rose in protest at having to put up $1.25 per acre for their claims or lose them. Many of them went heavily into debt to save their claims. Many others plunged deeply into land speculation. This speculation, however, was based on the potential productivity of Nebraska's soil.

AGRICULTURAL AND INDUSTRIAL BEGINNINGS

Prior to the panic of 1857, aside from speculation, there was very little serious interest in agriculture or industry in Nebraska. Commerce and industry, for speculative reasons, excited much more interest than agriculture. Farming simply didn't seem to be lucrative enough, and the principal interest in land was as an instrument of speculation. Pressed by the panic, however, many turned to farming; some because they could find nothing else to do, some because it would pay better than any other kind of business. As late as the fall of 1858, however, it was charged that:

Scarcely any produce enough to support themselves. Hundreds of acres of land, entered and owned by men who live among us, are allowed to lie

[6]Everett Dick *The Sod House Frontier* (New York: Appleton-Century Company, 1937), p. 90.

idle doing no more good to the community than when the land was owned by the native savages. . . .[7]

In the spring of 1859 it was noted that the flour mill of Pollard and Sheldon at Weeping Water falls was regularly delivering sacks of meal for shipment out of the territory by steamboat. By 1862, editors could exult over the change that had taken place in the territory. Now, they observed, the territory was exporting enough agricultural produce to more than counterbalance goods imported, and exchange for the first time was running in favor of the territory.

The only comprehensive view of early territorial agriculture is that provided by the census of 1860:

Acres improved	118,889
Cash Value of Farms	$3,851,326
Implements & Machinery	$205,664
Horses	5,197
Milch Cows	6,995
Working Oxen	12,594
Other Cattle	8,608
Sheep	2,355
Swine	25,369
Wheat, bu.	147,867
Indian Corn, bu.	1,482,080
Oats	74,502
Irish Potatoes, bu.	162,188

From this it is clear that the diversified agriculture of the Middle West was being extended across the Missouri. Corn, grown in the region long before the first white settler arrived, was the dominant crop from the beginning, and the first crop planted on any piece of ground was almost invariably sod corn. The process was simple: break the sod; plant the corn by cutting holes through the sod with an axe and dropping the kernels beneath the sod. Simple and laborious. Fortunately, sod corn required little or no cultivation, and given a reasonable amount of rain, the yield was good. Wheat, soon to become the second most important crop, was found to be well suited to much Nebraska land. There was a good market, both at home and abroad, and the territorial press, ever alive to the problems of agriculture, constantly urged their readers to plant more wheat.

[7]Nebraska City *News*, September 25, 1858, quoted in Morton and Watkins, *op. cit.*, II, 265.

Though farming by 1860 had proved itself to be the most dependable way to make a living in Nebraska, it was not without its hazards. Drouth, a periodic problem in Nebraska, was much more serious than the territorial promoters were apt to admit. The records are somewhat scanty and perhaps unreliable, but seven of the thirteen territorial years appear to have brought less than average rainfall; and in 1859, 1860, 1863, and 1864 the average annual rainfall was not over sixteen inches. Grasshoppers, usually associated primarily with the middle Seventies, plagued the territorial farmer as well, and 1857, 1860, 1865 and 1866 seem all to have been bad grasshopper years. Indeed, with grasshopper years alternating with drouth years, farming in territorial Nebraska was a precarious occupation, ameliorated perhaps only by the fact that the average farmer operated largely on a subsistence basis and, while in debt for his land, was not operating on the high-cost commercial basis that characterized the industry in later years.

From almost the beginning there was considerable official and editorial interest in agriculture as Nebraska's principal industry. Acting Governor Cuming recommended the formation of "industrial societies" in every county to develop agricultural and other productive resources; a territorial board of agriculture, established by the legislature in 1858, held the first territorial fair at Nebraska City, September 21 to 23, 1859, at which "the display in the various departments of agriculture, manufactures, arts, stock, &c., was highly creditable; and although limited in number were unsurpassed in quality especially as to horses, cattle, swine, grain and vegetables."[8] Various editors—notably Robert W. Furnas of the Brownville *Advertiser* and J. Sterling Morton of the Nebraska City *News*—were deeply concerned with the problems of agriculture and devoted many columns to advice and encouragement for those engaged in what was essentially an experimental enterprise. The influence of Furnas and Morton, and others like them—James T. Allan, D. H. Wheeler, and O. P. Mason, to name but three—in encouraging agriculture as Nebraska's leading activity can hardly be overemphasized. Circumstances may have dictated the choice of farming as an economic activity, but these men helped to develop it as a way of life.

Then, as for years later, farming overshadowed other economic activity. The 1860 census indicates the subordinate role of manufacturing in the territory. There were only 107 manufacturing establish-

[8] Robert W. Furnas, *President's Report, Board of Agriculture* (Omaha City, 1860), p. 5.

ments, with a total capital investment of only $266,575, employing 336 persons and turning out products valued at $607,328. The leading industry was the sawmill which employed more than half of the labor and turned out more than half of the product. Next in importance was the gristmill, and third the shoemaker. All of the establishments were small, and industrial enterprise as a whole was little more than an expanded home manufacture supplying consumers goods for a local market. Though a committee of the first legislature called attention to "the vast coal beds which lie embosomed in our beautiful territory . . . coal enough for empires and to spare . . . granite . . . large specimens of almost pure copper ore, easily obtained . . ." and though as late as 1869 Governor Butler could refer to the "rich and apparently inexhaustible supply of pure and easily manufactured" salt in the Lancaster salt basin, the territory simply did not have the raw materials to sustain heavy industry of any kind; and it was apparent before the end of the territorial period that Nebraska's industry would consist largely of the processing of agricultural products. Such factories as did exist for other purposes were finding it increasingly more difficult to compete with products shipped in from the East, and many discontinued operation.

SCHOOLS AND CHURCHES

Among the more important acts of the first territorial legislature was legislation providing for free public schools. The free public school act, passed in March, 1855, created the office of territorial superintendent (combined with that of territorial librarian) and provided for the selection of county superintendents by popular vote. Each county superintendent was to divide his county into districts and notify the residents to organize schools for the support of which he was authorized to levy a tax of not less than three nor more than five mills on all property in the county, the proceeds to be distributed among the various districts on the basis of white children between the ages of five and twenty-one. Most of the control was centered in the local districts, each governed by a three-member board. Most of the initiative appears to have rested there, too, and the development of public schools varied greatly from place to place in the territory. Everywhere the first schools were very unpretentious, and during the panic of 1857 many closed down altogether. When this happened, churches or private teachers usually stepped into the breach to provide some sort of schooling for the children of parents who were interested enough to pay direct fees. Frequently, too, private schools preceded the public schools altogether; and when public schools were organized—or reorganized—the first step generally consisted of granting public funds for the support of the existing private school. In the early years, many children were denied altogether the opportunity to attend school: in 1859, out of a total of 4,767 children of school age, only 1,310 attended any school at all during the year, and seven counties reported no schools whatever.

Though effective interest in the public schools lagged at times, many communities appear to have had great enthusiasm for universities, colleges, academies, and seminaries. Part of this, of course, was pure town company promotion—it was impressive to have the distinction, at least on paper, of enjoying higher educational facilities. Within two years after the territory was opened for settlement, the legislature had chartered seven colleges and universities, and all together, territorial legislatures chartered twenty-three institutions of higher learning. The only one of these in existence in any form today is Peru State College, organized by the Methodists in 1866 as Peru Seminary and College. The first such institution chartered was Simpson University at Omaha. The first to give collegiate work was Fontanelle University opened in 1858 by the Congregationalists as the nucleus of the little interior settlement of the same name. Within a year it was apparent that the college could not flourish and after a struggling existence it closed its doors in 1873. The fortunes of the town paralleled those of the college, and Fontanelle dwindled from a town of five hundred (good-sized for territorial Nebraska) to a crossroads village.

Churches, like schools, faced an uphill struggle to get started and keep going. As the Reverend George W. Barnes, a pioneer Baptist preacher in Omaha, wrote:

There were but few Christians among that varied population, and religion met only a left-handed favor. The great mass seemed in a terrible hurry to build their houses, and push their various enterprises to success and wealth. A very large proportion seemed to have come to make a speedy fortune, then return east and enjoy the same. Everything was made to bend that way. The Sabbath was painfully disregarded. You could hear the whiz of the saw, and the click of the hammer, at all hours of day and night for

the whole week. The Lord's day found only a few who honored its
claims. . . .[9]

Though Baptists, Presbyterians, and Catholics had been active in the
missionary field for two decades, the Methodists were the first to establish regularly organized churches for the benefit of the settler. The first
regularly established church in the territory appears to have been the
Methodist Church at Nebraska City, established in October, 1854, with
the Reverend W. D. Gage (for whom Gage County later was named)
as pastor. The Baptists, Catholics, Christians, Congregationalists, Epis-
copalians, and Presbyterians soon followed. By 1860, the census showed
sixty-three church organizations, divided as follows:

Denomination	*No. of Organizations*
Baptist	3
Christian	2
Congregational	4
Episcopal	3
Lutheran	2
Methodist Episcopal	32
Presbyterian	14
Roman Catholic	3

Until a church could be built—which was likely to be some time—
services usually were held in the homes of members. The Methodists,
with their itinerant circuit riders, were particularly well organized to
serve the needs of frontier communities, and for that reason probably
developed more rapidly than other denominations. Moreover, the Methodists were ardent revivalists, and protracted revivals were much-enjoyed
institutions in a frontier community. Where there were station churches
with buildings, the revivals usually began just after the corn was shucked
in the fall and lasted three or four weeks. Even more popular were the
camp meetings—protracted revivals held in the open during the summer months. The camp meeting combined a vacation with a period of
spiritual refreshment, and families who could afford them took tents to
the meeting place, usually a grove on the banks of a stream. The prairie
camp meetings do not appear to have suffered from the excesses which
characterized those held in the Appalachian forests, but the ministers
made the prairies ring with a strong emotional gospel.

[9]George W. Barnes, "Pioneer Preacher—An Autobiography," *Nebraska History*,
XXVII (April–June, 1946), 79–80.

Churches also formed the nucleus for certain territorial settlements, though not so frequently as in the Seventies, when ministers negotiated with the railroads for tracts of land on which to settle their flocks. St. Johns, for example, an early Dakota County settlement, was established in 1856 by Catholics from Dubuque, Iowa, under the leadership of Father Jeremiah Trecy.

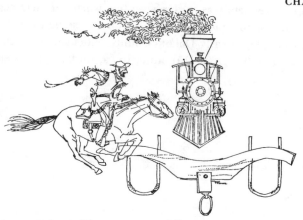

CHAPTER 9

From Trail to Rail

NEBRASKA TERRITORY, organized to make possible a Platte Valley route for the transcontinental railroad, was indeed on America's great road west. Overland emigration, which had built territories and even states in the Far West, continued—at a reduced rate, to be sure—but the summer of 1859 saw the Platte Valley alive once again with gold seekers, headed this time for the elusive riches believed to lie buried in the sands of Cherry Creek, where Denver was to arise almost overnight. The military posts, the Colorado mining camps, and even the diggings in far-off Montana created a heavy demand for goods that could best be supplied through the Platte Valley, and overland freighting developed into one of Nebraska territory's biggest businesses. The western demand for mail and passenger service was exceeded only by the demand for freighted goods, and the territorial years saw exciting developments in "fast" transportation taking place in the Platte Valley: the stage coach, the Pony Express, and finally the telegraph and the railroad. The heavy increase in population during the early years of statehood was made possible by the technological advances taking shape during the territorial years. A generation conditioned by more than a century of technological revolution finds it difficult to appreciate the rapidity with which the transformation from wagon to railroad took place on the Plains in the 1860's. But it was a rapid transformation—and a far-reaching one. In many respects it is the central fact of Nebraska's territorial history.

THE STEAMBOAT

Along the Missouri River, the impact of technology already had been felt when the territory was organized. Steam ferries were in operation at Omaha and Bellevue. Steamboats, first seen on the river as far north as the mouth of the Platte in 1819, when Major Stephen H. Long brought the *Western Engineer* up to Council Bluffs,[1] had been plying its course with some regularity since 1831. In that year the *Yellowstone*, owned by the American Fur Company, ascended the river as far as Fort Tecumseh (later Fort Pierre), going the next year to Fort Union, three miles above the mouth of the Yellowstone River. The success of these two voyages prompted the American Fur Company to abandon keelboats for steamboats altogether, and the use of the steamboat—expensive but admittedly effective—was an important factor in the company's acquisition of a virtual monopoly on the fur trade of the Far West.[2]

Occasionally the company had two boats on the river, but normally it sent only one vessel upstream each season. Though there was an increasing number of boats on the lower river, until about 1846 virtually the only ones on the upper river were those engaged in the fur trade. The Mormon emigration and the California gold rush resulted in the penetration of a few non-fur trade boats as far as Council Bluffs and Winter Quarters. Council Bluffs remained a port of call, and after 1854 the steamboats touched at the ambitious little settlements springing up on the west side of the river. River traffic increased steadily during the Fifties, reaching its zenith in 1859, the year of the Colorado gold rush. Unfortunately, no comprehensive statistics are available, but scattered figures will indicate the traffic's growth: in 1857, twenty-eight steamboats arrived at Sioux City before July 1; by August 11, 1859, 128 steamboats had arrived at Omaha-Council Bluffs.

Though they carried great and varied quantities of freight, many of the boats were designed primarily for passenger trade, and in the heyday of Missouri River steamboating some of them were little short of floating palaces. The largest were about 250 feet long with a forty-foot beam and a full-length cabin capable of accommodating from 300 to 400 passengers, in addition to a freight capacity of from 500 to 700 tons. Powered by two ponderous engines, such a boat cost between

[1]See p. 45.
[2]See p. 49.

$50,000 and $75,000. Trimmed with gilt and glass and painted a dazzling white, the river queen was indeed a proud vessel as she churned her way against the turbulent waters of the Missouri. Inside, the carpeted saloon and the well-appointed staterooms provided the utmost in luxury for those who could afford it. The big boats carried a crew of from seventy-five to ninety, presided over by the pilot, who was the true aristocrat of the western waters. It took skill and experience to guide a boat along the treacherous Missouri, and the pilots, who had a tight little union known as the "Pilots' Benevolent Association," sometimes drew as much as $1,200 per month. Even with the best pilots, accidents were frequent and losses heavy. All told, over four hundred vessels were sunk or damaged, with losses amounting to almost nine million dollars.

For the river towns of Nebraska territory, the steamboats provided an indispensable connection with the outside world. They brought settlers; they carried goods to stock the frontier stores and to be shipped across the Plains in heavy wagons; they brought mail and newspapers. Little wonder that the first boat up the river in spring provided the occasion for an impromptu celebration, with the entire town emptying itself on the river landing to greet debarking passengers, watch the freight being unloaded, dance to the ship's orchestra, and (for the favored few) enjoy a nip with the captain.

During the 1860's the Missouri River steamboat business went into a serious decline. The Civil War greatly disrupted the trade. More important, the railroads began to provide overwhelming competition: the Hannibal and St. Joseph reached the Missouri in 1859, the Chicago and Northwestern in 1867. The steamboats simply could not meet railroad competition, and postwar river traffic was confined largely to servicing points not yet reached by the railroad. The arrival of the Great Northern at Helena in 1887 delivered the final blow.

OVERLAND FREIGHTING

The heavy emigration to California, Oregon, and Utah in the Forties and Fifties, the Colorado gold rush of 1859, and the opening of the Montana diggings in the Sixties created an almost insatiable demand for goods of all kinds. Adding heavily to the demand were the military posts established throughout the West to protect trails and settlements from the Indians. California and Oregon could be supplied by ship, but the most feasible way to get goods to Colorado, Utah, and Montana was through the Platte Valley, the route of the emigrants. If Nebraska's river towns were established too late to serve as outfitting points for the emigrants,[3] they developed into important freighting terminals as steamboats unloaded goods at their wharves to be transshipped by wagon across the Plains.

Drawn by six to twelve yoke of oxen and loaded with three to five tons of freight, the heavy wagons carried an amazing variety of goods: food, grain, clothing, whiskey, mining machinery, lumber, arms, ammunition—anything for which there was a demand or for which a demand might be created. One freighter took a load of cats to Denver, disposing of them at a good profit to miners who sought companions and mousers. Another filled his wagon box with frozen eggs at Omaha in the fall and hauled them to Denver. Two enterprising Germans loaded a similar wagon with frozen oysters at Omaha, peddling them along the way at $2.50 per quart. Another specialized in hauling apples, which commanded as much as $15 per bushel in Denver. Still others drove flocks of turkeys and sheep and herds of cattle from the Missouri to Denver. The big companies, however, concentrated on grain, food, and military supplies for the Army, serving as carriers rather than speculators.

The freighting business embraced everything from the farmer or small merchant who loaded a single wagon with goods and set out for Denver to the large companies employing hundreds of men and doing millions of dollars worth of business each year. Of those regularly engaged in the business, sixty-four have been identified as operating out of Nebraska City at one time or another, and twenty-four out of Omaha. Prominent in the Nebraska City trade were Russell, Majors and Waddell; Coe and Carter; the Gilman Brothers; Hosford and Gaynon; John Coad; Ben Holladay; Wells, Fargo and Company; Hawke, Nuckolls and Company; A. and P. Byrum; Moses Stocking; R. M. and D. P. Rolfe; H. T. Clarke and Company; Moses Sydenham; and many others. Among the Omahans were Edward Creighton, William Paxton, and Major Frank North.

By its very nature, however, the freighting business tended to concentrate itself in a relatively few large firms. Costs were high; profits, though occasionally large, were speculative; and in order to bid on government contracts, the most dependable source of income, the freighter

[3]They did, of course, develop a considerable emigrant business, particularly during the Colorado gold rush when Omaha boomed as an outfitting point.

needed hundreds of wagons and thousands of oxen. The standard "bull outfit" consisted of a train of twenty-five freight wagons and one mess wagon, representing an investment of from $18,000 to $20,000 and requiring 300 to 320 head of oxen, including extras, and a minimum crew of about thirty men. The wagon boss received about $75 per month and the teamsters about $25. In addition, all were rationed, at a cost of about forty-five to fifty cents per day. An individual farmer could shuck a load of corn, haul it to Fort Kearny, and be well paid for his time, but a man had to have considerable financial backing to operate a freighting train—and the big outfits, of course, had several trains on the trail at once.

Largest of all the freighting firms was Russell, Majors and Waddell, which in the late Fifties virtually monopolized military freighting on the Plains. Alexander Majors and William H. Russell, both veteran freighters, formed a partnership in 1855 to carry military freight from Fort Leavenworth to the posts of the Plains and the mountains. When they secured in addition the contract to supply Albert S. Johnston's Army of Utah in 1857, they added another partner, William B. Waddell. The new contract necessitated the establishment of an additional terminal up-river from Fort Leavenworth, and the partners chose Nebraska City, transforming it in one season from a struggling frontier settlement to a major river port. Russell, Majors and Waddell bought 138 lots on which they constructed houses, wagon shops, foundries, boarding houses, and warehouses. All told, the company spent more than $300,000 developing its terminal. Majors, who superintended the firm's operations in Nebraska City and on the trail, announced that he would need eight thousand yoke of oxen and about twelve hundred men. Actually, he advertised for sixteen thousand yoke of oxen and fifteen hundred men. The river landing was busy with steamboats unloading huge quantities of freight. The uphill grade of Nebraska City's main street was pulverized by the grinding of heavy wheels.

Initially, the route west from Nebraska City followed what was known as the "Ox-Bow Trail," crossing Salt Creek at Ashland and following the Platte River to Fort Kearny. This was generally unsatisfactory—it was a roundabout route and much of it traversed the eastern Platte River bottoms, impassable for freight wagons when wet—and before he located at Nebraska City, Majors required the town to agree to lay out and develop a road directly west to Fort Kearny. Nebraska City failed to keep its promise and finally, in the spring of 1860, Majors, having invested so heavily in the town that he could not afford to move the terminal, assumed the burden himself, hiring Augustus Harvey to survey a direct route. Harvey found a well-beaten path as far as Olathe (now Saltillo) on Salt Creek. From Salt Creek he plowed a furrow due west to Fort Kearny. Wagons, coming along later, straddled the furrow, and before the season was out the Nebraska City-Fort Kearny cutoff was well established. Later the cutoff came to be known as the Steam Wagon Road, commemorating the ill-starred effort of one General J. R. Brown to run a wood-burning steam locomotive across the treeless plains to Denver, an effort which ended when the wagon broke down on its maiden run a few miles out of Nebraska City.

The freight wagon like the steamboat fell in the wake of the railroad, though, of course, until the advent of the motorized truck local freighting was all done by wagon. The importance of overland freighting in the economic development of Nebraska territory, however, can hardly be overemphasized. The river towns developed almost in proportion to the amount of steamboat or freight wagon transfer business they were able to secure, and Nebraska City's success in this activity established it as the second most important town in the territory, giving it a more important relative position than it has enjoyed since. The big operators provided an outlet for crops and livestock produced in the territory and employment for thousands of men. Small-scale freighting ventures helped many a farmer and small merchant to keep going and at times to develop into a businessman of considerable stature. All along the trail, road ranches developed to provide the freighters with feed for their oxen, food and diversion for themselves. Some of these developed into the large cattle ranches of a later day, others into towns.

STAGE COACH AND PONY EXPRESS

The West desired mail as much as it did freight service, and almost from the beginning of settlement in California, Oregon, and Utah, the government was bombarded with requests for improved mail service. The agitation attached itself to the growing sectional controversy and particularly to the question of the ultimate route of the Pacific railroad. Initially, mail to California came by ocean. This, however, provided no service to the mountain settlements and was generally unsatisfactory to Californians, who by the 1850's were demanding overland mail service as the only adequate solution to their problem. To many, however, regular mail service over the long, hard overland route to California seemed impracticable, and in the early Fifties the government could be persuaded to supply such service only to the mountain settlements.

In 1850, United States mail service was established between Independence and Salt Lake City, and the next year from Salt Lake City to Sacramento. The service, particularly to the East, was far from satisfactory. The contract provided for a monthly mail, but the contractor, using the same wagon and team for the entire journey, frequently failed to keep the schedule and during the winter virtually suspended operations. When the government finally established through service to California in 1857, it used the southern route, of no value to the Utah settlements. By 1858, however, as the result of a generous expansion of postal facilities in the West, the central route had a weekly mail from Independence to Placerville by way of Salt Lake City. It was soon evident that the overland mail service, whatever the route, was an expensive operation, and when in 1859 the western service generally was greatly curtailed, that on the central route was reduced to a semimonthly basis.

The West, of course, wanted more not less mail service, regardless of the cost to the general government, and in 1859 the newly-established mining communities of the Pikes Peak region added to the demand. To meet this demand, William H. Russell conceived the then daring idea of a stage coach express to the Pikes Peak region. Though his partners refused to join what they considered a wild scheme, Russell with the aid of John S. Jones went ahead, establishing the Leavenworth and Pikes Peak Express along the Republican-Solomon route. The "L. & P. P." was in financial difficulty from the beginning, and Russell, Majors and Waddell bailed the enterprise out, transferring it to the Platte Valley route so that they could combine it with their Salt Lake mail service. Further service on the Platte Valley route was provided by the Western Stage Company, which ran a weekly mail over the Military Road from Omaha to Fort Kearny, extending its service to Denver in September, 1860.

Meanwhile, Senator William M. Gwin of California had persuaded William H. Russell to launch a pony express between St. Joseph and California as a means of dramatically demonstrating the superiority of the central route. Russell's partners, still making up losses for the Pikes Peak Express, were not particularly enthusiastic over this latest brain-child of their ebullient colleague, but finally they were induced to agree to make good his pledge to Gwin, who, in turn, had promised to obtain a government mail contract for the Pony Express. Having made their decision, Russell, Majors and Waddell began preparations to launch the service at the earliest possible date, and on April 3, 1860, to the accompaniment of celebrations at both ends of the line, the first riders set out from Sacramento and St. Joseph. Riders, station keepers, and ponies functioned with brilliant precision to bring the first mail through both ways in the scheduled ten days.

The Pony Express generally followed the route of the Oregon-California Trail, along which stations of logs, stone, or adobe were built at intervals of about fifteen miles. Riders covered seventy-five to a hundred miles, although horses were changed at each station. Both riders and horses were the best obtainable. The horses for the most part were half-breed California mustangs, noted for their dependability, endurance, and speed; the riders were young men hired for their light weight, strength, courage, horsemanship and marksmanship—the pick of the frontier. Throughout the summer and fall, the Pony Express maintained its ten-day schedule fairly well. By autumn, the transcontinental telegraph extended west as far as Fort Kearny and east to Fort Churchill, Nevada, and telegraphic messages carried between these two points by the Pony Express spanned the continent in record time—news of Lincoln's election, for example, got across the country in eight days, the run between Fort Kearny and Fort Churchill being made in six days. During the winter, when the operations were watched with great interest as a test of the practicability of the central route for year-around use, the schedule was extended to fifteen days between terminals and eleven days between telegraph stations. Though this schedule was seldom kept—the average time between Kearny and Churchill was 13.8 days—only one trip was missed altogether, and the Pony Express was able to maintain supremacy over the Butterfield Line operating on the southern route.

As spring came on, the Pony Express made decided improvement—but by spring its days were definitely numbered, its function limited to shuttling messages across the ever-narrowing gap between the termini of the transcontinental telegraph. When the lines were joined at Salt

Lake City on October 24, 1861, the Pony Express ceased to operate altogether. Financially, the Pony Express was never a success. Though the rates were high—$5.00 per half ounce, later reduced to $1.00 plus postage—the costs of operation were still higher, and even when occasionally loaded to capacity the Pony Express could not pay for itself. The oft-promised government mail contract failed to materialize, and Russell, Majors and Waddell completed their financial destruction (well begun in the Pikes Peak Express venture) with the Pony Express. Nationally, however, the experiment was a definite success: it demonstrated the practicability of the central route at all seasons of the year; it blazed the path for the first transcontinental railroad; it helped tie California to the Union cause in the first difficult months of the Civil War. It remains one of the great acts in the drama of the West.

The Civil War added importance to the Platte Valley route. The Butterfield Overland Mail was transferred from the southern to the central route, and to help hold California to the Union, daily service was inaugurated under a contract that was to cost the government a million dollars a year. Letter mail was to go through in twenty days, other mail in thirty-five. For a variety of reasons, Butterfield could not keep his schedule, and the whole operation was denounced as a fraud and a humbug. Ben Holladay purchased the line in 1862 and, despite Indian difficulties in 1864,[4] greatly improved and extended the service. Wells, Fargo purchased the lines in 1866 and continued to operate them until completion of the transcontinental railroad, when the stagecoach, like the freight wagon, was transformed from a transcontinental to a local carrier.

Throughout the Civil War, however, the Concord coaches rolled through the Platte Valley on their daily transcontinental schedule. Manufactured by Abbott-Downing of Concord, New Hampshire, the swaying coach, drawn by four to six horses or mules, was as much an institution on the Plains as the covered wagon. As many as nine passengers could be accommodated inside, and in times of great rush others rode on top. Mail and express were carried in large leather pouches at the front and rear. Speed varied greatly, although in the Platte Valley a coach could make ten miles per hour, and six miles per hour, including stops, was considered to be average. Rates increased steadily during the Civil War, and at the end of the conflict passage from the Missouri

⁴See pp. 135–137.

River to Denver cost $175—nearly twenty-seven cents per mile. This was transportation only. Meals were extra. Samuel Bowles, a Massachusetts editor who went through in 1865, described the facilities as follows:

. . . every ten or fifteen miles is a stable of the stage proprietor, and every other ten or fifteen miles an eating-house; perhaps as often a petty ranch or farm house, whose owner lives by selling hay to the trains of emigrants or freighters; every fifty or one hundred miles you will find a small grocery and blacksmith shop; and about as frequently is a military station with a company or two of United States troops for protection against the Indians. This makes up all the civilization of the Plains. The barns and houses are of logs or prairie turf, piled up layer on layer, and smeared over or between with a clayey mud. The turf and mud make the best houses, and the same material is used for military forts and for fences around the cattle and horse yards. Their roofs, where covered, are a foot thickness of turfs, sand, clay, and logs or twigs, with an occasional inside lining of skins or thick cloth. Floors are oftenest such as nature offers only; and, as at some of the Washington hotels, the spoons at the table do not always go around. Mexican terms prevail: an inclosure for animals is called a "corral"; a house of turf and mud is of "adobe"; and a farm-house or farm a "ranch."

Our meals at the stage stations continued very good throughout the ride; the staples were bacon, eggs, hot biscuit, green tea and coffee; dried peaches and apples, and pies were as uniform; beef was occasional, and canned fruits and vegetables were furnished at least half of the time. Each meal was the same; breakfast, dinner and supper were undistinguishable save by the hour; and the price was one dollar or one dollar and a half each. The devastations of the Indians last summer and fall, and the fear of their repetition, form the occasion and excuse for enormous prices for everything now upon the Plains. . . .[5]

More important, Bowles clearly saw the destiny of the Platte Valley: "This valley of the Platte, through these Plains, is the natural highway across the Continent. Other valleys and routes have similar advantages, but in minor degree: this unites the most; for it is central—it is on the line of our great cities and our great industries, East and West, and it is the longest, most continuous. A smooth, hard stage road is made by simply driving over it; a railroad awaits only sleepers and rails. . . ."[6]

[5]Samuel Bowles, *Across the Continent* (Springfield, Mass., 1865), pp. 20–22.
[6]*Ibid.*, p. 20.

TALKING WIRES AND THE IRON HORSE

On June 16, 1860, Congress authorized the Secretary of the Treasury to subsidize a telegraph line from the western border of Missouri to San Francisco at the cost of $40,000 per year for a period of ten years. Hiram Sibley, president of Western Union and principal inspiration for the act, immediately went to work to complete a line and secure the subsidy. W. H. Stebbins was employed to build up the Missouri River from St. Joseph to Omaha, and out along the Platte. By August 29 the line was at Brownville, its first Nebraska station, prompting "a general jollification. . . . Bonfires, illuminations, fire balls, music, burning gunpowder, speeches and toasts were the order of the evening. . . ."[7]

By September 5, the line was open to Omaha, and it had been stretched west to Fort Kearny in time to bring news of Lincoln's election to the post and the waiting Pony Express. Meanwhile, on November 18, Edward Creighton, general agent of Western Union, who had built many miles of telegraph east of the Mississippi, left Omaha by stage to make plans for extending the line farther west. During the winter a California company was formed to cooperate with Western Union by building the western end of the transcontinental line, and to build the eastern end Western Union organized the Pacific Telegraph Company under the liberal incorporation laws of Nebraska territory. The two lines were to join at Salt Lake City.

During the spring of 1861, Stebbins completed the line from Fort Kearny to Julesburg. Creighton then divided the construction force into two crews—one under Stebbins was to build east from Salt Lake City, and the other under Creighton himself, west from Julesburg. It was a great summer for Ed Creighton, whose name was to become intimately identified with Omaha's development. Though it was July 2 before the first poles were set west of Julesburg and the company despaired of meeting the deadline of July 31, 1862, Creighton completed the line to Salt Lake City by October 20—by the twenty-fourth the west end was in and the wires were joined. Creighton's great problem, of course, was that of supply; and hundreds of wagons were used to transport wire, insulators, tools, and provisions west from the Missouri River. On the treeless Plains poles were also a problem, and in one instance they were

[7] *Nebraska Advertiser,* August 30, 1860.

hauled 240 miles. Cedar poles from the canyons at Cottonwood Springs near North Platte were used for miles along the line.

Meanwhile, the transcontinental railroad—Nebraska territory's initial reason for being—gradually was taking shape. The project languished during the Fifties, largely because of sectional controversies over the route—controversies which were to be settled only by the Civil War. On July 1, 1862, Congress chartered the Union Pacific Company to build the eastern end of a transcontinental railroad and provided assistance for the Central Pacific Company, organized a year earlier, to build the western end.

To Nebraskans and Iowans the matter of greatest moment was the location of the eastern terminus. Council Bluffs had promoted the organization of Nebraska territory and Omaha as the capital of that territory largely to further her railroad interests. Omaha, suffering from alternate periods of prosperity and depression, pinned her economic hopes on securing the transcontinental railroad. It was a great day then, December 2, 1863, when Peter Dey, chief engineer of the Union Pacific, received a telegram in Omaha announcing that President Lincoln, fulfilling the responsibility placed on him by the Act of July 1, 1862, had fixed the initial point of the road on the "western boundary of the State of Iowa, opposite Omaha—opposite section 10, in township fifteen, north of range thirteen, east of the sixth principal meridian, in the territory of Nebraska."

Legally this put the eastern terminus in Iowa, but for all practical purposes the plum had fallen to Omaha. Ground breaking ceremonies were held that very day with Governor Alvin Saunders wielding the ceremonial spade to the accompaniment of guns and cheers. A number of dignitaries took part in the proceedings, including George Francis Train, whose spectacular international career was being interrupted for a while in Omaha, and who said, "The President shows good judgment in locating the road where the Almighty placed the signal station, at the entrance of a garden seven hundred miles in length and twenty broad." The day's festivities concluded with supper at the Herndon House, served promptly at one-thirty in the morning.

For more than a year after this auspicious beginning, nothing was done. The Act of 1862 had provided a grant of ten sections of public land and a government loan for each mile of track laid, the loan to be $16,000 for each mile on the plains, $32,000 for each mile in the foothills, and $48,000 for each mile in the mountains. Generous as this may seem, it was not enough to attract capital for building a railroad across the desert wastes to California, and it was not until Congress in 1864 —under heavy pressure from the railroad—doubled the land grant and relegated the loan to the status of a second mortgage that money became available. Congressman Oakes Ames of Massachusetts and his brother Oliver, important Boston bankers, provided much-needed assistance. Thomas Durant, the U. P.'s chief executive, devised a scheme, in the Credit Mobilier of America, whereby company officers, congressmen whose influence was needed, and others could make their fortunes from the construction operation, and this brought still additional capital— capital that returned annual dividends of about one hundred percent! The Credit Mobilier's fantastic operations, by means of which the officers of the Union Pacific and their friends profited at the expense of the railroad, the small stockholders, and even the government itself, developed into a national scandal that was to be a major factor in anti-railroad politics of later years.

By the time the Civil War had ended, the Union Pacific was at last ready to move. Money was available, and so was labor. Supplies were more difficult to obtain. Tie-cutting crews denuded the Missouri Valley of trees for miles up and down the river from Omaha. When this supply ran out, ties were shipped in from the East. Until 1867, when the Chicago and Northwestern reached Council Bluffs, everything had to be shipped to Omaha by steamboat, and even after the rails reached the eastern bank of the Missouri, materials had to be ferried across the river. West of Omaha, the railroad could haul its own rails, ties and other supplies, but the grading crews and others who worked ahead of the rails had to be supplied by wagon. Not the least of the company's problems were the Indians, who looted supply wagons and attacked construction crews in western Nebraska, Colorado, and Wyoming. Once construction had well begun, however, General Grenville M. Dodge, who succeeded Dey as chief engineer, pushed it steadily toward completion. Although only forty miles of track had been laid by the end of 1865, the rails reached Kearney by August, 1866, and North Platte by November.

As the road pushed west, base towns were established at the end of the track to facilitate the handling of supplies, men, and equipment— in Nebraska, at Fremont, Fort Kearny, North Platte, and Sidney—boisterous little towns loaded with prostitutes and gamblers ready to prey on the Irish workmen who came to town on payday. As "end-o-track" moved on, the terminal towns became mere way stations, but all of them were to develop into prosperous small cities. Also, as the tracks went west, pioneer Platte Valley settlements literally moved from their original location to one on the railroad; Ben Holladay's stage runs steadily became shorter; and observers marvelled at the speed with which General Dodge pushed his great project through.

On November 13, 1867, the rails reached Cheyenne. On May 10, 1869, they joined those of the Central Pacific at Promontory Point, a little west of Ogden, Utah. The nation was united by rail. The Platte Valley, the funnel through which America had been channeled into the West, had become an important link in the iron chain binding East and West. It could now become a homesite as well. The technological transformation that would make possible the settlement of the Plains west of the Missouri—the new state of Nebraska—had been completed.

CHAPTER 10

Politics and the

Struggle Over Statehood

THOUGH PALLID in comparison with the bloody conflicts raging in the twin territory to the south—and for that reason often ignored—politics in Nebraska territory were lusty, the debates frequently acrimonious, and the proceedings often characterized by the excesses common to a frontier society. Early pioneers seem to have come to Nebraska in significant numbers for the express purpose of carving political careers for themselves in the new territory; others to use politics as one means to financial gain. They lost no time in getting about their business. The same issue of the *Nebraska Palladium*, for example, that reported the arrival of Silas Strickland from Tennessee carried a notice that he was announcing his candidacy for election to the territorial House of Representatives. J. Sterling Morton had attended two political meetings and had made a political speech before he had been in the territory a week.

PERSONAL AND SECTIONAL POLITICS

Insofar as party labels were concerned, Nebraska's early politics were all Democratic. The territory had been created by a Democratic Congress and a Democratic Administration, and her first governors, secretaries, judges and other appointive officials were all good Democrats, being thus rewarded by President Pierce for faithful party service or appointed to strengthen the Democratic cause. The initial counties all bore good Democratic names, excepting only the father of his country: Burt, Cass, Dodge, Douglas, Forney, Pierce, Richardson, and Washington. Within the territory, however, party lines were not sharply drawn, and political contests were decided on personal and sectional considerations, particularly the latter. Individual towns struggled for preferment; counties south of the Platte made common cause against those north of the river. The first legislature contained twenty-seven Democrats and twelve Whigs, but they had not been elected on the basis of political affiliation, and no contemporary mention seems to have been made of party strength. Likewise, the delegate to Congress—the most important position in the gift of the territorial electorate—was elected without regard to party, and candidates appealed for sectional rather than party support.

The legislature, however, soon became embroiled with the executive. This was not unique in Nebraska but was common in all the territories. The federally appointed executive represented outside control; and even though—as usually was the case—he tried to act in the best interests of the territory, he was the symbol of an inferior political status which most territorial residents were anxious to escape. Legislators, elected by the people of the territory, looked upon themselves as the champions of the people against federal authority. In Nebraska, legislative independence was strengthened by the doctrine of "popular sovereignty," which, though applied only to the institution of slavery in the organic act, was popularly construed as a mandate for the widest possible exercise of local self-government. Moreover, the provision in the organic act which permitted laws passed by the territorial legislature to take effect without submission to Congress for approval greatly strengthened the legislative arm in Nebraska.

Squatter sovereignty was good frontier doctrine, and it was easy to rally local public opinion against acts of the executive on the grounds that they encroached upon that sovereignty. Thus, those who opposed Cuming's selection of Omaha as the territorial capital denounced his act as a denial of popular sovereignty, the basis of government in the territory:

The doctrine of popular sovereignty is a good doctrine, our faith is in it, and we had expected that here in its new home it would be developed prop-

erly, and by its benign influence, put down the cant and hypocrisy which
has ever opposed it. But our hopes have thus far proved futile. And though
the world abroad may envy us our privileges, it cannot know, and if it could,
is too incredulous to believe, that by a conspiracy, headed by one rascal,
those privileges and rights have been snatched from us. . . .[1]

Later, when Acting Governor J. Sterling Morton assumed the right
to appoint the public printer—hitherto selected by the legislature—
that, too, was denounced as a denial of popular sovereignty.

So even good men found it difficult to function effectively as territorial executives, and it was perhaps even more difficult to get good
men to accept the appointment. The position of governor paid only
$2,500 per year. Nebraska was far from the beaten path and an ap-
pointment there hardly was looked upon as a steppingstone to greater
things. The country was new and life was hard. Shortly after his arrival,
Judge Edward R. Harden of the territorial supreme court wrote his
wife, who had remained at home in Georgia: "I will start for home,
on the very first boat that comes up in the Spring . . . and unless my
views, and feelings and opinions undergo a great change, I shall not
return. It is a poor country no Timber, sickly, and out of the world
and settled up with Savages."[2]

Consequently, the appointments often went to the young and inexperienced, or to political hacks who needed to be rewarded for faithful,
if relatively insignificant, service. Cuming and Morton, who served as
acting governor, were both young, inexperienced, and hot-tempered.
Mark W. Izard had good intentions but little else. Samuel W. Black
was able, but stories that he was in his cups much of the time reduced
his effectiveness. The only man of stature and experience to serve the
territory as governor during the period prior to the Civil War was
Douglas' close friend, William A. Richardson of Illinois, an influential congressman who had had a large part in the struggle to get the
Kansas-Nebraska Act through the House, and who prior to his appointment had been the Democratic candidate for governor of Illinois.
He served, however, for less than a year (January 12 to December 5,
1858), resigning in protest against Buchanan's pro-slavery policy in
Kansas.

[1]*Nebraska Palladium,* February 7, 1855.
[2]Ruth K. Nuermberger, ed., "Letters from Pioneer Nebraska by Edward Randolph
Harden," *Nebraska History,* XXVII (January–March, 1946), 27.

PARTY POLITICS AND THE CIVIL WAR

Local dissatisfaction with the acts of federally appointed officials naturally tended to develop into opposition to the party in power. The strong pro-southern, pro-slavery attitude of the Buchanan Administration, which alienated Douglas and many northern Democrats and gave powerful ammunition to the burgeoning Republican party, provided additional grounds on which to base opposition to the Democrats, particularly in a territory whose settlers were preponderantly from the North. This, combined with Buchanan's attitude on the public lands,[3] made difficult indeed the position of Administration Democrats in Nebraska territory.

The opposition was slow to commit itself to the Republican party. As early as 1858, J. Sterling Morton, Secretary of the Territory and an ardent Administration Democrat, could refer to the "irresponsible, Black Republican, nigger-loving legislature," but those who opposed the Democrats in the delegate campaign of 1859 organized as the People's party, and carefully avoided use of the word "Republican." They sought merely to provide a voice for all "those citizens of Nebraska who disapprove the policy of the national government during the last six years." Their candidate for delegate to Congress was Samuel G. Daily of Peru, a vigorous campaigner.

The Democrats held their first nominating convention in 1859, too, selecting Experience Estabrook, prominent Omaha lawyer and former United States attorney for the territory, as their candidate for delegate. The Democrats won control of the legislature, and by a narrow margin of three hundred votes elected Estabrook to Congress. Daily immediately contested the election on charges of fraud, and the Republican House of Representatives found that while there had been fraud on both sides, there was less on Daily's, and allowed him to take over the seat. This was an old story in Nebraska. Almost every delegate had been faced with a contest. Indeed, as the *Nebraska Advertiser* complained, "One great reason why so little has heretofore been secured for Nebraska is that she has never yet had a delegate so situated that he could work for the territory; he has always devoted the most of his time to watching and defending his seat."[4]

[3] See p. 91
[4] November 17, 1859.

By 1860, the issues were more clearly drawn. The People's party definitely adopted the name "Republican" and in its convention at Plattsmouth arrayed itself enthusiastically behind Lincoln and Hamlin. For delegate, it nominated Samuel G. Daily. The Democrats, meeting in Omaha, nominated J. Sterling Morton, Secretary of the Territory, and—despite his twenty-seven years—easily one of the most prominent men in Nebraska. Both parties campaigned enthusiastically for federally supported internal improvements in the territory. The Republicans, in addition, insisted strongly that the election of Lincoln was essential to prevent slavery from encroaching further upon freedom. The Democrats, embarrassed by the split in their party nationally, contended that inasmuch as residents of the territory had no vote in the presidential election, the only issues worth considering were local ones. Morton, sensing Buchanan's unpopularity in the territory and his own vulnerability as a Buchanan appointee, early in the campaign declared himself to be a Douglas Democrat—a declaration vigorously disputed by the Republicans and particularly by Robert W. Furnas, editor of the influential Brownville *Advertiser*, who had been a Douglas Democrat but joined the Republicans in 1860.

This first contest between Republicans and Democrats in Nebraska brought together two of the best stump speakers in the territory. Daily, thirty-seven, a lawyer who also engaged in the sawmill business, had been an active "free soiler" in Indiana before emigrating to Nebraska. He had served a term in the territorial legislature and had been a leading spirit in the organization of the Republican party. Morton, though ten years his opponent's junior, was even better known. He was a brilliant speaker and an aggressive debater. According to the custom of the time, the campaign consisted of a series of joint debates, followed avidly by the territorial press, with each correspondent seeking to add to his favorite candidate's triumphs in debate through the magic of his own pen.

When the returns were in, Morton was declared elected by a vote of 2,957 to 2,943—a margin of fourteen. Daily immediately filed notice of contest, making twelve specific charges of fraud and irregularity. Morton responded with a vigorous denial and countered his opponent's dozen charges of fraud and irregularity with seventeen of his own. The two men spent the winter collecting evidence to support their charges, and it soon became clear that there was plenty of evidence on both sides. Territorial elections were conducted in a free and easy manner, and a little manipulation was the rule rather than the exception. To complicate matters further, Governor Black, who had become estranged from Morton both personally and politically, issued a second certificate of election to Daily. When the House of Representatives finally got around to considering the matter in May, 1862, it was almost impossible to determine who was rightfully entitled to the seat. The House decided the question on purely partisan grounds and gave the seat to Daily.

The Civil War demoralized the Democrats in Nebraska, as it did all over the North. Forced by the necessity of preserving the Union to make common cause with the Republicans against their former partisans, they nevertheless refused to forget their differences with the radical elements of that party. Democratic refusal to disband the party for the sake of unity against the common enemy was looked upon as giving aid and comfort to the enemy, and it was easy to reason that because the Southerners who were attempting to destroy the Union were Democrats, all Democrats were disunionists and disloyal. The change of Administration, too, robbed the Democrats in Nebraska of assistance in the form of federal patronage. Lincoln replaced Governor Black— who went back to Pennsylvania to lead a regiment and who ultimately was killed in battle—with Alvin Saunders of Mount Pleasant, Iowa; Morton was succeeded as Secretary by Algernon S. Paddock, who had emigrated to the territory in 1857 and had been active in the formation of the Republican party.

Surprisingly, the Democrats were able to maintain considerable strength in Nebraska during the Civil War, and it was not until the state began filling up with Union veterans that the party fell into the position of a hopeless minority. The Civil War was not popular in Nebraska, largely because the demands of the war reduced the garrisons at Fort Kearny and elsewhere on the Plains to the point where the entire frontier was exposed to Indian attacks. Led by Morton—who at times skirted dangerously close to copperheadism—the Democrats kept up a steady drumfire of criticism against Lincoln's conduct of the war and against what they liked to refer to as "black Republican rascality." At times they came close to success: Daily won re-election as delegate in 1862 by a margin of only 136 votes; Butler defeated Morton for the governorship in 1866 by only 145 votes. But the tide was running against them and these "near misses" only pointed up the fact that in their intransigent opposition to Lincoln's program they were shooting wide of the mark insofar as most Nebraskans were concerned.

Aside from the overriding necessity to preserve the Union, the Republicans were greatly aided in Nebraska by the enactment in 1862 of a free homestead law, a measure which the previous Democratic Administration had consistently opposed. In 1864, the Republicans, who had adopted the Union party label, won an overwhelming victory as Phineas W. Hitchcock defeated Dr. George L. Miller in the race for delegate. Though Dr. Miller had been inclined toward a moderate course, he had been saddled with an extreme platform in the territory and with a national party flying in the teeth of overwhelming popular opinion. The impressive Republican victory of 1864 convincingly demonstrated that the people of the North had had enough of political sniping at the conduct of the war. In the nation the Republicans went on to a successful conclusion of the war and the preservation of the Union; in Nebraska, they turned their attention to bringing the territory into the Union as a state.

THE STRUGGLE OVER STATEHOOD

Nebraskans, schooled in the American tradition of political expansion, regarded territorial status as temporary and looked forward to early statehood. The politicians, however, were conscious of the importance of timing in the achievement of the generally desired goal, and their attitude was determined by their chances of securing the offices that would be filled as a result of statehood.

As early as 1858, the Omaha *Times* urged that the question be submitted to the people. In 1859 both parties declared for immediate statehood, and on January 11, 1860, the legislature authorized a special election to be held March 5 to determine whether a convention should be called to frame a state constitution. At this juncture, the politicians of both parties became somewhat wary of the proposition and so complicated it with sectional and partisan questions that as election day drew near it became apparent that it would be impossible to get a true expression of public sentiment on the main issue. The Republicans elected forty of fifty-two delegates to the constitutional convention, but at the same time the voters declared against forming a state government; so no convention was held.

Following this fiasco, the issue remained dormant until January, 1864, when most of the legislature, Republicans and Democrats alike, memorialized Congress to pass legislation making statehood possible. Congress on April 19 responded with an act authorizing the people of Nebraska to form a state government. Republicans in Congress, looking upon Nebraska as safe for their party, had pushed the enabling act through in the hope of getting reinforcements from west of the Missouri. Governor Saunders ordered an election of delegates on June 6 to a constitutional convention to meet July 4. The dormant Democrats came out swinging against statehood, indicating that the real leadership of the party was not in the legislature. They had a convincing argument: taxes would be increased, for in addition to the amount already paid the people of the state would have to raise the amount supplied by the federal government. The argument was effective. An overwhelming majority of the delegates elected were opposed to statehood, and when the convention met in the territorial capitol in Omaha it adjourned immediately without forming a constitution.

The proponents of statehood were not to be turned aside by this surprise defeat. Though the issue had not been debated in the legislative campaign of 1865, Governor Saunders devoted a considerable portion of his message to the eleventh legislature, January 9, 1866, to the advantages of early statehood. He called attention to the fact that "Nevada, with a much less permanent population than Nebraska, has already become one of the independent states of the Union" and declared that he had "the assurances of many of the most intelligent and influential men of both political parties that the people of the Territory are anxious to have this subject acted upon at as early a day as practicable." A constitutional convention was unnecessary—after all, they had had two unhappy experiences with that method of procedure. He suggested that the legislature itself might adopt a constitution and submit it to the people for approval.

Though the legislature appears to have had little initial enthusiasm for statehood, the Governor and other Republican officials in the territory apparently were determined to push it through. A voluntary committee, the composition of which is not definitely known, met secretly to draft a constitution. Consisting of both Democrats and Republicans, it probably included Governor Saunders, Secretary Paddock, Chief Justice William Pitt Kellogg, William A. Little, Hadley D. Johnson,

Experience Estabrook, and O. P. Mason. When they had completed
their work, they turned the document over to J. R. Porter—the only
Democrat of prominence in the legislature favoring statehood—who
introduced it in the Council on February 5. Under pressure from Governor Saunders and other federal officials, the issue was made a party
matter and the constitution was pushed through the legislature in a
way that would have been unusual for even the most minor, noncon-
troversial measure. On the day it was introduced the constitution was
referred to a special committee consisting of Porter and two others,
who reported it back favorably later in the day, but in time to enable
the Council to pass it before adjourning. The vote was seven to six,
with President Mason casting the deciding ballot. Four days later the
constitution was approved by the House, and on the ninth Governor
Saunders signed the bill. The constitution had not been printed for
the use of members of either house, no amendments had been permitted,
and in the lower house it was not even referred to a committee.

Few of the legislators had more than a foggy notion of the constitution's provisions. When the document finally became available for examination, it was found to be simply an instrument to establish a state
government, with very little provision for its functioning. Because the
argument of expense had been used so effectively in 1864, the idea
behind the constitution appears to have been to set up as cheap a government as possible. The Governor, for example, was limited to a salary
of $1,000 per year, with the salaries of other officials established in
proportion: Auditor, $800; Secretary of State, $600; Treasurer, $400.
The justices of the supreme court were to get $2,000 per year, and
members of the legislature $3.00 per day, with the sessions being lim-
ited to forty days.

The constitution had been accompanied by a joint resolution providing for a special election, June 2, at which the voters were to approve
or disapprove the instrument and to vote for state officers who were to
take office if the constitution were adopted. The Republicans adopted
a platform favoring the constitution and nominated a ticket headed by
David Butler of Pawnee City, who had emigrated to the territory from
Indiana in 1859 and had served in the legislature. The Democrats, as
usual, were divided as to what course they should take. One faction,
headed by J. Sterling Morton, was in favor of refusing to nominate a
ticket, basing their whole campaign on opposition to the constitution.

Others, particularly Dr. George L. Miller, editor of the newly established but already powerful Omaha *Herald,* argued that it would be unwise to stake everything on opposition to the constitution. Statehood could not long be delayed: the territory was filling up; settlement had advanced well beyond the river counties; the people, growing in wealth and numbers, would not long deny themselves the advantages of statehood and equal representation in Congress. In the end, the Democrats nominated Morton for governor and adopted a platform which was noncommittal on the constitution.

This first campaign for state offices in Nebraska was characterized by all the excitement that had marked territorial political struggles. The press of each side struck out at the other in a fury of frenzied partisanship. The opposing candidates denounced each other with unbridled license. In addition to Morton, who was judged by friend and foe to be the most gifted political entertainer in Nebraska, the Democrats had the services of George Francis Train, eccentric world traveller temporarily residing in Omaha, who stumped the territory in the first white suit ever seen in Nebraska. Butler, on the other hand, was no mean debater, and his seemingly unaffected sincerity was more useful in reaching the sensibilities of the majority than was Morton's brilliant wit. His favorite expression, "I thank God from my heart of hearts," was combined with an effort to impugn his opponent's loyalty in the late war—the bloody shirt was to prove an effective weapon in Nebraska politics.

The results were close, and as had been true so many times in the past, were determined by those who counted the votes rather than by those who cast them. The Cass County board of canvassers threw out the entire vote of Rock Bluffs precinct—107 for Morton, 50 for Butler—on technical grounds, but allowed the heavily pro-Butler vote at Plattsmouth to stand, even though the same technical irregularity had prevailed. At the same time the almost unanimously Republican soldier vote from Fort Kearny was allowed to stand. Thus counted, the official returns showed the constitution approved by a vote of 3,938 to 3,838 and Butler elected, 4,093 to 3,984. The Republican victory was complete: their entire ticket, except O. P. Mason, running for Chief Justice, was elected; ironically, William A. Little, who defeated Mason, died before he could qualify and Mason was appointed in his stead.

While Nebraska had a curious mixture of state and territorial legislatures, the controversy was transferred to Washington. The Nebraska constitution restricted the suffrage to free white males. This was not an oversight occasioned by the manner in which the constitution was rushed through the legislature: the House of Representatives had voted down a resolution to strike the restriction from the constitution by the resounding margin of thirty-six to two. Negro suffrage had been debated by territorial legislatures all during the war, but it had never been more than an academic question in Nebraska, where there were few, if any, potential Negro voters. Even so, the preponderance of sentiment against it in 1866 is surprising—although the vote may merely have indicated an unwillingness to amend the constitution. In any event, the Republican Congress was surprised and disappointed to see a constitution coming from a presumably safe territory like Nebraska that did not reaffirm the position on which the Republican majority had attacked the President.

Senator Edmunds of Vermont moved to amend Wade's bill admitting the state, to provide that the act would take effect "with the fundamental and perpetual condition that . . . there shall be no abridgement of the exercise of the elective franchise or of any other right to any person by reason of race or color, excepting Indians not taxed." The Radical Republicans, led by Edmunds and Sumner, denounced the constitution as a "rebel document" and would have nothing to do with it unless the restriction were removed. The moderates, led by Wade and Sherman, did not feel that it was of much importance. After all, twenty of the twenty-six states then comprising the Union had similar restrictions. The important consideration was that the state be admitted without further delay: its population already was well in excess of that of most new states, and the public lands rapidly were being taken up. Others—notably Reverdy Johnson of Maryland—argued that Congress had no constitutional right to interfere with suffrage requirements established by a state. The moderates, however, gave way to the Radicals, and the bill passed the Senate with the Edmunds amendment. The Senate also accepted an amendment added by the House to the effect that the legislature should be convened and "by a solemn public act . . . declare assent of said state to the said fundamental condition," whereupon the fundamental condition should be considered a part of the organic law and the state should then be admitted without further congressional action. President Johnson, already at loggerheads with the Radicals, vetoed the measure on constitutional grounds. Congress promptly passed the bill over his veto on February 9.

In accordance with the Act, Governor Saunders called the state and territorial legislatures into special session on February 20 to consider the "fundamental condition." In a session lasting only two days, the legislature promptly passed the necessary act, negating the restrictive provision in the constitution. General John M. Thayer, who had acted as an intermediary between Congress and the territory, carried a certified copy of the Act to Washington, and on March 1, 1867, President Johnson reluctantly signed a proclamation admitting Nebraska as the thirty-seventh state.

CHAPTER 11

The Indian Dispossessed

THE KANSAS-NEBRASKA ACT, extending territorial organization over all of the northern Plains, completely and finally broke down the concept of an Indian country west of the Missouri. The semi-sedentary tribes along the river, already under the influence of the white man's culture, acquiesced without a struggle, and by mid-1854 had ceded their lands to the Government. Though the Pawnees occasionally harassed travellers and outlying settlements, they, too, gave up without organized resistance. The nomadic tribes to the west—particularly the Dakotas, Cheyennes, and Arapahoes—were not so tractable. At Fort Laramie in 1851, in return for a guarantee of annuities, a number of them agreed to certain tribal boundaries, to keep the peace, and to permit the Government to build roads and forts in their country. The territory assigned the Dakotas included all land in Nebraska north of the North Platte; that south of the North Platte was recognized as belonging to the Cheyennes and Arapahoes. Though some members of these tribes were content to loaf around the forts and live off the annuities, the restless young men and most of the leaders found the situation far from satisfactory. For years they had watched the white-topped wagons rolling along the Platte with increasing apprehension, driving away the game and filling the valley with the white man's diseases. Among them there was a growing disposition to regard the boundaries established at Fort Laramie in 1851 as final and, if need be, to make a last-ditch fight to preserve their rights to western Nebraska, the Black Hills, and the Big Horns. The need, of course, arose, and in the final occupation of the Plains and the mountains the whites had to overcome the most serious opposition they encountered in the whole of America's westward expansion. Many of the battlefields of this last-ditch struggle were beyond the borders of Nebraska, but the struggle is important in the history of the state and must be given at least passing consideration.

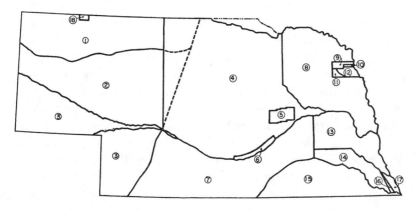

INDIAN LAND CESSIONS IN NEBRASKA

15 Kansas	 1825	8 Omaha	1854	5 Pawnee. . . .	. 1875
16 Oto	 1830	4 Pawnee.	. . . 1857	1 Sioux, N. Chey-	
17 Oto	 1830	3 Arapaho &		enne, & Arapaho 1876	
14 Oto & Missouri	1833	Cheyenne.	. . 1861	11 Omaha.	. . . 1882
7 Pawnee.	. . . 1833	9 Omaha.	. . . 1865	12 Omaha.	. . . 1882
6 Pawnee.	. . . 1848	10 Omaha.	. . . 1874	18 Sioux	 1892
13 Oto & Missouri	1854	2 Sioux	 1875		

THE EASTERN RESERVATIONS

As has been indicated, the tribes in eastern Nebraska, never warlike or aggressive, readily acquiesced to the white man's demand for their land. Their history in Nebraska from the beginning of white occupation is brief and uninspiring, and perhaps can best be treated by a consideration of the difficulties of each tribe, or group of related tribes.

Aside from the Kansas cession of 1825, which included a claim to what is now south-central Nebraska, the earliest cession in Nebraska was that of the Otos and Missourias, who at Prairie du Chien in 1830 ceded for $3,000 a tract of land between the Nemahas, estimated at 128,000 acres, for the benefit of Oto, Iowa, Omaha, Yankton and Santee half-breeds. Here provision was made for the allotment of lands in severalty to recognized half-breed claimants—the first such allotment to Indians in the United States—and the tract soon developed into a land-grabber's paradise, encumbered with a tangled skein of title law that still complicates legal matters in Richardson County. The Otos and Missourias ceded additional lands in 1833 and gave up the remainder of their Nebraska lands in 1854, reserving only a strip of land in the Blue Valley, ten miles wide and twenty-five miles long. Before many years, white settlers began to look longingly at the fertile lands of the Oto reserve. The Otos and Missourias, destitute and diminishing in numbers, had neither the ability nor the inclination to develop the lands agriculturally, and Nebraskans began to bring pressure upon their representatives in Congress to reduce the size of the reservation or abandon it altogether. During the 1870's Congress authorized sale of part of the reservation; in 1881 the remaining lands were opened to entry and the tribes were removed to Indian Territory (Oklahoma). The Iowa, Sauk, and Fox—related to the Oto and the Missouria—were given a common reservation which, though primarily in Kansas, extended to the Nemaha in the southeastern corner of the state. This land ultimately was allotted to the Indians in severalty.

When the Omahas ceded their lands in eastern Nebraska, March 16, 1854, they were given a reserve along the Ayoway River with the understanding that if this should prove unsuitable they would be given other lands. They found the reserve unsatisfactory, and were given a tract, eighteen by thirty miles, fronting on the Missouri River in what is now Thurston County. Though much of the land was hilly and unsuited to farming, the Omahas raised fairly good crops in the river bottoms and with the aid of government assistance managed to get along. At least their condition looked good to the Winnebagoes, who, starved out and dried out at their reservation on Crow Creek in South Dakota, began in the fall of 1863 to "visit" the Omahas in increasing numbers. Agent Robert W. Furnas, with the consent of the tribe, did what he could to assist the destitute Winnebagoes, but their presence posed a serious problem. In 1865 Furnas took a delegation of Omaha chiefs to Washington, where they agreed to cede part of their reservation to the Winnebagoes. The Omaha-Winnebago reservation still remains in Nebraska, although most of the land has been allotted to individual members of the tribes.

The Poncas, who since the time of first white contact had lived near the mouth of the Niobrara, relinquished all the land they owned or claimed in 1858, except a small reserve along the Niobrara. Harassed by the Sioux and unsuccessful in agriculture, the Poncas had a difficult time of it. Their difficulties were compounded by a blunder in the Treaty of Fort Laramie, 1868, which unwittingly included their reservation in lands assigned the Sioux. These warlike nomads now made annual raids on the unfortunate Poncas, who lost more than a fourth of their population in unsuccessful efforts to defend themselves. The Government finally solved the problem in 1877 by arbitrarily removing the Poncas to Indian Territory. Within a year after this forced removal from lands to which they had title in fee simple, a third of the tribe was dead and most of the survivors were sick. Returning to Nebraska in 1879 to bury the remains of his son, Standing Bear, chief of the Poncas, and those accompanying him were arrested by soldiers and started back to Indian Territory under armed guard. While camped near Omaha, Standing Bear was interviewed by T. H. Tibbles, and as a result of the ensuing publicity Andrew J. Poppleton and John L. Webster, two of Omaha's best-known lawyers, offered their services on behalf of the Poncas. In a celebrated ruling on their petition for a writ of habeas corpus, Federal Judge Elmer S. Dundy declared that "an Indian was a person within the meaning of the law" and that Standing Bear was being illegally held. The noted chief was freed and allowed to return to northeast Nebraska, where he lived out his life. The plight of the Poncas attracted wide attention, and a commission appointed by President Hayes in 1880 to inquire into the matter worked out an arrangement whereby those who wanted to return to Nebraska (approximately one-fourth of the tribe's 833 members) were allowed to do so, being allotted lands along the Niobrara in severalty.

The Pawnees, Nebraska's most important tribe, were the only group of semi-sedentary people who gave the Government any trouble whatever, and they very little. In 1833, the Pawnees ceded all their lands lying south of the Platte. In 1848 they sold an eighty-mile strip along the Platte, including Grand Island, and in a treaty negotiated at Table Creek, just north of Nebraska City, September 24, 1857, they ceded all their remaining lands in Nebraska, except a fifteen by thirty mile tract along the Loup. Prior to the time they went on the reservation in what is now Nance County, the Pawnees had been a source of irritation to the whites. They were not particularly warlike, but their penchant for plunder resulted in numerous losses by travellers on the overland trails and by settlers. They continued to waylay travellers even after they accepted reservation status, and in the spring of 1859 caused general alarm in the Elkhorn Valley, forcing many settlers to abandon their cabins. The territorial militia was called out, but the Pawnees gave up the offending braves without a struggle and promised to keep the peace.

At Table Creek, the Government had promised to protect the Pawnees from their hereditary enemies, the Sioux. This protection, however, was soon withdrawn, and by 1860 the Pawnees were again suffering harassment at the hands of their wide-ranging foes. The whites, too, were constantly encroaching upon their territory. As a result, agitation developed within the tribe for removal to Indian Territory, where a party of Republican Pawnees had been kindly received by the Wichitas in 1870. The massacre of a hunting party under Sky Chief near present-day Trenton by Oglala and Teton Sioux in 1873 convinced many of the Pawnees that it was useless to try to remain in Nebraska, and by 1875 most of them had removed to Indian Territory. In 1876 their reservation in Nebraska was formally exchanged for lands in Indian Territory.

To complete this discussion of the disposition of the Indians in eastern Nebraska, mention should be made of the Santee Sioux, who in 1866 were assigned a small reservation in Knox County. Aside from a few acres set apart for agency buildings, the lands were ultimately assigned to the tribesmen in severalty.

INCIDENTS AND REPRISALS

Insofar as the western tribes were concerned, the Treaty at Fort Laramie was supposed to bring peace. From the beginning, however, it was an uneasy peace, little honored by the whites and little understood by the Indians. The Senate started off by reducing the number of years for which the annuities were to be paid from fifty to ten, then ratified the treaty without resubmitting it to the tribes concerned. Even so, the tribes faithfully observed the terms of the treaty, despite the fact that, as the Commissioner of Indian Affairs reported in 1852, they continued "to suffer from the vast number of immigrants who pass through their country, destroying their means of support, and scattering disease and death among them." Indian officials continued to report the tribes as "generally quiet and peaceable," but underneath a seemingly placid surface smoldered an explosive irritation, just waiting to be touched off. The spark was struck by the hoof of a lame cow, and though not strong enough to kindle a general war, it did set off scattered fires which burned first one area and then another, and, after a decade, erupted into a general conflagration.

On August 17, 1854, a footsore cow belonging to a party of Mormons enroute to Utah strayed into the camp of the Brule Sioux, who with most of the other Sioux were assembled along the North Platte east of Fort Laramie awaiting an issue of goods under the Treaty of 1851. One of the Brule braves killed the cow and the animal was promptly eaten. The next day the Mormons stopped at Fort Laramie and complained to the commandant, who immediately sent a detachment of men to the Brule camp with orders to bring in the offender. Heading the detachment of twenty-nine men and two cannon was twenty-one year old Lieutenant John Grattan, fresh from Vermont and West Point and burdened with a contempt for the Indians born of ignorance and inexperience. The Bear, chief of the Brules, tried to reason with Lieutenant Grattan, saying that he would try to get the young man to give himself up—it was a great disgrace for a Dakota to be taken prisoner. The Bear, having to speak through Grattan's drunken interpreter, failed to get his point across, and the Lieutenant, impatient with the whole proceeding, broke off the discussion, withdrew, and opened fire on the encampment, killing The Bear. In the ensuing struggle, Grattan and his entire force were killed. The Indians, their inherent savagery aroused, went on to the nearby trading posts of Bordeaux and Chouteau, pillaging them and threatening worse.

Throughout the next year, the Dakotas terrorized travellers on the Platte Valley trail. In August, 1855, General William S. Harney set out from Fort Leavenworth with twelve hundred men and orders to restore peace on the trail. At Ash Hollow on September 3 Harney came upon Little Thunder's band of Brules. Harney parleyed with Little Thunder until his cavalry was in place, then gave orders to attack, killing 136 of the tribe and capturing the rest. After this needless massacre —which had the effect of instilling fear and distrust into the hearts of the Dakotas—Harney went on to Fort Laramie, dragging his captives in chains. From Fort Laramie he proceeded to Fort Pierre, where he spent the winter. On his own authority, he assembled the Tetons at

Fort Pierre and forced them to agree to a treaty restating their willingness to permit white travel along the Platte Valley trail and agreeing to the establishment of a military road from Fort Laramie to Fort Pierre. Following this, Harney went down the Missouri to establish Fort Randall across from the mouth of the Niobrara.

Though Harney's conduct at Ash Hollow—by any but the most primitive standards—was inexcusable, his Sioux campaign of 1855–56 seemed to have the desired effect, at least insofar as the Army could determine. The Indians, from the military point of view, could be controlled only by the most stringent measures, and the fact that Harney, by applying such measures, had brought peace to the trail supported the military contention. Representatives of the Indian Service, and particularly Thomas S. Twiss, Indian Agent on the Upper Platte, stationed at Fort Laramie, bitterly opposed Harney's policies. The Army was in the saddle, however, and rode roughshod over all such objections: Harney even forbade Twiss to have any intercourse whatever with the Sioux, Cheyennes, and Arapahoes.

Harney's peace was short-lived. The Indians, though temporarily cowed, bitterly resented the treatment accorded them at the hands of the Army. Peace won by the sword would have to be preserved by the sword, and when the demands of the Civil War drained most of the nation's military strength from the Plains the smoldering fires of conflict burst once again into flame.

THE CIVIL WAR

Nebraskans responded with alacrity to President Lincoln's call for volunteers to put down the rebellion, ranking second among the territories in the number of men furnished the Union cause. The First Nebraska Cavalry, commanded by Brigadier General John M. Thayer, served at Fort Donelson and Shiloh; the Curtis Horse Cavalry fought in Tennessee and Alabama as part of the Fifth Iowa Cavalry. The real problem in Nebraska, however, during the Civil War was that of protecting the exposed frontier against Indian attack.

Alarmed by the Minnesota Sioux uprising during the summer of 1862, Nebraskans through their territorial government petitioned the War Department for authority to organize a regiment of cavalry for home defense. Permission granted, the Second Nebraska Cavalry was organized under the command of Colonel Robert W. Furnas. Initially, the twelve companies comprising the regiment were stationed at various points along the Missouri River from Falls City to Dakota City. In the summer of 1863 Furnas and nine companies joined Brigadier General Alfred Sully and the Sixth Iowa Cavalry in a campaign against the Sioux in Dakota Territory, a punitive expedition designed to prevent repetition of the Minnesota difficulties of the year before. At White Stone Hills, two hundred miles above Fort Pierre, on September 3, Sully's force surprised a Sioux encampment and in a bloody battle virtually wiped it out. Having thus demonstrated their strength, the two regiments returned southward, and the Second Nebraska was mustered out at Omaha on November 30.

Meanwhile, success at Gettysburg, relieving some of the pressure in the East, combined with the fear that the Confederates were trying to organize a general Indian uprising on the Plains, caused the Army to reinforce its strength in the West, and on September 19, 1863, eight companies of the Seventh Iowa Cavalry arrived in Omaha destined for the Plains. The Seventh Iowa pushed on to Fort Kearny, and then to Cottonwood Springs, an important point on the trail a short distance east of the forks of the Platte. In addition to its importance as a stopping-place for westbound emigrants and freighters, Cottonwood Springs was a great crossing for Indians going north and south. To break up this movement the Seventh Iowa established a post near the mouth of Cottonwood Canyon, first known as Camp McKean, and then, Fort McPherson. In April, 1864, the Eleventh Ohio Cavalry, consisting in part of Confederate prisoners who had taken the oath of allegiance and had enlisted with the understanding that they would be used only to fight Indians on the frontier, was ordered west to be distributed along the trail from Fort Kearny to Fort Laramie.

This additional strength was soon needed. Throughout the spring and summer of 1864 incidents, particularly along the South Platte in Colorado, presaged difficulty. Then, on August 7, Cheyennes, Arapahoes, and Brules launched a concerted attack upon stage coaches, emigrant trains, freight trains, stations, and ranches all along the central and western stretches of the Platte Valley. That day and the next they struck every stage station and ranch between Julesburg and Fort Kearny. Fortunately, few lives were lost because a warning had been telegraphed from Plum Creek where they hit first. The attack spread to the valley of the Little Blue; here there was no telegraph to warn the settlers and station keepers, and the loss of life was considerably greater. The entire Nebraska frontier was thrown into a state of panic. Almost all the settlers in the Platte and Little Blue valleys fled eastward, except the Germans at Grand Island who fortified the O. K. store and decided to entrench themselves. Stage coaches and freight wagons ceased operating altogether.

The First Nebraska Cavalry, recently returned from the South, was recalled from furlough and ordered to Fort Kearny. Major General Samuel R. Curtis, commandant of the Department of Kansas, which included Nebraska, came out from Fort Leavenworth with a small force and with Brigadier General Robert Mitchell, in command of the District of Nebraska, organized an expedition against the Indians. Though Curtis didn't have enough men to move against the Indians in force, he provided escorts for stagecoaches and freight wagons west of Fort Kearny and reopened traffic along the overland trail. Fort Plum Creek was established as an intermediate station between Kearny and McPherson. The Indians, somewhat awed by the presence of troops, made no further concerted attacks, but confined themselves to small, sporadic hit-and-run raids against isolated points. As one means of combatting the Indians, the Army in October fired the prairie from Fort Kearny to Julesburg, and as far south as the Republican. This checked the Indians for a while, but by November they again were committing depredations all along the trail.

Thus, at the end of the Civil War the Indian problem was more critical than it had been at any time since white penetration of the Plains had begun. The Indians were further inflamed when on November 29, Colonel J. M. Chivington, formerly presiding elder in the Nebraska Methodist Conference but then commanding the Third Colorado Cavalry, fell without warning on Black Kettle's band of Cheyennes encamped on Sand Creek in Colorado to await peace negotiations. This bloody massacre of a group who voluntarily had surrendered brought to an end any hope for early peace on the Plains. The Chivington outrage caused widespread concern in the United States and gave point to the contention that the Army's policies would never pacify the Indians. After an investigation of the Sand Creek affair, Congress in 1866 created a Peace Commission to remove if possible the causes of the Indian wars and to try to persuade the Indians to give up their nomadic ways and accept reservation status.

But the Indians were in no mood for peace. Cheyennes who had escaped from Sand Creek went north and south telling the news and inviting all Plains and mountain tribes to join them in a general war against the whites, and the Peace Commission found that it would be able to bring about the kind of peace it wanted only by the sword. The war raged both north and south. Only that in the North can be treated here, and it but briefly.

THE LAST ROUNDUP

The Sioux, with memories of Harney, Sibley, and Sully fresh in their minds, had new grievances: whites, drawn by the discovery of gold in Montana, were moving into the area by the thousands in direct violation of the Treaty of 1851. Early in 1865, the Government announced that it would open a road from Fort Laramie to Montana directly through the heart of the Sioux country. Red Cloud, great chief of the Oglalas, bitterly protested this latest violation of Sioux rights, and when his protests went unheeded, the Sioux took to the warpath. To overawe the Sioux and open the Bozeman Road to Montana, General Patrick E. Connor was sent into the Powder River country during the summer. The Powder River campaign did little but further infuriate the Indians, and early in the fall Connor's troops were recalled for another try at negotiation.

During the fall representatives of the Peace Commission had negotiated a series of treaties with various bands of Sioux around Fort Sully, and in the spring of 1866 General Grenville M. Dodge, commandant of the Department of Missouri (which now included Nebraska), persuaded the Brules and Oglalas to come into Fort Laramie for another conference. By June 1, peace terms had been worked out. At this juncture, however, Colonel Henry B. Carrington arrived with a large body of troops to open the Bozeman Road. Red Cloud and Man-Afraid-of-His-Horse withdrew from the conference, and once again the Sioux country was engulfed in war. Carrington went on to garrison Fort Reno and establish Forts Phil Kearny and C. F. Smith. The Indians, now thoroughly disillusioned, gave these isolated posts along the Bozeman Road a great deal of trouble; on December 21, 1866, they entirely wiped out the command of Captain W. J. Fetterman sent out from Fort Phil Kearny to relieve a wood train. Further south the Indians continued to harass travellers in the Platte Valley, and particularly the construction crews of the Union Pacific Railroad. To protect the railroad, Sidney Barracks was established, on November 19, 1867.

Meanwhile, in September, 1867, the Peace Commission sent runners through the Sioux country to invite the Indians into Fort Laramie for a conference. Only a few put in an appearance. Red Cloud sent word that there could be no conference as long as the whites maintained the Bozeman Road. He adhered firmly to this position, and when in April, 1868, he finally came in, troops were withdrawn from Forts Phil Kearny and C. F. Smith, and the Bozeman Road was officially closed—much to the disgust of Montana's miners. The Sioux agreed to confine themselves to the country north of Nebraska and west of the Missouri, with the understanding that they would be allowed to hunt on their old ranges. The Sioux also agreed to allow roads and railroads to be built through their country. Moreover, in accepting a restricted area they also accepted the principle of fixed reservations.

The Brules under Spotted Tail were placed on a reservation early in 1869 at the mouth of Whetstone Creek, eighteen miles northwest of Fort Randall. Red Cloud objected strenuously to going so far east, and finally in 1871 the Government agreed to establish his agency on the North Platte River, thirty-two miles below Fort Laramie. Spotted Tail, dissatisfied with his location on the Missouri, in 1871 persuaded the Government to relocate the Brules on the White River in northwest Nebraska. A permanent agency in the Platte Valley was, of course, out of the question, and the next year Red Cloud also agreed to accept a White River location near present-day Crawford, about fifty miles upstream from the Brules. The Army in Nebraska, though hit hard at Beecher's Island by combined forces of non-treaty Cheyennes, Arapahoes, and Sioux on September 17, 1869, was able to devote most of its time to patrol and scouting, enlivened occasionally by entertaining a visiting notable on a buffalo hunt, as General Sheridan entertained the Grand Duke Alexis in 1872.

The Indian problem, however, was far from being settled. Many of the young men refused to recognize the proceedings at Fort Laramie and were contemptuous of the whole reservation idea. These non-treaty Sioux, under the leadership of Crazy Horse and Sitting Bull, and the northern Cheyennes roamed their former ranges at will, causing great concern to the military, who felt that around them a new Indian war would develop unless they could be brought under control. Also, the whites were impatient with the terms of the treaty, particularly after word got around that there was gold in the Black Hills. The Army tried for a while to keep prospectors out of the Hills, but with very little enthusiasm or success, and by the middle Seventies there was a heavy traffic into this last sacred hunting ground of the Sioux from Sioux City, Sidney, and Cheyenne. The non-treaty Sioux moved further into the Hills, those on the reservations became increasingly more sullen and restless, and trouble seemed inevitable.

In 1874, while General George A. Custer was "exploring" the Black Hills, General Sheridan moved troops into the Sioux country of northwest Nebraska, establishing encampments at both the Spotted Tail and Red Cloud agencies. That at Spotted Tail (Camp Sheridan) was only temporary, but that at Red Cloud (Fort Robinson) became a permanent installation. At the same time, Fort Hartsuff was established on the Loup River northwest of Grand Island to quiet the fears of settlers in the Loup Valley. Efforts were now made further to restrict the Sioux. The Brules and Oglalas in 1875 agreed to relinquish their hunting rights south of the divide between the Niobrara and the Platte, but they steadfastly refused to cede any part of the Black Hills or to lease mining rights therein. Following this refusal, the Government served notice on the Sioux in Nebraska, Wyoming, and Montana to come into the reservations. The notice sent from Washington on December 6, 1875, provided that those who did not comply by January 31, 1876, would be considered hostile. The time allowed was so ridiculously short that even those who might have wanted to comply could not possibly have done so. Be that as it may, the non-reservation bands refused to comply; on January 31 the entire Sioux Nation was turned over to the War Department, and plans were promptly prepared for crushing the hostiles by force.

And great force it required. General Sheridan, in charge of the Sioux campaign, first attempted to launch a "winter campaign," such as had been so successful in the South two years earlier, but was driven back by the snow and cold. When in the spring his troops finally advanced, the hostiles, reinforced by men and supplies slipped to them from the inefficiently and/or corruptly administered agencies, offered bloody resistance. A band of Sioux under Crazy Horse forced Crook's troops to retire after a bloody battle at the mouth of the Rosebud, June 17, and on the twenty-fifth the main body of Sioux annihilated Custer's command on the Little Big Horn. For two months the Sioux eluded the forces sent out to bring them in, completely thwarting the efforts of Generals George Crook and Alfred Terry, immediately in command of the campaign. With dwindling strength and diminishing supplies of food, clothing, and arms, however, the Sioux could not keep up the unequal contest, and in October General Nelson A. Miles, who had come out from Fort Leavenworth to rejuvenate the flagging campaign, forced about three thousand of them to surrender. Later, others came in, surrendered their arms, and accepted reservation status. Crazy Horse, who finally brought nearly two thousand of his followers in the next spring, was killed at Fort Robinson on September 7, 1877, as he was resisting arrest on suspicion of trying to foment another war.

Meanwhile, the Northern Cheyennes, who had participated in the Battle of the Little Big Horn, had surrendered after a serious defeat at the hands of Colonel R. S. MacKenzie, November 25, 1876, and had been sent south to Indian Territory. In 1878 a small band under Dull Knife broke away from the reservation and made their desperate way north. They were captured and confined at Fort Robinson, and when on the night of January 9, 1879, they tried to escape, most of them were killed.

And so the Indian resistance was crushed. Their great war chiefs dead or broken in spirit, the Plains tribes turned from the wild nomadic ways of their ancestors to the way of the white man. The Brule and Oglala reservations in Nebraska were abandoned and the tribes were concentrated at Pine Ridge and Rosebud in South Dakota. Troops at Fort Robinson kept them under surveillance, and to protect settlers in northeast Nebraska, Fort Niobrara was established near Valentine in 1880. The settlers, however, hardly needed protection from the broken people trying to farm the barren, arid lands of western South Dakota —although fear that the Indians would once again go on the warpath was omnipresent throughout the northwest part of the developing state. This fear was heightened when the "ghost dance," a ritualistic worship of Wovoka, prophet of the Great Spirit who had come to restore the game and drive out the white men, spread through the reservations. Civilian authorities became alarmed in the fall of 1890 and called for military protection: General Miles came out from Chicago to take command of the situation; the Nebraska National Guard was ordered to the northwest part of the state. Sitting Bull, who had fled to Canada but finally had accepted reservation status, was believed to be at the bottom of the whole ghost dance disturbance, and when he was killed in a melee growing out of an attempt to arrest him at Standing Rock, the whole frontier was again thrown into a state of alarm—alarm that culminated in the wanton massacre of a band of Sioux at Wounded Knee Creek, northeast of Fort Robinson, on December 29.

The "battle" of Wounded Knee was the last armed conflict between the Army and Indians in Nebraska or surrounding territory. By the time it occurred, the state had been almost completely settled. The Army had crushed the spirit of the red man, and the settlers in an irresistible tide had spread over his lands. He was completely dispossessed.

CHAPTER 12

Establishing the State Government

THE NEBRASKA admitted to the Union as a state in 1867 comprised only a little more than a fifth of the area of the Nebraska organized as a territory in 1854. The territory's 351,558 square miles had included a vast area which, it was assumed in 1854 and for several years thereafter, would never be settled. This assumption was just as erroneous as the earlier belief that the whole region west of the Missouri would never sustain any but a nomadic population, and while settlers were occupying the lands along the Missouri and in the eastern Platte Valley, others pushed still farther west. On February 28, 1861, in response to demands from miners and others in the Rocky Mountain region, Colorado territory was organized, decreasing the area of Nebraska territory by 16,035 square miles. Three days later, in anticipation of ultimate statehood for the settled portion of Nebraska, the territory's area was reduced by 228,907 square miles through the creation of Dakota territory. The organization of Idaho territory in 1863 brought about a further reduction, so that when the state was admitted it included 75,995 square miles. One important change—the annexation of the Sioux reserve (now Boyd County) in 1890—and several minor changes increased the total land and water area of the state to 77,393 square miles.

The area admitted as a state was in 1867 upon the threshold of a rapid development that would transform it from empty prairie to a settled commonwealth. It was to be a development coincident with the growth of mechanized commercial farming, and was to be dependent almost entirely upon that activity. The state's economic, political, and social life were to reflect alternate periods of prosperity and depression in agriculture, and during the developing years those fluctuations were to be marked and often violent. Moreover, the early years of statehood were to constitute a period of trial and error experimentation, not only in the development of commercial agriculture and particularly in the distribution of its products, but in the development of agricultural techniques on the Plains.

Government, complicated by the demands of an unstable economy, was in the beginning to suffer from the fact that it had to operate under the hastily drawn and inadequate constitution of 1866. Even more serious, the years in which Nebraska's state government was being established were characterized by gross public immorality in financial matters and an all-too-general practice of using public funds for private gain. As a result, the state government soon became engulfed in scandals that vitiated its effectiveness and came close to threatening its very existence.

ORGANIZATION

As has been indicated, Nebraska between the adoption of the constitution, June 2, 1866, and admission to the Union, March 1, 1867, had a curious mixture of state and territorial governments. Governor Butler called the state legislature into session on July 4, 1866. The only business transacted before adjournment, July 11, was the election of two United States senators. As had been the case in the contest over the constitution and the election of general officers, the action of the Cass County board of canvassers in throwing out the heavily pro-Democratic vote of Rock Bluffs was decisive. The House and Senate, upholding this action, seated four Republican representatives and one Republican senator from Cass County instead of the five Democrats who would have been elected if the Rock Bluffs vote had been included; and by a straight party vote of 29 to 21, the legislature elected John M. Thayer and Thomas W. Tipton over Andrew J. Poppleton and J. Sterling Morton. The state legislature met in special session with the territorial assembly on February 20 and 21, 1867, to consider the "fundamental condition" imposed by Congress relative to admission,[1] so

[1]See p. 126.

that the special session which convened on May 16, 1867, for the enactment of general laws was actually the third session. Nebraska's transition from territorial status to statehood, because of the wrangle in Congress over its constitution, was more complicated than that of any
other Louisiana Purchase state.

In calling the special session of May 16, Governor Butler listed thirty-
one subjects for legislative consideration. Among them were: selection
and management of lands the state would get from the federal government; free schools and their support; creation of counties; revision of
the general incorporation laws; appropriations; encouragement of immigration; the location and construction of public buildings.

Probably the most important item of business—though by no means
given the most attention at the time—was the selection and management of state lands. Nebraska received a total of 3,526,591.84 acres
from the federal government, for the following purposes:

Common School Endowment	2,797,520.67
Public Buildings at Capital	12,751.05
Penitentiary	32,034.01
State University	45,439.93
Agricultural College	89,140.21
Saline Lands	48,893.37
Internal Improvements	500,812.00

This gift of land was one of the primary arguments in favor of statehood; the fact that good lands in the eastern part of the state were rapidly being taken up was advanced as an imperative reason for early
statehood. As it was, by the time the state government got around to
locating its lands, the railroads, purchasers, and homesteaders had indeed occupied a large portion of the choicest, most accessible land,
and the state was required to locate much of its land in the northern
and western areas. The lands set aside for the erection of public buildings and the penitentiary were the first selected and sold. The internal
improvement lands were almost immediately absorbed by various railroad companies, some of which had been organized solely to get benefits under the act, although grants of a thousand acres each were made
to Gage and Saline counties for the construction of bridges across the
Blue River. The disposition of the saline lands was involved and complicated, but most of them were sold to provide an endowment for the
normal school at Peru. The state held on to its university and agricul-

tural college lands until about 1880, after which date the landed endowment was gradually converted from real estate to cash. The common school lands—by far the most important part of the gift—became involved in a succession of political disputes continuing to the present day. Initially, the state proposed to build up its school endowment through the sale of these lands, but this plan was beset with so many abuses that in 1897 sale was forbidden and a system of leases substituted. Ranchers in the central and western part of the state, where most of the school lands were located, were dissatisfied with the lease system from the beginning, and finally in 1965 the legislature, over the veto of Governor Frank B. Morrison, repealed the ban on sale. By this time it could be argued that investment of the proceeds from sale of the lands in securities would provide a more productive endowment for the common schools than the land itself.

Of more immediate interest to the politicians of the new state was the location of the capital. As had been true in the early years of the territory, the capital question tended to overshadow all public problems. Actually, there was little need for a change: the territorial capitol at Omaha, constructed in 1857–58, was highly suitable and probably could have been used for a number of years with only minor repairs; considering transportation facilities and the distribution of population, Omaha was better located than any other point that could have been selected. Removal, nevertheless, was made the first order of business. South Platte legislators were determined almost to a man that the capital should not remain in Omaha. Omaha newspapers charged that they obtained sufficient votes for their removal scheme by supporting a land grant to the North Nebraska Airline Railroad, whose incorporators were virtually all state officials and members of the legislature from north of the Platte.

Be that as it may, the legislature after a spirited contest passed a bill providing that the Governor, the Secretary of State, and the Auditor should constitute a commission to locate the seat of government on a section of land within "The County of Seward, the south half of the counties of Saunders and Butler, and that portion of the county of Lancaster lying north of the south line of township nine." The Commissioners were to have the site surveyed and platted, and then sell lots at public auction, the proceeds to be held as a state building fund. In the original bill, the seat of government was to be known as "Capitol City." This unfortunate name was dropped when Senator J. N. H. Patrick of Omaha, in an effort to draw South Platte Democratic votes away from the measure, moved the substitution of "Lincoln." The name still was anathema to many Democrats, but sectional loyalty overrode political considerations, and South Platte Democrats promptly approved the new name. The Act further provided that the state university and state agricultural college, "united as one educational institution," as well as the state penitentiary, should be located at Lincoln.

THE NEW CAPITAL CITY

The bill relocating the seat of government was approved on June 14, and on the eighteenth Governor Butler, Secretary of State Thomas P. Kennard, and Auditor John Gillespie assembled at Nebraska City to make preparations for a personal examination of the area named in the legislation. Having secured an outfit and employed Augustus F. Harvey as surveyor, the Commissioners set out on their tour, July 18. They made a cursory survey of all eligible sites, and on the twenty-ninth returned to the vicinity of Yankee Hill and Lancaster, on the banks of Salt Creek. At Lancaster "the favorable impressions received at first sight . . . were confirmed." They described it thus:

We found it gently undulating, its principal elevation being near the center of the proposed new site, the village already established being in the midst of a thrifty and considerable agricultural population, rich timber and water power available within short distances, the center of the great saline region within two miles; and, in addition to all other claims, the especial advantage was that the location was at the center of a circle of about one hundred and ten miles in diameter, along or near the circumference of which are the Kansas state line, directly south, and the important towns of Pawnee City, Nebraska City, Plattsmouth, Omaha, Fremont, and Columbus.

The removal act had directed the Commissioners to locate the capital on state lands. Title to the lands selected by the state had not yet been confirmed by the federal government, and fearing delay or even possible title failure, the Commissioners entertained a proposition from various people residing in the vicinity and the Lancaster Seminary Association, whose building had burned in 1866, to donate land for the new city. Meeting in the house of W. T. Donavan, of Lancaster, on the afternoon of the twenty-ninth, the Commissioners unanimously agreed to accept the proposition.

Sites further south or east might have been preferable, but the Commissioners' obsession with the potential value of the saline deposits carried the day for Lancaster, and the capital city was located directly in the salt basin. Later inhabitants were not so favorably impressed with the basin and Lincoln developed almost solely to the south and east, as far away from the salt deposits as possible. There are many legends connected with the salt basin—of Indians, trappers, and others coming great distances to secure their supply of this precious mineral —and from early territorial days there had been an interest in developing the commercial value of the deposits. Little had been realized, however, and the town of Lancaster had a population of less than thirty when it became Lincoln. But hope was still high. In addressing the legislative session of 1869, the first to meet in the new capitol, Governor Butler said: "Although comparatively little has been accomplished in the actual production of salt, that little has settled beyond question, if indeed further proof was needed, that we have, within sight of this hall, a rich and apparently inexhaustible supply of pure and easily manufactured article. It will be directly and indirectly a source of wealth to the state whose great value no one can fully estimate."

That "rich and inexhaustible supply" produced nothing but lawsuits, and the only tangible evidence of salt remaining today is a saltwater swimming pool at the west edge of the city.

Omahans and many others living along the Missouri north of the Platte severely criticized the choice and spoke disparagingly of the new city's prospects. "Nobody will ever go to Lincoln," prophesied the Omaha *Republican*, "who does not go to the legislature, the lunatic asylum, the penitentiary, or some of the state institutions." Founded on fiat, with "no river, no railroad, no steam wagon, nothing," it was destined for isolation and ultimate oblivion.

The Capital Commissioners, however, went ahead with the building of their paper city. On August 14, 1867, they formally announced their decision; the next day Harvey and A. B. Smith began surveying the site; on the seventeenth the Commissioners gave notice that the first sale of lots would be held September 17. Meanwhile, they had reserved twelve acres each for the capitol, the state university, and a city park; in addition, lots had been set aside for ten different churches, the Lancaster County courthouse, a city hall and market space, a "state historical library association," public schools, the Independent Order of Good Templars, the Independent Order of Odd Fellows, and the Ancient Free and Accepted Masons.

Initial lot sales were highly disappointing. September 17 was cold and rainy and that may have dampened the ardor of bidders beset by doubts that the enterprise could ever succeed. The first lot offered brought only twenty-five cents on an appraised value of forty dollars, and the entire day's sales amounted to only about one-tenth of the Commissioners' expectations. Realizing that something must be done to prevent the whole project from collapsing, the Commissioners arranged secretly with James Sweet and a group from Nebraska City to bid the appraised value for every lot up to $10,000 worth of lots, with the understanding that any party bidding more than the appraised value on any lot should have it, and with the further understanding that unless $15,000 worth of lots were sold in addition to the $10,000 held by the Nebraska City Trustees, the whole thing would be called off. Under the impetus of this forced bidding, the second day was much more successful, and at the end of the five-day sale in Lincoln, $34,342.25 worth of lots had been sold, at prices ranging from forty to one-hundred-fifty dollars. Sales at Nebraska City and Omaha during the next two weeks added $19,750.50, and the success of the project seemed assured.

The Commissioners now went ahead with the construction of the capitol. There were no architects in Lincoln and those in Omaha paid no attention to advertisements for such service. Finally, in response to an advertisement in the Chicago *Tribune,* James Morris of that city prepared a plan for a central structure, with wings to be added. It was not very imposing, but it was the only plan received; so it was accepted. The Commissioners were aware of the fact that if they didn't have the capitol ready for the legislature by January, 1869, it was probable that no legislature would ever meet in Lincoln. They got only one bid in response to the advertisement for construction, and, again, under the pressure of time, they accepted it. With the contract let, the next problem was finding materials. Finally, a limestone quarry near Beatrice proved productive of satisfactory stone, and all of the teams that could be hired were put on the road to haul the stone to Lincoln. This was slow at best, but by December 1, 1868, the capitol was ready for occupancy. It had cost $75,000, when it was supposed to have been built for $40,000, and was so poorly constructed that it had to be replaced

Nebraska City's River Front, 1865 (*from a drawing by Alfred Mathews*)

Nebraska City's Main Street, 1865 (*from a drawing by Alfred Mathews*)

Pony Express Rider
(*from a painting by
W. H. Jackson*)

Stages and Telegraph
Poles, Cottonwood Springs
(*from a drawing by
Carl P. Bolmar*)

Building the Union Pacific Railroad (*from a drawing by A. R. Waud*)

FROM TRAIL TO RAIL

Alexander Majors, Freighter

General Grenville M. Dodge,
Builder of the Transcontinental Railroad

Edward Creighton,
Builder of the Transcontinental Telegraph

THREE BUILDERS OF THE WEST

First Territorial Capitol,
Omaha, 1855

Second Territorial Capitol,
Omaha, 1858

First State Capitol,
Lincoln, 1868

NEBRASKA'S CAPITOLS

Second State Capitol,
Lincoln, 1888

Present Nebraska State Capitol

NEBRASKA'S CAPITOLS

Logan Fontenelle, Omaha

Spotted Tail, Sioux

Standing Bear, Ponca

Red Cloud, Sioux

FOUR INDIAN LEADERS

Beef Issue at
Pine Ridge

Fort Kearny

The Dead
at Wounded Knee

THE INDIAN WARS

Lincoln,
about 1868

Lincoln,
about 1889

Below: Lincoln
Today

GROWTH OF THE CAPITAL CITY

after a dozen years of service.

With the capitol built and the legislature actually in session, Lincoln's prospects considerably improved. The legislature gave a further push by an act, approved the last day of the session, February 15, 1869, chartering the University of Nebraska. The beginnings of that institution, which was to play an important role in the development of Lincoln, were as uncertain and confused as those of the capital city itself, and even before its doors were opened, it was subjected to severe criticism. The State Teachers Association contended in 1870 that the establishment of a university was impracticable, and that the state should concentrate instead on the building of preparatory and subordinate schools; internal wrangling among the regents as to the management of the prospective institution and even as to the wisdom of its establishment hampered its chances for success; sectional jealousy from towns that wanted the university worked against it as established in Lincoln. Nevertheless, construction went ahead, and in the fall of 1871, the University with its faculty of five and its one building was ready to receive students.

Meanwhile, the much-to-be-desired railroad connection was achieved when the Burlington and Missouri River Railroad in the summer of 1870 built from Plattsmouth to Lincoln and began striking off in a southwestwardly direction to connect the capital city with the rapidly developing South Platte country. That, and the construction of the capitol, the university, a penitentiary, and an insane asylum seemed to provide evidence that the paper city was going to become a reality. Throughout 1867 investors had been hesitant about risking money in the enterprise, but beginning in 1868 an increasing confidence developed, and by 1870 the town had a population of 2,500. It was off to a good start, but its future was by no means secure: scandals in state government, associated in the public mind with the Lincoln promoters, threatened the capital city's existence and, for a time, that of stable state government.

SCANDAL AND IMPEACHMENT

In their haste to construct the capitol and develop the city of Lincoln, the Capital Commissioners on occasion ignored the letter of the law; at other times they proceeded in a manner that, to say the least, was highly irregular. As has been indicated, they accepted the gift of the people of Lancaster instead of locating the capital on state lands as the law directed. Then, in their effort to encourage land sales, they allowed certain buyers, including themselves, to speculate in Lincoln town lots without advancing money for them. Finally, the Commissioners had refused to turn receipts from lot sales over to the state treasurer as the law required on the grounds that he (Augustus Kountze) was an Omaha man and probably would not release the money for construction of public buildings in Lincoln. Kountze had declared that inasmuch as the Commissioners had not filed bonds with him, as required by the law, he would receive money but would not honor their requests for payment.

Though Democratic and anti-Lincoln newspapers hammered away at the Commissioners' irregularities, the legislature of 1869, meeting in the new capitol in Lincoln, generally approved their activities. The Lincoln lot sales had brought in much more money than had been expected, the capital city enterprise was a success, and the state was experiencing great growth. Most of this, it was agreed, was due to the energetic work of Governor Butler and his associates (all of whom had been re-elected in 1868), and most people seemed inclined to overlook the fact that they had overstepped the law. Even the fact that the capitol had cost almost twice as much as had been approved was excused by the statement that the Commissioners had "been governed by an honest purpose to subserve the best interests of the state." Unfortunately, the Governor and his associates acted as though they assumed the state would continue to be indulgent of their technical irregularities in appreciation of their great service to the public.

The air over the state soon became heavy with charges. The Governor, it was declared, had entered into a contract for the construction of the University building without the consent of the Board of Regents at a figure in excess of the amount appropriated; the contract for the insane asylum had been let in excess of the amount appropriated to a contractor who could not give bond and who at the same time was erecting "palatial residences" for the Governor and the Secretary of State; the Governor had lent the school funds to friends, with inadequate security, as personal or political favors—some $40,000 which were to be invested only in United States or state securities; he had speculated illegally in Lincoln lots and had greatly profited therefrom. These and other charges—including the acceptance of bribes from contractors, railroads, and private individuals—were freely and ominously discussed. Even as the Governor was campaigning for a third term in 1870, impeachment sentiment was strong in the legislature and a joint committee of both houses was appointed to investigate "all of the public activities" of the Commissioners. The Committee's report, while indicating that there was ground for many of the charges, generally absolved the Governor and his associates of evil intent: speculation in Lincoln lots, for example, was looked upon as "an act of faith" in the capital city; furthermore, the Commissioners had "rightly found" the appropriations too small to build public buildings.

Butler himself treated the appointment of the committee solely as the work of his political enemies designed to destroy him both as a private citizen and as a public official. The stories, he declared, were mere gossip. He did not deny that he had exceeded instructions, but declared that the exigencies of the situation demanded that he do so and that at all times he had acted in the best interests of the state. Typical, perhaps, was his response to the charge of illegally lending state funds to private individuals. He argued that United States bonds were depreciating rapidly, and that the individuals to whom he lent the money provided better security. Besides, it was to the state's interest to use the money to keep business flourishing in the state.

The people apparently accepted the Governor's explanation, for though his majorities were smaller than other Republican candidates, he was re-elected to a third term in 1870 over John R. Croxton by a vote of 11,126 to 8,648. Butler's enemies, and they were many even in his own party, were not so easily satisfied, and when the eighth session of the legislature convened in 1871, Edward Rosewater, a Republican from Omaha, introduced an entirely new element in the charges against the Governor by asking him to account for funds collected from the federal government for school lands sold prior to the state's admission. The Governor replied that he had collected the money, amounting to $16,881.26, and had deposited it with the State Treasurer. When neither the Treasurer's nor Auditor's books showed any account of the transaction, the Governor was confronted with the question again, and this time admitted that he had not deposited the money but had borrowed it for his own use—assuring the legislature, however, that it was adequately secured by mortgages on Pawnee County land.

Here, the Governor's opponents realized, was a charge they could push effectively, and though influential voices continued to argue that impeachment proceedings would be expensive and would cast great discredit upon the new state, the House of Representatives on March 6 approved eleven articles of impeachment against the Governor. The first charge—and the only one on which the Senate voted to convict— was that the Governor had appropriated school funds collected from the federal government to his own use; the remaining ten articles simply revived old charges. The trial before the Senate revealed an incredible laxity in the handling of the state's financial affairs. Auditor John Gillespie, who by this time had turned against Butler, was impeached for malfeasance in office, but was not convicted. James Sweet, who had succeeded Kountze as State Treasurer, was severely criticised but not impeached. He and Nelson Brock, his deputy, owned a bank in which they deposited all state funds. Apparently, they not only failed to keep these funds segregated from their private accounts but did not even identify them as state accounts: state deposits were carried under the name of "John Rix," thereby making it impossible to determine from an examination of the books that the bank's deposits included any state funds, much less discover what was done with the money. Much of it, the trial brought out, was lent on real-estate mortgages at usurious rates of interest.

On June 1, the Senate voted, nine to three, to convict the Governor of the charge of misappropriating state funds; on the remaining charges they voted acquittal. The punishment, adopted by a vote of eleven to one, was simply removal from office. Secretary of State William H. James (Nebraska's constitution did not provide for a lieutenant governor), who had been serving as Acting Governor since the proceedings began, filled out the remainder of the term. Governor Butler retired to his farm in Pawnee County, continuing his stock raising as successfully as if he had never left it. The legislature authorized a commission, consisting of the Governor, Secretary of State, and Treasurer, to take a deed for land to settle the state's claim against him. In 1874 that commission took a deed for 3,392.16 acres in Pawnee, Jefferson, and Gage counties, believed to be the amount necessary to settle total claims against Butler amounting to $23,633.74. Actually, when the last sale was made in 1895, the land had brought a total of $27,635.32. After a number of unsuccessful attempts, Butler's friends in the legislature finally got the impeachment proceedings expunged from the record in 1877, although they were unsuccessful in getting an appropriation to reimburse him for losses suffered at the hands of the state! In 1882 Butler was elected to the state Senate as an Independent, and in 1888 was the Union Labor party's candidate for governor.

One cannot survey the record of the case and the time without coming to the conclusion that the people generally did not expect rigid honesty in the handling of public affairs, and that Governor Butler was as much unfortunate as he was maleficent. In the minds of many, his great service in building the state and its new capital city overrode any irregularities in the performance of that service. These irregularities, however, cast a shadow upon the capital city and all the public institutions located there and for a number of years greatly hindered their development.

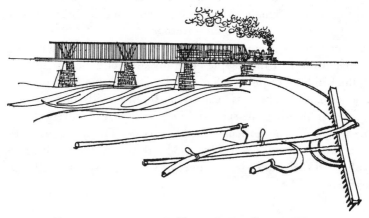

CHAPTER 13

Settlement—The Major Factors

THE YEARS immediately following the Civil War brought the beginning of a flow of emigration into Nebraska which, despite political and economic uncertainties, continued almost unabated for two and a half decades. When the flow began to subside in the Eighteen Nineties, the state had almost acquired what was to be a relatively static population. The census figures dramatically show both the expansion and the levelling off:

Year	Population	Year	Population
1860	28,841	1910	1,192,214
1870	122,993	1920	1,296,372
1880	452,402	1930	1,377,963
1890	1,058,910	1940	1,315,834
1900	1,066,910	1950	1,325,510
		1960	1,411,330

Our concern here is with the expansion of the late Sixties, the Seventies, and the Eighties—and the forces which brought it about.

The most important factor was the construction of railroads through the state, making possible settlement away from the Missouri River, the only navigable stream in the area. The Union Pacific, which as early as August, 1866, was carrying passengers and freight as far west as Kearney, was completed to Cheyenne in May of 1868, and a year later joined the Central Pacific to span the continent. Completion of a bridge across the Missouri at Omaha in 1872 made it possible for the

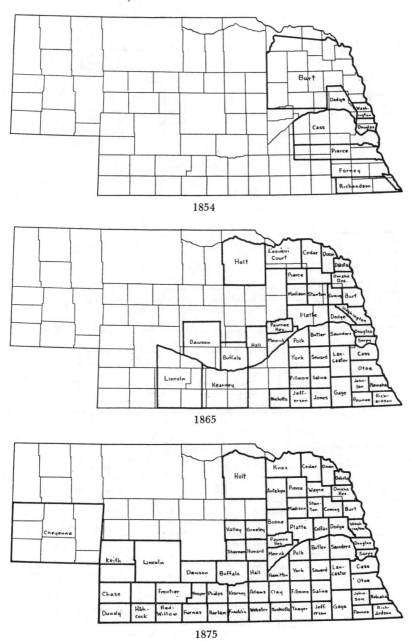

1854

1865

1875

GROWTH OF COUNTIES IN NEBRASKA

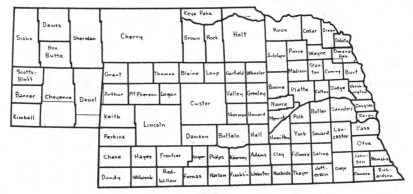

1885

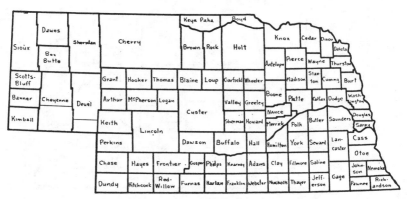

1895

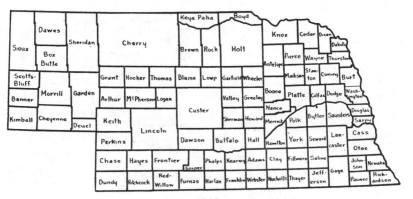

1913

GROWTH OF COUNTIES IN NEBRASKA

Union Pacific to make connections with the roads crossing Iowa. The Burlington, starting from Plattsmouth in July, 1869, reached Lincoln a year later and in 1872 joined the Union Pacific at Kearney; by the end of 1881 the road had built through the Republican Valley and on to Benkelman, almost at the state's western border. The Midland Pacific, soon to become part of the Burlington system, connected Nebraska City and Lincoln in 1871 and later built westward through Seward, York, and Aurora to Central City. The St. Joseph and Denver entered Nebraska in 1870 and reached Hastings two years later. The Atchison and Nebraska built through the southeastern corner of the state to Lincoln in the early Seventies. North of the Platte, the Sioux City and Pacific built from Missouri Valley, Iowa, to Fremont; and the Omaha and Northwestern reached Blair. The Fremont, Elkhorn, and Missouri Valley built up the Elkhorn Valley, and the Union Pacific constructed various branches connecting with its main line.

A second major factor in the settlement of the state was federal land policy, which—theoretically, at least—made it possible for the settler to acquire a landed estate solely through his own labor. Expressed through the Homestead Act and related legislation, this policy made available the land which the railroads had made accessible. A third significant factor was the colonization activity of the railroads, combined with an intensive advertising campaign conducted by both private and public agencies.

Nebraska land, thus made accessible, available, and known, was a strong impelling force; combined with expelling forces at work in the East and in Europe—unemployment, lack of opportunity, and just plain restlessness—it brought about the great expansion of the late Sixties, the Seventies, and the Eighties.

THE LAND LAWS

When President Lincoln signed the Homestead Act on May 20, 1862, the West realized one of its great historic ambitions. Nebraskans, who since the organization of the territory had done all in their power to promote the legislation, looked upon its enactment as the long-awaited answer to a heartfelt prayer. In his message to the legislature in 1864, Governor Saunders spoke exultantly of the nation's future under the Act:

What a blessing this wise and humane legislation will bring to many a poor, but honest and industrious family. Its benefits can never be estimated in dollars and cents. The very thought, to such people, that they can now have a tract of land that they can call their own, has a soul-inspiring effect upon them, and makes them feel thankful that their lots have been cast under a government that is so liberal to its people.

The Act provided that "any person who is the head of a family, or who has arrived at the age of twenty-one years, and is a citizen of the United States, or who shall have filed his declaration of intention to become such . . . and who has never borne arms against the United States government or given aid and comfort to its enemies" could upon the payment of a ten dollar fee file a claim upon as much as a quarter-section of unappropriated public land; and that after having "resided upon or cultivated the same for the term of five years immediately succeeding the time of filing," and "if at that time a citizen of the United States," the claimant could receive a final patent from the government.

Although amended many times—principally to extend its privileges —the Homestead Act remained in force substantially as passed, and was looked upon as the cornerstone of the nation's public land policy. The Pre-Emption Act of 1841, under which many of Nebraska's early territorial pioneers had secured their land,[1] also remained in force (until its repeal in 1891), but was relegated to a position of supplemental importance: one would not pay $1.25 per acre for land that he could secure free of charge—he would, however, if able, add to his homestead through the purchase of an additional quarter-section at the minimum price.

Another supplemental land law was the Timber Culture Act, approved on March 3, 1873, which provided that the same class of persons who could homestead could acquire an additional quarter-section by planting forty acres of the same to trees and tending them for ten years. Later this time was reduced to eight years, and the required acreage of trees to ten. This act, introduced by Nebraska's Senator Phineas W. Hitchcock, was primarily designed to encourage tree-planting on the Plains, and was closely associated with other similar efforts in Nebraska: Arbor Day had been established the year before; in 1869 the legislature had exempted one hundred dollars worth of property from taxation for every acre of forest trees planted and kept in cultivation.

[1]See p. 89.

The nation's first entry under the Homestead Act was that made by Daniel Freeman, a soldier in the Union Army home on furlough, to a quarter-section lying along Cub Creek northwest of Beatrice. The story of that filing has been somewhat confused in the frequent retelling (even his military service has not been documented), but apparently Freeman, who had selected the land a few days earlier, persuaded the Register of the Land Office at Brownville to open up shortly after midnight on January 1, 1863, the date the law went into effect, and receive his entry before he had to leave early on New Year's Day to join his regiment.[2]

Freeman was followed by many others. The Brownville *Advertiser* remarked, January 3, 1863, that since the Homestead Law had gone into effect, there had been "a rush to take advantage of its benefits." The extent and nature of the "rush" can perhaps best be shown by means of a statistical statement. (See table, page 167.)

An examination of the figures in the table reveals that of 131,561 entrymen who filed original homestead entries on 18,393,541 acres of the public domain in Nebraska between 1863 and 1895, only 68,862 had received final patents by 1900, and the total acreage which had been finally transferred to individual homesteaders up to that time amounts to only 9,609,922 acres. In other words, only about fifty-two percent of the original homestead entries were carried through to the final patent. Moreover, including the Kinkaid homesteads of the early twentieth century,[3] only a little more than half of the public domain in Nebraska actually passed to settlers.

Why, one might ask, did the public land policies—and particularly the Homestead Act—fall so short of expectations? A great deal of work needs to be done before we can arrive at a definite answer to this question, but a few tentative conclusions may be suggested in the light of the information available.

In the first place, a "free farm" in itself by no means assured the success of the farmer. A successful farm operation required both capital and experience. While many who homesteaded were experienced farmers, they had very little capital, and much of their experience—in Europe and the more humid regions of the United States—was found

[2]The United States Government reacquired the Freeman homestead in 1936, and established it as Homestead National Monument of America.

[3]See pp. 258–260.

HOMESTEAD ENTRIES IN NEBRASKA, 1863-1900

	Original		Final	
Year	*No.*	*Acres*	*No.*	*Acres*
1863	349	50,775	....	....
1864	769	114,649	....	....
1865	812	114,875	....	....
1866	1,456	203,980	....	....
1867	1,628	225,856	....	....
1868	2,844	325,459	...	....
1869	3,596	376,860	277	41,687
1870	4,583	509,062	285	42,134
1871	6,021	713,306	437	61,465
1872	5,970	696,620	649	91,466
1873	6,189	742,884	1,658	220,420
1874	5,165	615,424	2,818	321,743
1875	2,281	265,548	2,828	344,345
1876	1,984	237,786	3,590	418,962
1877	1,345	163,312	3,507	422,147
1878	3,015	407,949	3,897	456,075
1879	4,905	703,750	2,960	349,373
1880	5,648	827,112	2,559	315,501
1881	2,545	365,922	1,611	202,241
1882	3,223	471,939	1,925	258,393
1883	4,728	716,509	1,768	241,511
1884	8,887	1,362,186	2,595	375,128
1885	11,293	1,748,841	2,658	393,239
1886	10,269	1,590,410	2,121	328,968
1887	7,120	1,098,636	1,949	292,874
1888	5,439	839,675	2,184	331,409
1889	4,105	622,626	3,017	467,373
1890	3,141	475,183	4,207	651,732
1891	1,969	288,480	3,918	611,116
1892	3,999	604,320	2,770	431,590
1893	3,270	484,357	2,900	451,773
1894	1,712	245,477	2,204	342,155
1895	1,301	183,773	1,671	255,845
1896	1,101	154,930	1,227	185,245
1897	1,309	191,701	1,000	153,094
1898	1,882	271,725	1,205	181,246
1899	2,452	351,449	1,189	178,092
1900	3,141	456,855	1,278	191,580
Total	141,446	19,820,201	68,862	9,609,922

to be of little use on the Plains. Moreover, the Homestead Act lured many settlers into areas where a quarter-section simply would not support a family; and even in areas where a quarter-section was normally sufficient, the homesteaders seem to have been particularly unfortunate in the land they acquired. In Wayne County, for example, 33.11 percent of the land settled by homesteads and timber entries was poorer land; no other group received such a high percentage of inferior land. It is little wonder that many failed in the venture.

In the second place, the Homestead and Timber Culture acts frequently were perverted from their original purposes. The provision in the Homestead Act allowing commutation for cash was used by speculators and other large operators to acquire vast tracts to which they were not entitled in the spirit of the law. The process was simple: hirelings would file homestead claims, then after six months commute or purchase them for the minimum price of $1.25 per acre ($2.50 per acre in the railroad areas); title would then pass to the employer who had put up the money. Further compounding the evil, repeated filings were made in violation of the provision in the law which limited each person to one entry. In Nebraska, 2,634,240 acres were commuted for cash, and mostly for speculative purposes. The Timber Culture Act, under which final patents were issued on 2,456,969 out of 8,876,351 acres on which original entries were filed, was subject to even more flagrant abuse. To be sure, in many areas it was impossible to grow trees even with the best of care; but in many more instances the Act was used simply to increase holdings with little effort being made to produce timber. In his annual report for 1883, the Commissioner of the General Land Office wrote:

My information leads me to the conclusion that a majority of the entries under the timber-culture act are made for speculative purposes, and not for the cultivation of timber. Compliance with the law in these cases is a mere pretense. . . . My information is that no trees are to be seen over vast regions of country where timber culture entries have been most numerous.

Again, in 1885, he quoted from a field inspector as follows:

I have traveled over hundreds of miles of land in western Kansas, Nebraska, and central Dakota, nearly one-fourth of which had been taken under the "timber culture Act," without seeing an artificial grove even in incipience, and can scarcely recall an instance in any one day's travel where the ground had been more than scratched with the plow for the purpose of planting trees.

Finally, the Homestead and other related acts designed to provide farms for actual settlers suffered from the fact that they were simply added to an already incongruous land system which sought to use the public domain to further a variety of social purposes; the provision of bounties for those who had served in the nation's wars, the construction of railroads and other internal improvements, and the furtherance of education. Whether by accident or design, legislation enacted to further these ends resulted in the transfer of vast quantities of the public domain to large, monopolistic, and speculative holders. The use of military warrants, with which 1,333,760 acres were entered in Nebraska, already has been discussed.[4] Railroad lands, definitely in competition with government land, will be treated in the pages immediately following. Here, however, mention should be made of certain other aspects of federal land policy by which large holdings were acquired.

Particularly noteworthy was the use of agricultural-college scrip, which under the Morrill Act of 1862 states could receive in lieu of public lands within their borders for the endowment of their agricultural colleges. Twenty-seven states—principally those which had no public domain remaining—chose scrip in lieu of land. The scrip was sold, generally in large blocks, and the money used to provide a permanent endowment. Much research still needs to be done on the use of agricultural-college scrip, but such evidence as is available indicates that the 1,123,200 acres located in Nebraska by such means passed largely into the hands of speculators who had secured the scrip from various eastern states at very favorable prices.[5] Likewise, a large portion of the Indian lands sold in the state (599,018 acres) appears to have gone to speculators.

From the foregoing, then, it is clear that while the Homestead and other related acts were designed to encourage settlers in the settlement

---

[4] See p. 92.

[5] Nebraska, incidentally, was much more fortunate in the management of its agricultural college lands than were many eastern states. The state's 89,140 acres of agricultural land, located primarily in northeastern Nebraska, were sold for an average price of $8.37 per acre; many states sold their scrip for much less: Rhode Island, forty-two cents; Kentucky and North Carolina, fifty cents; New Hampshire and Ohio, fifty-three cents; Indiana, fifty-four cents. Moreover, much of Nebraska's land went to relatively small purchasers, although a total of 14,555 acres were divided among five purchasers, the largest acquiring 3,777 acres. (Agnes Horton, "Nebraska's Agricultural College Land Grant," *Nebraska History*, XXX [March, 1949], 50–76.)

of Nebraska—and other Plains states as well—they did not play the important role expected of them, and the state, like the territory before it, continued to be a paradise for the land speculator.

RAILROAD COLONIZATION

Approximately 16.6 percent of Nebraska's total acreage was given to various railroad companies, either by the federal government or by the state, as follows:

From the United States	*Acres*
Union Pacific	4,846,108.18
Burlington and Missouri River	2,374,090.77
Sioux City and Pacific	38,227.84
Central Branch Union Pacific	2,560.03
St. Joseph and Grand Island	380,768.96
Total	7,641,755.78
From the State (Internal Improvement Lands)	
Fremont, Elkhorn, and Missouri Valley	100,030.32
Midland Pacific	100,384.08
Brownville and Fort Kearney	19,989.12
Sioux City and Pacific	47,327.10
Burlington and Missouri River	40,104.77
Omaha and Southwestern	100,010.00
Omaha and Northwestern	80,416.24
Burlington and Southwestern	20,000.00
Atchison and Nebraska	12,841.54
Total	531,103.17
Grand Total	8,172,858.95

The Union Pacific and the Burlington, the state's two major railroads, were given alternate sections extending back twenty miles from each side of the track, or a total of twenty sections of land for each mile of road constructed. Except in the area along the Missouri River and a few isolated places elsewhere, the Union Pacific was generally able to locate its lands in the forty-mile strip along its tracks. Had the Burlington done this, however, its grant would have overlapped that of the Union Pacific; hence the Burlington secured a ruling which enabled it to locate land elsewhere in lieu of that along the road itself; its land as finally located lay north and south of the Union Pacific grant.

Once the railroads had located and patented their land, they were, of course, anxious to dispose of it as quickly as possible and at the highest possible price. The problem was somewhat complicated, however, by the realization that the development of farms and towns upon which a profitable carrying trade could be based was of even greater significance than the immediate returns from land sales. The land departments, therefore, tried to establish prices and terms which would produce as much immediate revenue as possible and at the same time encourage settlement on the railroad lands. In their pricing policies, they were aided by the fact that a homesteader could acquire only eighty acres within the area of a railroad grant, and that pre-emptions and commutations within the same area were at a minimum price of $2.50 per acre rather than the $1.25 which obtained elsewhere. During the thirteen years, 1871–1883 inclusive, the Burlington got an average of $6.05 per acre for its land, and the Union Pacific, $4.27 per acre.[6] Both roads gave long-term credit.

The land departments of both roads conducted vigorous promotional campaigns. They stationed immigration agents in the principal cities of the East and in the countries of northern and central Europe; they distributed brochures by the millions describing the beauties and prospects of Nebraska; they sent lecturers around the country extolling the virtues of Nebraska; they cooperated with the State Board of Agriculture and with other agencies in exhibiting Nebraska's products at fairs and expositions; they conducted special "land-seeking" excursions with the understanding that if the excursionist decided to purchase land, his fare could be applied to the payment. Indeed, they utilized almost every device known to the advertising trade of the nineteenth century in the promotion of their Nebraska land.

The land departments devoted considerable attention to encouraging group removals to Nebraska, and many of the state's communities were settled on that basis. The Union Pacific, for example, located a large group of people of Swedish descent on its lands in Saunders and Polk counties in 1869–70; and in 1870 a group of sixty families from Nova Scotia came to Colfax County. The Burlington likewise located large group settlements on its lands, many from foreign countries—among them the "Russian Colony" in Lincoln. Frequently groups were organized around a church—particularly the Lutheran and Roman Catholic

---

[6] The Union Pacific's land grant, of course, extended all the way across the state, and much of it lay in the sub-humid region of the central and western area, whereas virtually all of the Burlington's land lay in the more humid section.

—with the emigration directed by the pastor; and frequently they were organized by individuals as business enterprises, as, for example, the "Soldier's Free Homestead Colony" of Ohio, which settled Gibbon, and those organized by James N. Paul and John J. Cozad. The Burlington, through its subsidiary, the Lincoln Land Company, carried on systematic town development, particularly along its line through the Republican Valley.

By 1905, all of the Burlington's lands in Nebraska had been sold and paid for. The Union Pacific had 12,307 acres remaining unsold in the state in 1921 and continues to retain about this acreage to the present. The two roads had disposed of more than seven million acres to private purchasers—almost seventy-five percent as much as was taken free of charge under the Homestead Act. The railroads did not altogether abandon their interest in their land and its purchasers with sale, but continued to carry on agricultural improvement programs, working closely with the University of Nebraska and various agencies of both the state and federal governments. George W. Holdrege, general manager of the Burlington's Lines West, was particularly active in agricultural development work, supporting the revolutionary dry farming experiments of Hardy W. Campbell.

THE GREAT ADVERTISING CAMPAIGN

State government joined the railroads in promoting settlement. In his message to the legislature in 1869, Governor Butler urged the establishment of a bureau of immigration, and in 1870 the lawmakers established a Board of Immigration to consist of five members chosen by the legislature for two-year terms. The Board was given $15,000 and authority to appoint four "agents of Immigration" to be assigned to duty "in this country, or in foreign countries." There was some dissatisfaction with the work of the Board of Immigration, and after an initial burst of enthusiasm support for its work sharply declined. The Board itself was abolished in 1877.

More effective, perhaps, was the work of the State Board of Agriculture, which under the leadership of Robert W. Furnas developed the State Fair into an effective annual agricultural exposition, and with the State Horticultural Society, sent exhibits of Nebraska fruit and grains to expositions throughout the East. The railroads cooperated by providing free transportation. J. Sterling Morton, a member of both boards, an agriculturist of wide reputation, and the paid publicist of the Burlington, performed particularly effective liaison work between the railroads and the state boards.

A major obstacle to the settlement of the state was the widely held belief that much of the trans-Missouri region was unsuited to agriculture. Dolorous descriptions from explorers and others of "the Great American Desert" lying east of the Rockies[7] had found their way into periodical and newspaper literature and had created a generally unfavorable impression of the Plains. The promotional activity of the railroads and the various state agencies was designed primarily to demolish this impression. The exhibits, the brochures, and the lectures demonstrated by statistic and example that the desert concept was nothing but a mischievous myth. Moreover, for the skeptical there was the word of no less an authority than Dr. Samuel Aughey, Professor of Natural Sciences at the University of Nebraska, that the state's rainfall, already adequate, was actually increasing!

Dr. Aughey, who prior to joining the first faculty of the University in 1871 had combined his scientific studies with the ministry and land speculation, set forth his views in a book entitled *Sketches of the Physical Geography and Geology of Nebraska* (Omaha, 1880). From his experience as an old settler—he had been in the state since 1864—and from the experience of others, it was clear to him that rainfall in Nebraska was increasing. There were many phenomena to demonstrate the validity of the assertion: the appearance of new springs, the appearance of water in old creek beds, the increasing size of the streams of the state, and changing vegetation. From experimentation on a farm about a mile east of Lincoln, Dr. Aughey concluded that the cause of Nebraska's increasing rainfall was to be found in "the great increase in the absorptive power of the soil, wrought by cultivation." He wrote:

Anyone who examines a piece of raw prairie closely, must observe how compact it is. Everyone who opens up a new farm, soon finds that it requires an extra force to break it. There is nothing extraordinary about this. For vast ages the prairies have been pelted by the elements and trodden by millions of buffalo and other wild animals, until the naturally rich soil became as compact as a floor. When rain falls on a primitive soil of this character, the greater part runs off into the canyons, creeks and rivers, and is soon through the Missouri on its way to the Gulf. Observe now the change

[7]See pp. 3–4.

which cultivation makes. After the soil is broken, the rain as it falls is absorbed and retained to be given off by evaporation, or to produce springs. This, of course, must give increasing moisture and rainfall.

The theory that "rainfall follows the plow" was indeed provocative. C. D. Wilber popularized it in *The Great Valleys and Prairies of Nebraska and the Northwest* (Omaha, 1881), widely circulated by the railroads. Orange Judd, widely known and highly respected editor of the *Prairie Farmer*, published in Chicago, expounded it further in an address at the Nebraska State Fair on September 16, 1883. Speaking from a platform of baled hay, Judd extolled the virtues of Nebraska as an agricultural state and advanced the view that an important feature of Nebraska's climate was that its rainfall was increasing annually as a result of the extension of agriculture westward. Nebraska stood to benefit not only from its own development but also from that of Kansas: "as neighboring Kansas settles up and breaks its prairie sod away out to its western border those parching winds that formerly came up into Nebraska, and still come at some points, will be heard of no more."

Agriculture, then, would provide its own solution to the problem of the Plains. Those who disagreed were promptly shouted down. When, for example, the Department of the Interior in 1879 published Major J. W. Powell's report, *Lands of the Arid Region*, in which the hundredth meridian was designated as the western limit of agriculture and the area between that and the line where twenty-eight inches of annual rainfall stopped was classed as a marginal region, Nebraska's indignation knew no bounds. The state agricultural and horticultural societies requested Professors Aughey and Wilber to draft a reply. This they did, suggesting that the condemnation of the western part of the state was inspired by cattlemen who wanted to keep farmers out. They declared further that the soil of the area was as productive as any in the country, and that the only element lacking for successful agriculture was an adequate supply of moisture—which soon would be remedied: "the present rate of increase in rainfall . . . will in a comparatively short time fit these regions for agriculture without the aid of irrigation."

The proponents of increased rainfall, aided immeasurably by the fact that during the early Eighties Nebraska experienced a series of comparatively wet years, seem to have carried the day. At least, many were willing to take a chance at homesteading the relatively sub-humid lands of the central part of the state—lands that bitter experience was to demonstrate could not be farmed by the methods applied to the humid regions east of the Missouri. The acquisition of that experience was a major factor in Nebraska's economic and political history.

CHAPTER 14

The Seventies—Growing Pains

THE SETTLEMENT FORCES at work in the West brought profound changes to Nebraska in the decade immediately following the close of the Civil War. Population, which had increased to 122,993 by 1870, was estimated at 250,000 in 1874. At the same time, thirty-seven new counties were organized—thirty-one of them in the years 1870–73. Prior to the end of the war, county government, save for omnibus Lincoln County at the forks of the Platte and a strip along the north side of the Platte to Grand Island, did not extend much beyond seventy-five miles west of the Missouri. By 1874 the entire South Platte region was solidly organized through Frontier and Hitchcock counties; organization north of the Platte, except for the Indian reservations, had been extended to the eastern edge of the Sandhills; Keith County had been organized west of Lincoln County, and the southern portion of the panhandle was established as Cheyenne County.

Except in the range country, this growth generally represented the westward extension of conventional, humid-region diversified agriculture. Much of the land occupied during the period was sub-marginal for this activity, even in good years—and the middle Seventies saw serious distress that brought the experiment near the brink of complete failure. Almost pushing it over was the depression which hit agriculture—indeed, all activity—during those same years. Moreover, agriculture on the prairie-plains was not "corn and 'tater patch" subsistence

169

farming, but a commercial enterprise which employed an increasing amount of machinery, requiring a corresponding increase in capital; and each time the farmer substituted a machine for a hand tool it usually meant going further into debt. The land was free, but it would not produce enough to pay the cost of farming it.

Political instability, growing out of the scandals of the Butler Administration and the inadequacies of the constitution, combined with economic instability to produce a period of grave uncertainty in the middle Seventies. Particularly distressing to the farmer who lived in his little soddy and worked his parched fields for little or no return was the apparent collusion between the politicians and the groups to which he was constantly in debt: the railroads, the banks, and the commercial classes generally. Though it was to be a decade before the Nebraska farmer was to rise in organized rebellion against the forces he believed to be oppressing him, he was becoming steadily more willing to lend an ear to those who denounced the Government, the railroads, the bankers, and the "middlemen."

Attitudes formed in the Seventies tended to become more rigid as the years wore on. As Addison E. Sheldon, who during those years was growing up on a Seward County farm, later wrote:

> In these years was created the Soul of Nebraska—characteristic mind, vision and form of action. Soil and sun and wind, hardship and conflict, spirit, institutions, debates and experiences shaped the type of man who still lives upon these prairies. The blendings of different racial stocks, begun then, still goes on. But the Nebraska type was created in the '70s. . . . The soul of Nebraska remains in dominant feature the product of the pioneer '70s.[1]

INITIAL GROWTH

Approximately fifty-four percent of Nebraska's population increase during the Seventies resulted from the growth of counties established prior to 1870. Homesteads and railroad lands were still available in these counties, and in some—notably Dodge, Douglas, Gage, and Lancaster—small cities were developing into nuclei of an urban population. Yet, to those with little or no capital, the more significant opportunities seemed to lie further west, and about forty-six percent of those

[1] Addison E. Sheldon, *Nebraska: The Land and the People* (Chicago: Lewis Publishing Company, 1931), I, 579.

living in the state in 1880 resided in the counties created during the years 1870–1874.

Particularly marked in the early Seventies was the extension of population up the Republican Valley. Prior to 1870 the region had been little affected by the white man: it lay outside the main stream of overland emigration. While providing an easy route, it seemed to lead nowhere; trappers and traders, visited the region but generally moved on to more profitable fields; the Indians, driven out of the other great valleys on the Plains, stubbornly resisted white efforts to penetrate this last haven where the buffalo and other wild game were still plentiful. In 1870, however, exploratory and settlement expeditions were organized in a number of the Missouri River towns to go out into the Republican Valley.

First in the field was the Rankin Colony, organized in Omaha in the fall of 1869. They established themselves at Guide Rock and began to build a house, but an Indian scare drove all except two away before the house was completed. The first permanent settlement in the valley was Red Cloud, established in the summer of 1870 by Silas Garber—soon to become governor—and a party from Beatrice. Another Omaha group, known as the Thompson Colony, explored the valley in the fall of 1870 and returned the next spring to found Riverton. A branch of the Rankin Colony, forming a separate organization known as the Republican Valley Land Claim Association, settled at Franklin City in the fall of 1870, but the town never materialized and present-day Franklin grew out of the town of Waterloo, established by the Plattsmouth Town Company. Another Plattsmouth company was organized in 1872 to found Bloomington. Also in 1870, Victor Vifquain—the first Nebraskan ever to receive the Congressional Medal of Honor—led a party west from Nebraska City. Most of them quit in disgust, but a few remained and erected Melrose Stockade. In February, 1871, a group of Union Pacific laborers from Cheyenne explored the valley, returned to Cheyenne, and recruited settlers to establish Alma. Later in the year, a group led by Dr. John McPherson, a wealthy Brownville doctor, established Republican City.

One of the best known of the colonizing companies was the Red Willow Colony, also known as the Republican Valley Land Company, organized in the fall of 1871 at Nebraska City. This colony sent out an exploring party under Royal Buck, which, after encountering difficult weather and even more difficult Indians, pushed on to Red Willow Creek to organize the town of Red Willow in December. The company, capitalized at $100,000, had visions of organizing a large city in the valley. The town was laid out on the plan of Lincoln with streets one hundred feet wide, a newspaper was started, and the company worked feverishly to promote its new city. For a variety of reasons, however, the venture failed. The Republican Valley Land Company also was active in the establishment of Indianola and Bartley, but in these ventures it ran afoul of competition from the Lincoln Land Company, incorporated in 1880 as a subsidiary of the Burlington, and an important force in the urban real-estate boom of the Eighties.[2]

The prospect of a railroad in the valley provided a significant impetus to the settlement of the region. This prospect did not materialize until the Burlington built along the river in 1878–1882, and the settlers of the Seventies had to make the long trip overland to the Union Pacific, or, after 1873, to the Burlington at Lowell. The area along this South Platte extension of the Burlington was developed by the Eastern Land Associates, organized in 1870 by high officials of the Burlington to develop the lands along its main line. The Associates were primarily responsible for the development of the railroad's "alphabetical towns" west of Lincoln: Crete, Dorchester, Exeter, Fairmont, Grafton, Harvard, Inland, Juniata, Kenesaw, and Lowell.

In the Republican Valley as elsewhere individual settlers pushed out ahead of the colonies and the railroads. In the fall of 1870, Galen James went out from the Melrose Stockade to live at the junction of the Beaver and the Sappa. Cambridge's first settler was Hiram Doing, who arrived in 1871. In 1872 George Hunter and E. S. Hill settled on the site of Indianola. The village of Culbertson was settled in 1873 as a headquarters for cattlemen.

Meanwhile, the Union Pacific continued to develop its lands in the Platte Valley. By 1873 it had settled forty groups, or 2,113 families, in its land grant as far west as the eastern edge of Buffalo County, although the larger groups concentrated on the cheaper lands south of the Platte or west of Colfax County. Most of these settlers were of Scandinavian descent. During the next four years, activity fell off considerably, and only one large group settled on Union Pacific lands—348 families of Swedes from Illinois, who occupied a large tract in Phelps and Kearney

[2]See pp. 200–204.

counties. Group settlement in 1878 did not extend beyond the Cozad settlement of 1873. Smaller groups were active in taking up the lands east of Central City.

Further north, Norfolk, founded in 1866 by a group of Germans from Wisconsin, began to develop as a trading center for growing settlements along the Elkhorn, particularly after the Fremont, Missouri Valley and Elkhorn built up the valley to Wisner in 1871 and to Neligh in 1880. Further up the valley, General John J. O'Neill, eccentric Irish leader who had served a term in prison for participation in the Fenian invasion of Canada, founded a community bearing his name as an Irish colony in 1874. He later established similar colonies at Atkinson and in Greeley County.

Religious groups were active in the settlement process of the early Seventies. Many of the Scandinavian groups were led by Lutheran pastors. The Catholics were active in Platte and Cedar counties. York was founded by Congregationalists. A group of Seventh Day Baptists established a colony in the Loup Valley. Large Mennonite colonies were founded south and west of Lincoln, particularly under the leadership of Peter Jansen.

It was a polyglot population, frequently set off in communities dominated by one particular national group. Many of these groups had little contact with other sections of the state, continuing to maintain Old World customs and traditions. Official state papers were even printed in their various languages. By 1880, 97,414, or 21.53 percent of the people in Nebraska, were foreign born; an additional 168,538 were of foreign stock. The Tenth Census showed the origin of the foreign born as follows:

Germany	31,125
Sweden	10,164
Ireland	10,133
Bohemia	8,858
England and Wales	8,831
British America	8,678
Denmark	4,511
Russia	3,281
Austria	2,346
Scotland	2,230
Norway	2,010
Switzerland	1,579
Poland	1,128
France	749

DISTRESS AND DOUBT

Hope ran high in the new state during the early Seventies as settlers poured across the Missouri by the thousands to claim farms for themselves. New towns staked out on the Plains vied with each other for preferment, and almost every one of the thirty-one counties organized during those years had a county-seat fight in its history. The various local struggles were somewhat reminiscent of the territorial struggle for the capital carried on among the river towns two decades earlier. The struggle was all the more intense because of the roseate hue on the horizon of the future. In almost every instance, the first year's crops were good enough to convince those who had planted them that their future in the new land was assured. To be sure, marketing difficulties in the region beyond the railroad absorbed almost all the profit; but the railroads were coming—everywhere—and it was only a matter of time until those who had pioneered in the experiment would come into their reward.

Then in September, 1873, the investment house of Jay Cooke and Company of New York failed, precipitating a panic that swept across the country like a prairie fire fanned by a high wind. Agricultural prices tumbled, and in some instances Nebraska farmers could find no market whatever for their wheat and corn. As if this were not sufficient, in July of the next year the plains from Canada to Texas were overrun by vast hordes of Rocky Mountain locusts, which descended in ominous black clouds upon the pioneer farms and literally ate them off the face of the earth. Almost every pioneer story of the period has its account of the grasshopper infestation. Addison E. Sheldon's is typical:

In a clear, hot July (July 26) day a haze came over the sun. The haze deepened into a gray cloud. Suddenly the cloud resolved itself into billions of gray grasshoppers sweeping down upon the earth. The vibration of their wings filled the ear with a roaring sound like a rushing storm. As far as the eye could reach in every direction the air was filled with them. Where they alighted they covered the ground like a heavy crawling carpet. Growing crops disappeared in a single day. Trees were stripped of leaves. Potatoes, turnips and onions were pursued into the earth. Clothing and harness were cut into shreds if left exposed. Wheat and oats were mostly in the shock, but the grasshoppers covered the shocks, cut the bands and gnawed the grain.

Everywhere the earth was covered with a gray mass of struggling, biting grasshoppers. Turkeys and chickens feasted on them. Dogs and swine learned to eat them—the latter making them their chief food for many days.

It was hard to drive a team across a field because the swarm of grasshoppers flew up in front, striking the horses in the face with a force that made them wild.

We thought when they were filled they would fly away. Not at all. . . . Each one laid about one hundred eggs. Then they died and the ground was covered with their dead bodies.[3]

Though weather records for the years prior to 1876 are very incomplete, the grasshoppers apparently delivered the final attack on crops already withering under the effects of a serious drouth. The "hard times" were bad enough before the drouth and the grasshoppers, but so long as the farmers had their sod corn and garden stuff, they could at least feed themselves and their livestock. With these gone, however, the situation was indeed desperate—and the future was made to seem hopeless by the knowledge that the soil was filled with eggs which would hatch a hundred times as many grasshoppers the next spring. Particularly discouraged were those who were trying to raise their first crop. Many sold or gave away their claims and returned east; on the tattered covers of their wagons they scrawled:

> Eaten out by grasshoppers
> Going back East to live with wife's folks.

At first, public officials and newspapers—concentrating on the promotion of settlement—were inclined to minimize the seriousness of the situation. On August 21, Governor Robert W. Furnas issued a report to the public which, while admitting that "at quite a number of points on the extreme borders . . . help will be required soon," stated that information derived from correspondence with county officials and from personal observation "warrants the assertion that while our crops are shorter than for several years before, there is by no means a failure, or even ground for serious alarm." J. Sterling Morton was confident that exhibits of Nebraska's products at the State Fair and at eastern expositions would "knock stories of starvation in Nebraska higher than Beecher's Life of Christ."

But as reports of destitution began to pile up from all parts of the state it became apparent that something would have to be done, and done quickly. To avoid calling a special session of the legislature, Governor Furnas asked a number of well-known citizens to meet with him

[3] *Nebraska: The Land and the People*, I, 494.

in Lincoln on September 18 to find a means of dealing with the situation. This group incorporated the Nebraska Relief and Aid Society to collect money, provisions, clothing, seeds, and other supplies for distribution among the needy of the state. Various Nebraskans toured the eastern states soliciting aid and, despite competition from Kansans on the same mission, secured cash donations amounting to $74,000— twenty-eight percent of which went for expenses and freight charges. In addition, the Relief and Aid Society collected and distributed supplies valued at from $350,000 to $400,000, most of which was carried free of charge by the railroads. General E. O. C. Ord, commanding the Department of the Platte, on his own authority—later legalized by Congress—issued large quantities of damaged and unserviceable army clothing and equipment to destitute settlers, and in the spring of 1875 the federal government, through the Army, distributed rations valued at $41,316.72 to 49,817 persons. The Grange tried to provide relief for its own members, concentrating its activities on the purchase of seed in the spring of 1875. Churches and other groups also made efforts to relieve the destitute.

Grasshoppers continued to menace prairie-plains agriculture through 1876. Various devices and techniques, including a variety of grasshopper traps, were brought forth to control them, and in the fall of 1876 the governors of ten western states met in Omaha to consider the problem. This convention called upon the federal government to take action to eliminate pests and urged the states to offer bounties, modify game laws to prevent the destruction of insect-eating birds, prevent prairie fires, and encourage tree culture—the last as a means of "promoting moisture and harboring birds." The grasshopper problem, however, solved itself, at least partially and temporarily. So, too, did the drouth; and from 1877 through the remainder of the decade the state got more than the mean of 22.84 inches of annual rainfall, enjoying a "wet cycle" which continued through the Eighties. Immigration, which had all but ceased during the grasshopper-drouth years, began again. The production of corn, which had fallen from 7,000,000 bushels in 1873 to 3,500,000 bushels in 1874, jumped to 28,000,000 bushels in 1875, and increased steadily to 62,000,000 in 1879. Wheat, the second crop, had not been so seriously affected by the drouth and grasshoppers. The annual production remained between three and four million bushels through the middle Seventies and then increased markedly to over 13,000,000 bushels in 1878, largely as a result of extending wheat culture into the counties of the southwest.

Through it all, however, the farmer's relative economic position steadily worsened. In the face of increased costs of production and a potentially higher standard of living—given a sufficient cash income—farm prices generally declined during the decade, as the following Nebraska farm prices on December 1 will show:

Year	Wheat	Corn	Oats	Barley	Rye	Potatoes	Tame Hay
1870	.57	.32	.27	.58	.48	.50	5.03
1871	.81	.22	.22	.41	.49	.29	4.28
1872	.69	.16	.14	.35	.35	.25	3.37
1873	.69	.26	.24	.76	.49	.90	4.14
1874	.54	.66	.45	.78	.67	.93	4.27
1875	.56	.17	.19	.39	.45	.17	3.18
1876	.72	.25	.21	.29	.37	.29	3.09
1877	.81	.18	.15	.26	..	.39	3.55
1878	.49	.16	.17	.33	.24	.23	3.28
1879	.84	.21	.23	.37	.41	.36	3.23

This decline in farm prices was reflected in assessed values. While 4,431,390 acres of farm land were assessed at $53,709,829 in 1870, more than 13,000,000 acres were assessed at only $75,000,000 in 1879. In other words, the assessed value of land declined during the decade from $4.79 to $2.86 per acre.

The farmer seemed to be at a disadvantage wherever he turned. High freight rates reduced the price of his products and increased the cost of the farm machinery and other commodities he had to buy. Short of cash, he had to support his purchases with mortgages on his crops or his land. At best, he had to sell his crops immediately after harvest at any price the local speculators were willing to pay. Should his crops fail, he was likely to find himself confronted with a judgment against his land which stood in a fair way to absorb his entire equity. Even in good years, he was fortunate if he could meet his bills and his debts and still retain title to his land.

Some of the farmers made an effort to alleviate their condition through the Patrons of Husbandry, or the Grange, established in 1869 as a social and educational institution and first organized in Nebraska in 1872. The Grange grew rapidly: by the end of 1872 fifty local Granges had been organized; by the early part of 1874 twenty thousand members were reported. The meetings of the Grange soon developed into forums for the discussion of social and economic questions, and it wasn't long before the organization was combining action with discussion. Direct participation in business seemed to promise the greatest benefits, and the Nebraska Grange adopted methods of cooperative buying used by the organization in other states. It even attempted to manufacture farm machinery. A state purchasing agent was appointed, with offices in Lincoln; county Granges formed cooperatives for the purpose of buying and selling farm products and dealing in farm machinery, lumber, and coal; in certain instances, local Granges also established cooperative stores. A Grange Plow Factory was established at Plattsmouth. and a header—widely used before the development of the self-binder —was manufactured at Fremont.

All these enterprises failed. The reasons were many and varied: inadequate resources; mismanagement; an unwillingness on the part of members to give them sustained support—many were perfectly willing to buy from the dealer who was underselling the Grange store simply to drive it out of business; and the agricultural depression which left the farmers unable to buy, even at the low prices and favorable terms offered by the Grange. With the failure of its economic enterprises, the Grange generally went into a decline: after 1875 hardly any local Granges were organized; after 1876 the order declined rapidly in Nebraska.

By 1876 the Grange had achieved one of its major political objectives, and that, too, may have contributed to its decline. That objective was a provision in the new constitution providing for the regulation of railroads, which by the middle Seventies had emerged in the minds of many farmers as the principal oppressor of the farm population.

POLITICAL REFORM—THE CONSTITUTION OF 1875

The scandals culminating in Governor Butler's impeachment[4] left an ugly stain on the opening pages of the new state's political history. It was a penetrating stain, and cast its blot on the record for some time after the Governor had been removed from office. The Governor's irregular methods seemed to permeate all the state's fiscal affairs, and the public buildings at Lincoln stood out as stark monuments to the slipshod way in which he had handled the public's business. All had

[4]See pp. 149–153.

cost more to build than had been appropriated for their construction; all were so poorly built that they began falling down almost as soon as they were occupied. The insane asylum burned to the ground on April 17, 1871, while a legislative committee was recommending repairs to correct its bulging walls. The University building needed a new foundation and extensive repairs on the superstructure within six years after it was opened.

All this, many outstate politicians and editors argued, was due to the venality of what they liked to call "the Lincoln ring," a group whose membership was unidentified, but which included, it was generally assumed, the principal state officials and the leading businessmen of the new capital city. The most radical of the critics contended that the only adequate solution to the problem was the removal of the capital and all state institutions from Lincoln. This naturally retarded the growth of the state's institutions—particularly the University, which in addition to its internal difficulties was under constant fire from a wide variety of groups within the state, especially certain religious groups who looked upon it with horror as a "godless" institution.

Even the most able and conscientious men would have found it difficult to administer the state's affairs under the hastily drawn and inadequate constitution of 1866.[5] Designed to provide as cheap a government as possible, it came close to providing no government at all, and though there was little agreement as to the nature of the reforms needed, almost all groups in the state were certain that the basic law should be overhauled. The politicians argued that the ridiculously low salaries— the Governor, it will be recalled, was limited to $1,000 per year— made it difficult to attract good men for public office; Lincoln interests felt that the capital should be permanently located by a constitutional provision; a substantial and influential group felt that more encouragement should be given railroads and other business projects; a growing number were insistent that constitutional protection be given the taxpayer against exploitation by reckless public officials, both state and local; others wanted to make constitutional provision for woman suffrage, prohibition, and compulsory education.

All these objectives and others besides had representatives in the fifty-two delegates to the constitutional convention who assembled in the jerry-built state capitol on June 13, 1871—less than two weeks

[5]See pp. 123–124.

after Governor Butler had been removed from office. It was soon evident that it would be impossible to secure agreement on many of the issues before the convention. Debate was heated, and many of the issues were decided by a bare majority. Throughout the proceedings, partisan politics reigned triumphant, and valuable time was occupied with such questions as whether the impeached Governor should be given "the privileges of the floor of the convention" (defeated, 28 to 15), and with such matters as an investigation of the management of the insane asylum, an inquiry into the selection of state lands, and an investigation of the expenditures of the state board of agriculture.

After two months of wrangling, the convention adjourned on August 19, having adopted a constitution which in the main followed the Illinois constitution of 1870, a Granger document affirming the right of the legislature to regulate railroads and seriously restricting the rights of local governments to provide financial aid to corporations. The governor's salary was increased to $3,000 per year and other salaries were raised accordingly, with the provision that they could be readjusted after five years. The capital was to "remain at the city of Lincoln" until 1880 and until "otherwise provided by a law designating some other place therefor, which shall be submitted to, and be approved by a majority of the electors voting thereon." Five proposals were submitted to the voters separately, to become a part of the constitution only if specifically approved: (1) a definition of the liability of stockholders in a corporation as twice the amount of stock held; (2) prohibition of county and municipal aid to corporations; (3) compulsory education; (4) a provision requiring the legislature to submit the question of prohibition to the voters; and (5) woman suffrage.

The voters completely rejected the work of the convention. The railroads—already a dominant factor in the state—were absolutely opposed to the regulatory features of the constitution and were able to line up an imposing array of leading politicians of both parties against it. A "sleeper" providing for the taxation of church property valued in excess of $5,000, inserted at the insistence of certain Protestant groups who looked askance at the fine churches being constructed by the Catholics in Omaha and elsewhere, provoked widespread opposition among the state's considerable Catholic population. There was a general fear that the constitution, which raised salaries and created the offices of lieutenant governor and attorney general, would create too

David Butler, First Governor

Phineas W. Hitchcock,
United States Senator

Charles H. Gere,
Founder of the Lincoln *Journal*

Algernon S. Paddock,
United States Senator

Edward Rosewater,
Founder of the Omaha *Bee*

EARLY STATE LEADERS

University Hall, 1871

City Campus Today

THE UNIVERSITY OF NEBRASKA

Freeman Homestead, First in the United States

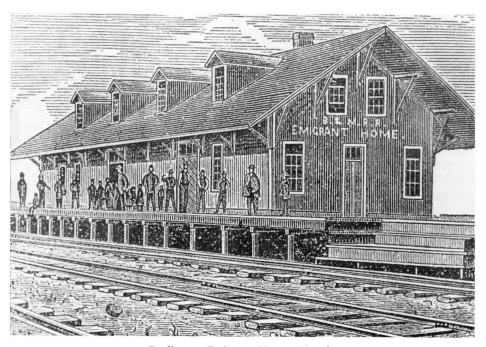

Burlington Emigrant House, Lincoln

OCCUPYING THE LAND

"Uncle Swain Finch Fights Grasshoppers"

"Wire Cutters"

TWO OF THE HOMESTEADER'S PROBLEMS

The Newman Ranch on the Niobrara

Cattle at a Sandhills Lake

THE RANGE CATTLE INDUSTRY

A Dugout on the
South Loup River

"Alone on
the Plains"

Sod House
near Merna

ON THE SOD HOUSE FRONTIER

The Windmill
Was Important

A "Ranch-Style"
Soddie

The Haumont
Sod House
near Broken Bow

ON THE SOD HOUSE FRONTIER

Major Frank North

Captain Luther North

William F. Cody ("Buffalo Bill")

Captain James H. Cook

RANCHERS AND FRONTIERSMEN

expensive a government. At the special election called for the purpose, the constitution was turned down, 8,627 to 7,986. None of the separate proposals fared even this well. The vote is worth recording as a key to public sentiment on the issues of the day:

	For	Against
Liability of Stockholders	7,425	8,580
Prohibition of Aid to Corporations	6,690	9,549
Compulsory Education	6,289	9,958
Submission of Prohibition to Voters	6,071	10,160
Woman Suffrage	3,502	12,496

Rejection of the constitution only intensified the problems facing the new state. When the legislature which had provided for the constitutional convention and removed the Governor adjourned on June 7, 1871, it did so with the provision that it re-convene on January 9, 1872. There was some doubt that the legislature had the authority to re-convene itself in this way, and Acting Governor James undertook to settle the question by declaring the legislature adjourned, *sine die*. A part of the body, however, refused to adjourn, and stayed on, occupying itself with an effort to impeach the Acting Governor. The session ended in confusion when James shut off the coal supply from the legislative chambers. Another act in the serio-comic opera ensued when Isaac Hascall, President of the Senate, took advantage of Governor James' absence from the state on a trip to Washington to re-convene the legislature. The Acting Governor hurried home and issued a counter-proclamation, but some of the members assembled in accordance with Hascall's call, only to find the doors of the legislative chambers barricaded against them. Somehow they managed to get in, but, finding it impossible to transact business, departed.

Meanwhile, government—both state and local—continued to provide evidence that the need for a basic change was great: Robert W. Furnas, whose election as governor in 1872 had put down an incipient "liberal Republican" movement, was involved in a spectacular libel suit against the Omaha *Herald*, which had charged him with accepting a bribe; taxes were delinquent to the point where the state's whole revenue system was imperiled; local governments continued to vote bonds recklessly for railroads—almost four and one-half million dollars of local debt was outstanding in 1874—and many of the bonds were virtually unsalable; the newspapers were full of charges of bribery and sundry corruption levelled against many of the state's leading political figures. All this evidence contributed to the growing demand for a constitutional convention. To it was added a rising demand from the new counties in the west for additional representation in the legislature.

The Republicans acceded to western demands in 1874 by nominating Silas Garber, who three years earlier had helped establish the settlement of Red Cloud—and a proponent of a new constitution—as their candidate for governor. In his inaugural message—nomination by the Republicans was tantamount to election—Governor Garber urged the legislature to act speedily upon the desire of the people as expressed in a ballot on the question that a constitutional convention be called. The legislature provided for the election of delegates, and on May 11, 1875, sixty-nine delegates assembled in the crumbling sandstone capitol to draft a new constitution. They met in an atmosphere of gloom. Hard times were everywhere. As the delegates assembled, the principal item of news was the hatching of grasshoppers across the state.

Economy was the watchword. A resolution requiring the Secretary of State to furnish each delegate with three dollars worth of postage stamps was voted down in haste; in lieu of hiring a chaplain, the convention decided to ask ministers of the various Lincoln churches to open the daily sessions with prayer; a shorthand report of the proceedings was dispensed with as too expensive, with the result that there is no verbatim report of the convention. Another resolution—adopted—directed that the committees use "nothing but pure, unadulterated English" in drafting the various sections of the constitution.

The convention adjourned on June 12, after having adopted a constitution modelled very closely on the Illinois constitution of 1870. Likewise, it closely paralleled the rejected document of 1871. The clause providing for church taxation was dropped, as was the railroad right-of-way restriction. Both had been potent factors in the defeat of the earlier constitution. Other provisions gave the right of appeal to the supreme court in every lawsuit, separated the supreme court and the district courts, enlarged the legislature to eighty-four members in the House and thirty in the Senate with a provision for further enlargement after 1880, enlarged the executive department by the creation of the offices of lieutenant governor and attorney general, provided for increased salaries, added a section on education, provided limitations on county taxes, and limited state debt to $100,000.

The constitution retained the Illinois provision giving the legislature power to regulate the railroads, and this was bitterly opposed by the railroad interests of the state. J. Sterling Morton, for example, called the provision "this red flag of communism." Despite opposition of this sort, however, the people adopted the constitution by the overwhelming margin of 30,332 to 5,474. Two separate propositions, providing for the location of the capital in Lincoln and a preference vote for United States senators, also were approved.

The adoption of the Constitution of 1875 signalled an end to the era of uncertainty in the state's affairs. Fortunately, too, economic conditions improved somewhat in the late Seventies and early Eighties, giving government under the new instrument a fighting chance. The farmers, reasonably satisfied with the constitution's regulatory provisions, seemed content for a time to expand their holdings and vote the Republican ticket. Within a decade, however, they were to find that authorization to regulate railroads was a far cry from the achievement of effective regulation. That, combined with a growing discontent over economic conditions generally, was to develop in the state's agricultural population a spirit of rebellion such as the dark days of the middle Seventies had never seen.

CHAPTER 15

The Range Cattle Industry

WHILE THE GRANGERS settled the valleys and uplands of eastern and central parts of the state, cattlemen occupied the wide expanse of the western areas. Except where grangers and cattlemen came in conflict, the development of the range cattle industry was so far removed from the general agricultural development of the state—in spirit and in deed —as to warrant separate treatment, a treatment further justified, perhaps, by the fact that the cattle industry was to become Nebraska's most important economic activity.

The development of the range cattle industry on the Plains was coincident with the extermination of the bison. So long as these shaggy beasts occupied the Plains, there could be no room for cattle. Moreover, while bison remained plentiful, the Indian had the wherewithal to maintain resistance against white encroachment. With the bison gone, however, the rich grasses of the Plains were available for cattle, and the Indians were forced onto restricted reservations where they could not menace white occupation of the range. The extermination of the bison occurred after the discovery in the early Seventies that their hides could be used in the manufacture of harness, belting, shoes, and other leather goods. To satisfy the demand thus created, commercial hunters went out on the Plains in gangs, armed with high-calibre, long-range rifles, and in a few short years they literally wiped the bison off the face of the earth. Conservative estimates place the kill on the

Plains at more than ten million during the years 1870–1885. Moreover, this was simple, wanton destruction. Whereas the Indians had used virtually all of the animal, the commercial hunters took only the hide, leaving the carcass to rot where it fell. In the late Eighties, a number of men eked out a living by gathering bison bones and hauling them into Kearney, North Platte, and other rail points, whence they were shipped east to be used in the making of phosphates and carbon. Before the commercial hunters got them all, the bison furnished great sport for big-game hunters. A particularly celebrated hunting excursion was that arranged by General Sheridan for the Grand Duke Alexis of Russia south of Fort McPherson in 1872.

Small herds of cattle grew up along the Platte Valley trails before, during, and immediately after the Civil War, as strategically located operators of "road ranches" developed a substantial business out of the exchange of fresh cattle for trail-worn animals; the large-scale, postwar range cattle industry, however, had its origins in Texas. As Professor Edward Everett Dale put it:

Any history of the cattle industry in the West must begin with Texas since that state was the original home of ranching on a large scale in the United States, and from its vast herds were drawn most of the cattle for the first stocking of the central and northern plains.[1]

Texas had been a cattle country almost from the days of its earliest settlement. The long-horned cattle brought in by the Spanish thrived under the climate and range conditions of Texas, and in addition to those in herds, many ran wild. Almost as much as the physical factors, the land system of both Spain and Mexico—involving large grants to individuals and groups—fostered cattle raising. It was easy to raise cattle in Texas; the problem was finding a market for them. This problem was partially solved in the pre-war years by driving them to New Orleans, Galveston, and other Gulf ports, and to northern markets such as Chicago and Cincinnati. The Civil War cut off the established markets and otherwise disrupted the industry. The cattle, however, continued to thrive and at the end of the war thousands of wild cattle roamed the plains of the Lone Star State. At the same time, a brisk demand for beef in the North and in Europe made it possible to get forty or fifty dollars in Chicago for a fat beef that would bring only six or

[1]Edward Everett Dale, *The Range Cattle Industry* (Norman: University of Oklahoma Press, 1930), p. 21.

seven dollars in Texas. The problem was getting the beef to market. Even before the war there had been great opposition to the cattle drives in Missouri and Illinois; after the war that opposition extended to eastern Kansas and Nebraska. The solution was found in driving cattle to shipping points along the westward moving rails of the Kansas Pacific and the Union Pacific—an activity which also resulted in the development of ranches on the northern Plains, much nearer the market areas.

THE LONG DRIVE

Prior to 1870, only a few of the cattle pointed north out of Texas were driven as far as Nebraska—approximately 15,000 out of 260,000 in 1866—and while a few were ferried across the Missouri at Brownville, Nebraska City, and Omaha, most of them were bought by the government to feed the Indians on Nebraska reservations. The Union Pacific did not have adequate shipping facilities and most of the cattle destined for rail shipment stopped at Abilene, Kansas, on the Kansas Pacific. During the winter of 1869–70, however, Union Pacific officials began to interest themselves in the possibility of shipping Texas cattle from some point along their line in Nebraska. Drovers, dissatisfied with both rates and service on the Kansas Pacific, definitely were interested; and when the Union Pacific was able to work out a uniform rate with the Burlington and Rock Island on the haul from Omaha to Chicago, about twenty-five percent less than the rate from Abilene to Chicago, the way was opened for the southern drovers to move into Nebraska.

The next question was the location of the shipping point. Both Schuyler and Columbus pressed hard for it, but Schuyler, at the upper end of the Blue River trail, won the victory—a victory which transformed the sleepy little frontier village into the first of Nebraska's cow towns. Between 40,000 and 50,000 head of Texas cattle were sold at Schuyler during the summer of 1870 and the town's population jumped from less than a hundred to approximately six hundred. Plattsmouth, with its Burlington connection to Chicago, vied with Schuyler for the Texas trade, but while the Missouri River town offered the cowboys more in the way of diversion, the trail into Plattsmouth was not so good as the Blue River trail and probably not more than five thousand longhorns were shipped from there in 1870. By 1871 heavy settlement in the lower Platte Valley prevented easy access to Plattsmouth, and it almost passed out of the picture as a cattle market.

Schuyler's boom, too, was about over, as the Blue Valley filled with settlers who were quick to invoke Nebraska's herd law to keep the drovers out. By 1871 trail's end had shifted westward to Kearney. Two years later it had moved still further west—this time to Ogallala, gateway to the northern Plains and for more than a decade Nebraska's cowboy capital.

Ogallala, established as a way station by the Union Pacific, seemed destined for several years to be little more than a section house and water tank in the vast emptiness of western Nebraska. By 1873, however, Louis Aufdengarten was doing a thriving business at his "Drover's Store," supplying professional hide hunters and a few ranchers with, as his advertisement in the North Platte *Enterprise* put it, "Groceries, Dry Goods, Provisions, Cigars, and Liquors." That same year the Lonergan brothers opened a "men's store," and L. M. Stone, a "hotel." These men and a few others climaxed their work in 1873 by organizing Keith County, moving a small frame house from Brule to serve as the courthouse. As late as the summer of 1874, however, it was reported that the county records were "floating around" in North Platte, and the continued existence of the prematurely organized county seemed most uncertain.

Aufdengarten, the Lonergans, and Stone had faith in their enterprise, however, and in the summer of 1874 that faith seemed well on the way to being justified: the Union Pacific built a cattle pen and loading chute just west of town in an effort to maintain the profitable trade they had enjoyed at Schuyler, Kearney, and other eastern points. Between 60,000 and 75,000 Texas cattle were driven into Ogallala in 1875; by 1876 the number had jumped to over 100,000, where it remained until the middle Eighties. Schuyler and Kearney never became boisterous cow towns, but Ogallala not only lived up to the tradition of the wild and wooly West—it helped make it. As Norbert Mahnken put it, "Gold flowed freely across the tables, liquor across the bar, and occasionally blood across the floor as a smoking gun in the hands of a jealous rival or an angered gambler brought an end to the trail of some unfortunate cowhand on the stained boards of 'Tuck's' Saloon."[2]

The trail into Ogallala was an extension northward from Dodge City, Kansas, of what was known as the Western Trail, which, as settlement

[2]Norbert Mahnken, "Ogallala—Nebraska's Cowboy Capital," *Nebraska History*, XXVII (April–June, 1947), 85.

moved west in Kansas, replaced the old Chisholm Trail running from San
Antonio to Abilene. The Western Trail started at Bandera, Texas,
crossed the Red River at a point known as Doan's Store, then pushed
on to Dodge City, the Santa Fe's boisterous shipping town on the Arkansas River. Some of the longhorns were left there, but most of the
younger animals were driven on to Ogallala. From Dodge City the
trail angled north and west to Buffalo Station, about sixty miles west
of Hays on the Kansas Pacific. The next stop was Ogallala. The last
leg of the journey was the most difficult, principally because of the
lack of water. Streams were few and far between at best, and the drovers
frequently found that many of the smaller streams on which they were
depending had dried up. The last day's drive—some thirty miles from
Stinking Water Creek to the South Platte—was almost the worst of
the whole journey for the trail-weary cowhands.

The "long drive" came to an abrupt end in the middle Eighties as
settlers in northwestern Kansas and southwestern Nebraska invoked
herd laws to keep the cattle out, and as quarantine laws, passed at the
insistence of the northern cattlemen against the spread of Texas fever,
blocked off the longhorns from the South. By the time this happened,
however, a new industry had been built in western Nebraska and eastern Wyoming, an industry that literally had come up the trails from
Texas.

OCCUPYING THE NEBRASKA RANGE

As mentioned above, the first Nebraska cattlemen were the operators
of road ranches along the Platte who dealt in working oxen—men like
James E. Boyd near Kearney, and Jack Morrow near the forks of the
Platte. The early beef cattle industry developed in the lower panhandle
between the North and South Platte, the region between the Platte and
the Republican, the Platte Valley near Fort Kearny (and the islands in
the river itself), and in the valley of the South Loup, now southern
Custer County. These areas all had good pastures; they were protected
from the Indians by Forts Kearny, McPherson, Mitchell, and Laramie,
and by the patrols along the line of the Union Pacific; they were near
the terminals of the Texas trails; and they were accessible to markets
in the region (the Indian agencies) and the Union Pacific.

J. W. Iliff probably ranged cattle in the western Platte Valley from
the early Sixties on. Edward Creighton, builder of the transcontinental

telegraph and Omaha's pioneer millionaire, ranged working oxen on the western Plains as early as 1859, and was in the beef cattle business in a big way in 1867—in that year he drove three thousand head from Schuyler to the western part of the state. Another of the early operators was R. C. Keith of North Platte, who began stock raising in the autumn of 1867 with five American cows, greatly expanding his herd in 1869 with the purchase of one thousand Texas cows. Coe, Carter and Bratt, who had run cattle near Cheyenne in 1868, brought twenty-five hundred Texas cattle to the Platte Valley near Fort Kearny in 1869. There were many others: Texans who had driven cattle up the trail; freighters who turned to the cattle business when competition from the Union Pacific ruined their business; eastern farmers who turned to ranching when they found that grazing was more profitable than general farming; scouts, hunters, and army men; easterners and Europeans, out for a fling and a quick killing. Their names are woven securely into the fabric of the old West—names like John Bratt, William F. Cody (Buffalo Bill), Captain James H. Cook, the Newman brothers, Frank and Luther North, and Colonel James H. Pratt.

As the initial range areas filled up, the industry spread elsewhere, impinging in places upon the settled part of the state. When settlement, which had pushed up the Republican Valley into Furnas, Red Willow and Hitchcock counties, receded somewhat during the drouth and grasshopper years of the middle Seventies, the cattlemen moved in, establishing ranches in parts of the area and extending westward into Dundy County. To the north, cattlemen established themselves on the upper stretches of the Elkhorn, particularly in Holt County.

For several years the cattlemen avoided the Sandhills like the plague. To be sure, they had occupied the Loup valleys in the eastern part of the hills in the early Seventies, and from North Platte west, John Bratt, the Keystone Cattle Company, and the Bosler brothers had penetrated the region from the south. The interior, however, remained little known and greatly feared until 1879. In the spring of that year, Frank North decided to take a herd straight through the hills from the roundup on Blue Creek to his home ranch on the Dismal. After going about thirty-five miles through supposedly dry country, he came upon a lake, around which were about seven hundred head of cattle in much better shape than those he had gathered on the roundup. At about the same time, the Newman brothers had a similar experience. A blizzard in

March had driven about six thousand head past their line-riders into the hills; so the manager decided to make a desperate attempt to save some of them. When the snow melted in April he sent a roundup into the hills, and after working five weeks the crew brought out about eight thousand head of Newman cattle and an additional thousand head of unbranded cattle, descendants of animals that had drifted into the hills in previous years. If these experiences were not enough to convince cattlemen that they were overlooking the best range in the West, the winter of 1880–81 provided conclusive proof. During the heavy storms of that season, thousands of cattle died in the Platte Valley, but the Cody-North ranch lost only a few on its range back in the Sandhills.

In the middle Eighties the Sandhills developed into an important segment of the cattle country—not by the big organizations, which generally remained out of the hills, but by small operators who came in with only a few cattle and grew up with the country: men like Thomas Lynch, "Dad" Abbott and his son Arthur J., the Haney brothers, J. M. Gentry, James Forbes, J. H. Minor, Sidney Manning, and R. M. "Bud" Moran. Grant County was organized in 1887, less to serve the needs of a growing population than to meet the demands of cattle owners for local law enforcement. Originally, the only accessible market was provided by the Indian agencies in northwest Nebraska and southwest Dakota, but the extension of the Burlington through the area in 1887–88 opened up new markets to the east.

Meanwhile, stories of the easy money to be made in the range cattle business circulated widely in the East and in Europe—exciting stories which described the possibility of parlaying an investment of $5,000 into a net gain of $40,000–$50,000 in four years. General James S. Brisbin's *The Beef Bonanza; or, How to Get Rich on the Plains* (Philadelphia: J. B. Lippincott & Company, 1881) set forth facts, figures, and directions whereby the neophyte could quadruple his investment in a few years and all the while make an annual return of as much as twenty-five percent. Indicative of the book's direction are such chapter headings as: "Estimated Fortunes," "Millions in Beef," "The Money to be Made," "Great Land and Great Owners." The stories of great profits combined with tales of high adventure provided an irresistible lure, and millions of dollars were poured onto the Plains by easterners and Europeans who sought to set themselves up as cattle barons. It was inevitable, perhaps, that under the circumstances the range cattle industry should head for an early collapse. Unsound financing was combined with the even more serious overstocking of the range, to create a precarious situation unable to withstand even the slightest adversity —and when adversity came, it was by no means slight. The great blizzards which roared across the Plains during the winters of 1885–86 and 1886–87 literally wiped out many of the newly established herds, and with them the fortunes of their owners. Again, the Sandhills were not hit quite so severely as the rest of the country. Moreover, most of the ranchers in the hills were seasoned westerners who understood the limitations of both their range and their money. The Sandhills provided the basis for the revival of the cattle industry in the early Nineties —a revival that was to continue relatively unchecked for more than half a century.

But wherever it revived, the cattle industry was not the old range industry. Blooded stock—Shorthorns, Herefords, and Angus—replaced the unsatisfactory Texas longhorn. Fenced land replaced the open range. Supplemental feed was added to grass, to produce more and better beef and to tide herds over the hard winters. Haying became as much a part of the cowboy's regular activity as riding the range, and the great flats interspersed among the hills came to be dotted with stacks of wild hay.

COWBOY AND CATTLEMAN

Although almost every farmer raised a few cattle, the cattle industry, in the strictest sense, generally was carried on by large-scale operators. By 1900, for example, the Sandhills, which had been initially occupied by small, one-man ranches, had come to be dominated by large organizations. Some big companies—such as the Spade, 101, and UBI (British)—had come in; many of the early settlers had developed into large-scale cattlemen: the Haney brothers, Abbott, Forbes, Lynch, and Yeast, to name but a few. By the 1930's, Sandhills ranches comprised as many as sixty thousand acres; a "medium-large" ranch included from ten to twenty thousand acres, with herds running from twelve to fifteen hundred head. Many who had taken homesteads under the Kinkaid Act[3] had sold out to the cattlemen.

Initially, the ranchers simply ran their cattle on the public domain, for which privilege they paid neither taxes nor rent. This range, of

[3]See pp. 258–260.

course, was theoretically "open"; but the cattlemen, by mutual agreement and through friendly local governments and the influence of their associations, generally were able to control the range as they saw fit, keeping out any who tried to encroach upon it. Particularly obnoxious were the "nesters" who ventured into the range country to take quarter-section homesteads, build their little soddies, and fence their land, thus breaking up the open range. Wire-cutters became standard equipment for the cowboys, and when harassment would not drive the homesteaders away, some of the ranchers resorted to stronger methods, including, on occasion, outright murder.[4]

Except in the Sandhills, however, the badlands of the northwest, and certain small areas elsewhere, the homesteaders by persistence and sheer force of numbers gained the ascendancy. They extended from county to county the provisions of the herd law, which was adopted in 1871 to make it mandatory to restrain cattle from wandering at will over the prairie, but with the provision that it could be suspended locally by action of county officials. Frontier County provides a good example. The county was organized by cattlemen in 1872 for the express purpose of making a stock country out of the region south of the Platte and north of the Republican. The county seat was given the appropriate name "Stockville." A decade later, however, A. S. Shelley, one of the county's cattleman founders, could write in his diary: "Report that Monty [Clifford] and Jack [Lynch] went among the Grangers on the creek and said that they were satisfied that free Range was lost anyhow and that they would give them support on the Herd law if they would give them their support for Judge and Sheriff and other county offices."

Further strengthening the homesteader's hand was federal legislation, adopted in 1885, making it illegal to enclose the public domain. For a number of years, cattlemen in western Nebraska and elsewhere had fenced in large tracts of the public land as a means of keeping homesteaders from occupying it. The Brighton ranch in Keith County, for example, had fenced in 125,000 acres; again, when the Coad brothers sold their ranch in 1883, they listed four enclosed pastures, the largest of which embraced 143,000 acres. The government made no serious

[4]Perhaps the most notorious incident in the homesteader-cattlemen conflict in Nebraska was the hanging and subsequent burning of Luther Mitchell and Ami Ketchum, Custer County homesteaders, in 1878 by a gang led by I. P. Olive, one of the wealthiest ranchers in the state. (See S. D. Butcher, *Pioneer History of Custer County* [Broken Bow, Nebraska, 1901], pp. 43–62.)

effort to enforce the law against illegal fencing until the administration of Theodore Roosevelt, and even Roosevelt had difficulty. As an "example" case, he ordered action against two of the largest offenders in the country, Bartlett Richards and William G. Comstock, president and vice-president of the Nebraska Land and Feeding Company, which operated the Spade, Bar C, and Overton ranches, comprising more than 500,000 acres in Cherry, Sheridan, and Box Butte counties. In November, 1905, they pleaded guilty before Federal Judge Munger in Omaha to the charge of having illegally fenced 212,000 acres of government land, but asked for leniency inasmuch as they were removing the fences. They got leniency: Judge Munger fined them each $300 and costs and sentenced them to six hours in the custody of the United States marshal; the marshal did not keep them in his own custody but turned them over to their counsel who took them to the Omaha Club to spend the time. Roosevelt was furious. He removed the district attorney and the United States marshal and expressed regret that he did not have the power to remove Judge Munger. Later, the two men were convicted of conspiring to secure title to public land through fraudulent entries, and both were sent to jail. They were allowed the choice of any Nebraska jail, and chose the Adams County jail at Hastings, where special cells had been fixed up for their comfort!

Much of the range country, of course, simply was not suited to general farming, and by World War I many of the homesteaders who had moved in under governmental protection had been driven out by natural forces, their homesteads for the most part being purchased by the large ranchers.

Other means of controlling the range cattle industry were provided by a system of brand inspection and by the roundup. At first, the cattlemen's associations registered and inspected the brands; in 1877 it was made a function of state government, and it continues to be a governmental function. The Nebraska Brand Committee, created by the legislature in 1941, consists of the Secretary of State as chairman, and four active cattlemen as members. In the days of the open range, the roundup was essential to the control of the industry. Carefully supervised by the cattlemen's associations, a spring roundup was held for the purpose of branding calves, and a fall roundup for gathering cattle for shipment to market. The roundup was a great social institution as well as an economic necessity, bringing the cowboys together and giving them opportunities to vie with one another in feats of derring-do. As the open range disappeared, so did the roundup, and by World War I it was a thing of the past.

Though today cowboy and cattleman still hold sway over the Sandhills and much of the rest of western Nebraska, it is on an entirely different basis than in the days of the old range industry. The ranches still maintain horses, but many of their former functions have been taken over by the truck, the jeep, and the light plane. The old West lingers on only in the rodeo, dress, and memory.

CHAPTER 16

The Eighties—Progress and Prosperity

THE EIGHTIES were good years in Nebraska, years of progress and prosperity unparalleled in the early history of the state. Rain, the *sine qua non* of prosperity in Nebraska, fell in relative abundance: the average annual rainfall for the whole state during the decade was 24.18 inches, compared with the mean of 22.84 inches; for the eastern section, 28.83 inches, compared with a mean of 27.74 inches; and for the central portion, 25.00 inches, compared with a mean of 22.28 inches. Rainfall seemed particularly abundant in the central section where most of the new lands were being opened—the theory that "rainfall follows the plow" appeared to be demonstrating its validity.

Under the impetus of favorable conditions and aggressive promotion,[1] settlers poured in by the thousands, increasing the state's population from 452,402 in 1880 to 1,058,910 in 1890.[2] Twenty-six counties were organized, extending county government to virtually all parts of

[1]See pp. 165–168.

[2]There has been a widespread belief that the census returns for 1890 were heavily padded in certain Nebraska cities. Though apparently there was some padding, it does not appear to have been so heavy as generally believed. See Edgar Z. Palmer, "The Correctness of the 1890 Census of Population for Nebraska Cities," *Nebraska History*, XXXII (December, 1951), 259–267

the state and leaving only Boyd, Thurston, Garden, and Arthur as yet unorganized.[3] Both reflecting and making possible the growth of settlement was the great increase in railroad mileage: from 1,868.40 in 1880 to 5,144.48 in 1890. A major factor in that increase was the extension of the Burlington through the Republican Valley and the Sandhills.

In summarizing the progress of the decade, Addison E. Sheldon wrote:

In it came the largest addition to our population; the greatest increase in our production; the furthest extension of railway mileage; the greatest change in the physical aspects of our state. More land was taken by settlers in this period, more livestock added, larger increase in crops of all kinds, more new towns were founded, more postoffices were established, more schools were created, more churches built, more homes constructed than in any other decade of Nebraska history.[4]

Agricultural Development

Farming, which had been established as *the* way of life during the Seventies, continued to dominate the state's economic life, and Nebraska went far toward making the transition from an unoccupied frontier to a major food producing area. A total of 19,585,382 acres of the public land was taken during the decade, leaving only approximately 11,000,-000 acres still unclaimed, virtually all in the Sandhills. The Burlington sold 937,100 acres of its land, most of it in the first four years of the decade; and the Union Pacific, 6,913,539 acres, including over four million in 1884. Much of this activity was purely speculative, but still the total number of farms increased from 63,389 in 1880 to 113,608 in 1890; the improved acreage from 5,504,702 to 15,247,705; the valuation from $147,193,723 to $511,799,810. Agricultural settlement, except in the Republican Valley, had not extended much west of Grand Island in 1880, and there was still considerable land available east of that point; by 1890 agricultural settlement had pushed clear across the state, and—though the pioneer settlers were not yet aware of it—virtually all of the free arable land had been occupied.

[3]Boyd County was organized in 1891 from land added to the state in an adjustment of the South Dakota boundary; Thurston County in 1892 in an area formerly occupied by the Omaha Indian Reservation.

[4]Sheldon, *Nebraska: The Land and the People,* I, 661–662.

While population doubled during the decade, food production tripled, as can be seen from the following statistics for production of principal crops in 1879 and 1889 in the census reports of 1880 and 1890:

Crop	1879	1889
Corn	65,450,135 bu.	215,895,996 bu.
Wheat	13,037,116 bu.	10,571,059 bu.
Oats	6,555,875 bu.	43,843,640 bu.
Barley	1,744,686 bu.	1,822,111 bu.
Rye	424,348 bu.	1,085,083 bu.
Potatoes	2,164,521 bu.	9,181,616 bu.
Hay	786,722 tons	3,115,398 tons

The same trend is reflected in the number of livestock on farms:

	1879	1889
Cattle	758,550	2,142,597
Horses	204,864	626,789
Mules	19,999	46,512
Swine	1,241,724	3,815,647
Sheep	199,453	209,243

As will be observed from the foregoing, corn, the first crop planted by the pioneers, continued to be the state's most important crop, and from 1879 to 1889 Nebraska jumped from eighth to fourth place among the corn states of the union, producing in the latter year 10.2 percent of the nation's entire crop. A number of factors account for the persistent supremacy of corn: (1) many of the earlier settlers were from the corn producing states of the East and naturally thought of farming in terms of corn; (2) from the very beginning corn yielded well—the early settlers, it must be remembered, occupied that part of the state where temperature, rainfall, and other characteristics were well suited to the production of corn; and (3) there were no satisfactory alternative crops from which to choose—spring wheat was generally unsatisfactory, winter wheat was still in the experimental stage, the feeding value of barley was little appreciated, oats were considered primarily as horse feed and not as a cash crop

Corn maintained its ascendancy despite the fact that its relative purchasing power was lower than wheat, oats, or barley. The production factors mentioned above account in part for this; also important was the belief that corn fed to livestock would yield a good return. It was noted that a bushel of corn would make ten to twelve pounds of pig, and it became an empiric rule that hogs at $5.00 a hundred could be grown profitably on fifty-cent corn. The price ratio was almost always satisfactory. Agricultural journals and farm spokesmen constantly talked about the "corn-hog" ratio and the importance of hogs that could be marketed at two hundred pounds at six to eight months—"mortgage lifters," they were called. In his last report as president of the State Board of Agriculture, in 1876, J. Sterling Morton wrote:

> We cannot raise too much corn. No matter what corn may be worth as corn in the market. It may be worth five cents or nothing at all. But transmuted to beef, pork, or mutton, it will always pay the husbandman a handsome and satisfactory return. This should be, and must be, if it will grow prosperous, a stock-feeding state. Wheat growing for exportation will not pay. It wears out the soil, the men who till it, and the reputation of the State; the first by taking away part of its productive power each year; the second by hard work and fretting over poor compensation; and the last by the pronounced and unyielding poverty of its citizens.

Wheat found little favor among Nebraska farmers until about the turn of the century. The soil and climate of Nebraska seemed to be unsuitable for spring wheat and for such varieties of winter wheat as most of the farmers were willing to plant. The Mennonites who came to the south-central part of the state in the Seventies and Eighties got good yields from the Turkey Red winter wheat they brought with them from Russia, but most farmers were slow to adopt it. Moreover, the millers looked with disfavor upon the hard winter wheat because their equipment was designed for the processing of soft spring wheat. With the development of new milling processes, and an appreciation of the possibilities of Turkey Red and other hard winter varieties developed by the College of Agriculture, and a realization—prompted in part by declining livestock prices and corn yields in the Nineties—that greater crop diversification was needed, wheat came into its own in the early years of the twentieth century as a strong second crop. By 1899 Morton, who had severely criticized wheat two decades earlier, was writing of winter wheat:

> The success which has come to the farmers, within the last five years of its cultivation, leaves no room for speculation upon the problems of wheat culture on these vast and rich areas. The fact arms our people for a new advancement and the advantage of diversifying production as a measure of both profit and safety, whose probable benefits it would be impossible to estimate.[5]

[5] *The Conservative*, January 19, 1899.

The Eighties saw Nebraska farmers taking advantage of the general improvement in farm machinery that had been occurring in the United States since the Civil War. Horses replaced oxen as a motive power, and in the Eighties the sulky plow was introduced. Spike-toothed harrows began to come into the state in the late Seventies and early Eighties; the disc harrow was not in general use in Nebraska until after 1900. There were improvements in planting, too: the end-gate seeder replaced the sowing sack, to be replaced, in turn, by the force-feed drill; for corn, walking one-row markers and single-row planters were introduced in the late Seventies, replacing the hand planter and the crude homemade marker, and in the late Eighties the two-row marker became available. Contributing greatly to the expansion of corn production was the cultivator: first there was the one-horse, two-shovel cultivator which could cover only one side of the row at a time; by the late Seventies, however, the shovels were so arranged that the row could be straddled. Although some of the most prosperous farmers used riding cultivators as early as 1880, this convenience was not generally adopted until after 1900. Indeed, many of the older farmers looked askance at the riding cultivator. Some of them felt that it made a man soft to use one and that sitting down to work was an evidence of laziness.

Reapers were used in Nebraska in territorial times, but they only cut the grain and laid it on a platform from which it had to be raked by hand. Later a self-rake was added, but still the grain had to be picked up from the ground and tied into bundles by hand. Twine binders came into use in Nebraska in the early Eighties. Threshers began to appear in the state in the early Seventies. The first ones simply knocked the grain from the straw but did not separate. Later, separators and a winnowing device which separated the grain from the chaff were developed. The early separators were horse-powered, with the most common type being the sweep power drawn by five teams of horses. Threshing was done from a stack or from racks, although the early machines had to be hand-fed, one bundle at a time. Threshing under these conditions was hard work at best. To the joy of the hired hands and the discomfiture of the owners, however, the routine was interrupted by frequent breakdowns. By the middle Eighties steam began to replace horses as the motive power for threshing. An even greater improvement was the development of the traction engine which could move the separator from place to place as well as power its operations.

Most of the corn in the state was harvested from standing stalks in the field—and by hand. Nebraska's pioneer farmers did have a husking peg—a small, round piece of hard wood sharpened at one end, some six inches in length, held in the hollow of the right hand and kept in place by a loop of buckskin or soft leather—but husking corn remained an unpleasant and seemingly never-ending task in the late fall and winter months.

Throughout the period, Nebraska's leading agriculturalists continued their program of popular education. As earlier, they placed great stress upon the importance of tree culture, both fruit and forest, and in 1885 J. Sterling Morton's birthday, April 22, was designated Arbor Day and made a legal holiday. To be so honored while in the prime of life— and by a legislature composed largely of his political opponents—was an indication of the unusual esteem in which the people of Nebraska held the founder of Arbor Day. The University's College of Agriculture was opened in 1882, but much of the early popular education in farming was carried on by the State Board of Agriculture and its affiliated organizations, particularly the State Horticultural Society. In 1884 Dr. Charles E. Bessey arrived from Iowa State College to begin his long and distinguished career as professor of botany at the University of Nebraska. Immediately after his arrival he began a state-wide investigation of plant life, instituting a program of "scientific" and "popular" experiments. In 1886, the Board of Regents authorized the establishment of the Experiment Station, appointing Dr. Frank S. Billings as its director. Dr. Billings was expected to spend most of his time trying to devise a remedy for hog cholera.

THE URBAN BOOM

Measured in terms of product value, Nebraska's manufactures increased from $12,627,336 in 1880 to $93,037,794 in 1890. This seven-fold increase is reflected in the following statistics:

	1880	1890
Establishments	1,403	3,014
Capital	$4,881,150	$37,569,508
Employees	4,793	23,876
Wages	$1,742,311	$12,984,571
Materials	$8,208,478	$67,334,532

These figures by no means indicate that Nebraska was developing into an industrial commonwealth, but they do help illustrate the general growth of the decade. Most of the industry was concentrated in Omaha, which already was beginning to assume a metropolitan aspect sufficient to set it off from the rest of the state.

Pacing Omaha's industrial development was the meat-packing industry—and, indeed, meat products counted for more than one-fourth of the state's entire manufactured products in 1890. Omaha had had commercial stockyards since 1867 and a number of small packing houses since 1871, the most important of which was that of James E. Boyd, organized in 1872; but the modern large-scale packing industry dates from the establishment of the Union Stock Yards Company in 1884. At first, skeptics were inclined to doubt that the Omaha yards could ever become more than transit and feeding places for stock enroute to Chicago; the railroads, preferring the longer haul, discouraged the packing industry in Omaha. Yet Omaha's location in the center of the corn belt and its direct communication with the great grazing regions of the West, and the energy with which John A. McShane, president of the Stock Yards Company, set out to develop a packing industry, carried the day. Significant, too, was the success which attended the shipment of dressed beef in refrigerator cars.

The first big packer to locate in Omaha was George P. Hammond of Detroit, who opened a plant near the yards on May 19, 1885. It was a great day for Omaha, and many of the city's leading citizens rode out in their carriages to see McShane kill the first steer and hog. In 1886 the Anglo-American Provision Company began operations in a plant built by the Stock Yards Company, further encouraged by five years free run of the yards, a $200,000 subsidy, and a personal gift from McShane of $25,000 worth of stock in the Omaha Land Company. That same year, Sir Thomas Lipton made a brief foray into the Omaha packing business but departed when he found that western farmers could not supply hogs from which he could make English bacon. The Armour-Cudahy Packing Company bought Lipton out, and in 1890 the Cudahys bought the Armour interests. Rounding out the list of big packers who moved into Omaha in the Eighties was Swift and Company, which opened an Omaha plant in 1888 after the Stock Yards Company had given it $100,000 in stock, $100,000 in cash, and eleven acres of land. Armour did not re-enter the Omaha field until 1898.

Accompanying the growing packing industry was the revitalization of some of the city's older industries and the organization of a variety of new ones. The old Omaha and Grant Smelting Company, organized in 1870, consolidated with a Denver company in 1882 and increased its business manyfold. By 1892 it was employing a thousand men, and its products were valued at more than $21,000,000 annually. It was drawing ore from as far away as Canada and Mexico and was reputed to be the largest plant of its kind in the world. The Carter White Lead Works, using the pig lead of the Omaha smelter, increased its capital five hundred percent from 1880 to 1889; a linseed oil company reached an annual production valued at a million and a half dollars, and a pioneer soap factory expanded its operations ten-fold during the decade. There were many new establishments: brickyards, clothing factories, food processing plants, breweries, and distilleries.

In short, Omaha was booming. Its population of 30,000 in 1880 increased to 61,000 in 1885, and then in the next three years doubled again. Real-estate additions were platted for miles on all sides of the city. A 614-acre farm which once sold for $2.50 per acre brought $1,000 per acre. The whole populace—reeling under the heady influence of new industry, highly publicized visits of Eastern capitalists, and a growing population—seemed convinced that the dirt of Omaha's streets had a peculiar and magnetic charm.

Omaha was not alone. Lincoln, too, enjoyed a boom during the Eighties. As an ebullient contemporary writer put it: "Day by day it has grown and thriven, adding some new industry or social element, until the winter of 1886–1887, when like a mountain stream, bounding free from its frozen embrace, and leaping with mad delight to meet the warm sunshine, has this capital city sprung into national fame and great prosperity."[6] In 1885 its population stood at 20,000; two years later it had doubled, and enthusiastic residents prophesied a population of 100,000 by 1890. New additions were laid out; the city began to assume a metropolitan air, with an electric light plant, a water system, street railways, and a few blocks of paved streets. Its citizens, however, still used the University campus as a pasture for their livestock.

The boom spread to the smaller cities. Beatrice, envisioning itself as a city of fifty thousand, extended its city limits and promoted a street railway to carry residents into town from the new subdivisions. In Nor-

[6] *Western Resources*, February, 1887, p. 36.

folk, the Elkhorn Valley Investment Company employed all the methods of professional boomers—parades, celebrations, conventions, and advertisements—to attract new industry and new population. Kearney, under the aegis of H. D. Watson, founder of the famed Watson ranch, enjoyed perhaps the most spectacular excitement of any of the smaller cities. Hastings, trying hard to outdo Grand Island, manufactured a short-lived but exciting boom. Even the small towns, aspiring to have a canning factory, a flour mill, and a creamery, were affected with the spirit of boom.

Indeed, that spirit was highly reminiscent of the speculative spirit of the middle Fifties. Progress was in the air. The good crops, the railroads, the growing population all suggested great things. Any town could become a commercial center or a great railway metropolis, or both. A score of villages coveted the state capital, and not a few believed that in time the greatness of the new West would necessitate the abandonment of Washington for a national headquarters on the Plains. Raw villages indulged in rosy dreams of greatness, and gas lights twinkled where the coyotes should have been left undisturbed.

Everywhere the dreams of greatness were implemented with borrowed money: counties and towns issued bonds to assist railroads and other enterprises; corporations issued stock; individuals assumed mortgages. And the loans were by no means wrung from reluctant hands. There was a great demand in the East for western mortgages and many companies sent out solicitors, paying large commissions on loans placed. As the manager of one large investment company, which ultimately failed with liabilities of over $10,000,000, testified: "It is a fact that during many months of 1886 and 1887, we were unable to get enough mortgages for the people of the East, who wished to invest in that kind of security. My desk was piled high every morning with hundreds of letters, each enclosing a draft, and asking me to send a farm mortgage from Nebraska."[7]

The fever was not confined to Nebraska, but spread all through the West. A contemporary observer wrote:

During the years from 1880 to 1887, and in some cases 1890, the date of the climax, varying in different sections, there developed in Minnesota, the Dakotas, Nebraska, Kansas, Texas, in all the states and territories farther

[7]C. M. Harger, "New Era in the Middle West," *New Harpers Magazine*, XCVII (July, 1898), 276–277.

West, and in some parts of Iowa, Wisconsin, and Missouri, a fever of speculation in real estate, which affected the whole population, destroyed all true
sense of value, created an enormous volume of fictitious wealth, infected
with its poison all the veins and arteries of business, and swelled the cities
to abnormal proportions.[8]

When the bubble burst in the late Eighties its repercussions were
felt all over the country. Money lenders took over such property as had
secured their mortgages, but their hope of profit was gone. Farmers
were forced to take out chattel mortgages—if indeed they could get
mortgages at all—to protect their land. Cities everywhere exhibited
crumbling derelicts which stood out as stark monuments to their speculative spree. There had been prosperity—but whose prosperity?[9]

LIFE ON THE SOD HOUSE FRONTIER

While city dwellers were beginning to enjoy "modern conveniences,"
and prosperous farmers in the eastern counties constructed comfortable
frame houses in pleasant groves, most of the newer settlers, occupying
the central and western portions of the state, eked out a precarious
existence under the most primitive conditions. Much of their difficulty
in day-to-day living stemmed from the shortage of those two basic commodities, wood and water. The shortcomings of the environment in
these two respects permeated all of life, and efforts to overcome them
provided in many respects a new frontier experience for the westward-
moving people of the United States as they modified their ways of living to meet the demands of the new country.

There was a basic change in housing. Pioneers in the wooded regions
found it a simple matter to get together enough logs for a rude cabin
or even quite a comfortable dwelling. On the Plains, however, it took
great ingenuity or considerable expense to gather enough timbers for
the basic supports. The walls were made of sod—or "Nebraska marble"
as the early settlers liked to call it—and the sod house became the enduring symbol of the new frontier. Sod houses varied from dugouts
that were little more than caves to rather pretentious, two-story affairs,
although the average sod house was a simple one-room, frame-supported
structure. The most prosperous pioneers shingled their roofs or cov-

[8]H. J. Fletcher, "Western Real Estate Booms, and After" *Atlantic Monthly,* LXXXI
(May, 1898), 689–704.

[9]See pp. 207–219.

ered them with tar paper, but most sod houses were roofed with earth or sod. The hard-packed earth usually served as the floor. Occasionally the inside walls were whitewashed or covered with old newspapers, and a cloth was stretched across the top to provide a ceiling. Although far from an ideal place in which to live—the problem of keeping it clean was particularly burdensome—the sod house was fairly cool in summer and warm in winter. Indeed, in these respects it frequently was more satisfactory than the poorly insulated frame house which replaced it as soon as the settler could afford to make the transition.

Another problem posed by the shortage of wood was that of providing fuel, for cooking and for heating during the severe winters. Buffalo chips and later cow chips provided an easy answer, albeit a somewhat unsavory one, and there was a constant search for an adequate substitute for wood. Coal was available in the railroad towns, but few if any of the homesteaders could afford it. The wild prairie hay, seemingly the only abundant commodity, had some possibilities, and hayburning stoves were developed to facilitate its use. Hay, however, was far from satisfactory: it burned too rapidly to provide a steady fire; and the great quantities required to keep a stove going for a day posed something of a fire hazard if kept in the house. Corn cobs and corn stalks were used, and at times the price of corn was so low that throwing the ears into the fire seemed the best use to make of them. There was considerable interest in sunflowers as a wood substitute. One advocate argued that it was possible to grow enough sunflowers on an acre to provide sufficient fuel to cook for an ordinary family for a year, and that two acres would produce enough sunflower stalks to furnish any family with all of its fuel requirements for a year, "if provided with a tight house."

Likewise, the shortage of wood made fencing difficult. The rail fence of the Eastern pioneer was, of course, out of the question. Osage orange hedges were found to be a fairly satisfactory substitute in the eastern counties, but they would not grow in the central and western portions of the state. A sod fence was reasonably satisfactory for a small yard or corral, but it was unsightly and difficult to construct. The only satisfactory answer was barbed wire—and barbed wire, developed in the 1870's, was an important technological factor in the occupation of the Plains.

The problem of procuring water for domestic use and stock was in many respects more acute than that of securing wood for fuel and construction. Fuel, save for cooking, was not needed during the summer, but water was a desperate daily necessity the year around. Until a homesteader could sink a well, he had to haul water from the nearest source of supply—frequently several miles away. In some favored localities an adequate supply could be found at depths of from twenty to forty feet, but on the high plains, away from the streams, it was necessary to dig from three hundred to six hundred feet to reach water. This was frequently prohibitively expensive; so the homesteader managed to get along on water hauled in barrels and the little he could catch during the infrequent rains. Well digging was expensive because it was dangerous and laborious; and well diggers occasionally became noted characters on the Plains.[10]

Combined with these difficulties were climatic extremes which taxed the endurance of even the most resolute—hot, dry winds in summer and icy blasts in winter. The exposed soddies were particularly vulnerable to the blizzards that roared across the barren plains with unrelenting fury. The great blizzard of January 12, 1888, which took a heavy toll of both animal and human life in all the northern Plains states, is still commemorated as a major catastrophe.

Above all, perhaps—particularly for the women—was the loneliness. All too often, the pioneer housewife on the sod house frontier could see nothing at all between her little soddy and the horizon—not another human habitation, not even a tree. Little wonder that she grasped eagerly at any opportunity for social intercourse—church, working bees, and all-day visits. If life was difficult for the men who pioneered the Plains, it was almost unbearable for the women.

[10]See Addison E. Sheldon, "A Hero of the Nebraska Frontier," *Nebraska History and Record of Pioneer Days,* I (February, 1918), 5.

CHAPTER 17

The Eighties—Whose Prosperity?

BEFORE THE DECADE was out, the speculative prosperity of the middle Eighties had collapsed, leaving in its wake a trail of weed-grown additions, empty buildings, and foreclosed farms. Even during the height of the boom it was apparent that one group—the farmers—was not sharing in the general prosperity. To be sure, land was available, money was easy, and crops were plentiful—but prices remained low, and in general the decline begun in the Seventies continued throughout the Eighties and developed into a sharp downward spiral in the late years of the decade. These price figures tell the story:

Year	Wheat	Corn	Oats	Barley	Rye	Potatoes	Tame Hay
1880	.75	.25	.26	.42	.57	.61	3.61
1881	.97	.39	.37	.55	.71	.98	4.50
1882	.67	.33	.25	.42	.40	.33	3.25
1883	.70	.24	.20	.37	.35	.30	3.50
1884	.42	.18	.19	.33	.32	.29	3.48
1885	.57	.19	.19	.33	.33	.36	3.51
1886	.47	.20	.19	.31	.32	.40	3.75
1887	.53	.30	.21	.37	.35	.58	4.23
1888	.83	.22	.19	.52	.48	.36	3.75
1889	.52	.17	.15	.30	.25	.20	3.10

Prices such as these could hardly support an expanding agriculture financed at high rates of interest. For a time the farmers, busy with breaking new sod and encouraged by increasing production, failed to voice any effective organized protest against their worsening economic position; but by the end of the decade they were fully aroused and prepared to set the prairies afire with a far-reaching political revolt.

The Politics of Prosperity

As in most northern states, the Republicans had dominated politics in Nebraska since the Civil War. The stigma of being the party of rebellion was too much for the Democrats to overcome among an electorate dominated by Union veterans who consistently heeded the admonition of Republican orators to vote as they had shot. Moreover, among Nebraskans the Republicans could point with pride to substantial national achievements of great local significance: the Republicans had enacted the free homestead law after Democratic administrations had consistently opposed it; Republicans had made possible the Pacific railway and other railroads which made the land accessible to homesteaders and opened the way for settlement of the state.

The people indeed seemed ready to follow the advice of Governor Saunders to "obey the injunction of the sacred writer by rendering 'honor to those to whom honor is due,'" and the Democrats could hardly have prevailed even if they had been united. Moreover, the Democratic party was far from united: it was rent by a violent personal feud between J. Sterling Morton and Dr. George L. Miller, two of its most prominent leaders;[1] it was torn by division between those who wanted to combine with the Greenbackers, Anti-Monopolists, and other radicals, and those who insisted that the salvation of the country lay only in getting back to the fundamental principles of Jefferson and Jackson. Under these circumstances, the Republicans were able to stay in power even during the difficulties surrounding the Butler scandals and the failure of the Constitution of 1871; and with the adoption of a new constitution in 1875, their continued success seemed assured. They regularly elected the governor and other state officers, most of the congressmen, and large majorities in the legislature who in turn regularly sent Republicans to the United States Senate.

For governor, the Republicans usually chose bright young men with an obvious future or faithful old wheel horses who deserved recognition for prior service. Albinus Nance, who served as governor from 1879 to 1883, was one of those bright young men. He emigrated to

[1]See Olson, *op. cit.*, pp. 299ff.

Nebraska in 1871 from Illinois, where he had attended Knox College and been admitted to the bar, settling on a homestead near Osceola. He was only 'twenty-three when he arrived in the state, but in 1874 he was elected to the legislature. He was re-elected in 1876 and chosen Speaker of the House of Representatives. In the same year he was chairman of the Nebraska delegation to the Republican National Convention. In 1878, at the age of thirty, he won the Republican nomination for governor and, of course, the subsequent election. Unfortunately, he followed the example of many other bright young men and left the state, moving to Chicago shortly after the expiration of his second term to spend the rest of his life dealing in railroad securities. James W. Dawes, who succeeded Nance, was only thirty-seven years old when elected governor in 1882. Dawes, also a lawyer, came to Nebraska from Wisconsin in 1871, the year of Nance's arrival. He settled at Crete and immediately began combining his law practice with politics. He served as a member of the constitutional convention in 1875 and the next year went to the state Senate and became chairman of the Republican State Central Committee, and, in 1880, Nebraska's representative on the Republican National Committee. Though strictly a machine politician, Dawes was a good campaigner and an able orator—as is witnessed by the fact that in both 1882 and 1884 he defeated J. Sterling Morton, the ablest and best-known candidate the Democrats could possibly have put forward. As in the case of Nance, however, the governorship ended Dawes' active participation in state politics: he practiced law in Crete until 1898, when he left the state to spend the rest of his active life as an Army officer.

In John M. Thayer, their candidate for governor in 1886, the Republicans went from youth to old age. Sixty-six when elected, General Thayer, a hero of Shiloh and Fort Donelson, had been United States Senator and state commander of the GAR; he had also served four years as governor of Wyoming territory.

The United States senatorships, distributed by the legislature, usually went to men of more standing in the party than those selected for governor: Phineas W. Hitchcock (1871–1877), Algernon S. Paddock (1875–1881, 1887–1893), Alvin Saunders (1877–1883), C. H. Van Wyck (1881–1887), and Charles F. Manderson (1883–1895). Hitchcock, Paddock, and Saunders were territorial pioneers, and all had been prominent in territorial politics: Hitchcock had served as delegate to

Congress; Paddock and Saunders had served as secretary and governor of the territory, respectively, from their appointment by President Lincoln in 1861 to the admission of the state in 1867. General Van Wyck did not settle in Nebraska until 1874, although he had had property interests in the state for several years prior to his removal, and he brought with him a distinguished Civil War record and eleven years' service as a congressman from New York. He had large interests in Otoe County and early gained the friendship of Edward Rosewater, editor of the powerful Omaha *Bee*. Manderson, likewise, was a relative late-comer, moving to Omaha from Ohio in 1869. He had commanded an Ohio regiment in the Civil War, however; was a lawyer of prominence and means; and enjoyed wide support among the old soldiers.

The senatorial contests were protracted affairs, occupying the attention of the legislature to the exclusion of all else for weeks at a time. On occasion, the Democrats and Anti-Monopolists by uniting on one candidate could have elected a United States senator; but they were never able to compose their differences—indeed, the Democrats could not even agree among themselves—and the Republicans always were able to carry the day by agreeing finally on one candidate, although it usually took many ballots for one of their number to develop sufficient strength to cause his opponents to withdraw. The atmosphere of the capital city during a senatorial contest usually was oppressive with intrigue. The leading candidates ensconced themselves in hotel suites at twenty dollars a day. Board bills of the hangers-on, paid by the candidates, often ran to five hundred dollars a day. Hotels and saloons reeked with the smoke of free cigars strewn with a lavish hand by the generous candidates. It seemed that each train brought a fresh pack of politicians, big and little, all wanting to have some part in the manufacture of a senator. The hotels were filled to overflowing. The overflow, if important enough, spilled into the twenty-dollar suites; if unimportant, into the lobbies. One reporter declared that during the heated contest of 1883, the lobby of the Commercial Hotel usually was so full that if one wanted to invite a man to have a drink, he did it in a whisper else his invitation would get a dozen takers instead of one.

It was generally conceded that the officers of the two large railroads serving the state, the Union Pacific and the Burlington, wielded much influence in the election of senators from Nebraska. The extent of this influence was never demonstrated, nor even its presence absolutely confirmed; yet it undoubtedly existed, and to a considerable degree, because all the politicians in the state acted in senatorial matters with an eye to the two railroads, and no man was elected to the Senate during this period over the opposition of the railroads. In the case of Van Wyck, however, the railroads and the more conservative elements of the Republican party soon came to realize that they had put their money on the wrong horse. Though known as "a Burlington man" at the time of his election, he soon developed maverick tendencies, aligning himself with the opposition on all the major issues of the day. As a result, the regular Republicans developed a hatred for him which has not been equaled in Nebraska politics, except in the later case of George W. Norris.

Locally, the prohibition issue intruded itself into the political picture with considerable vigor. The voters had decisively turned down a proposal to submit the prohibition question to the people in 1871,[2] but in the late Seventies, widespread abstinence agitation under the leadership of John B. Finch, combined with apprehension over the influence of the liquor interests in politics, brought prohibition to the fore as a political issue; and in 1886 the Prohibition party nominated candidates for governor and the other principal offices. Their gubernatorial candidate, H. W. Hardy, prominent businessman who had served as mayor of Lincoln, polled 8,175 votes out of a total of 138,209. In 1888 it took all night to defeat a prohibition plank in the Republican platform, but the Prohibition candidate for governor got only about 4.5 percent of the vote as compared with Hardy's approximate 6 percent of two years before. Though the Prohibition party as such never had a chance, prohibition sentiment grew steadily, and in the Nineties became inextricably interwoven with the politics of the two major parties.

RUMBLINGS OF DISCONTENT

Though the organization of the Prohibition party indicated some discontent with the political status quo, prohibition during this period was not a major issue. The major issues arose out of the unfavorable economic position in which the farmers of the state found themselves. The fundamental factor in that position was debt. The West, including Nebraska, was consistently a debtor region: the area's meager capital had been strained to the limit to establish commercial farming; addi-

[2]See p. 181.

tional capital required to keep it going had been secured by wholesale mortgaging, both public and private. Moreover, in Nebraska, agriculture was the only basic industry. The older areas had become industrialized and had tended to change their point of view, but in Nebraska, though Omaha and Lincoln (particularly Omaha) developed into urban centers with some industry, they were dependent upon agriculture and their points of view remained agricultural. Furthermore, agriculture in Nebraska was conducted on a shoestring, and any deviation from full production or minimum prices could throw the whole industry—and the state—into a position from which it was impossible even to service its debt, let alone reduce it. Those deviations occurred with ominous regularity, with the result that the wolf—in the form of a mortgage or bond holder—seemed always lurking just outside the door. Nebraskans, then, were fair game for anyone who had a proposal which would seem to benefit the debtor.

Moreover, the farmers were convinced that they worked longer hours, under more adverse conditions, and with smaller compensation for their labor than any other group on earth. For these conditions, the farmers blamed "some extrinsic baleful influence." Their difficulty, they were sure, lay basically in the low prices received for the products they had to sell. A rather considerable body of opinion believed the cause to lie in overproduction. Most farmers, however, refused to admit overproduction—how could they, with their papers filled regularly with stories of mass starvation all over the world?—but felt that the trouble lay in "barriers to consumption."

Chief among these barriers were the railroads. Settlement had been made possible in many parts of the state only by railroad construction, and its continuance, to a great degree, was dependent upon the railroads. Possibly it was this dependence which made the farmer so sensitive to any signs that the railroads were being operated for other interests than his own—and of signs there were aplenty. Most obvious were the high freight rates. It cost a Nebraska farmer a bushel of wheat to send another bushel to market. Local rates (short hauls) were particularly high, and in this the farmer saw a discrimination against himself in favor of the large, long-distance shipper. The principal cause of high rates—in the minds of the farmers—was monopoly. Each town usually had only one railroad, and its monopolistic character was self-evident; in areas served by two or more railroads, business was divided and rates were maintained by mutual agreement.[3] Corollary causes of the high rates, so the agrarian argument ran, were the necessity to pay high dividends on watered stock and the natural tendency of the monopolistic railroads to discriminate in favor of other monopolies and against the farmer.

Added to high freight rates were the taxes levied to pay off construction subsidies granted to the railroads—and all too often, it seemed, without value received. So eminent a conservative as J. Sterling Morton, for example, declared that the Brownville, Fort Kearney and Pacific Railroad was organized for the sole purpose of "public plunder through Brownville bonds."[4]

Moreover, the railroads themselves successfully resisted efforts on the part of local governments to tax the lands which had been given them by the federal government. This was bad enough in areas which had the benefit of railroad transportation as a result of those gifts, but in northeastern Nebraska, where the Burlington had located thousands of acres of "lieu lands," thus removing them from the homestead lists without providing any transportation advantages, the situation was particularly disconcerting.[5] Moreover, the farmers came to feel that the federal land-grant system had been merely a device whereby the railroads had been given the best agricultural lands in the state at the expense of the homesteaders.

Giving color to the charges against the railroads was their political activity. Their voice in the selection of United States senators was freely discussed; they lobbied openly and effectively against legislative efforts to implement the provision in the Constitution of 1875 providing for railroad regulation. Particularly objectionable was the railroad practice of issuing free passes to every public official who wanted them, from dog-catcher to governor—the "free pass bribery system." As one antirailroad author characterized it,

For thirty years the politics of Nebraska has been policed and the government of the state controlled by railroads. This railroad control of politics

[3]See Robert E. Riegel, "The Omaha Pool," *Iowa Journal of History and Politics,* XXII (October, 1924), 569–582.

[4]For the history of this extraordinary enterprise, see James J. Blake, "The Brownville, Fort Kearney and Pacific Railroad," *Nebraska History,* XXIX (September, 1948), 238–272.

[5]See Ray H. Mattison, "The Burlington Tax Controversy in Nebraska Over the Federal Land Grants," *Nebraska History,* XXVIII (April–June, 1947), 110–131.

and state government is procured through a conspiracy. The conspiracy is between the railroad managers and the politicians. The purpose of the conspiracy is to procure for the railroads, through the politicians, control over the state government. The price paid to the politicians for their part in the conspiracy is the free pass.[6]

Though the railroads epitomized all that was wrong with politics and the economic system, there were other groups against whom farm complaints were directed. The elevators, usually operating as monopolies, acted in a highhanded fashion, downgrading grain and shading prices to their own advantage. They had very close arrangements with the railroads, too, as farm groups which tried to operate elevators of their own found when they attempted to get trackage and cars. Bankers and mortgage holders were another obvious source of oppression, particularly in the lean years. To many farmers, however, they simply were the instruments of an inadequate currency and credit system. Interest payments on mortgages drained off cash needed for immediate activities, and short-term loans were virtually unavailable. Closely allied was the supply of circulating money, and a significant segment of farm opinion in the post-Civil War years could always be found advocating measures which seemed to promise an increase in the amount of currency available. There was some feeling, too, that the protective tariff worked to the advantage of the corporations at the expense of the farmer, although the tariff never became an overriding issue in Nebraska politics.

The basic issue revolved around the railroads. The issue came to the fore in the session of 1881, after the State Board of Equalization, in response to a legislative recital of the problem in 1879, had come up with a long report to show that many of the roads were operating at a net loss and thus the only appropriate action was a reduction in their taxes! A special Senate committee on railroads came out with a strong report calling attention to rebates, pooling, and rate discrimination, but all the legislature managed to do was to memorialize Congress to enact laws correcting unjust discriminations and excessive charges on the part of interstate railroads. Actually, of course, the federal approach to railroad regulation ultimately was found to be the only satisfactory one in many respects, but at this time the legislative memorial seemed like little more than passing off responsibility. The Constitu-

[6]George W. Berge, *The Free Pass Bribery System* (Lincoln: Independent Publishing Company, 1905), p. 9.

tion of 1875 had given the legislature power to regulate railroad rates, and a growing number were demanding that the lawmakers exercise that power. Lawmakers were reluctant to do so, however. Moreover, if rates were to be regulated, a commission of some sort would have to be set up, and the constitution specifically prohibited the creation of additional salaried offices. A legislative committee to which the problem was referred in 1883 came to the conclusion that the constitution would have to be amended—the legislature as a whole again confined itself to memorializing Congress on the question and submitting an amendment to the constitution authorizing the creation of a railroad commission.

The people, feeling that the problem could be solved without the creation of additional boards and salaries, turned down this proposal, two to one. The legislature then attempted to solve the problem within the limitations of the constitution by creating a railroad commission consisting of the attorney general, secretary of state, and auditor, with the understanding that secretaries authorized them by the constitution should be appointed to do the work. The commission was given the authority to regulate the railroads in a general, but quite innocuous, manner. Opponents of the act charged that it was a farce, a measure designed solely to forestall significant regulation. The three secretaries, appointed entirely from political considerations, had little knowledge of the problem and less inclination to do anything that would cause the railroads to test the constitutionality of their offices and possibly put them out of their $2,000-per-year jobs—comfortable berths in Nebraska during the 1880's. As had been implicit in the memorials to Congress, effective railroad regulation was in many respects outside the province of state government, but no determined effort would be made to achieve any regulation until a complete change had occurred in the political complexion of the state.

There were other signs of discontent. Omaha, developing into an industrial community, began to feel the stress of labor troubles. In 1882 a strike for higher wages by laborers on a large grading enterprise in the Burlington's yards (the "Camp Dump Strike") spread rapidly to other industries and soon degenerated into a riot as the strikers attempted to maintain a picket line—a riot that was quelled only after the National Guard was called out.

Throughout the decade there were strong signs of discontent with the "regular" Republican approach to the problems facing the state, but this discontent, while weakening the party's hold on state politics, never developed into effective opposition. Within the party, mavericks like Senator Van Wyck, Editor Rosewater, and Attorney General William Leese were read out of the organization, shouted down, or quietly set on the shelf. Outside the party, there seemed to be no organization around which an effective opposition could develop. The Democrats were badly divided, and Democratic leadership seemed even less sympathetic than the Republicans with the problems of the farmers and the workingmen. Remnants of the Greenback party—which had polled almost a fifth of the total vote in 1878—joined with dissident Republicans and other independent spirits to form an "Anti-Monopoly" party, but while it was able to muster nearly a fifth of the vote in 1882, it suffered from lack of leadership and soon collapsed. Actually, the Republicans came closer to defeat in 1882 than they did at any time in the decade. Morton, the Democratic candidate for governor, and E. P. Ingersoll, the Anti-Monopolist, together received more votes than did the victorious Dawes; P. D. Sturdevant, on whom the Democrats and Anti-Monopolists united, was elected Treasurer—the first Democrat to win an office since statehood, except Chief Justice William A. Little, who died before he qualified. Together the two parties won control of the Senate and came within four seats of getting control of the House. In 1884 the Anti-Monopolists joined with the Democrats to nominate Morton for governor, but the Sage of Arbor Lodge could develop little enthusiasm among the rank and file of the Anti-Monops, and Dawes easily won re-election. The only other instance when the GOP armor was pierced occurred in 1886, when Democrat John A. McShane, founder of the Omaha stockyards and a prominent Catholic layman, was elected to Congress.

THE FARMERS ALLIANCE

The opposition was soon to find an effective voice in the Farmers Alliance. That organization, founded in Illinois in 1879, was first established in Nebraska in 1880, when an Alliance was formed near Filley in Gage County. Later in the year, another Alliance was formed at Alda in Hall County. The early history of the organization in Nebraska is difficult to trace, but a state Alliance was formed at Lincoln in 1881, with E. P. Ingersoll of Johnson County as president, and Jay Burrows, who had been instrumental in organizing the Filley Alliance, as secretary. The stated purpose of the Alliance was to secure cheaper transportation and in general "to wage war on capital." The convention adopted resolutions urging the legislature to pass laws to enforce the constitutional provisions permitting railroad regulation.

At first, the Alliance did not flourish. A second state meeting was called for August 3, 1882, but it had not been well advertised, and, being held in the midst of the harvest season, brought an attendance of only fifteen persons. The meeting adjourned to a joint session with the Anti-Monopoly League at Hastings on September 27. Out of this came the Anti-Monopoly state ticket, headed by E. P. Ingersoll.[7] The Alliance was in a decline nationally, too. Although at the time of the second annual convention in 1881 it claimed 24,500 members—with Nebraska the leading state—and a membership of over one hundred thousand in 1882, there were so few in attendance at the annual convention in 1883 that the group decided not to meet the next year. The mid-Eighties witnessed some revival. A national convention was held again in 1886, and in that year over two hundred local Alliances were chartered in Nebraska. Custer County led with fifty-seven, Frontier came second with eighteen, Hamilton and York had sixteen each, and then followed Antelope, Holt, Sherman, Hall, Hitchcock, Buffalo, Saunders, and others. In 1887 the State Alliance was reorganized as a secret society, with rituals and objectives somewhat similar to the earlier Patrons of Husbandry. There was much activity throughout 1888, yet at the annual meeting of the State Alliance in January, 1889, only fourteen counties were represented by about a hundred delegates. It was apparent that more work was needed. The state organization authorized its officers to do field work to increase the membership, and under the leadership of J. H. Powers of Trenton, the new president, five hundred locals were chartered during the year.

The State Alliance also authorized the establishment of a newspaper at Lincoln. Jay Burrows, chairman of the State Executive Committee and one of the leading figures in the whole Alliance movement—he had been elected president of the national Alliance in 1887—left his farm near Filley and moved to the capital city to develop *The Alliance* (later changed to *The Farmers' Alliance*) into a dynamic and influential organ. In addition to its own paper, the Alliance enjoyed the support

[7]See p. 216.

of a growing number of newspapers in all parts of the state: in 1888 approximately eighteen out of 499 weekly newspapers were friendly to the movement; by 1889 the number had risen to 113.

Though the stated objectives of the Alliance, as reorganized in 1887, were educational and philanthropic, the organization could not have avoided political action had it wanted to. Local meetings held in homes and country schoolhouses throughout the state almost inevitably developed into political forums. Senator Van Wyck urged independent political action. So menacing had the organization become that the "Old Guard" in the state Senate was moved to pass the following resolution introduced by Church Howe of Nemaha County, who himself had vacillated between radicalism and regularity:

Whereas, certain persons, associated under the title of the Nebraska Farmers' Alliance have publicly stated that the financial obligations of the farmers of Nebraska are an oppressive burden to said farmers, and that the general economic condition of the state is the reverse of prosperous, therefore be it

Resolved, That it is the opinion of the senate of the state of Nebraska, that the so-called Farmers' Alliance, being a private and non-representative body, has no right nor title to speak in behalf of the farmers of the state . . .,

Such resolutions, of course, only served to spur on those who believed that the Alliance must get into politics on an independent basis. The declaration of principles had pledged the organization to "labor for the education of the agricultural classes in the science of economical government in a strictly non-partisan spirit," and many of the leaders —notably Burrows—argued that the only hope of success lay in working through the old parties. Many of the members, however, developed different opinions. In their thinking, there was no hope in either of the old parties. The Democrats were still the party of rebellion; they were dominated by the Catholics and opposed to prohibition, which many of the Protestant farmers favored; the intransigent conservatism of their leaders made cooperation with the Democratic party seem impossible. The Republicans, because of their treatment of all who expressed progressive ideas, seemed equally hopeless. The only hope was independent action, and many people joined the Alliance precisely because they expected independent action to be taken. As early as 1889, the Alliance in several counties had run independent tickets and in some instances had succeeded in electing them. Accordingly, when a state convention of Alliance county presidents and organizers was held in Lincoln on April 22, 1890, it decided that if the strength of the Alliance increased sufficiently state-wide independent action would be justified.

And its strength did increase. By July 1, Alliance authorities estimated that the organization included about fifteen hundred locals with a membership of over fifty thousand. A total of 174 papers was on their side. The time was ripe for independent action.

CHAPTER 18

The Populist Revolt

ON JANUARY 15, 1890, the Omaha *Bee* wrote: "The remarkable growth of the State Farmers' Alliance during the last year is a gratifying evidence of an awakening among the producers. . . . Organization among the farmers has become an urgent necessity. Confronted on every side by combines and trusts, they are forced to unite to protect themselves from the grasping greed of corporations. It is to be hoped that strong, conservative men will be placed at the helm of the alliance—men who know the right of the producers and who will demand and secure just treatment from the transportation companies of the state."

There were strong men at the head of the Alliance, but they were not conservative men. They were radicals, ready and able to take such action as the demands of their difficulties seemed to indicate. By 1890 those difficulties appeared to call for heroic action. For almost a decade, the farmers of Nebraska and other Plains states had been given good crops by a bountiful Nature—but as their crops increased their prosperity decreased. The great crop of 1889—the best in a decade—brought with it some of the lowest prices the farmers of Nebraska had yet received.[1] After a winter spent pondering the problem of fifty-cent wheat, ten- to twenty-cent corn, and fifteen-cent oats, a sizable portion of Nebraska's farmers were willing to believe what Alliance orators had been saying for years: the root of their difficulty lay in the man-made

[1] See p. 207.

barriers interposed between producer and consumer for the benefit of Eastern capitalists.[2] This conclusion determined elections and shaped legislation so long as the depression lasted.

The situation was made all the more urgent in 1890 because Nature added to the farmers' man-made burdens. Nebraska received only 17.15 inches of rain that year, well below the minimum required for even reasonably good crops, and the lowest since 1864. Normally, the farmers could meet philosophically adversity brought on by Nature, but the hot, dry winds that parched Nebraska's crops in the summer of 1890 —coming as they did upon the heels of a depression born of plenty— only served to increase the desperation with which the farmers of Nebraska viewed their plight. They could not do much about Nature, but man they believed they could handle, and the summer of 1890 found the farmers of Nebraska engaged in a determined struggle to secure control, in so far as was humanly possible, of their own political and economic destiny. Though the resulting movement found much of its support and many of its leaders in Nebraska, it was by no means confined to the state. It spread all through the Plains states and even into the older Middle West. American society had been completely changed by the post-Civil War technological transformation. Commercial agriculture—brought into being, in part, by that transformation—was for the first time making a serious effort to come to grips with the problem of existence in a society that was becoming steadily more industrialized.

THE ELECTION OF 1890

As has been pointed out, the leaders of the Farmers' Alliance initially had no desire to engage in independent political action. Indeed, many of them resisted it as folly and as the surest way to destroy the effectiveness of their organization. But, as pressures mounted from the growing number who joined the organization because they felt that the leadership of the old parties offered no hope, the Alliance leaders not only gave into the demand but assumed control of the new movement. The April 22 meeting of county presidents and organizers[3] was followed by another meeting at Lincoln in May, attended by state officers and county representatives. Many of the leaders still believed that their best course was work through the old parties, but the desire for a new

[2]See pp. 216–219.   [3]See p. 219.

party was so strong that the meeting decided to test sentiment by issuing a call for a people's convention. The call as finally issued was signed by the president of the State Farmers' Alliance and the head of the Knights of Labor. It was accompanied by a "declaration of principles," written by Burrows, which supporters were invited to sign. This declaration called for the free coinage of silver, abolition of the land monopoly, governmental ownership of railroads and telegraph lines, and an adjustment of taxation so that "our laboring interests will be fostered and wealth bear its just burdens." Within thirty days, more than fifteen thousand voters had signed the petition. There could be no doubt now about sentiment, and a formal call was issued for a People's State Independent Convention to meet July 29 at Lincoln to nominate a ticket supporting the "declaration of principles" in the call.

More than eight hundred delegates, representing seventy-nine counties, assembled at Bohanan's Hall in Lincoln on the appointed day. Hundreds of visitors were on hand to witness the launching of the new party. Though the convention refused to adopt the "declaration of principles" which had accompanied the call as the new party's platform, the instrument adopted closely paralleled the original document, with the addition of planks calling for an increase in the amount of money in circulation to fifty dollars per capita, a freight-rate law with rates no higher than those in force in Iowa, a liberal service pension for old soldiers, the adoption of the Australian ballot, and an eight-hour day, except for agricultural labor. The Knights of Labor were primarily interested in the eight-hour day, but the farmers insisted that it should not be applicable on the farms. The only serious division in the convention occurred over the nominee for governor. A considerable block of delegates wanted Charles H. Van Wyck, former Republican Senator who had been defeated for re-election by the corporations and the regulars. Alliance leaders, however, lead by Burrows, opposed Van Wyck as being too wealthy and too much the professional politician to be the leader of a common people's movement. They put forward in his stead John H. Powers of Trenton, president of the Farmers' Alliance, a Civil War veteran, and a modest man who lived in a sod house on his homestead in Hitchcock County. Addison E. Sheldon, one of the Populist movement's most sympathetic chroniclers, called Powers' nomination "a victory of the idealists in the convention over the opportunists." Van Wyck, a tested politician, undoubtedly was a stronger vote-getter than Powers, "but John H. Powers more accurately represented the spirit of the new political movement than Senator Van Wyck."[4] First-district Populists nominated Van Wyck for Congress, but he refused to make the race. Most of the other nominees on the state ticket were old Anti-Monopoly war horses who had spent their political years leading lost causes and whose reputation for fidelity to the principles of the new movement had been tested in many an Anti-Monopoly campaign.

But this was no lost cause being hatched in Bohanan's Hall. The convention had numbers, it had strength of purpose, and it had confidence. As the *Nebraska State Journal*, the new movement's most vitriolic journalistic critic, wrote, "a more sanguine lot of politicians one could never dream of meeting. Each individual delegate is endowed with the belief to a degree of dead moral certainty that the political world is his oyster."[5]

The leaders of the old parties were obviously disturbed. They could refer sarcastically, as the *Journal* did, to "horny handed sons of toil" and "venerable hay seeds," but they were in trouble and they knew it. In January, Governor Thayer had made a blundering attempt to solve the transportation problem by addressing a pleading letter to the railroads of the state, calling attention to the corn piled on the ground that could not be moved because of the high freight rates and urging them to lower rates as an experiment. This, of course, only increased Alliance certainty that the Republicans were completely captive to the railroads. When this letter failed to have the desired effect, Thayer further compounded his troubles by issuing a call for a special session of the legislature to consider a maximum-rate law, then revoking it after being flooded with opposition communications.

Republicans, meeting in Lincoln a week before the Populists took over the capital city, had wrestled manfully with the problem posed by the rising agrarian tide—as Church Howe put it in opening the convention, "the old ship is leaking and men are wanted to man the pumps" —but they had failed to come up with any convincing solution. Their platform made a few concessions to popular demands in declaring for the Australian ballot (which a Republican majority in the last legislature had voted down), a reduction of freight and passenger rates, the aboli-

---

[4] Sheldon, *Nebraska: The Land and the People*, I, 682.
[5] *Nebraska State Journal*, Lincoln, July 29, 1890.

tion of free passes, legislation defining the duty of corporations to employees, the prohibition of illegitimate increase of stock or capital by corporations, abolition of railroad and elevator discrimination in the handling of grain, more rigid usury laws, a recognition of the right of labor to organize, a noncommittal tariff plank, the remonetization of silver, an opposition to land monopoly, the establishment of a system of postal telegraphy, and a more liberal pension system. The platform also denounced the trusts. To man the pumps as its candidate for governor, the convention, after an all-night session, chose L. D. Richards, prominent Fremont banker who had long been a leader in the GAR.

The Democrats, meeting in Omaha on August 14, joined the other two parties in denouncing the trusts, thus making it unanimous. Their special fire, however, was reserved for the Republicans who, they declared, had squandered the public domain and perverted the results of victory in the Civil War. They, too, favored the Australian ballot, the remonetization of silver, bigger pensions, and the right of labor to organize. They also demanded an amendment to the Constitution providing for the direct election of United States Senators and the repeal of laws which enabled the Governor to call out the militia in the event of labor troubles. They nominated James E. Boyd, prominent Omaha meat packer and an arch-conservative, as their candidate for governor.

The Democrats came to grips with an issue which both the Republicans and Populists tried to duck—prohibition. Constant agitation throughout the Eighties had greatly increased prohibition sentiment, and the legislature by one vote in the House and two in the Senate had placed a prohibition amendment on the general election ballot in 1890. The Prohibition party, which had fielded a ticket in every election since 1884, entered the lists again with B. L. Paine, prominent Lincoln merchant, as its candidate for governor. Many of the Populists were dry, but their convention decided that the prohibition issue was too controversial for injection into the party's initial campaign. They also argued that any effort to make prohibition an issue in the campaign would play into the hands of the railroads and other corporate interests. Many Republicans likewise were prohibitionists, but party leaders—aware of the fact that the German and Bohemian vote which they needed for victory was strongly against the amendment—successfully stamped out an effort to commit the organization. In line with this policy, Richards, though personally dry, consistently refused to take a stand on the issue, thus losing votes from both wets and drys. The Democrats, of course, knew where they stood—first, last, and always. They were against prohibition, their platform flatly said so, their candidate was a well-known anti-prohibitionist.

The campaign produced excitement such as the state had never seen. After the hot winds had withered away the crops, energy which normally would have been spent in harvesting went into politics—as the more outspoken Alliance orators were fond of proclaiming, "We farmers raised no crops, so we'll just raise hell." Thousands thronged to hear the fiery Populist orators proclaim farm grievances and point the way to victory. A Populist picnic at Cushman Park in Lincoln, on September 1, drew 20,000 people; at Wymore, on September 23, 1,050 farmers' wagons were counted in the parade; at Hastings on the same day, 1,600 were counted. While waiting for the orators to begin, the assembled throngs sang rousing campaign songs, usually set to familiar tunes—songs like "Goodbye, Old Party, Goodbye," "A Mortgage Has Taken the Farm, Mary." A good example was "The Hayseed," sung to the tune of "Save a Poor Sinner Like Me."

> I was once a tool of oppression
> And as green as a sucker could be
> And monopolies banded together
> To beat a poor hayseed like me.
>
> The railroads and old party bosses
> Together did sweetly agree;
> And they thought there would be little trouble
> In working a hayseed like me.
>
> *   *   *
>
> But now I've roused up a little
> And their greed and corruption I see,
>
> *   *   *
>
> And the ticket we vote next November
> Will be made up of hayseeds like me.

The opposition resorted to the same tactics, and A. L. "Doc" Bixby, famed columnist of the Lincoln *Journal,* produced this quatrain:

I cannot sing the old songs,
My heart is full of woe;
But I can howl calamity
From Hell to Broken Bow.

Though in some areas Democrats and Populists supported a fusion candidate, on the state level Democratic leaders joined the Republicans in sneering at the third party while they talked the tariff and waved the bloody shirt respectively before small audiences. The ridicule, however, only served to aid the Populist cause. The Lincoln *Journal* could refer to Populist candidates as "hogs in the parlor," and the Omaha *Bee* could call them "political thugs," but such vilification only drew new converts to the Alliance cause, as its members shouted that they were being persecuted in their battle for human rights.

When the election returns came in, the Republicans for the first time since statehood found that they had been cast aside. The Populists secured clear control of the Senate, with eighteen members to eight Democrats and seven Republicans; in the House there were fifty-four Populists, twenty-five Democrats, and twenty-one Republicans. Not a single Republican was sent to Congress: the first district sent William Jennings Bryan, a young Lincoln lawyer who had been given the Democratic nomination simply as a gesture of goodwill, there being no hope that he could be elected; the second district elected William A. McKeighan, the fiery Red Cloud orator who had received both Populist and Democratic nominations; the third district was represented by Omar M. Kem, a Populist from Custer County. For state offices below governor, Republican name candidates generally struggled back into office. In the gubernatorial race, James E. Boyd eked out a narrow 71,331-to-70,187 victory over Powers. Richards ran third with 68,878, and Paine got a mere 3,676 votes. Boyd's victory resulted largely from the fact that he piled up an overwhelming lead in Douglas County, where opposition to prohibition outweighed all other issues in the campaign. The Omaha Business Men's Association, organized largely to oppose the amendment, comprised most of the leading businessmen of the city. The *World-Herald* and the *Bee* both opposed prohibition; indeed, the *Bee* lost much of its effectiveness as a Republican paper in the campaign as a result of its concentration on the prohibition issue. On the amendment, the wets carried the day, 111,728 to 88,292. In Douglas County the vote was 23,918 against the amendment to 1,555 for it.

Victory and Frustration

Republicans and Populists immediately raised a cry that Boyd had been elected by fraudulent votes in Omaha. The Populists contested the election on the basis of those votes, but unfortunately they got trapped into the tactical error of contesting both Republican and Democratic votes in Douglas County, thus uniting the two old parties against them, and in the joint session of both houses of the legislature called to canvass the election returns, the new party's members were completely outmaneuvered, with the result that the returns were officially approved as they had been initially reported. Meanwhile, Boyd had taken the oath of office as governor in a notary's office, but Governor Thayer, taking note of the contest pending before the legislature, refused to surrender the office. He not only had himself guarded in his office by policemen but called out the state militia, for the purpose, he said, of preserving order and saving the legislature from the annoyance of noise in the corridors. The contest was finally decided in Boyd's favor and the new Governor was permitted to deliver his message to the legislature on February 6.

Boyd was to have further trouble. Though Thayer had surrendered his office, he had filed a writ of quo warranto in the state Supreme Court to remove Boyd on the grounds that he was not a citizen. Boyd's father had come to America from Ireland bringing with him his son, who was still a minor. The elder Boyd failed to take out his first naturalization papers until 1890, long after his son had grown to manhood. Thayer argued that under these conditions naturalization of the father could not give citizenship to the son. On May 5 the state Supreme Court sustained Thayer's contention and he was reinstated in office. Boyd immediately appealed to the United States Supreme Court, and on February 1, 1892, that tribunal reversed the Nebraska court and declared Boyd a citizen. One week later he resumed the governorship.

The incident left a bad taste in the mouth of many Independents, who felt that their farmer-legislators had been outmaneuvered by shrewd lawyers from Omaha and Lincoln. More frustrating still was Governor Boyd's adamant stand against Populist efforts to regulate the railroads. Those efforts took the form of a bill introduced by Representative Fred Newberry of Hamilton County to reduce rates on most of the goods shipped on Nebraska railroads to correspond with those generally enforced in Iowa. Backed by a solid Independent vote and some help from both Democrats and Republicans, the bill got through the house by a vote of 78 to 17. It was apparent that in the Senate the contest would be much closer. One Independent member, Senator W. M. Taylor of Loup County, was induced by railroad lobbyists—for a fee, it was charged—to leave his post and the state, thus cutting the Populist vote by one. Following this, the opponents of the bill kept the Senate in continuous session for seventy-five hours under roll calls and points of order in an effort to wear out its friends. Finally, however, the bill got through by a vote of 23 to 7. Governor Boyd promptly vetoed it on the grounds that to reduce rates in Nebraska to the Iowa level where the tonnage was more than four times as great would bankrupt every road in the state. The supporters of the bill weren't able to get the necessary three-fifths majority to pass it over the Governor's veto. Boyd's action, of course, only served to intensify Populist insistence that their sole hope lay in independent action—the Democrats were as much friends of monopoly as were the Republicans.

Though frustrated in their efforts to regulate railroads, the Populists did enact other measures in which they had considerable interest: the Australian ballot, a free textbook law, a public-fund deposit law, mutual insurance acts, and a repeal of the sugar bounty law ending state subsidies for the beet sugar industry. They also passed an act establishing eight hours as a legal day's work except on farms, but this was subsequently held invalid by the Supreme Court. They made a material reduction in state expenditures, corresponding in some degree to the reduced income of the state's taxpayers.

The presidential year 1892 found the Populists full of fire and ready to go on to complete victory. Third-party successes throughout the West had greatly heartened Independents everywhere and they resolved to put a national ticket in the field. Their national convention at Omaha was attended by some thirteen hundred enthusiastic delegates. They adopted a platform reiterating traditional Populist demands and then nominated General James B. Weaver of Iowa, the old Anti-Monopoly-Greenback war horse as their candidate for President.

To head their state ticket, Nebraska Populists chose Senator Charles H. Van Wyck, whom they had spurned two years earlier as unsuited to lead a common people's movement. The selection of Van Wyck represents a change in the direction of the Populist party. Started primarily as a radical agrarian organization, it had failed to get enough of the farm vote to put it into a position of absolute ascendancy. Now the Populists were trying to bid for the support of middle-class business and professional men. The Republicans nominated Lorenzo Crounse, who had served on the state Supreme Court and as a member of Congress and who at the time of his nomination was serving as Assistant Secretary of the Treasury in Washington. He was nominated against his wishes as a compromise candidate who could unite the warring factions of the party and get the GOP back on the victory trail. The Democrats, more badly split than ever, came up with J. Sterling Morton, a conservative who had denounced Boyd's veto of the Newberry bill as bad politics, but who in general agreed with his opponent on most basic issues. More ominous than the personal squabble between Morton and Boyd was the rift in the party on the monetary question. A sizable portion of Democrats were now coming to feel that the steady decline in prices could be halted only by the remonetization of silver. Morton stood four-square against any departure from the gold standard, and in this he was solidly behind the national standard-bearer, Grover Cleveland.

Somehow the momentum generated in 1890 failed to carry over into 1892, and Populist orators seemed unable to stir up the same enthusiasm they had created in 1890 for issues that were by now a little shopworn. In the state, Harrison won a narrow victory over Weaver, and Cleveland ran a poor third. Republicans took the governorship, too, with Crounse getting 78,426 votes to Van Wyck's 68,617. Morton, who had campaigned almost solely against Van Wyck and had greatly aided Crounse's cause by so doing, ran a poor third, although he got approximately 20,000 votes more than Cleveland. Bryan, McKeighan, and Kem were all returned to Congress, but Republicans won in each of the three new districts created as a result of the reapportionment following the census of 1890. Republicans also won control of both houses in the legislature, although a combination of Democrats and Populists could defeat them. This combination went into effect to elect William V. Allen, a Populist judge from Madison County, to the United States Senate[6] and to enact the Newberry bill into law.

[6]An interesting discussion of the role of William Jennings Bryan, who withdrew as a candidate and lined up Democratic support for Allen, thus assuring his election, will be found in Paolo E. Coletta, "William Jennings Bryan and the Nebraska Senatorial Election of 1893," *Nebraska History*, XXXI (September, 1950), 183–203.

THE POPULISTS ELECT A GOVERNOR

Drouth and low farm prices combined in the early Nineties to increase agrarian unrest. Then in 1893, the country fell into the grip of a paralyzing, world-wide depression. Cleveland's answer to the problem of the depression was negotiation with Wall Street bankers to maintain the price of gold, and repeal of the Sherman Silver Purchase Act, by which the Treasury had been committed to purchase four and a half million ounces of silver each month. The nation's most ardent advocate of the official Administration policy was J. Sterling Morton, the Nebraskan who was serving Cleveland as Secretary of Agriculture. Throughout the West, however, and particularly in Nebraska, the rank and file of the farmers had long since come to the conclusion that one of their basic problems was the gold standard and that their only hope for getting out of the economic morass in which they found themselves was the free coinage of silver.

The silver issue split the Democratic party in Nebraska wide open. While Secretary Morton plugged for the gold standard, Congressman Bryan—whose silver tongue already had won him a large following— was in the thick of the fight against Cleveland's monetary policies. Initially, the party was securely in the hands of the conservative supporters of Morton and the Administration. The off-year convention of 1893, despite a personal appeal from Bryan and a warning that he would leave the party if it did not adopt his views, gave enthusiastic endorsement to the Administration and demanded the repeal of "that vicious law, the Sherman Silver Act." Congressman Bryan went back to Washington asserting that he had been sacrificed upon the altar of gold and greed, but he did not leave the party. Rather, he remained a Democrat, hoping to bring enough Populists into the party to enable him to defeat the Administration's adherents. He took a long step toward securing control of the party when he became editor, on September 1, 1894, of the Omaha *World-Herald,* the state's most powerful Democratic paper. This move, the Administration's bungling in the matter of patronage, the continuing depression, and the almost total crop failures of 1893 and 1894 (the state got only 16.26 inches of rainfall in 1893, and 13.54 inches in 1894) enabled him to take control of the party in 1894. Under his leadership, the Democratic convention that year fused with the Populists to nominate Silas A. Holcomb for

governor and the entire Populist state ticket; it also endorsed Omar
C. Kem and William McKeighan, Populist congressmen. The only
Democrat of prominence of whom the convention approved was Congressman Bryan, whose course in the House of Representatives was
given high praise, and whose candidacy for the United States Senate,
official blessing. Administration Democrats bolted the convention and
nominated a ticket of their own headed by Phelps D. Sturdevant, but
from the outset there was little hope that they would make even a good
showing.

The campaign was as confused as it was furious. The Republicans
rode roughshod over National Committeeman Edward Rosewater to
nominate a slate of standpatters headed by Thomas J. Majors, pioneer
soldier and farmer from Nemaha County who long had been an active
force in Republican politics. Rosewater indignantly resigned his place
as national committeeman in a letter branding Majors as "the pliant
tool of the railroads . . . whose nomination was procured by the combined influence of corporation cappers, professional bribe givers, jury
fixers and impeached state house officials," and placed the *Bee* behind
Holcomb. With the combined support of the *Bee* and the *World-Herald,*
the Populists and the Democrats, Holcomb defeated Majors, 97,815 to
94,613; Sturdevant got a mere 6,985, and the Prohibition candidate
came along with 4,440. The Republicans won all other state offices,
however, and elected all their candidates to Congress, except in the
sixth district where Kem, now a Demo-Pop, was re-elected. They won
complete control of the legislature, which on the first ballot sent John M.
Thurston, general solicitor of the Union Pacific Railroad, to the Senate.

Though Holcomb was re-elected in 1896, and William A. Poynter,
a Boone County Populist, was chosen governor in 1898, the Populists
as an independent third party were never able to get complete control
of the state government. Both of their successful gubernatorial candidates were also the nominees of the Democratic party. Moreover, even
in 1897, the only time when the Republicans had control of neither
the legislature nor the executive office, the control was exercised by
fusionists. This was bitterly disappointing to many of the old-time
Populists who fervently believed that the farmers' only hope lay in independent, third-party action. They, however, were unable to stem the
tide flowing from the logic of American politics and the magnetic personality of William Jennings Bryan.

CHAPTER 19

Political Realignment

THOUGH THE FARMERS, through the Peoples party, had changed the pattern of politics and had achieved some voice in state government, they had by no means improved their economic position. Indeed, the farmers in the early Nineties were worse off than they had been in the Seventies when they had been hit by grasshoppers, drouth, and depression, or in the Eighties when bountiful crops brought steadily lower prices. In the early Nineties, the state suffered from protracted drouth and farm prices fell to new lows. There was some improvement in both prices and production in the late years of the decade, but conditions were so unfavorable that immigration, which had more than doubled the state's population in the Eighties, virtually ceased, and population increased only from 1,058,910 in 1890 to 1,066,300 in 1900. The following figures tell part of the story:

Year	Inches Rainfall	Corn Production	Price	Wheat Production	Price	Oats Production	Price
1890	17.15	70,694,112	.48	15,014,250	.76	34,997,615	.39
1891	30.61	70,608,114	.26	18,356,805	.73	34,101,768	.23
1892	24.29	63,708,064	.28	18,444,975	.50	28,103,592	.23
1893	16.26	61,931,024	.27	20,106,240	.40	28,893,360	.22
1894	13.54	66,085,536	.50	17,605,110	.49	25,403,016	.36
1895	19.02	68,343,248	.18	14,787,024	.40	39,911,696	.14
1896	25.85	298,599,638	.13	19,390,602	.58	34,092,631	.11
1897	23.68	241,268,490	.17	27,452,647	.69	51,731,095	.15
1898	20.61	158,754,666	.22	34,679,309	.47	56,245,042	.20
1899	19.55	175,816,641	.23	18,848,100	.49	51,731,132	.22

These general figures, however, do not tell the whole story. They do not, for example, tell the story of the central part of the state, where rainfall deviated downward even more seriously than it did in the state as a whole—a fact which may help somewhat to explain that section as the center of Populist activity. Likewise, these general figures do not tell the story of personal distress as it unfolded through the experience of individual farmers attempting to work their way out from under a crushing burden of debt contracted during the relatively flush times of the Eighties. Charles H. Morrill, a prominent pioneer who both experienced and witnessed the hard times of the period, describes them as follows:

In the year of 1893 crops in Nebraska were almost totally destroyed by drouth and hot winds. Then came the panic and financial stress, which paralyzed business. In 1894 Nebraska was doomed to have another crop failure. Farmers were obliged to ship in grain and even hay to feed their stock; many sacrificed their livestock by selling at very low prices. Some farmers shot their stock hogs to prevent their starving. Financial conditions grew worse and the entire state was almost in the grip of actual famine. Farmers could not pay interest on their mortgages; nor could land be sold at any price. One eastern loan company offered to sell me forty quarter sections at $200.00 each.

Labor, likewise, had benefited little from the independent political action in which it had participated. The Supreme Court had held invalid a Populist law declaring eight hours as a legal day's work in Nebraska, but for many the question was purely academic—the great problem was finding work of any sort. The financial depression growing out of the world-wide panic of 1893 and—particularly in Nebraska cities—reflecting the depressed condition of agriculture threw many people out of work and depressed the wages of those who were fortunate enough to find a job.

Into this picture William Jennings Bryan stepped with the full force of his magnetic personality. By taking for his own the coinage issue which had been paramount in Populist thinking since 1890, Bryan captured the Democratic party in Nebraska in 1894 and at the same time brought many of the Populists into the Democratic fold. In 1896 he did the same thing nationally. Bryanism thus replaced Populism as the voice of agrarian discontent, and the Democratic party, in Nebraska and the nation, was transformed from an organization of conservatives who looked with horror upon the expanding role of government under the Republicans to an organization which accepted not only the reality but the desirability of this expanded governmental role—insisting, however, that government must act in behalf of different groups than it had since the Civil War under the Republicans. Within the Republican party, too, there was a growing insistence that government assist the farmer and the laborer at least as much as it did the capitalist. In Nebraska and other northern Plains states, the Populists had secured many of their adherents from dissident elements in the Republican party. While they could support a third party, many of them found it virtually impossible to join the Democrats. Instead, they went back to the old party and tried to reform it from within. We have, therefore, paralleling Bryanism in the Democratic party, a growing progressivism within the GOP.

THE REPUBLICANS RECOVER CONTROL

Bryan's nomination for the presidency in 1896 created great excitement in Nebraska—the ultra-conservative Lincoln *Journal,* for example, greeted the news with the first two-column headline in its history. With the presidential nomination, Bryan's control of the Democratic party in Nebraska remained secure. He was even more the darling of the Populists than he was of the Democrats, and it was easy for him to promote fusion again in 1896 as he had in 1894. This fusion extended in a limited degree to the national campaign, too; the Populists also named Bryan as their standard-bearer, but they could not tolerate conservative Arthur Sewall of Maine for vice-president; so they confused the issue by naming Thomas E. Watson of Georgia as their candidate for the vice-presidency. Joining in the fusion, at least informally, were many silver Republicans who could not accept the nomination of William McKinley for president or that of J. H. McColl of Dawson County, regarded as extremely friendly to the Union Pacific, for governor.

With this strength behind him, Governor Silas Holcomb easily won re-election. Bryan defeated McKinley, 115,999 to 103,064, thus bringing Nebraska's electoral votes into the Democratic column for the first time in history. Also for the first time in history, the Republicans lost all the state offices. In the congressional races, fusionists won four seats and Republicans two. The fusionists gained an overwhelming majority in both houses of the legislature—twenty-six to seven in the Senate, and seventy-two to twenty-eight in the House.

The destruction of Republican control, begun in 1890, was complete by 1896—but the GOP was not destined to stay long out of power. The fusionist legislature of 1897 passed a variety of reform measures: an act providing for the use of initiative and referendum (the first in the United States),[1] acts regulating stockyards, telephone and telegraph companies; a law forbidding corporations to contribute to political campaign funds and another against grain elevator combinations; and an act forbidding further sale of the state school lands and providing that they should be leased forever, the income to be used for the annual support of the schools.[2] They failed, however, to deal effectively with railroads, against whom so much fusion oratory had been directed; bills to abolish free passes and reduce passenger rates to two cents per mile were sidetracked or defeated. Again, in 1899, the fusionists elected a state ticket headed by Populist William A. Poynter, but the Republicans controlled the legislature, and the fusionists were unable to abolish the hated free pass system. Indeed, it seemed that politicians' attitudes toward the free pass were determined by whether they were in office or out of it. The Omaha *Bee,* which continued to argue that the farmers only hope lay in the reform of the Republican party, commented:

Never in the history of Nebraska has the State House been filled by such a rapacious free pass brigade as since the offices were occupied by the Popocrats. According to the authority of the recognized organ of the party, there is but one official on the state payroll who does not ride on free railroad passes, and it is notorious that popocratic office holders high and low have not only been taking pleasure junkets at the expense of the railroads, but have travelled about on public business on free passes and charged up mileage in the expense accounts turned in to the state treasurer.

There were signs, too, that the great depression was passing. The rains came again, and despite good crops, prices improved a little.[3] Unemployment declined and hope stirred once more throughout the nation. Whether this represented, as the Republicans claimed, the Mc-

[1] See Adam C. Breckenridge, "Nebraska as a pioneer in the Initiative and Referendum," *Nebraska History,* XXXIV (September, 1953), 215–224.

[2] This brought to an end one phase of the heated controversy over the state school lands. See Sheldon, *Land Systems and Policies in Nebraska,* pp. 210–285 *passim.*

[3] See p. 232

Kinley Administration's stabilization of the economy and the saving of
the country from the horrors of Bryanarchy, or whether it represented,
as some of the fusionists maintained, the completion of a process of
liquidation by which most of the heavily mortgaged people had been
sold out at panic prices to start life over again, made little difference.
The period of stress was over and many people fell once again into
their old habits, which politically in Nebraska meant voting Republican.

Moreover, the nation's attention was occupied with war. Though
Union veterans were still around—albeit in dwindling numbers—the
war with Spain was the first international conflict in half a century.
The war took on something of the aspect of a great crusade, and though
Nebraskans who served in the Philippines or in the disease-ridden training camps of Chickamauga Park soon became disillusioned, McKinley's
position as a national leader was greatly strengthened. The war posed a
particular problem for Bryan. Struggling hard to keep himself in the
limelight and thus retain control of both the Democrats and the Populists, Bryan offered his services to the Government. When these were
declined by his erstwhile opponent, he persuaded Governor Holcomb
to appoint him Colonel of the Third Nebraska Regiment, which saw
service in Florida and Cuba. Bryan's military career did little to en-
hance his reputation, and he was constantly overshadowed by Theodore Roosevelt, seemingly given carte blanche by the Administration.
Bryan turned his attention from the silver issue to imperialism, but
while most Nebraskans had little enthusiasm for bearing the white man's
burden, and while the conservative Democrats generally agreed with
the Great Commoner's anti-imperialist views, he could not stir up much
articulate support for his program of anti-imperialism either in Nebraska
or the nation.

The Republicans, who had regained control of the legislature in
1898, fought hard to restore themselves completely to power in 1900.
Nebraska was a key state in that first election of the twentieth century.
Not only was it the home state of the Democratic presidential nominee
(Bryan easily secured the nomination again in 1900) but the seats of
two United States Senators were at stake. M. L. Hayward of Nebraska
City, who had been defeated by Governor Poynter in 1898, had been
elected Senator over William V. Allen in 1899, only to die before he
could qualify. Both Democrats and Populists were devoted to Bryan,
but neither group was willing to surrender its party organization to the

other. As a result, they went along with a fusion ticket which had within it the seeds of its own destruction. The fusionists had not distinguished themselves for their ability to work together in the legislature; they had never been able to agree to hold a single convention; they had always argued about candidates. It was only the magic of Bryan's name that held them together.

Though their victory was far from complete, the Republicans were able to rejoice when the returns for 1900 came in: McKinley defeated Bryan, 121,835 to 114,013; Charles H. Dietrich, a Hastings banker, defeated Poynter by the narrow margin of 861 votes; and the Republican candidates for other state offices won by similarly narrow margins. The fusionists retained four of the six congressional seats, but the Republicans secured a considerable majority in the legislature: in the Senate there were nineteen Republicans, twelve fusionists, and two Democrats; in the House, fifty-three Republicans, thirty fusionists, ten Democrats, and three Populists. In the joint convention which would choose the two senators, the Republicans had a margin of nine, even if the fusionists, Democrats, and Populists could have worked together —which was impossible.

It soon developed that even the Republicans would have difficulty in holding together. There were simply too many strong candidates. Among the leading contenders were John M. Thurston, seeking re-election; D. E. Thompson, Lincoln millionaire and superintendent of the Burlington lines west of the Missouri; the redoubtable Edward Rosewater; and former Governor Lorenzo Crounse. In addition there was a host of others, each hoping that lightning would strike him should a compromise candidate be necessary. On the fusion side the leading contenders were Senator Allen, who had been appointed by Governor Poynter to fill out Hayward's term; and Gilbert M. Hitchcock, a son of Republican Senator Phineas W. Hitchcock, but now editor of the Democratic Omaha *World-Herald*. Much of the struggle centered around D. E. Thompson, who had secured almost absolute control of Republican politics in the capital city but who was bitterly opposed by Charles H. Gere, editor of the powerful Lincoln *Journal*. The balloting, which began on January 5, did not end until March 29, providing those who urged the popular election of senators one of their strongest arguments. The struggle was finally ended when Thompson withdrew in favor of Governor Dietrich, and the opposition forces agreed upon J. H. Millard, prominent Omaha banker put forth by Thompson, as their other candidate.

Lieutenant Governor Ezra P. Savage, who became governor when Dietrich went to the Senate, immediately got his party in trouble by pardoning Joseph S. Bartley, former State Treasurer who had been found in default in the sum of $555,790.66, and who had been sentenced to twenty years in the state penitentiary and fined $303,768.90. But the Republicans themselves took care of Savage. They indignantly refused to renominate him—even though his most ardent critic, the Lincoln *Journal,* admitted, "Outside of his unpopular and perhaps premature exercise of the pardoning power, the Governor has been the chief of one of the most upright and certainly the most efficient bodies of state officers that Nebraska has had for years." They selected instead John H. Mickey, a farmer and banker from Osceola, a man who generally was looked upon as opposed to the Republican machine, an able and public-spirited citizen.

Fusion was even more difficult for the Democrats and Populists in 1902 than it had been in prior years. They met in separate halls in Lincoln on the same day, and though Bryan addressed both conventions, counselling a fraternal spirit and united effort in a common cause, it was clear from the outset that unity would be difficult to achieve. The Democrats demanded as the price of fusion the head of the ticket, inasmuch as they had supported Populists since 1894. Specifically, they wanted C. J. Smyth, who had served as attorney general and who had been well liked by the Populists. The Populists, for their part, wanted M. F. Harrington of O'Neill, who had been a Democrat before he became a Populist and who generally was looked upon as one of the ablest lawyers and stump-speakers in the state. Bryan apparently wanted William H. Thompson of Grand Island, and after a stormy all-night session in a conference committee from the two conventions, his desire, as in the past, prevailed. Thompson conducted a vigorous campaign, but he couldn't divert the drift back to the Republican party. Many Republicans who had supported the Populists now felt that the Independent movement had been taken over completely by Bryan and the Democrats; and with a candidate of the caliber of Mickey at the head of the ticket they found it easy to get back into the fold. Even so, the vote was close, attesting somewhat to the fusion candidate's personal popularity: Mickey, 96,471; Thompson, 91,116. Prohibition and Socialist candidates received 3,396 and 3,157 votes respectively, making the total against Mickey a little larger than the vote cast for him. The Republicans elected their entire state ticket, a comfortable majority in both houses of the legislature, and all but one of their congressional candidates. In the second district, Gilbert M. Hitchcock defeated Congressman David H. Mercer, in part because the former got the support of his journalistic rival, Edward Rosewater of the Omaha *Bee*. Rosewater had tried unsuccessfully to prevent Mercer's renomination in the Republican primary and refused to support him in the general election—largely because Mercer had tried to intrude himself as a compromise candidate against Rosewater in the heated senatorial struggle of the year before.

PROGRESSIVISM AND THE GOP

Whatever influence the Populists had ever possessed as an independent party—in Nebraska and the nation—declined rapidly after 1892. Nationally, they had fused with the Democrats to nominate Bryan in 1896 and again in 1900. They could not accept Parker, the Democratic nominee in 1904, and by 1908 they had become somewhat disillusioned with Bryan's leadership; they put their own candidates in the field in both those years but their disappointing showing in 1908 (only about 29,000 votes) resulted in their complete dissolution as an independent party. In Nebraska, their only victories had been those they shared, through fusion, with the Democrats. In Nebraska as in the nation, fusion spelled disaster for those who hoped to maintain the Populists as an independent third party. As one of their newspaper supporters, John C. Sprecher of Schuyler, observed in 1904: "The Populists have to go back twelve years to get a vote to base their representation upon, as fusion has been a confusion as to votes. A year or so more of fusion and they won't need to go back for a vote because there won't be any delegates to elect. The Populist party has reached the point where it is nothing with fusion and nothing without it." For their off-year convention in 1905, they could assemble only about fifty delegates in a dingy little room on East "O" Street in Lincoln.

While they died out as an independent party in the early years of the twentieth century, their ideas lived on in both of the old parties, which in the early years of the twentieth century seemed to be vying with each other to implement the Populist assumption that the government should be truly representative of the people, that long established control of politics and economics by the few should be broken. As the great historian of the frontier, Frederick Jackson Turner, once phrased it, "Mr. Bryan's democracy, Mr. Deb's socialism, and Mr. Roosevelt's Republicanism all had in common the emphasis on the need of governmental regulation of industrial tendencies in the interests of the common man; the checking of the power of those business titans who emerged successful out of the competitive individualism of pioneer America."[4]

In Nebraska, Bryan not only took over the Populists; he changed the Democratic party from an organization dominated by ultra-conservatives like Morton, Miller, and Boyd to an organization in which all but the most ardent agrarian reformers could feel at home. The Republicans, too, began to feel the impact of Populist doctrine, as old-timers who had joined the Populists briefly began to drift back, and as youngsters, nursed on the heady debates of the Populist period, began to make their voices heard in the party's councils. The presence of Theodore Roosevelt in the White House naturally strengthened the hands of the progressives within the state, but the logic of events locally also demonstrated forcibly that if the Republicans were to maintain their control they would have to move toward the Progressive position. In 1904, George W. Berge, author of the celebrated *Free Pass Bribery System*,[5] and fusion candidate for governor, almost defeated Mickey's bid for re-election despite the landslide majority for Roosevelt over Parker.

The Republican progressives clearly saw that if they were to achieve control of the party they must break railroad domination of its affairs. Railroads, the principal "big business" in the state, had long been the object of reform denunciation. Despite their oratory, the fusionists had been unable to do much toward curbing railroad influence—the roads kept issuing free passes to politicians, watching over the sessions of the legislature through the agency of highly paid and skillful lobbyists, and keeping local politics in order by retaining influential attorneys at all the county seats. Their unseemly struggle for two United States senators in 1901 had greatly irritated many citizens. Moreover, that struggle, in which the Union Pacific and the Burlington, instead of dividing the

[4]Frederick Jackson Turner, *The Frontier in American History* (New York: Henry Holt and Company, 1920), p. 281.

[5]See pp. 213–214.

two senatorships, decided to fight it out for control of both, presaged a breakup of the railroad machine. It also was an important factor in the demand for a change in the method of electing senators. Governor Dietrich, usually looked upon as the Burlington's senator, got involved in a nasty difficulty resulting from his removal of the Hastings post office into a building of his own and his collection from the state of the governor's salary for a few weeks while he was also United States Senator. He was hauled into District Court on both counts, and though acquitted on technicalities, it was clear that Dietrich and railroad influence would do the party no good. His was the short term, and when it ended the Republican state convention endorsed Elmer J. Burkett for his seat over the opposition of the railroads. The electorate approved the choice in the preferential ballot, and the GOP-controlled legislature of 1905 elected Burkett without so much as the formality of a caucus. The next year, through the influence of Senator Burkett, the state convention adopted an anti-free pass resolution, despite railroad efforts to defeat it.

By the summer of 1906, progressivism was sweeping over Nebraska like a prairie fire. On June 16, Senator George L. Sheldon of Nehawka, who had declared, "We have had too much of railroad government in Nebraska," and Attorney General Norris Brown of Kearney, who had been carrying on an active campaign against lumber dealers' associations, line elevators, and other large business groups, announced that they would seek the Republican nomination for governor and United States senator respectively. They made a series of public addresses which sounded more like old-time Populist fireworks than anything that had been heard in the state for more than a decade, uniting in a declaration to the effect: "There never will be a square deal in this state until the railroad machine is overthrown and its pernicious free pass system abolished." With Roosevelt carrying on an aggressive campaign against millionaire land-grabbers and corporation consolidations, and the Lincoln *Journal*, which in former years had been the faithful supporter of party machine and railroad rule, carrying the torch for the aggressive anti-railroad Republicans, the progressives carried the day. The state convention nominated Sheldon for governor and endorsed Brown for the Senate. Their platform, very similar to that of the Democrats, embodied many of the early Populist doctrines and was a strong anti-railroad, anti-corporation document.

The Democrats, who after Parker's resounding defeat were once again in Bryan's lap, also came out strongly for reform, as they had been doing in their state platform many years, but nominated Ashton C. Shallenberger of Alma, an old-line machine Democrat generally looked upon as being under the railroad influence, as their candidate for governor. The Populists were persuaded to endorse Shallenberger only after an impassioned speech by George W. Berge in his favor. The Democratic convention also connived with Gilbert M. Hitchcock, who was running for Congress but who wanted to be United States senator in case the Democrats should take over the legislature, to refrain from endorsing anyone for the Senate. Sheldon defeated Shallenberger 97,858 to 84,885; all Republican candidates for state offices were elected by large majorities; and the Republicans got a majority of both houses of the legislature and elected all congressmen, except in the second district, where Hitchcock, largely because of his great local popularity, defeated John L. Kennedy, who had beaten him two years earlier.

On December 12, 1906, W. B. Rose, Chairman of the Republican State Committee, addressed a letter to the Republican members of the incoming legislature warning them of the tricky manipulations by which the railroad and corporation lobbies might be expected to attempt to block the reform measures promised in the Republican state platform. Whether they needed the warning or not, the members of the legislature went ahead to redeem their campaign promises with the result that the legislative acts of 1907 marked more important and permanent changes in the political structure of the state than those of any other session. In a very real sense they brought to fruition the revolution in public thought which began in 1890. Among the major items entered in the statute books were: a state-wide compulsory primary, a Child Labor Act, an Anti-Free-Pass Act, a Two-Cent Passenger Fare Act, and an Anti-Discrimination Act. They also created and defined the power of a state railway commission, established a state bureau for the investigation of insect pests and plant diseases, created a board of pardons, prohibited brewers from holding any interests in saloons, and memorialized Congress to amend the Constitution to provide for the popular election of the United States senators.

Possibly the most important in the long run was the direct primary law. There had been primaries of sorts since the 1870's, but they were purely voluntary. The senatorial fiasco of 1901 had aroused great interest in primary legislation. Adam McMullen of Beatrice had led a direct primary fight in the session of 1905 but nothing had been accomplished. With both parties committed to the primary in 1907, however, it was easily put through. In 1909 presidential electors were added to the primary system, and in 1911, delegates to the national conventions, national committeemen, and a presidential preference. The primary was not the great cure-all its proponents had promised it would be, and frequently over the years the Nebraska legislature has changed the operation of the primary system in an effort to make it work to the satisfaction of all.

DEMOCRATIC ASCENDANCY

The campaign of 1908 went forward in an atmosphere of reform, albeit a rather confused and confusing atmosphere. Nationally, the Republicans, led by the relatively conservative Taft, were able to carry the day against the Democrats, once again under the banner of the nation's outstanding western liberal, William Jennings Bryan; in Nebraska, Governor George L. Sheldon, perhaps the most liberal chief executive in the history of the state, was defeated for re-election by the relatively conservative Ashton C. Shallenberger. There were a number of factors in this reversal of the trend back to the Republicans. In the first place, Bryan at the head of the ticket was favored over Taft. Then, on two local issues, bank guarantee and county option, Shallenberger campaigned much more effectively than Sheldon. The panic of 1907 had spotlighted the importance of guaranteeing bank deposits. Oklahoma territory had had such a law since 1903, and under the leadership of Bryan, the Democratic national convention adopted a plank favoring national bank guarantee. Similarly, the Democratic state platform favored a state guarantee law, and Shallenberger, who got the Democratic nomination again, campaigned vigorously in its behalf. Sheldon had also declared himself in favor of a bank guarantee law, but his position was greatly weakened when the Republican state convention voted down the proposal by a resounding three-to-one majority. Sheldon also got himself in trouble on the liquor issue. He had tried to push a county option law through the legislature in 1907, but it failed. He continued his fight for county option into the election campaign with the result that he lost many wet votes which might normally have been expected to go to the Republican candidate. Shallenberger, on the other hand, straddled the issue, letting wets think he opposed county option and the dry Populists think he favored it. As a result, he unseated Sheldon, 132,960 to 125,976. While the Republicans generally won other state offices, Bryan secured the state's electoral votes; the Democrats elected three congressmen and secured a clear majority in the legislature.

The Democrats in the legislature of 1909, assisted by some progressive Republicans, set out to redeem their campaign promises. They passed a bank guarantee law, changed the primary from a closed to an open election, provided for the election of judges and educational officers on non-partisan tickets, enacted the "Oregon Pledge Law," which required candidates for the legislature to pledge that if elected they would vote for the candidate for United States senator receiving the highest preferential vote. The liquor issue intruded itself into the session in an unusual and unexpected way. County option was defeated in the House and did not come to a vote in the Senate. The real fireworks arose over an eight o'clock closing law which got through both houses and, despite great pressure from the liquor interests who had supported him, received the signature of Governor Shallenberger.

Shallenberger's approval of the eight o'clock law cost him renomination in 1910. Mayor James C. Dahlman of Omaha, colorful former cowhand and a well-known opponent of any sumptuary legislation on the liquor question, entered the lists against him, and with the support of wet Republicans who were able to move into the Democratic primary as a result of the open primary law passed in 1909, squeezed out a 500-vote victory over the Governor. The Republicans, meanwhile, nominated Chester H. Aldrich, a David City lawyer and a former state senator, who campaigned as the advocate of county option and with the full support of the Anti-Saloon League. "Mayor Jim" made an aggressive, colorful campaign, promising to serve his supporters free beer on the state house grounds on the day of his inauguration, and with the tide generally running toward the Democrats, he confidently expected election. He failed to take into account, however, that many of the Populists were ardent prohibitionists and let their views on that issue overcome any other Democratic predilections. Moreover, the most powerful man in the party, William Jennings Bryan, refused to support Dahlman for governor. Bryan, personally a dry, had long compromised the prohibition issue with his predominantly wet colleagues, but by 1910 he had come out strongly in favor of the Anti-Saloon League position. As a result, while Gilbert M. Hitchcock defeated Elmer J. Burkett in the senatorial preference vote and the democrats elected three congressmen and the majority of both houses of the legislature, Aldrich and the Republican state ticket went in by handy majorities.

The Democratic legislature ignored Aldrich's demand for a county option law, concentrating instead on other issues. Perhaps the most important achievements of the legislature of 1911 were the submission of an amendment providing for the initiative and referendum and another providing for a non-partisan Board of Control with powers of government over seventeen state institutions, thus removing them from the spoils system.

Meanwhile, the fight between the insurgent progressives and the regulars for the control of the Republican party seriously threatened its position in Nebraska. Representative George W. Norris of McCook had led the insurgent Republican fight against Speaker Cannon. The national prominence he attained as a result of that struggle enabled him to move into a position of leadership among the insurgent Republicans of the state. The Roosevelt bolt from Taft further complicated the Republican position. By nominating progressive candidates—Norris for the Senate, and Aldrich, who had been one of the governors who had urged Roosevelt to make the independent race for re-election—the Republicans were able to hold their state ticket together. They could not keep Roosevelt off the ballot on the national ticket, however, and the Republican vote for president was so badly split that Woodrow Wilson easily carried the state. John H. Morehead, a relatively conservative Democrat from Falls City, defeated Richard L. Metcalfe, Bryan's candidate, in the Democratic primary for governor, and former Governor Shallenberger beat W. H. Thompson, another Bryan candidate, for senator. (Bryan's advocacy of county option and his long association with lost causes nationally had cost him much of his former influence in the Democratic party of the state, as the anti-Bryan forces were marshalled under Arthur Mullen of Omaha, a former Populist and one of the state's ablest lawyers.) While Wilson was winning the state's electoral votes and Morehead the governorship, George W. Norris, already proving his ability to attract Democratic votes, ran comfortably ahead of Shallenberger in the senatorial preference; and in compliance with the "Oregon Pledge Law" the legislature, which had a strong Democratic majority in the House—the Republicans had a small majority in the Senate—went through the formality of electing him.

The Democratic tide continued to roll. Though Morehead was opposed for re-nomination by Metcalfe and Berge, the state convention made a great show of loyalty, and Morehead—who had developed into a strong administrator and despite his conservative tendencies had worked earnestly for the initiative and referendum and the Board of Control—easily defeated R. B. Howell, his Republican opponent, and carried with him the Lieutenant Governor, Secretary of State, Auditor, Treasurer, and Attorney General. The Democrats elected three congressmen and a sizable majority in both houses of the legislature.

It was clear now that the Democrats, who had come to power on the shoulders of William Jennings Bryan, were maintaining at least a precarious control of state affairs without his assistance. Bryan, who had alienated a large portion of the party in 1910 on the county option issue, further alienated many of the regulars when he split with Woodrow Wilson over policy toward the European war and resigned as Secretary of State. The dominant forces in the party now were Hitchcock, Mullen, and Morehead. The extent of this group's control is perhaps best shown in the primary campaign of 1916. Prohibition was now a burning issue. A prohibition amendment to the constitution was before the voters of the state, and Bryan was doing everything in his power to turn the Democratic party from its former habits. Yet the anti-prohibition forces easily took over the Democratic primaries, renominating Senator Hitchcock, and nominating for governor Keith Neville, thirty-two year old rancher and banker from North Platte, over Charles W. Bryan, the Great Commoner's brother. Surprisingly enough, Hitchcock and Neville were elected by comfortable margins although prohibition was adopted by an even greater margin. Prohibition was an issue, but it was only a side issue. Wilson, by virtue of his "New Freedom," which had embodied many of the ideas for which Nebraska liberals had been fighting for years, and of his record of having "kept us out of the war," which appealed to the state's large German population, carried the day again for the Democrats in Nebraska. The Democrats got their usual three congressmen and an overwhelming majority in the legislature.

Though Governor Neville had opposed prohibition, he had promised to enforce such a law to the best of his ability if one were adopted and he urged his brethren in the legislature to enact a law implementing the new amendment without delay.

But Nebraska's attention, like that of the nation, was being turned to other than domestic issues. Wilson had kept us out of the war, but he could not prevent the war cloud hovering on the horizon from engulfing the nation.

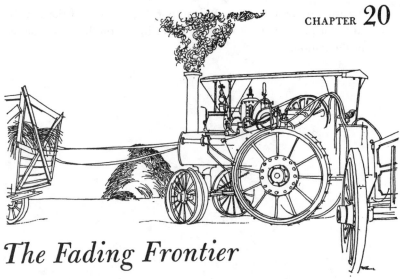

CHAPTER 20

The Fading Frontier

IN WHAT HAS long been considered one of the most significant papers ever presented by an American historian, Frederick Jackson Turner, addressing a meeting of the American Historical Association being held in connection with the World's Columbian Exposition in Chicago in 1893, called attention to a statement in the reports of the Superintendent of the Census for 1890 that "the unsettled area has been so broken into by isolated bodies of settlement that there can hardly be said to be a frontier line." He noted that it marked "the closing of a great historic movement . . . the colonization of the great unoccupied West." Though an unsettled area of considerable extent that was not to be filled in until after the turn of a century remained in northwest Nebraska, the settlement period in the history of the state by 1890 was in many respects over. Surely the years between 1890 and the outbreak of the first World War—or, for census purposes, 1910— saw the passing of frontier conditions as they had existed during the pioneer years.

There was great growth during the period, particularly after 1900, but even considering the settlement of northwest Nebraska that growth was not primarily in terms of population. The state's population increased only from 1,058,910 in 1890 to 1,192,214 in 1910, or only about 12.7 percent. In terms of population, the period is characterized by redistribution rather than growth. Particularly marked was the beginning of a trend toward the cities which has continued slowly but steadily to the present time: virtually all of the population increase went to the cities; the number of places with more than twenty-five hundred inhabitants increased from 16 to 27; the percent of total population classified as rural decreased from 59.2 to 53.5. Total wealth during the period increased by more than two hundred percent—from $1,275,685,-514 in 1890 to $3,794,986,781 in 1912, a per-capita increase of from $174.49 to $375.77.

To a degree, the initial phase of the experiment in occupying the prairie-plains of Nebraska had been completed. The fact that the hard times of the Seventies brought no great political upheaval may be explained in part by the thought that those hard times were looked upon somewhat as difficulties besetting any new country. By the same token, the great political changes accompanying the depression of the Nineties may be partly explained by the fact that the state's population had assumed some degree of permanence and had accepted the realization that it would have to try to work out its destiny with what it had. As Willa Cather put it:

These years of trial, as everyone now realizes, had a salutary effect upon the new state. They winnowed out the settlers with a purpose from the drifting malcontents who are ever seeking a land where man does not live by the sweat of his brow. The slack farmer moved on. Superfluous banks failed, and money-lenders who drove hard bargains with desperate men came to grief. The strongest stock survived, and within ten years those who had weathered the storm came into their reward.[1]

Earlier chapters have discussed the trials. This discussion will deal primarily with the reward.

ON THE FARMS

Despite a trend to the towns, Nebraska remained preponderantly an agricultural state; and agriculture during this period, particularly after the turn of the century, was characterized by great growth and the development, to a degree, of at least temporary stability.

A part of the story can be told in the following figures on number of farms, acres, and values:

[1]Willa Cather, "Nebraska: The End of the First Cycle," in Virginia Faulkner, ed., *Roundup: A Nebraska Reader* (Lincoln: University of Nebraska Press, 1957), p. 7.

	1890	1900	1910
Number of farms	113,608	121,525	129,678
Acres of land in farms	21,593,444	29,911,779	38,622,021
Percent of land area in farms	43.9	60.8	78.6
Acres of improved land	15,247,705	18,432,595	24,382,577
Percent land area improved	70.6	61.6	63.1
Total value of farm property	$511,799,810	$747,950,057	$2,079,818,647
Value land and buildings	$402,358,913	$577,660,020	$1,813,346,936
Value implements and machinery	$ 16,468,977	$ 24,940,450	$ 44,249,708
Value livestock	$ 92,971,920	$145,349,587	$ 222,222,004
Value per farm, all property	$ 4,505	$ 6,155	$ 16,038
Value land and buildings per acre	$ 18.63	$ 19.31	$ 49.95

Moreover, it appeared that the old bugaboo—the mortgage—had re-treated somewhat from its earlier position. The amount of mortgage debt increased from $37,678,132 in 1890 to $62,373,472 in 1910, but the percent of debt to value decreased from 32.4 to 21.8. Offsetting that somewhat—and reflecting the heavy loss of farms during the depression of the Nineties—was the increase in tenancy from 24.7 percent in 1890 to 38.1 percent in 1910.

While some of the great increase in general farm values—and particularly land values—was the result of an increased number of acres in farms, most of it was brought about through an increase in both production and price. The first ten years of the twentieth century brought relatively abundant rainfall—each year except 1907 more than the annual mean of 22.84 inches, and an average of 25.54 inches—resulting in correspondingly good crop yields. To be sure, not all crops were uniformly good every year, but no part of the state suffered from prolonged drouth or repeated ravages of insect pests. A general price increase accompanied the good yields. Between 1899 and 1910 the price of wheat increased 67 percent, oats 78 percent, corn 140 percent, and hogs 133 percent. Fortunately, too, at least part of this represented a net gain in agriculture's economic position, for the price of goods purchased by farmers increased only about 30 percent during these same years. This is explained in part by the fact that the price of manufactured goods did not fall as low during the depression of the early Nineties as did the price of farm products.

New discoveries, labor saving inventions, improved varieties and strains of crops and livestock contributed to increased productivity. Horses and mules still provided the motive power—except for the steam engines which pulled the grain separators—but farmers generally began to use riding implements. The gang plow replaced the walking plow and the one-bottom sulky. The riding cultivator came into general use. New barns made it easier to care for livestock. The blow stacker, manure spreader, horse fork, and other laborsaving equipment took a great deal of the drudgery out of farm life, and larger machinery reduced the hours of labor. Though some farm homes could boast an oil stove, carpet sweeper, sinks, and running water, the farmer's wife generally had to do much of her work in the same old way. For the most part she had moved from her soddie into a frame house, but she still drew water from the well and spent long hours over the kitchen range preparing food for the family and hired help.

There was some improvement in existing crops, such as the replacement of late maturing oats with early maturing varieties, but the most notable developments came in the introduction of basically new crops, notably winter wheat and alfalfa. The development of winter wheat had a particularly marked effect upon the state's agricultural economy. As has been pointed out, though spring wheat never yielded very well, Nebraska farmers generally had been slow to adopt the winter varieties.[2] The Mennonites had had good success with Turkey Red brought with them from Russia, but the generality of the farmers had to have its superiority demonstrated before they were willing to accept it. Newspapermen like Dr. George L. Miller and J. Sterling Morton actively promoted the production of winter wheat. George W. Holdrege of the Burlington, "always optimistic and ready to try anything which will benefit Nebraska," did a great deal to encourage experimental planting of the new varieties. The state experiment station, beginning in 1902, worked to produce varieties of Turkey Red that were well adapted to conditions in various sections of the state. The milling industry became interested in winter wheat in the late Nineties and began to adjust its equipment to take care of the increased quantities being marketed. There were other factors—particularly the introduction of the press drill, which made it possible to plant and seed deeper, thus enabling it to get a good growth before winter came. As a result of all this activity there was a steady increase in the production of winter wheat. The Depart-

[2] See p. 198.

ment of Agriculture in 1901 changed Nebraska's classification from a spring wheat state to a winter wheat state, and in that year Nebraska was exceeded only by Kansas as a winter wheat producer. In 1899 spring wheat acreage constituted 96.86 percent of total wheat acreage; in 1909 winter wheat accounted for 91.25 percent of the total. Likewise total wheat acreage increased. From 1899 to 1901 there were about 450,000 additional acres planted to wheat in Nebraska.

Another development of great significance was the introduction of alfalfa. This crop had been introduced in 1875 from Utah and was first grown in 1876 by S. P. Baker of Curtis in Frontier County. During the Eighties it was raised in some of the southwestern counties and in the Nineties H. D. Watson pioneered the raising of alfalfa on his huge ranch west of Kearney. Watson, the father of Kearney's short-lived urban real-estate boom,[3] not only planted thousands of acres to alfalfa but encouraged other farmers to raise it because of its value as a forage crop. In 1894 the Agricultural Experiment Station issued a bulletin setting forth the qualities of alfalfa as a forage crop and as a soil-building plant. This bulletin was widely distributed and induced many farmers who had never heard of alfalfa to try it. As farmers began to experiment with alfalfa they readily realized its value in filling an important need in the cropping system of the state, enabling farmers to readjust their crop system to maintain soil fertility and engage in livestock production on a larger scale than ever before. No other plant except Turkey Red wheat changed the agriculture of the state in so short a time.

Sugar beets, for which there had been alternate enthusiasm and disgust, began to make some impression on the agricultural economy of the irrigated North Platte Valley. There had been interest in sugar beets as a means of diversifying the agriculture and increasing the industrial potential of the state since the late Eighties. The state had offered bounties to encourage the production of beet sugar. A sugar factory had been established in Grand Island in 1890 and a few years later other factories were located at Ames and Norfolk. Generally, however, they had been unsuccessful and the raising of sugar beets was a tiresome job, requiring much hard labor.

The livestock industry recovered rapidly from the depression of the Nineties. The development of a serum for hog cholera, long the bane

[3]See p. 203.

of the swine industry, greatly reduced the ravages of that disease, and the number of hogs on Nebraska farms increased from 1,316,047 in 1895 to a high of 2,435,351 in 1907, after which there was a decline. The cattle industry likewise developed rapidly during the early years of the twentieth century, reaching a peak of over three million cattle on the farms of Nebraska during the three years 1907–1909. The growth in alfalfa greatly influenced the cattle industry, and the alfalfa counties in the Platte Valley became extensive cattle feeding centers. Likewise, under the leadership of the Agricultural College, considerable attention was given to the cattle industry as a means of building up the soil. Dairying also increased markedly: in 1901 there were 556,359 milk cows in the state and by 1909, 897,000, an increase of 61 percent. The introduction of the hand cream separator and the Babcock tester were important factors in the development of dairying.

But most significant of all during this period of farm prosperity was the growing realization that Nebraska had certain limitations as an agricultural state and that farmers as well as any other group needed to apply their best brains to the problems before them. As early as 1895, W. J. Whitmore, president of the Improved Stock-Breeders Association, delivered an address on "The Lessons of the Drouth," in which he bade good riddance to those who had departed the state, but warned:

Do not misunderstand me to mean that every portion of Nebraska is reasonably sure to raise good crops of farm products in a majority of years. Probably many parts will not; but experience is merely determining what portions are adapted to certain pursuits and what to others. . . .

There is wealth in our state, in her consummate combination of soil and climate, for those who know enough to get it. The progress of civilization is opening new fields for the play of intelligence. The scope of knowledge that enabled the farmer of fifty years ago to not only earn a living, but to hold his rank among the agencies of society and keep a touch of elbow with the marching column of progress, now would leave him far behind, a hopeless and despairing loser in the race for power and supremacy. . . .

The time has come when the farmer must mix brains with his soil or fall to the rear.

And there were many who were mixing brains with the soil. Hardy W. Campbell, encouraged by George W. Holdrege, conducted successful dry farming experiments in the western part of the state. The State Board of Agriculture, under the leadership of men like Robert W. Furnas, who continued until his death in 1905 to be the state's outstanding agricultural spokesman, and W. R. Mellor continued to urge farmers to try new methods. The University of Nebraska, its College of Agriculture and Experiment Station, steadily developed scientific investigation of some of the principal factors entering into the development of agriculture. Geologist Erwin H. Barbour and botanist Charles E. Bessey (who persuaded President Roosevelt to establish a national forest in the Sandhills!)[4] not only engaged in scientific investigation but worked ceaselessly to convince their fellow Nebraskans of the importance of scientific farming. Under the leadership of the University, farmers' institutes were held in many counties, to be superseded after 1914 by agricultural extension work carried on with both federal and state funds.

As Nebraska agriculture moved into its wartime boom, there were still farmers who disdained the assistance of the Agricultural College and the county agent, declaring that they "weren't farming now half as well as they knowed how," but most of them had accepted the warning that they had better mix brains with their soil.

IN THE TOWNS

The depression of the Nineties caught the cities and towns in a paralyzing grip. Symptomatic of the paralysis was the condition of banking. Bank deposits went down from $53,674,113 in 1892 to $27,264,-537 in 1896, and creditors of Nebraska banks had over five million dollars tied up in 101 failed institutions. There were spectacular failures which destroyed confidence not only in the system but in the men operating it—that of the Capital National in Lincoln, for example, which put its president in the federal penitentiary at Sioux City and was a leading factor in the defalcation of State Treasurer Joseph Bartley. Factory buildings stood empty, store windows showed only dismal "for rent" signs, street railway tracks built to the new subdivisions rusted from lack of use. Population which had skyrocketed in the Eighties came to a standstill or declined: even allowing for the seriously inflated figures in 1890 from some of the cities, it is clear that there was very little urban growth during the Nineties and in some instances there was actual decline—in Beatrice, Plattsmouth, and Nebraska City,

[4] For a summary of Professor Bessey's work in connection with the Nebraska National Forest, see Raymond J. Pool, "Fifty Years on the Nebraska National Forest," *Nebraska History*, XXXIV (September, 1953), 139-180.

for example. Omaha's major links with the industrial world—the railroads and the big packers—became restive under federal restrictions, and its streets echoed in the hot summer of 1892 with fearful Populist oratory. Nevertheless, the city set about with the typical "American go-aheaditiveness" which the first paper published in the town had ascribed to it, to rebuild its fallen fortunes. The suburbs of Dundee and Benson were founded, and South Omaha, home of the great packing industry, increased greatly in population. The businessmen formed a Chamber of Commerce and the Knights of Ak-Sar-Ben was organized "to promote patriotism among the citizens."

Under the leadership of Gurdon W. Wattles, a former Iowa banker who had come to Omaha on the eve of the financial panic of 1893, the Knights set out to lick the depression by demonstrating to all the world that it did not exist. Out of this effort grew the Trans-Mississippi and International Exposition of 1898. When incorporated in 1896, it seemed like one of those hopeless gestures that could bring nothing but defeat and disappointment. Yet under Wattles the organization went ahead. Congress was persuaded to appropriate two hundred thousand dollars when the association raised a like amount; Nebraska appropriated one hundred thousand dollars; and other states, another $138,000. Out on the Kountze tract a group of glittering white buildings whose architecture was "freely inspired by the classic and the renaissance" and which had no relation whatever to the life of the Plains, arose to house the exposition. From Little Egypt to Cass Gilbert's monument to agriculture and the huge plaster warrior in a chariot drawn by four lions and inscribed simply OMAHA, the exposition bravely described the bright new future. President McKinley opened it June 1, 1898, by pushing a button which in turn sent electric current flowing across the nation to set the machinery in operation. Later the President came out to view the wonder—and to be viewed by some ninety-eight thousand Midwesterners. The exposition was a great success—even financially—and it helped convince Omaha at least that the depression was over.

The early years of the twentieth century saw another flurry of prosperity in Nebraska's metropolis. The Omaha Grain Exchange was organized to develop the city into an important grain market. Fancy new residential districts—such as Happy Hollow and Fairacres—were platted and occupied. Omaha school children learned to count off the industrial successes of the town in rapid succession—"Omaha macaroni

is sold in Italy. . . . Omaha pig lead is sold all over the world." Stockyard
receipts, which had developed into an important barometer of the city's
economic activity, showed the following gains:

	1890	1900	1910
Cattle	615,337	828,204	1,223,533
Swine	1,702,723	2,200,926	1,894,314
Sheep	153,873	1,276,775	2,984,870
Horses and Mules	5,069	59,645	29,734
Totals	2,477,002	4,365,550	6,132,451

Through it all, Omaha remained lusty and wide open as it had during the days when it was a jumping-off place for the West. True, sporting
bloods no longer raced their horses up and down Farnam Street, and
Gurdon W. Wattles was a different type of civic leader from Bill Paxton or Count Creighton, but there was plenty of entertainment for the
farmers and the boys from the small towns who came in to have a look
at city life. Jim Dahlman, colorful ex-cowboy from the west end of the
state, was elected again and again as mayor of the new city arising out
of the depression. "Mayor Jim," as he was affectionately called, was
an avowed friend of personal liberty—and this meant the open saloon.
Though he got his start under William Jennings Bryan, the Great Commoner broke with him when the Mayor, running for governor on the
Democratic ticket, denounced prohibition. Tom Dennison, a gambler
driven into politics to protect his business, became the city's political
boss. Omaha was still the Wild West, but its wildness was of a little
different variety.

Lincoln, too, came out of the doldrums. There was very little industry, but its growing wholesale houses and retail stores served an
ever-widening territory. With the capitol and other state institutions
firmly established, the University flourishing, and small communities
developing north, east, and south, the city's prospects looked good even
to hardheaded businessmen in the depths of the depression—Charles
G. Dawes, for example, noted in his diary on January 3, 1893: "I have
the northwest corner of 13th and O Streets constantly in mind. . . .
I am as sure of its rapid and permanent increase in value as I am that
the day follows night."

Life in the capital city was considerably different from that in Omaha.
Dominated by the University—which under the leadership of men like

Andrews, Pound, Bessey, Barbour, and Howard was developing into one of the major institutions of the West—and surrounded by church schools like Nebraska Wesleyan, Cotner University, and Union College, Lincoln came to attract a different sort of people. The solid burghers of the capital city frowned on the high jinks tolerated in Omaha, and Lincoln's social life centered around its discussion clubs, literary societies, the opera house—proclaimed the most ornate Romanesque building west of Chicago—its thirty-eight churches and thirteen temperance societies. William Jennings Bryan, though his political views disturbed many of the more conservative citizens, occupied a place of prominence in the city's life. He built a grand farm home east of the city and spoke repeatedly at local church gatherings, picnics, and banquets. Young Lieutenant John J. Pershing, Commandant of Cadets at the University, added sparkle to the city's social life. Among the students, Willa Cather was making an impression on her peers and on her elders with her brilliant pen, sharp tongue, and pronounced views.

Manufactures, two-thirds of which arose directly from the processing of agricultural products, reflected both the general urban gain and the fact that manufacturing played a relatively unimportant part in the state's economy.

MANUFACTURES, 1890–1910

	1890	1899	1904	1909
Establishments	3,014	1,695	1,819	2,500
Wage Earners	23,876	18,669	20,260	24,336
Value of Products	$93,037,794	$130,302,000	$154,918,000	$199,019,000
Value Added	$25,703,262	$ 34,377,000	$ 30,866,000	$ 47,938,000
Capital Employed	$37,569,508	$ 65,906,000	$ 80,235,000	$ 99,901,000
Cost of Material	$67,334,532	$ 95,925,000	$124,052,000	$151,081,000
Horsepower	23,479	41,825	46,372	64,466

Railroad mileage increased from 5,685.13 in 1900 to 7,879.19 in 1910. Double tracks had been laid on the main line of the Union Pacific and part of the Burlington. Most people depended upon the railroad for inter-town transportation, and upon horse-drawn vehicles for local transportation; but an automobile appeared on the streets of Lincoln about 1902. By 1905, the noisy, expensive, unpredictable horseless carriages were such a nuisance that the legislature passed a law requiring the operator of an automobile to halt on the highway until the driver of any frightened horse could get past. In 1906, 1,087 automobiles were

registered with the Secretary of State; by 1908 the number had jumped
to 4,200; and by 1910 to 15,000.

The frontier was indeed fading away.

THE KINKAIDERS IN WESTERN NEBRASKA

Northwest Nebraska, however, still remained a frontier area. The
Sandhills and high tablelands, originally shunned even by the cattlemen, had been proven unsuitable for farming on the basis of the standard, quarter-section homestead, and the only successful use made of
the Homestead Law in the area was by cattlemen who used it to secure
stream fronts and water holes. The Public Lands Commission of 1879
recommended a free homestead on grazing lands of four square miles;
but the cattlemen were satisfied with conditions as they were. If there
was to be a change, they wanted unlimited sale or leasing, and so the
idea slept. Congressman William Neville of North Platte introduced a
bill to provide a two-square-mile homestead in 1901, but it was killed
in the committee on public lands.

The idea of an enlarged homestead as a means of effecting more general distribution of grazing lands continued to be agitated, however,
and in 1902 President Theodore Roosevelt called attention to the in-
adequacy of the quarter-section homestead for much of the West.
Roosevelt made no specific recommendations, but Moses P. Kinkaid
of O'Neill, who had been elected to Congress from the sixth district
in 1902, set about trying to change the land laws for the benefit of homesteaders in his area. Despite opposition from the General Land Office
and from many congressmen who expressed the fear that the proposal
was simply another means for the cattlemen to secure additional fraudulent land holdings, Kinkaid, with a modicum of support from Senator
Charles H. Dietrich, was able to push his bill through, and President
Roosevelt signed it on April 28, 1904. Briefly, the Kinkaid Act provided that in thirty-seven counties of northwest Nebraska the homestead unit should not exceed 640 acres, with the provision that irrigable
lands should not be open to entry. Homesteaders could receive patents
for their lands after residence of five years and proof that they had placed
improvements to the value of $1.25 per acre upon the land claimed.

Many were skeptical, but the Alliance *Times,* published in the principal town in the area, reported that "the majority of citizens are hopefully waiting and sanguine that the outcome will be advantageous to

this section."[5] The General Land Office has no definite record of the number of Kinkaid patents granted prior to November, 1910, although some sixteen hundred patents were granted for approximately eight hundred thousand acres in the Kinkaid area by that date, part of them probably under the old Homestead Act, which also applied to the area. Between November, 1910, and July, 1917, a total of 18,919 patents were issued for 8,933,527 acres. After this time the acreage patented declined each year, although as late as 1941 one Kinkaid patent was issued for a forty-acre additional entry.

Population of the thirty-seven counties which had stood at 136,615 in 1900 jumped to 199,676 in 1910, and to 251,830 in 1920. Production of principal crops increased as follows:

	Corn	Wheat
1900	13,551,225 bu.	3,251,180 bu.
1910	25,953,801 bu.	4,332,089 bu.
1920	24,677,547 bu.	12,970,399 bu.

Unfortunately, no figures are available to indicate what percentage of original claimants carried through to final patent and continued to live on their Kinkaid homesteads. It is clear, however, that many found even the 640-acre homestead too small for satisfactory existence in the Sandhills and in certain parts of the high Plains. A section of land simply did not provide enough acreage to run cattle in an area where each animal required from fifteen to twenty acres. Likewise, many of the general farming experiences ended in failure. There was a steady increase in the average size of farms in the area, and the average went well beyond the section, indicating that the Kinkaiders either added to their holdings or—more probably—sold out to others who used the Kinkaid homesteads to add to their already large holdings. Generally the Kinkaiders, existing in their tar-paper shacks and little soddies, had a hard time of it, repeating the experience of other pioneers in the central portion of the state two decades earlier. They seemed to be a hardy lot, however, proud of their new country, and willing to make the best of it. Dry farming helped a good deal on the high tablelands, and in years when wheat both yielded well and sold well, life was fairly good. At least the generality were sufficiently well impressed with the law to send Moses P. Kinkaid back to Congress, again and again. He died in harness in 1922 while serving his tenth consecutive term. The spirit of

[5]May 10, 1904.

the people—and the key to Kinkaid's popularity—is perhaps best expressed in the words to this song, "The Kinkaiders":

You ask what place I like the best,
The sand hills, oh the old sand hills;
The place Kinkaiders make their home
    And prairie chickens freely roam.

Chorus (for first and second verses):

In all Nebraska's wide domain
'Tis the place we long to see again;
The sand hills are the very best,
She is queen of all the rest.

The corn we raise is our delight,
The melons, too, are out of sight.
Potatoes grown are extra fine
And can't be beat in any clime.

The peaceful cows in pastures dream
And furnish us with golden cream,
So I shall keep my Kinkaid home
And never far away shall roam.

Chorus (third verse):

Then let us all with hearts sincere
Thank him for what has brought us here,
And for the homestead law he made,
This noble Moses P. Kinkaid.

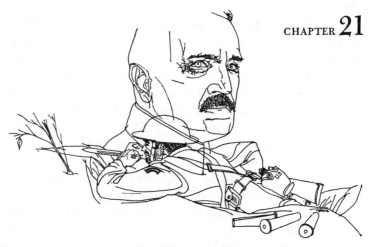

CHAPTER 21

Nebraska and World War I

DURING THE fateful months between August 4, 1914, and American entry into the war on April 6, 1917, the issues of preparedness, peace, and war were fought out in Nebraska as vigorously and with as much bitterness as perhaps anywhere in the nation, as the state's citizens—many of whom were born in one of the combatant nations and many more of whom had relatives and friends in war-torn Europe—reacted at least in part as European nationalists to the struggle across the Atlantic. Though from the beginning dominant sympathy was with the Allies, Nebraska had a strong German element numbering about two hundred thousand, of whom about thirty thousand were born in Germany and over sixty thousand were children of parents born there, and this group sympathized to a large degree with the cause of the Fatherland. This was particularly true of the more influential Germans in the state—the clergy, the editors of some forty German-language newspapers, and German leaders in other phases of Nebraska society—who made an effort to counteract influences favoring the Allies by presenting the German version of the origin of the war. Equally vigorous on the other side were the Czechs, second only to the Germans in numbers and in activity. The sympathy of the Poles likewise was strongly against the Germans. These groups were counteracted somewhat by the Irish who, though not particularly sympathetic to Germany, were strongly anti-British in their views.

261

In addition to these groups, there were many of the old Populist-progressives who believed that no good could come of war and that the nation's best interest lay in remaining aloof from the struggle in Europe. Typifying this group were William Jennings Bryan, who resigned as Secretary of State on June 7, 1915, in protest against Wilson's stiffening attitude toward the Germans and his increasing involvement with the Allies; and Senator George W. Norris, who participated in the filibuster against Wilson's armed ship bill and voted against American entry into the war.

Though there were some in Nebraska who openly rejoiced at the sinking of the *Lusitania,* as the struggle wore on and the nature of the German military machine seemed to reveal itself even more clearly, public opinion in Nebraska as in the nation kept pace with Wilson and in some instances preceded him on the road to war. Bryan's break with Wilson was a major factor in his loss of leadership in the Democratic party of the state. Norris' filibuster against the armed ship bill and his vote against the war resolution seriously reduced his popularity in the Republican party, and had his opponents been able to agree upon a candidate they undoubtedly would have defeated him in the primary election of 1918.[1] The campaign cry that Wilson "kept us out of war" was an important factor in the Democratic victory in November, 1916; but when, a few months later, the President led the nation into war, most Nebraskans were prepared to follow him.

THE HOME FRONT

Peaceful, prosperous America, which, save for a brief interlude in 1898, had gone its own way relatively unconcerned with the problems of the world, was in many respects psychologically unprepared for the world-wide struggle which, it soon became apparent, would require all the nation's vast resources. This lack of preparation temporarily threw the nation off balance to the point where it seemed that the only way a democratic nation could save the world for democracy was to negate much of the democratic tradition of individual liberty at home. In Nebraska, this lack of psychological preparation for the role of a democratic nation in a world-wide military struggle, the vigor of the prewar

[1] The vote in the Republican primary of 1918 for United States senator was as follows: George W. Norris, 23,715; Charles H. Sloan, 17,070; Ross L. Hammond, 16,948; William Madgett, 4,301; and Dave Mercer, 4,089.

debate, and the presence of many whose pro-German views were widely known resulted in excesses on the home front which make for anything but pleasant reading.

Under authorization from the legislature, Governor Neville immediately organized a State Council of Defense as an auxiliary of the federal Council of Defense, "to assist the Governor and state militia in doing all things necessary to bring about the highest effectiveness within our state in the crisis now existing and to coordinate all efforts with those of the National government and with those of the other states." County councils were organized everywhere with active leadership. The State Council had wide powers—it could carry on investigations, subpoena witnesses, compel the production of books and papers, and punish offending persons for contempt.

The State Council saw an immediate threat in the large German population. Not all the Germans were sympathetic to the Fatherland, but many of them were, and many of the leaders continued their prewar opposition to the struggle against Germany. This opposition was equipped with a substantial German-language press; it used the German language in everyday business and in its religious exercises. In addition, there were many in Nebraska besides the Germans who opposed the war—some because of hatred of war in all its forms, some because they believed it was not America's fight—and many of these, reared in an atmosphere of almost violent political discussion, were unwilling and/or unable to keep their views to themselves.

With taxes and the draft taking a heavy toll of the state's wealth and manpower, opposition in any form was unthinkable. The state and local councils of defense made every effort to whip the citizenry into line. While it is evident that the State Council of Defense brought heavy pressures to promote the sale of liberty bonds, enforce food and fuel rationing, and generally stamp out dissent, most of the wartime excesses on the home front seem to have been the work of overly eager individuals compensating perhaps for their own failure to be in uniform by calling attention to their neighbors' shortcomings. Then, too, the atmosphere was favorable for the settlement of personal grudges. If one didn't like a man, he could just call him a slacker. These people found a new use for yellow paint, liberally applying it to the houses and property of those they charged with being slackers.

Probably the most celebrated incident in the "battle of the home front" was the "trial" of various members of the faculty of the University of Nebraska before the Board of Regents on charges of failing to support the war. In response to complaints from various sources that certain members of the faculty were not in sympathy with the war, the Board of Regents held an open public hearing, inviting all citizens who had any knowledge of un-American utterances or actions on the part of members of the University faculty to appear. These hearings lasted over a period of two weeks and were reported at length in the press. All sorts of testimony, both relevant and irrelevant, was brought before the board, and that body found that while a majority of those reportedly attacked were in support of the war, two members of the faculty— Professor G. W. A. Luckey and Professor C. E. Persinger—had been so frank in their criticism that their usefulness at the institution was damaged to a degree that required their resignations.

Though the State Council of Defense could not be held officially responsible for many individual outrages against the American system, its adamant insistence upon absolute conformity in thought and action as necessary to win the war on the home front generally inspired the vigilante spirit. The State Council's special whipping boy was the Non-Partisan League, imported from North Dakota, where it had achieved spectacular success, in the same month (May, 1917) that the State Council itself had been organized. The League's platform, embodying much of the old Populist spirit, went a great deal further than the Populists had gone in demanding state action for the benefit of the farmers. Where the Populists had been content to call for the nationalization of railroads and telegraph lines, the Non-Partisan League demanded state stockyards, packing houses, cold storage plants, elevators, flour mills, creameries, beet sugar factories, and telephones. They also called for exemption of farm improvements from taxation, state hail insurance, rural credit banks operated at cost, and state inspection of dockage and grading of grain. The League developed much influence among the members of the powerful Farmers' Union and in many predominantly German rural communities. Within a few weeks, the League found itself engaged in a bitter conflict with the State Council of Defense. Though the Non-Partisan League strongly supported the war, its program was anathema to most of the men in the State Council, and that body made strenuous efforts to brand the League as unpatriotic. It curtly rejected the League's offer to promote the sale of liberty bonds; it got an opinion from the Attorney General that League organizers were not engaged in useful occupations; it branded as treasonable and seditious a book being circulated by the League in Nebraska —*The New Freedom*, by Woodrow Wilson!

The Attorney General's opinion brought the struggle to a head. With the assistance of attorneys C. A. Sorensen and C. C. Flansburg, the League brought an injunction suit against the State Council of Defense to prevent it from interfering with League meetings. The whole thing was compromised when the Non-Partisan League agreed to withdraw the circulation of its controversial war aims pamphlet and to hire only Nebraska organizers. The State Council of Defense agreed to permit Non-Partisan League meetings and to suspend the application of its regulation declaring the League's organizers to be engaged in other than useful occupations.

Governor Neville called the legislature into special session on March 26, 1918, to pass legislation which he felt was essential to the prosecution of the war. The Governor's program called for: (1) a plan for soldier voting; (2) protection of persons in military and naval service from collection of debts or mortgages during the war period; (3) acts defining sedition and sabotage and prescribing penalties; (4) provision for a home guard militia; (5) repeal of the Mockett Foreign Language Law; and (6) submission of a constitutional amendment limiting the ballot to full citizens. The Governor's program passed quickly, although many in his own party felt that the repeal of the Mockett Foreign Language Law was particularly unfortunate. This law, passed at the insistence of the German-American Alliance, of which Speaker Mattes was a prominent member, provided that when a petition of fifty signatures was presented to the Board of a school district, any foreign language designated in the petition must be established as a course of study. Governor Neville called it "vicious, undemocratic, and un-American." Many Democrats, also, thought the sedition law as prescribed by the Council of Defense was entirely too severe, and ten Democratic senators signed a remonstrance against it.

The campaign of 1918 found the Democrats in serious trouble. The German voters—feeling that they had been swindled by the Democratic cry that Wilson had kept the nation out of war, and bitterly resentful of the persecution they had suffered under Governor Neville's State

Council of Defense—turned solidly against the party in power. The Non-Partisan League saw in the election an excellent opportunity to get even with the State Council of Defense and strongly supported Republican candidates. There was much complaint about war profiteering, and the Democrats, being the party in power, bore the brunt of that complaint. As a result, Samuel R. McKelvie, thirty-four year old publisher of the *Nebraska Farmer,* the state's most widely read agricultural journal, and a former lieutenant governor, easily defeated Neville. Norris, who, as has been indicated, was renominated only because his opposition in the Republican party could not agree on a single candidate, won a similarly easy victory over former Governor John H. Morehead in the senatorial contest. The Republicans won all state offices, all congressional seats, and an overwhelming majority in the legislature. The voters also ratified an amendment to the federal constitution providing for woman suffrage, and approved the calling of a constitutional convention to revise the state's organic law. The prohibition question was another factor in the Democratic defeat. Long able to draw wet Republican votes as the party of personal liberty, the Democrats inexplicably had endorsed national prohibition in 1918. Though the special war session of the legislature had refused to ratify the national prohibition amendment, the legislature of 1919 quickly added Nebraska's name to a list of states ratifying the amendment.

NEBRASKANS IN THE ARMED FORCES

Though the Nebraska National Guard served as a unit on the Mexican border in 1916, Nebraskans in the armed forces during World War I—unlike their fathers and grandfathers in the Spanish-American and Civil Wars—did not serve in state-organized and controlled units. The decision to federalize the armed forces completely caused no little complaint among the politicians, but it did remove Army units from the realm of local politics. The 34th Division was composed of National Guard Units from Nebraska and other midwestern states, but it did not see service as a division, being broken up for replacements. Nebraskans, therefore, were scattered all through the Army up to the 89th Division.

There were, however, some distinct Nebraska units in the war: the 355th Infantry Regiment, called "Nebraska's own," the 314th Ammunition Train, and Nebraska Field Hospital No. 1. The first two were part of the 89th Division, and Field Hospital No. 1 was attached to the 42nd, the famous "Rainbow" Division. Field Hospital No. 1 was an historic and war-tried Nebraska National Guard unit which had first been organized on January 24, 1903. It functioned as Field Hospital No. 166 with the 42nd Division.

The 89th Division, of which the 355th Infantry was a part, was organized at Camp Funston in September and October, 1917. Generally a midwest division, composed of men from Kansas, Missouri, Colorado, South Dakota, Arizona, New Mexico, and Nebraska, it was known as both "The Middlewest Division" and "The Fighting Farmers." Most of the eight thousand men from Nebraska who entered the Division were assigned to the 355th Infantry, the 314th Ammunition Train, and to the three machine gun battalions organized with the Division. The Division was commanded by Major General Leonard Wood. The 89th Division arrived in France in June and played an important part in the final push ending the war.

Base Hospital No. 49 at Allereye in France was financed by Nebraskans and organized at Omaha by the University of Nebraska College of Medicine, its personnel being drawn largely from faculty and alumni. Its staff of four hundred men and women began work on September 12, 1918, doing an average of twenty surgical operations a day until the Armistice was signed. Nebraskans took pride in the fact that of all the American hospitals in Europe, this unit made the best record of saving life.

Nebraskans also took pride in the fact that the two men leading the military effort for United States both had close Nebraska relationships. General John J. Pershing, named Commander-in-Chief of the American Expeditionary Forces, had been Commandant of Cadets at the University of Nebraska and had studied at the University's College of Law. General Pershing had made a warm place for himself in the hearts of Lincolnites and Nebraskans, and generally considered Lincoln his home. His sister, Mae Pershing, continued to live in Lincoln. Charles G. Dawes, purchasing agent for the AEF, was also a Lincolnite. Though living in Chicago at the time of his appointment he had begun his law practice in Lincoln and retained financial interests in the capital city.

Many Nebraskans were decorated for bravery. Captain Nelson M. Holderman of Trumbull received the Congressional Medal of Honor and seventy-eight Nebraskans received the Distinguished Service Cross. The most decorated Nebraskan was Carl M. Lange, an enlisted man from Hartington. Lange received the Distinguished Service Cross and four French awards, one of them the *Medaille Militaire,* the highest honor France could give to an enlisted man.

All told, Nebraska sent 57,526 men and women to the armed forces —47,976 in the Army, 6,973 in the Navy, 547 in the Marines, 375 nurses. This group suffered 1,655 casualties. Fort Robinson saw service as a cavalry training center, and Fort Omaha was used as a balloon school.

WARTIME PROSPERITY.

Nebraska's primary contribution, however, was the production of food for the armed forces and the Allies—and in fulfilling that function the state prospered greatly. Indeed, aside from those who had men in the service or who had felt the ire of the State Council of Defense, the war years were years primarily distinguished by their great prosperity. The state's prosperity is reflected in the fact that Nebraskans bought $240,000,000 in liberty bonds, greatly exceeding the state's quota, and more war saving stamps, according to population, than any other state in the Union.

Farm prices, already higher than any Nebraska farmers had ever experienced, increased spectacularly during the war. The following figures on December 1 farm prices show the nature of that increase:

NEBRASKA FARM PRICES

Year	Wheat	Corn	Oats	Barley	Potatoes	Hay
1910	.80	.36	.28	.45	.84	8.90
1911	.87	.55	.43	.60	.92	9.70
1912	.69	.37	.30	.42	.51	8.40
1913	.71	.65	.38	.49	.78	8.70
1914	.95	.53	.40	.47	.54	6.90
1915	.84	.47	.31	.42	.42	5.80
1916	1.60	.78	.47	.75	1.50	7.10
1917	1.95	1.20	.61	.98	1.07	15.20
1918	1.97	1.28	.65	.85	1.18	17.20
1919	2.02	1.22	.65	1.00	1.90	14.00

Moreover, the purchasing power of the farmer's dollar was greater than it had ever been before. The year 1916 was the only one of the war years in which the index number of Nebraska farm prices fell below that of prices paid by farmers for manufactured goods.

Under the stimulus of high prices and the patriotic necessity for producing food to win the war, Nebraska farmers expanded both their acreage and production to unprecedented heights. Again, statistics tell the story best.

ACREAGE AND PRODUCTION

	Corn		Wheat	
Year	*Acreage*	*Production*	*Acreage*	*Production*
1910–15				
Average	6,537,736	160,303,583	3,294,586	58,014,087
1916	6,740,803	190,070,449	3,310,313	68,773,581
1917	7,932,650	223,488,778	902,255	12,602,574
1918	6,954,061	123,298,649	3,827,659	43,241,840
1919	7,039,811	182,250,823	4,383,731	61,234,602
1920	7,560,355	255,544,816	3,592,995	60,560,416

	Oats		Potatoes	
Year	*Acreage*	*Production*	*Acreage*	*Production*
1910–15				
Average	2,180,114	57,945,840	96,419	6,553,714
1916	2,174,236	83,791,558	74,796	6,505,959
1917	2,978,949	116,551,989	104,692	11,048,806
1918	2,530,877	56,215,487	121,432	10,497,998
1919	2,133,475	70,133,995	103,977	5,737,312
1920	2,400,062	83,037,162	85,439	8,435,554

	Alfalfa	
Year	*Acreage*	*Production*
1910–15		
Average	879,249	2,640,652
1916	1,127,642	3,412,465
1917	1,082,919	2,632,153
1918	1,164,941	2,527,834
1919	1,180,324	3,214,999
1920	1,232,947	3,527,689

Percentagewise, the greatest increase in cultivated acreage occurred in the western part of the state, where the number of cultivated acres doubled during the war. Most of this went into wheat, although there was some extension of corn westward into the marginal corn belt area of the central sections. The great increase in wheat was accounted for by its relatively high price, the discovery that the flatlands of the southwest and the high plains west of the Sandhills were excellent wheat producing areas, and the continued improvement of winter wheat strains adapted to western Nebraska. It was at this time that the southwest— Cheyenne, Deuel, Kimball, and Perkins counties, and parts of Banner, Garden, and Keith—developed into a specialized wheat producing area. The acreage increase was by no means confined to the western part of the state. Though percentage increase was much more spectacular there, 1,764,444 acres were added to the cultivated total in the eastern portion of the state, compared with 1,103,009 acres in the western portion.

Increased acreage was not the only factor in increased production. Climatic conditions during the war generally were favorable, except in 1916 when excessive summer rains seriously interfered with the harvest of small grain. Irrigation (to be treated later)[2] greatly stimulated the production of sugar beets, potatoes, and alfalfa in the North Platte Valley. Larger and improved farm machinery enabled the individual farmer to care for more acres better than he had in the past. New breeds, strains, and methods steadily were developed by scientists at the University's College of Agriculture. Practical education, greatly stimulated by the Smith-Lever Act and the development of the county agent system, provided additional information for the average farmer.

Nebraska's farmers were riding high, but in one important aspect they were sowing the seeds of their own destruction. With prices steadily rising, and in some instances guaranteed by the government—although generally prices in the open markets stayed above government guaranteed minimums—it was axiomatic that the more land a man could put under cultivation the greater would be his profits. So profits from the war years were not used to pay off existing mortgages or to improve existing holdings but were plowed into more land—and at ever-increasing prices. Actually, the spectacular increase in farm land prices did not occur until after the war. During the war there was some increase—as there had been since 1900—but farmers generally seemed to assume that once the wartime demand eased off, so would farm prices. When prices rose higher in 1919 than they had been in 1918, however, many persons came to believe that farm prices had reached a new high

[1]See pp. 311–315.

plateau, and land values rose rapidly in 1919 and 1920. In seven south-eastern counties, for example, land sold by warranty deed in 1915 brought $106 per acre; in 1916, $109; in 1917, $119; in 1918, $128; in 1919, $152; and in 1920, $180. Though detailed studies are not available, the same conditions seem to have existed throughout the state, and it has been estimated that the average increase in land prices for the entire state during the years 1917–1920 was seventy-two percent of the 1916 value.

Aside from high prices, an important factor in increased land values was the liberalization of credit available to farmers for the purchase of land. Local banks extended credit more readily on farm mortgages; farm loan associations, established under the Federal Farm Loan Act of 1916, made loans available at five to six percent on a long-term basis.

Mortgage debt increased 170.2 percent from 1910 to 1920. Part of this was justified by increased production, but a great part was wholly speculative in nature, dependent upon the permanent maintenance of wartime farm prices. When those prices were not maintained, Nebraska agriculture went into a tailspin from which it could not recover through-out the whole prosperous decade of the Twenties, and which so weak-ened it that the depression of the 1930's reduced the state's basic industry to the most desperate plight in its history.

Proportionately, there was a great increase in manufactures. From 1910 to 1920, the number of manufacturing establishments increased from 2,500 to 2,844; the number of wage earners increased from 24,336 to 36,521; the value of products from $199,019,000 to $596,042,498; value added by manufacture from $47,938,000 to $115,268,376; horse-power from $64,466 to $125,769. Manufacturing, however, continued to be a relatively unimportant part of the state's economy, and most of the manufactures consisted of the processing of agricultural products, with meat packing remaining the state's leading industry. The great demand for potash during the war and the discovery that some of the alkali lakes in the Sandhills could produce potash resulted in a brief flurry in that industry, as Antioch boomed to a bustling town of twenty-five hundred, with five factories working twenty-four hours a day. With the end of hostilities, however, the boom collapsed and a few dilapidated houses, ruins of five factories with rusting retorts, boilers, and steel skeletons were all that remained to remind the Sandhills of its short-lived industrial boom.

CHAPTER 22

Adapting Government
to the Machine Age

As A RESULT of the intermittent control of both the Democratic and Republican parties by the progressive elements in each—and occasionally, the combined action of these elements—the early years of the twentieth century saw the enactment of much legislation designed to give the people a greater voice in government, to give the government greater control over the large corporations which had risen with the industrial revolution to control the economic life of the state and nation, and to extend the functions of government for the benefit of the individual. All this resulted in a greatly expanded state government.

The Constitution of 1875 forbade the creation of any new executive offices. This prohibition was overcome by various subterfuges, none of which contributed to efficient administration. The situation was remedied somewhat by a constitutional amendment, adopted in 1912, which provided for a Board of Control of state penal, reformatory, and charitable institutions. This ended to a degree partisan administration of these institutions by the governor's office and concentrated their administration in a bipartisan, three-member board. To make possible a further overhaul of state government, the legislature of 1917 on general bipartisan lines had submitted a proposal to the voters for calling a constitutional convention, and that proposal had been endorsed by the people in the general election of 1918.

Meanwhile, the Republicans in 1918 had pledged the party to enact a civil administrative code to streamline the cumbersome governmental structure that had grown up as a result of the necessity of adding new functions to already existing offices· with the understanding that the actual administrative work would be done by deputies. Governor McKelvie interpreted the Republican landslide of 1918 as a mandate to enact the civil administrative code in advance of the constitutional convention and urged his party in the legislature to make it the first order of business. In his inaugural message, the Governor said:

Circumscribed by the restrictions of an antiquated fundamental law, we have sought to meet the constantly increasing needs of administration through the creation of boards, commissions, and additional offices. This has resulted in a system of government that reeks with divided responsibility, loose ends and overlapping functions.

This condition may be overcome through the application of a cabinet form of civil government, which centralizes responsibility and eliminates the large number of useless boards, commissions, and unnecessary offices. It is fashioned after our National administration, in which the various duties of law enforcement and control are grouped under common heads known as "Departments." These departments are presided over by heads who are known as "Secretaries," to be appointed by the Chief Executive, and confirmed by the Senate.

The code, McKelvie argued, was well within the present constitution, and was simply another way of administering the state's civil affairs under the constitution. To counter the argument of those who would wait for the constitutional convention the Governor said, "If the plan is practical, why wait for the constitutional convention to initiate it? . . . If the exercise of legislative functions is to await the action of the forthcoming constitutional convention, there is little for this legislature to do but adjourn." Though there had been bipartisan agreement that the state's administrative affairs needed overhauling and Democratic governors had repeatedly urged the centralization and consolidation of governmental functions, the Democrats—partly because McKelvie made his particular plan a partisan issue and partly because they were searching for an issue after their overwhelming defeat of 1918—opposed the code with all the vigor they possessed. They were joined by some Republicans of progressive persuasion who, indeed, led the fight against the bill in the legislature. Finally on the last day of the session the bulky, 430-page bill passed, having been introduced and ably fostered by Senator C. Petrus Peterson of Lincoln. It eliminated eleven boards and commissions and ten other subdivisions of various existing departments. It created the following six administrative departments: Finance, Agriculture, Trade and Commerce, Labor, Public Works, and Public Welfare.

Led by Charles W. Bryan, the Democrats continued to fire away at the code, and "The code, repeal it" was to be a campaign slogan of the Democratic party for the next ten years. Despite opposition, however, the administrative code continued to provide the format for the administration of those functions of state government not otherwise provided for by the constitution. In 1929 the Department of Finance was abolished and its duties given to the State Tax Commissioner. The code was further amended that year by the provision that the Secretary of Labor should be ex-officio Secretary of Public Welfare. In 1931, Governor Bryan, long the outstanding opponent of the code, decided to operate the activities of the Departments of Agriculture, Labor and Public Welfare without the appointment of secretaries. In 1933, the legislature complied with Governor Bryan's recommendation that the administrative agencies under the code be rearranged into the following six departments: Agriculture and Inspection, Labor, Health, Roads and Irrigation, Banking, and Insurance. This rearrangement did not change the duties of the several agencies in any material degree. In 1945 the Department of Aeronautics was established as one of the administrative departments, and in 1947 the Department of Veterans Affairs was likewise designated.

Further changes in the Fifties and Sixties reflected the growing complexity of state government. In 1957 the Department of Roads and Irrigation was split into the Department of Roads and the Department of Water Resources, and the Division of Motor Vehicles was elevated to the status of an administrative department. In 1961, the Legislature, following the mandate of a constitutional amendment adopted in 1958, replaced the Board of Control, which had functioned since 1912, with a Department of Public Institutions, which was given the management of all state charitable, mental, reformatory, and penal institutions. In 1963 the state penitentiary and the state reformatory were combined into the Nebraska Penal and Correctional Complex. Finally, in 1965 the Department of Administrative Services was established to coordinate the state's purchasing and accounting procedures.

THE CONSTITUTIONAL CONVENTION OF 1919–20

Though the administrative code had to a degree reorganized state government, there was still need for a constitutional convention. In addition to the prohibition against the creation of additional executive offices, the constitution limited the legislature in raising revenue to the general property tax, fixed rigid rules for legislative business which often were got around through subterfuges in the interests of more efficient procedure, severely limited state salaries, and above all prescribed a virtually impossible amending procedure which required for adoption a majority of all the votes cast at the election in which the amendment was considered. Only eleven of forty amendments submitted to the voters between 1875 and 1918 were adopted; many of those which failed did so not because of opposition but simply because too few had voted upon them to provide the requisite majority of all ballots cast. Those which were adopted received that majority through a subterfuge: with the adoption of the "party circle" law in 1901, and the primary in 1907, all straight party votes were counted as in favor of an amendment if the amendment had been endorsed by the party at the primaries.

One hundred delegates to the constitutional convention were chosen at a special election on November 4, 1919, in accordance with procedures adopted by the legislature of 1919. They were elected without party designation from the same districts and on the same basis as members were chosen for the state House of Representatives. The issues in the campaign were not clear, but in the main the contest seems to have been between the progressive and conservative elements in the state. In some districts, the Non-Partisan League endorsed candidates and the New Nebraska Federation, an organization of business groups, endorsed other candidates. There was some fear among conservatives that certain progressive elements urging the adoption of a one-house legislature and/or the establishment of a mere framework of government leaving the rest to the legislature would prevail, but these fears were set aside when the election returns came in. The general spirit of the convention was distinctly conservative. Included in the membership were forty-five lawyers, among whom were some of the most conservative members of the old order in Nebraska politics. Under the leadership of Arthur J. Weaver, Falls City farmer and attorney who was chosen president, the convention confined itself generally to the consideration of amendments designed to remedy the procedural defects in the Constitution of 1875. Convening on December 2, 1919, the convention remained in harmonious session until March 25, 1920, at which time it recessed until October 19, when it reconvened to adopt forty-one amendments which had been approved by the voters and incorporated into the constitution by a committee appointed for that purpose.

All forty-one amendments were adopted at a special election held on September 21, by margins of three or four to one among approximately one-sixth of the qualified electors voting. Among the amendments were those providing: that the constitution could be amended by a majority voting on each amendment if the affirmative vote was equal to thirty-five percent of the total vote cast; that the salaries of state officers and judges could be increased no oftener than once every eight years; and that no increase would be effective during the term of office in which it was voted. There were amendments providing for an increase in legislative salaries and for uniform and proportional taxes on tangible property, permitting classification of other property, and taxes other than property taxes. The amendments also provided for the creation of new executive offices by two-thirds vote of the legislature, for an executive budget, a Board of Pardons, and the office of State Tax Commissioner; for woman suffrage and soldier suffrage; for the election of University Regents by districts; for an increase in the number of state senators from thirty-three to fifty.

Since 1920, forty-nine amendments out of seventy-four submitted have been adopted. Of the seventy-four, thirteen were submitted by initiative and the remainder by the legislature. No amendments were approved during the first ten years under the new constitution, and only fourteen were adopted between 1930 and 1952, including: definition of the liability of stockholders in banks which had failed (1930), repeal of prohibition (1934), authorization of pari-mutuel betting (1934), provision for a unicameral legislature (1934), elimi-

William Jennings Bryan

John H. Powers

Silas A. Holcomb

William V. Allen

Omer M. Kem

William Poynter

C. H. Van Wyck

SOME POPULIST LEADERS

George L. Sheldon

E. J. Burkett

John M. Thayer

Norris Brown

SOME REPUBLICAN LEADERS

Erwin H. Barbour, Geology

Charles E. Bessey, Botany

George E. Howard, History

Roscoe Pound, Law

SOME UNIVERSITY LEADERS

Professor Samuel Aughey

J. Sterling Morton

Moses P. Kinkaid

George W. Holdrege

PROMOTERS OF SETTLEMENT

TRANS-MISSISSIPPI EXPOSITION, OMAHA, 1898 (*Rinehart photo*)

Steam Tractor and Plow

Steam Threshing

THE MACHINE COMES TO THE FARM

On the Farm, 1907

Merna, 1910

THE HORSELESS CARRIAGE

nation of the office of Commisisoner of Public Lands and Buildings from the list of constitutional offices (1936), provision that the State Superintendent of Public Instruction should be a member of the Board of Educational Lands and Funds (1940), abolition of the "closed shop" (1946), and five amendments approved in 1952 providing for a different method of taxing motor vehicles, providing for a State Board of Education, changing certain provisions regarding appointive offices and submission of constitutional amendments, and authorizing the legislature to provide for a constitutional convention.

The legislature refused to call a constitutional convention, but the need for overhauling the state's creaking constitution steadily increased. Reflecting an awareness of this need were both the number of amendments submitted and the number adopted. While in the thirty-two years between 1920 and 1952, only fourteen out of twenty-nine amendments (or just less than fifty percent) were approved, in the thirty-two years between 1952 and 1964, thirty-five out of forty-five (or a little more than seventy-five percent) were approved. Many of those approved were technical in nature—eleven related to taxation and nine to salaries and other conditions of employment of state officials. In 1962, four-year terms were approved for members of the legislature, the governor, and the lieutenant governor, and in 1964 the voters gave approval to adding the offices of secretary of state, auditor of public accounts, state treasurer, and attorney general to those having four-year terms. Bingo was legalized in 1958 and lotteries in 1962. A juvenile court was authorized in 1958. In 1960, cities and villages were authorized to issue revenue bonds to attract industry, and in 1962 the merit plan was adopted for the selection and retention of judges.

ADJUSTING TO THE AUTOMOBILE

One of the most pressing problems facing the state government in the postwar years was that of providing a road system to meet the needs of the automobile. At the time automobiles began to appear on Nebraska's city streets in the early years of the twentieth century, there were few indeed who thought that the imperfect, noisy, expensive mechanism would ever be more than a rich man's city toy; and as has been indicated,[1] the legislature's first action in connection with the automobile was an effort to reduce its nuisance characteristics. By 1920, however, there were 205,000 automobiles registered in the state, and by no means all of them in the urban areas. Indeed, though the western counties continued to rely heavily upon the horse as a means of transportation, the farming counties of the eastern and central portion of the state led the two principal urban counties—Douglas and Lancaster—in the ratio of automobiles per person.

It is not difficult to understand why the farmer eagerly took the automobile as his own. It represented individually owned rolling stock, reducing rural isolation and contributing to the well-being of the farmer and his family. It was much more expensive than the horse, but it was infinitely more satisfactory and the chores connected with its maintenance—once the thing was perfected—were fewer and less burdensome. In short, it opened up a whole new world for the farmer. Even during the years of readjustment from the wartime boom, the number of motor vehicles registered continued to increase. By 1925 there were 301,716, and by 1930, 367,410. There was a slight decline during the depths of the depression in the early Thirties, but beginning in 1933 the trend started upward again. By 1950 there were 441,632 automobiles registered in Nebraska, or an average of more than one car for every family in the state. By 1965 the number had jumped to 948,311.

The demand for good roads developed in direct ratio to the increase in the number of automobiles registered—as soon as a man became the owner of an automobile, he was an easy prospect for a good-roads association.

In 1904 Nebraska had designated public roads totalling 79,462 miles (compared with 102,661 miles in 1963), but most of these were little more than unimproved trails running along the section lines or wandering off from railroad points to fertile valleys. Only seventeen miles were improved with stone, and only six miles were surfaced with sand-clay. By 1909, total road mileage had increased to 80,338, but seventy-seven counties reported no improved roads, twelve had less than one hundred miles, and only one—Cedar—had more than one hundred miles of improved roads.

In horse and buggy days, road improvement and maintenance were

[1]See pp. 257–258.

largely township affairs, with the work generally being done by men of the neighborhood who came together to work out their three-dollar road tax at $1.50 per day. Interest in good roads rarely extended beyond the township, and that interest was seriously modified by the desire to keep local taxes as low as possible. When the automobile made possible easy travel from township to township, the discrepancy in roads was quickly noted and loudly complained against.

The first legislation resulting from good-roads agitation was the State-Aid Bridge Act of 1911 which provided that the State Board of Irrigation, Highways, and Drainage was to contribute ten percent of the expenditures for roads and bridges within the various counties. To finance the expenditure, the legislature passed a state-wide fifth-mill levy. In addition to the ten percent general contribution, the state paid one half of the cost of construction and maintenance of all bridges more than 175 feet long. The law also gave county commissioners greater power over roads and allowed them to use for road purposes the proceeds from property taxes, inheritance taxes, and license fees on motor vehicles.

Local taxes also increased, largely as a result of the demand for improved roads—they were eighty-two cents per capita in 1904 and $1.51 in 1914. By 1914 the state had 1,204.54 miles of improved roads, of which 1,131.10 were sand-clay. This was only 1.5 percent of the total mileage, however, and good-roads advocates were far from satisfied. In particular, they argued that local control of road building was inimical to the development of a sound highway system. As the Lincoln Highway Association, the leading organized advocate of good roads, put it: "The highways of America are built chiefly of politics, whereas the proper material is crushed rock or concrete." The Lincoln Highway Association, urging a transcontinental highway, sought to develop sentiment in favor of good roads by demonstrating just what good roads could do. In furtherance of the program, it secured from cement manufacturers an offer to supply free to any community three thousand barrels of cement if the community would appropriate adequate funds to construct an improved section of the Lincoln Highway in its region. The offer had been quickly accepted in Grand Island, Kearney, and Fremont, and by 1919, when the program was discontinued, it had created a popular demand for better highways in Nebraska.

It soon became clear that building good roads was not only too big a job for the counties, but for the states as well, and the federal government was called upon for both direction and financing in the development of the nation's highway system. The Federal Aid Road Act of July 11, 1916, provided federal funds on a matching basis for use in a construction of post roads, certain designated roads forming part of an interstate system. By 1921, 5,619.04 miles of road within the state had been selected as post roads, comprising the following major systems: (1) U. S. 20, extending west from Sioux City through O'Neill, Valentine, and Chadron, (2) U. S. 30, or the old Lincoln Highway, extending west from Omaha through Grand Island, North Platte, and Sidney; (3) U. S. 26, running from U. S. 30 at Ogallala to Scottsbluff and the west line of the state; (4) U. S. 38 (now 6), extending from Omaha through Lincoln, Hastings, and McCook to Colorado; (5) U. S. 77, from Sioux City through Fremont, Lincoln, and Beatrice to the Kansas line; and (7) U. S. 81, from Yankton through Norfolk, Columbus, York, and Hebron to the Kansas border.

By 1930, the Department of Roads and Irrigation had gravelled 5,000 miles and graded 3,300 more miles, although only 309.5 miles had been improved with rigid pavement, and an additional 28.8 miles with bituminous mat. Though travellers could complain about the bad roads across Nebraska, a start had been made toward the improvement of the road system, and fairly good "all-weather" roads connected the county seats and ran across the state.

The initial .65 mill levy established by the legislature for state road development in 1917 had been increased to three mills in 1919. In 1925, on the theory that motorists not only could pay for roads but were willing to do so, a two-cent gasoline tax was instituted (raised to four cents in 1930). By 1930 the state was receiving over nine million dollars annually from the gasoline tax. Local governments likewise increased the amount spent on roads, devoting much of the property tax and bond issues to local road construction.

With the depression of the Thirties, highway building became a basic project in federal work relief and pump priming activities. During the years from 1930 to 1941, the state highway system received $83,600,000 from WPA and PWA funds; the counties and townships received $66,-400,000; and the cities and villages, $11,394,563. In addition the regular federal aid program provided $160,394,563. The Department of Roads and Irrigation contracted work as follows:

Type	Mileage
Grading	4,236.9
Regrading	1,378.3
Rigid Pavement	860.6
Bituminous Pavement	2,640.2
Gravel Surfacing	4,182.1
Gravel Resurfacing	1,762.0

Though governmental costs generally increased following World War I, highway costs were the largest single item in state and county budgets, and the automobile thus had a terrific impact upon the state's public economy. Its impact was felt in many other areas, too. Small towns began to decline in population and importance as it became possible for neighboring farmers and the residents of the towns themselves drive to the county seats and regional cities to purchase everything from staples to luxuries. Local railroad passenger traffic almost disappeared, and local railroad freight felt the inroads of the motor truck. As a result, railroads began to abandon branch lines and seriously curtail service on others. Railroad mileage decreased from 6,174 in 1930 to 6,044 in 1940, 5,800 in 1950, and 5,721 in 1960.

POLITICAL ADJUSTMENT

With the enactment of many reforms that had been agitated during the Populist-Progressive period, the realization that many additional social questions were beyond state control, and the growing costs of state government as a result of expanded governmental functions, state politics in the postwar period tended to revolve around the question of taxes, state expenditures, and the exercise of regulatory powers already granted the state government. To be sure, national issues and national candidates had their impact upon Nebraska's politics—particularly in presidential years—but Nebraskans continued to exercise the independent spirit that had been developing over the years since 1890 by frequently crossing party lines and voting on state issues in a manner somewhat divorced from national issues.

The "executive budget" system provided a means whereby the governor could be held responsible, to a degree, for state expenditures; and though state expenditures accounted for only a relatively small portion of total taxes paid by the people, they served as a convenient statewide political whipping boy. Governor McKelvie, who was re-elected in the Republican landslide of 1920, presented the state's first executive budget to the legislature in 1921, and that body passed a law requiring the governor to submit a budget to the legislature each biennium.

In 1922, Charles W. Bryan, the Great Commoner's brother, defeated Republican Charles H. Randall for governor in face of a general Republican victory which resulted in the defeat of Senator Gilbert M. Hitchcock by R. B. Howell. The Democrats won three congressional seats, but state offices and a strong majority in both houses of the legislature were taken by the Republicans. Bryan's victory was based in part on his name—which was always good for a substantial block of votes in Nebraska—in part on the fact that he was able to pin responsibility on his opponent for the Revenue Law of 1921 which exempted intangible property from full taxation, and in part on his successful campaign against increased state expenditures which had resulted from McKelvie's budget. McKelvie himself had taken cognizance of this when he called the legislature into special session in 1922 to reduce appropriations for the second half of the biennium. Bryan also had campaigned vigorously for the repeal of the Administrative Code.

Bryan, who perhaps more than any other man helped to develop "the budget" into a political issue, presented the Republican legislature of 1923 with a document recommending a reduction of more than eight million dollars from the budget presented by outgoing Governor McKelvie. Characteristically, Bryan had based his budget on different figures from those McKelvie had used and upon the adoption of certain basic changes—including the repeal of the Administrative Code. After a winter in which the Governor and Republican members of the legislature tried to outdo each other in name calling, the legislature surpassed Governor Bryan in the matter of economy by appropriating $1,665,109 less than he had asked for. In his outgoing message, however, the Governor—who had temporarily abandoned state politics in 1924 to accept the Democratic nomination for vice-president—came up with a set of figures to show that the legislature actually had appropriated $1,203,978.08 more than he had recommended! He charged further that despite the failure of the Republican legislature to cooperate by reducing the number of state employees in the departments directly under his control from 610 to 272, he had saved the taxpayers nearly one million dollars. He recommended expenditures of $17,000,000 for the next biennium. Governor Adam McMullen of Beatrice, who had defeated J. N. Norton in 1924, ignored Bryan's budget altogether and submitted a request for $27,473,808.54. The legislature, in turn, increased this by about two and a half million dollars.

Bryan, who ran unsuccessfully for governor in 1926 and 1928—but, as will be seen, was successful in the early Thirties—kept the questions of taxation and governmental economy in a constant state of agitation. The failure of that agitation at election time can be explained in part by the fact that the Twenties generally were Republican years in Nebraska, and the Republicans had a relatively easy time of it on the state level—although the Democrats usually managed to pick up two or three congressmen in each election. In addition, however, Bryan's failure resulted in part from his refusal to use figures other than his own and from the fact that the Republicans were able to demonstrate that some of his more spectacular economies during the years 1923–25 were either not economies at all, but simply book juggling, or actions which resulted in serious crippling of state services and state institutions. The Republicans stayed in power in part because they recognized the demand for increased state services—particularly highway building, which Governor McMullen carried forward in an enlarged manner—and were willing to accept the responsibility for making increased appropriations for these services.

CHAPTER 23

The Great Depression

NEBRASKA JOINED the nation wholeheartedly in returning to "normalcy" after the war. Whereas Wilson had received a 41,000 majority in 1916, Harding rolled over Cox in 1920 by a majority of almost 128,000 votes. Though the Lincoln *Journal* assured its readers after the election that the nation was "measurably nearer entrance into the league" than it had been before Harding's victory, a general dissatisfaction with continued involvement in Europe's affairs—implicit in the desire for "normalcy"—played an important part in the Republican victory. Other factors, of course, entered in: the general desire for "a change"; German resentment of the war after German-Americans had voted for Wilson in 1916 on the ground that he had kept the nation out of war; dissatisfaction with the Democrats resulting from the fact that they were responsible for many of the infringements upon personal liberty during the conflict; and the ability of the Republicans to cement together the most conservative elements of their party and the radical elements in Nebraska society represented by Non-Partisan League votes. But the desire for "normalcy" was an important factor in the decision. This is emphasized by R. B. Howell's defeat in 1922 of Senator Hitchcock, who had led the fight in Congress for the League of Nations, in the same election that saw Charles W. Bryan elected governor.

Nebraskans, in short, generally joined the nation in a desire to forget Old World difficulties and get on with the enjoyment of the material benefits which the wonders of twentieth century technology were making available. The old frontier was gone and all but forgotten. The automobile had brought the farms closer together and closer to town. Main Street on Saturday night was lined with cars of farmers who had brought their families to town to shop and see a movie. Cornhusker football became front-page news and the businessmen of Lincoln decided to memorialize those who had died in the war by building a stadium that would hold 35,000 spectators. The old saloon was gone, but the ease with which youngsters as well as oldsters could obtain vile bootleg beverages caused many to wonder about the efficacy of the "noble experiment." To many of the oldsters who had built the state, the younger generation seemed completely pleasure-mad. Others were fearful of the impact of the new materialism on the state's future. As Willa Cather put it:

Too much prosperity, too many moving picture shows, too much gaudy fiction have colored the taste and manners of so many of these Nebraskans of the future. There, as elsewhere, one finds the frenzy to be showy; farmer boys who wish to be spenders before they are earners, girls who try to look like the heroines of the cinema screen; a coming generation which tries to cheat its aesthetic sense by buying things instead of making anything. There is even danger that that fine institution, the University of Nebraska, may become a gigantic trade school. The men who control its destiny, the regents and the lawmakers, wish their sons and daughters to study machines, mercantile processes, "the principles of business"; everything that has to do with the game of getting on in the world—and nothing else.[1]

Throughout the decade of the Twenties, the state exhibited many aspects of material prosperity; its citizens continued to buy automobiles, telephones, radios, and other modern conveniences; the cities increased in population and new buildings began to appear on their skylines. For agriculture, however, the Twenties were years of depression rather than prosperity; and because the state was almost wholly agricultural, the Twenties—even in the midst of relatively good crops and many superficial signs of prosperity—basically were depression years in Nebraska. These years so weakened the state's economy that when the crash came in 1929, to be followed by drouth and deep depression in the early Thirties, the economy came closer to complete collapse than

[1]Willa Cather, "Nebraska: The End of the First Cycle," *loc. cit.*, p. 7.

it had even during the beginning years of the Seventies and the bitter
years of the Nineties.

THE TWENTIES—DEPRESSION IN THE MIDST OF PLENTY

During the war the demand for food to feed the armed services and
the Allies had skyrocketed farm prices to heights beyond anything old-
time farmers had believed possible. When prices maintained their high.
levels after the shooting stopped, many farmers rubbed their eyes in-
credulously—but then decided that prices had reached a plateau and
would be maintained more or less permanently at wartime levels. In
the rush to cash in on the new prosperity, many mortgaged themselves
to secure additional, high-priced land on which to plant still larger
acreages. Then, in mid-1920, foreign demand for agricultural products
fell off sharply, and, in the case of wheat, government price guarantees
expired. The effect was startling. Wheat, which had sold for $2.02 per
bushel on December 1, 1919, brought only $1.31 per bushel on De-
cember 1, 1920. During the same period corn dropped from $1.22 to
$ .41, oats from $ .65 to $ .37, barley from $1.00 to $ .50, potatoes
from $1.90 to $1.20. Most farmers, pressed for interest payments on
their mortgages and on loans which many of them had taken to put
out their crops, had to market their 1920 crop in this period of suddenly declining prices, thus suffering heavy losses. Those who held on
to their grain in the hope that the recession was only temporary suffered even greater losses: by December 1, 1921, wheat was down to
$ .83 per bushel, corn $ .27, oats $ .21, and barley $ .28. Livestock
prices also tumbled: beef cattle which had brought $9.53 per hundred
in 1920 brought only $6.13 in 1921, hogs fell from $12.62 to $7.52,
lambs from $13.39 to $7.68. Though there was some recovery during
the decade and prices generally were above the 1910–14 level, they
did not regain their wartime heights, as the following table shows:

NEBRASKA FARM PRICES

Year	Corn	Wheat	Oats	Barley	Potatoes	Cattle	Hogs	Lambs
1910–14	$0.56	$0.81	$0.36	$0.51	$0.88	$ 5.91	$ 7.13	$ 6.33
1920	1.56	2.08	.68	.91	2.86	9.53	12.62	13.39
1921	.34	1.07	.25	.39	1.15	6.13	7.52	7.68
1922	.44	.97	.29	.38	1.65	6.39	8.04	10.93
1923	.66	.90	.36	.47	.67	6.79	6.59	10.76
1924	.69	1.00	.42	.56	.86	7.22	7.13	11.95

NEBRASKA FARM PRICES—CONTINUED

Year	Corn	Wheat	Oats	Barley	Potatoes	Cattle	Hogs	Lambs
1925	.89	1.44	.43	.64	1.16	7.09	10.86	13.26
1926	.65	1.31	.39	.53	1.94	7.96	11.54	12.29
1927	.74	1.16	.43	.51	1.49	8.90	9.31	12.30
1928	.78	1.07	.44	.60	.76	11.10	8.56	13.30
1929	.77	.97	.41	.52	.82	11.06	9.33	13.22

Of itself, the comparison between prices in the Twenties and the 1910–14 price level is misleading. More relevant are the index numbers, showing relative purchasing power:

Year	Corn	Wheat	Oats	Barley	Potatoes	Cattle	Hogs	Lambs
1910–14	100	100	100	100	100	100	100	100
1920	279	257	188	178	325	161	177	212
1921	61	132	69	76	131	104	105	121
1922	78	119	81	75	187	108	113	173
1923	118	111	100	92	76	115	92	170
1924	123	123	117	110	98	122	100	189
1925	159	177	119	125	132	120	152	209
1926	116	161	108	104	220	135	162	194
1927	132	143	119	100	169	112	131	194
1928	139	132	122	118	86	188	120	210
1929	138	120	114	102	93	187	131	209

Including these products and all others, the average farm price index in Nebraska from 1922 to 1929 was slightly less than thirty-five percent above the prewar level. During the same time, however, the wholesale price index averaged slightly more than forty-four percent above the prewar level. Another factor affecting the farmer's economic position—and even more, his outlook—was the high tax schedule. Most farm taxes were paid in the form of the general property tax, and at no time in the Twenties did levies fall below 122 percent of the 1913 levy. In 1927 the levy was 184 percent *higher* than that of 1913. Expressed another way, taxes which took 5.63 percent of average net farm income in 1914 absorbed 20.41 percent in 1922, 13.48 percent in 1924, 10.59 percent in 1928, and 8.69 percent in 1929.

Although gross farm income recovered somewhat in the late years of the decade, from studies available it appears that the net income per farm, after operating expenses had been deducted, averaged only $1,795, compared with an average of $3,087 for the years 1914–19.

Figures on the farmer's return for his labor were even more discouraging: he averaged only $245 per year during the Twenties; his return during the war period had been $1,610 per year. There was a corresponding decrease in farm values. In 1920 the total value of all farm property in the state was $4,201,655,992; in 1930 it was only $2,935,-029,721, a decrease of about thirty-three percent. The value of land and buildings decreased more than forty-eight percent. Though no complete studies are available, it is clear that there was a general decline in land prices: in seven southeastern counties land which sold by warranty deed at an average of $165.00 per acre in 1921 was selling for $115.00 in 1930, a decrease of 43.5 percent; in two east-central counties the average price fell from $134.00 to $114.00, a decrease of 14.6 percent; in one Sandhill county, from $29.00 to $10.00, a decrease of 190 percent.

Hardest hit of all were the farmers who were trying to pay off mortgages on land purchased at high prices during the war and immediate postwar years. Many tried to refinance their mortgages by borrowing from individuals, banks, or the farm loan banks, but while considerable credit was extended, it became increasingly more difficult for farmers to obtain loans. As a result, many either deeded their farms to mortgage holders or had them foreclosed. In the seven southeastern counties referred to above, there were 315 foreclosure sales from 1921 to 1930; in the two east-central counties, 156; in the one Sandhills county, 108. In addition, there were many token transfers which indicated hard times for the farmer. As Dr. H. C. Filley put it, "The large number of foreclosure sales and token transfers in 1922 and later years is an excellent index of the severity of the effects of the deflation upon Nebraska farmers."[2]

Though some businesses remained prosperous, agriculture's distress generally was reflected in all aspects of the state's economy. Particularly hard hit were state banks with assets tied up in real estate and crop mortgages, which they found increasingly more difficult to collect. Nearly 100 banks were forced to close their doors during 1924, 23 in 1926, 19 in 1927, 400 in 1928, and 106 in 1929. Most of the banks which failed were state banks with their deposits covered by the Bank

[2]H. C. Filley, *Effects of Inflation and Deflation Upon Nebraska Agriculture, 1914 to 1932* (University of Nebraska, Agricultural Experiment Station, Research Bulletin 71, 1934), p. 115.

Guaranty Fund, created by the legislature in 1911. During years of prosperity, the Guaranty Fund provided a measure of security for the state banks, but in the Twenties payments into the fund by member banks to guarantee the deposits of failed banks resulted in such a strain on the state banking system that the law was repealed in 1930. The Guaranty Fund Commission, created in 1923, operated a number of banks which would have closed under ordinary circumstances.

Manufactures, likewise, did not show any marked signs of prosperity during the period. The story is told in the following table:

MANUFACTURES, 1921-1929

Year	No. of Establishments	Wage Earners	Wages*	Cost of Materials*	Value of Products*	Value Added*	Horsepower
1921	1,381	27,530	37,287	242,425	328,348	85,923	......
1923	1,370	31,095	39,635	309,872	409,756	99,884	120,542
1925	1,306	27,200	36,021	348,397	443,308	94,911	133,708
1927	1,277	26,110	34,296	326,917	420,296	93,379	141,506
1929	1,483	27,933	36,648	359,378	478,330	118,952	168,542

*In thousands of dollars

Further reflecting the state's basic difficulty was the fact that population increased by only 81,591 during the decade. There was heavy emigration from the state—particularly to the west coast—and virtually all the meager increase went to the cities, continuing the trend toward urbanization begun in the first decade of the twentieth century. Whereas Nebraska's population in 1920 had been 68.7 percent rural, in 1930 it was only 64.7 rural.

All of this during a period of great national prosperity, at least on paper; of reasonably adequate rainfall—an averge of 22.26 inches compared with a mean of 22.84 inches; of average, or better than average, crop yields; of higher prices than at any period in history except during the war. If Nebraska was in depression in the midst of prosperity, it was clear that the state's economy, for one reason or another, was operating on a shoestring basis and would be unable to withstand any worsening of conditions, either natural or man-made. When both worsened suddenly and simultaneously, virtual paralysis set in.

THE COLLAPSE

Though some of the relatively few Nebraskans who had money enough to speculate on the stock market in a large way lost their fortunes in the Wall Street crash of October, 1929, its basic implications for Nebraska were to be found in the sudden collapse of farm prices following it. Nebraska's farm income was greater in 1929 than it had been in any year since the end of the war, but prices started to sag in the last quarter and continue to fall until December, 1932, when they were the lowest in the state's history—lower even than those of the middle Nineties. The following table shows December farm prices for the years 1929 to 1932:

DECEMBER FARM PRICES, 1929-1932

	1929	1930	1931	1932
Corn	.67	.52	.36	.13
Wheat	1.00	.54	.39	.27
Oats	.38	.27	.23	.10
Barley	.49	.33	.27	.13
Hay	8.00	6.90	6.90	4.10
Potatoes	1.20	.75	.50	.31
Beef Cattle	10.50	8.50	5.40	4.10
Hogs	8.20	7.10	3.30	2.30
Chickens	.148	.122	.112	.065

Compounding the distress was the fact that the farmer's relative price position in the economy as a whole became even worse than it had been during the Twenties. Based on a parity of 100 for the years 1910–14, the purchasing power of Nebraska farm products during the Twenties had averaged 87.22. In 1930, however, it fell to 83; in 1931, to 65; in 1932, to 54. The farmer faced the stern fact that though his prices had reached rockbottom, the prices he had to pay for goods he purchased had declined much less rapidly—even in 1932 they were still at 107.

Under the impetus of government support programs[3] prices began to edge up a bit during the Thirties. The depression, however, was far from over. Drouth, the periodic enemy of the Nebraska farmer, added its blows to an industry already reeling under the impact of world-wide financial distress. Although Nebraska did not suffer from the rather general drouth of 1930, the years 1931, 1932, and 1933 all brought subnormal rainfall and in 1934 the state received only 14.31 inches of annual rainfall—the lowest since 1864. Rainfall was normal in 1935, but again in 1936 it dipped down to 14.42 inches, and in 1937 was

[3]See pp. 297–301.

only 17.66 inches. The dry, powdered soil began to blow, as Nebraska and all the Plains states experienced a series of heavy dust storms which blotted out both sun and hope. This took care of the surplus problem. There was a good corn crop in 1932, but corn yielded only 3.2 bushels per acre in 1934 and 2.5 bushels in 1936, compared with an average of 24 bushels per acre for the years 1923 to 1932. Where production had averaged 223,843,000 bushels from 1928 to 1932 it was only 21,-363,000 in 1934 and 26,859,000 in 1936. Wheat, the second crop, exhibited a similar though not quite so drastic pattern. The yield per acre in 1934 was 7.8 bushels, and in 1936, 14.2 bushels, compared with an average of 15.4 bushels. Growing conditions for wheat actually were better in 1936 than they were in either 1935 or 1937. Total production amounted to 17,543,000 bushels in 1934 and 47,339,000 bushels in 1936; the average, 56,520,000 bushels. Part of the lower total production may be accounted for by reduced acreage under government programs,[4] but most of the disparity between the drouth years and the average for the five preceding years results from the low yield per acre.

Though the government ultimately stepped in to make it possible for thousands of farm mortgages to be renewed at lower rates of interest, thereby saving the farms for their owners, many lost their farms before that action was taken. Complete data are not available but certain statistics indicate the nature of the tragedy. From 1930 to 1935 the percent of total farms mortgaged decreased from 52.5 to 43.6, and farm mortgage debt decreased from $545,539,000 to $448,294,000. The percentage of farms operated by tenants increased from 47.1 to 49.3. In eleven southeastern counties there were 136 farm mortgage foreclosures in 1932, 8.2 percent of the total number of farm land transfers during the year; in addition there were 691 token transfers—most of them made because of fear of foreclosure—accounting for 41.5 percent of all transfers.

The depression in agriculture affected all other activities in this primarily agricultural state. The number of manufacturing establishments declined from 1,483 in 1929 to 992 in 1933; the number of wage earners from 27,933 to 19,483; wages paid, from $36,648,000 to $18,872,000. Though the number of wholesale trade establishments increased from 2,886 in 1929 to 3,409 in 1933, their net sales decreased from $1,053,-

[4]See pp. 297–301.

441,000 to $387,601,000, and their employees from 16,882 to 14,644. In retail trade the situation was the same: the number of stores increased from 17,637 in 1929 to 19,212 in 1933, but net sales decreased from $562,945,000 to $247,575,000, a decrease of 51 percent; employees decreased from 47,949 to 38,052; payrolls from $49,678,000 to $28,343,000.

At first Omaha tried to take the depression lightly, but the years of drouth and frozen credit struck one important activity after another. The city's livestock market slipped from second to third in the nation. The grain market was in a shambles. Heavy relief problems in the industrial city drained county finances, to be relieved only by the inflow of federal funds. In the milk strike of 1933 the roads into Omaha were picketed by farmers who overturned milk trucks. Lincoln, too, was paralyzed. Many business firms failed and the problem of unemployment became acute. There were many vacant buildings. The city's wholesale and retail trade, upon which it depended so heavily, was inactive. The city was treated to the frightening spectacle of farmers marching on the state capitol to demand a moratorium on farm debts.

There is little point in amassing further evidence. Everywhere the story was the same. As the authors of *Nebraska: A Guide to the Cornhusker State*[5]—themselves victims of the depression—put it:

> The condition of the farmers affected Nebraska merchants, lumber dealers, realtors, school teachers, laborers, and artisans. Housewives stocked their pantry shelves with the simplest essentials; construction lagged; school administrators curtailed their programs as tax receipts went down; day laborers, formerly sure of a place on Nebraska farms and in Nebraska industries, began the long trek of the unemployed.

POLITICAL REPERCUSSIONS

Insofar as state offices were concerned, Nebraskans throughout the 1920's followed their usual habit of voting Republican, save in 1922 when Bryan was elected Governor.[6] In the congressional elections, however, the Democrats managed, with one exception, to elect candidates consistently from three of the six districts. These three were John H. Morehead, first district; Edgar Howard, third district; and Ashton C. Shallenberger, fifth district. The only exception occurred in 1928 when

[5] New York: The Viking Press, 1939.
[6] See p. 282.

Fred G. Johnson defeated Shallenberger, and this was offset in the total statistics by the election of Democrat J. N. Norton from the normally Republican fourth district in 1926. The three perennially successful Democratic congressmen were all strong campaigners and all had large personal followings: Morehead and Shallenberger had served the state as Governor;[7] Edgar Howard, the inimitable poker-playing, Quaker-garbed editor from Columbus, was easily the most colorful figure in Nebraska politics.

But the success of Morehead, Shallenberger, and Howard was based upon more than a personal following. They represented three of the state's major farming areas, and their repeated re-election resulted, in part at least, from dissatisfaction on the part of the farmers with the efforts of Republican Administrations and Republican Congresses to deal with the farm problem. Conversely, the urban areas seemed quite well satisfied with Republican rule. Omaha, which before and after this period stood out as a Democratic stronghold, generally voted Republican; Lincoln, always a Republican stronghold, also voted Republican, but its pluralities in the congressional races were not sufficient to counterbalance the heavy Democratic vote in the rural counties of the first district. The fourth district, comprising the central South Platte section, was always a close battleground. The sixth district, including the Sandhills, was always safely Republican, repeatedly returning Robert G. Simmons to Congress as it had his predecessor, Moses P. Kinkaid.

Further reflecting farm dissatisfaction was the Progressive vote in the presidential election of 1924. Though LaFollette did not split the Republican party badly enough to result in Democratic victory, as Theodore Roosevelt had done in 1912, he did poll 106,701 votes, or twenty-three percent of the total. The combined vote of LaFollette and John W. Davis, the Democratic candidate, exceeded that of the victorious Coolidge by 25,405, and together equalled fifty-three percent of the poll. Senator Norris, who had been a thorn in the flesh of the Republican regulars since his fight against Speaker Cannon in 1910, openly supported LaFollette against Coolidge, and this fact accounts in some measure for LaFollette's success in the state. An indication that politics in Nebraska have always been complicated and that Nebraska voters have never slavishly followed party lines was Norris' re-election to the Senate as a Republican. Norris got 15,236 more votes

[7]See pp. 243–247.

than both of his opponents in the primaries (Fred G. Johnson and
Charles H. Sloan) combined and won handily over John J. Thomas,
who had the Progressive as well as the Democratic nomination. Norris
took a leading role in the farm fight against the Coolidge Administration and in 1928 supported Alfred E. Smith for the presidency—
although even his support was not sufficient to carry the day for Smith
in Nebraska, where the religious issue and prohibition entered signifi-
cantly into the campaign, and Hoover won a landslide victory of 345,-
745 to 197,959.

Norris was rewarded in 1930 by a desperate effort to beat him in
the primary through a trick designed to take advantage of the fact that
the law prohibited any identification whatever beside the names of
candidates appearing on the ballot. At the last minute, Norris' enemies
filed another George W. Norris, a grocery clerk at Broken Bow. The
filing reached the Secretary of State two days after the deadline had
expired, but because it had been postmarked at Broken Bow within
the prescribed time, Secretary Frank Marsh accepted it. Norris' friends,
led by Attorney General C. A. Sorensen, immediately brought action,
and an opinion by Chief Justice Goss that the filing was invalid kept
"Grocer Norris" off the ballot. But even with this skullduggery—which
aroused national indignation and brought a senate investigation—disposed of, Norris faced a desperate fight for re-election. It was clear that
the Republican National Committee wanted Norris defeated at any
cost; he had been even more critical of Hoover than he had been of
Coolidge. Large sums of money—some in excess of the amount allowed
by the Nebraska Primary Law—were poured into the campaign to elect
State Treasurer W. M. Stebbins, selected by the organization to oppose
Norris. Former Governor McKelvie, now a member of President
Hoover's Federal Farm Board, took an active part in the campaign.
Norris, however, rolled up an easy victory, 108,471 to 74,486.

In the general election, Norris faced former Senator Gilbert M. Hitchcock. Though Hitchcock received substantial support from many Republican leaders, though Democrat Charles W. Bryan defeated Arthur
J. Weaver for the governorship, and though the Democrats won, in
addition to their usual three congressional elections, the fourth district
(where Norton defeated Charles H. Sloan), Norris proved to be the
best vote-getter in the race, overwhelming Hitchcock, 247,118 to 172,-
795. It was evident that Norris not only had a greater hold on the rank

and file Republicans than did the party leaders, but that he was able to get a good many Democratic votes as well.

A vote for Norris was, of course, a vote against the Hoover Administration; but it is difficult to determine just what part the protest vote played in his election and what part his great personal following played. The same is true in the case of Bryan, Morehead, Howard, and Shallenberger. Norton's defeat of Sloan in the fourth district may, perhaps, be classed as a protest against the Hoover farm policies. Generally, however, 1930 was a Republican year in Nebraska. Republicans elected all state officers except governor, and though the Democrats picked up some strength in the legislature, the Republicans retained a majority of both houses. But as the depression deepened, it became apparent that the Republicans, as the party in power nationally, were going to be held responsible for the economic distress ravaging the state and nation. Senator Norris early came out in support of Franklin D. Roosevelt for president, and as the campaign wore on, many independent and progressive Republicans in the state joined him in support of the New York governor. Roosevelt rolled up a greater vote than had been given any candidate for president in the state's history and overwhelmed Hoover, 359,082 to 201,177. Bryan's victory over Dwight Griswold was much less impressive, but he and all Democratic candidates for state offices easily won election. Roosevelt had carried every county except Keya Paha and Lancaster; the Democrats for the first time since 1916 had elected their entire state ticket. The Democrats won the most complete control of the legislature they had ever enjoyed, electing all but two senators (both from Lancaster County), and all but seventeen representatives. As a result of the census of 1930, Nebraska had lost one representative in Congress, but the five elected were all Democrats —even Robert G. Simmons went down in defeat, being beaten in the new fifth district by Terry Carpenter. The Socialists also were on the ballot in Nebraska and polled a rather substantial vote for a minor third party: Norman Thomas got 9,876 for president, and John M. Paul, 6,733 votes for governor, Glenn Griffith, Socialist candidate for railway commissioner, polled 15,222 votes.

The Democrats had rolled up the most substantial protest vote in the history of the state. In the state—as in the nation—they were completely in power and assumed virtually sole responsibility for dealing with the economic distress which had the nation in virtual paralysis.

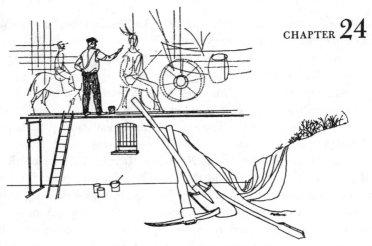

CHAPTER 24

Relief, Recovery, and War

NEBRASKA HAD RESPONDED to Franklin D. Roosevelt's dramatic campaign, calling for government action to bring about recovery and reform with the largest majority it had ever given a presidential candidate. And on that snowy March 4, 1933, as Nebraskans sat with their ears pressed to their radios to hear the new President tell them, "Only a foolish optimist can deny the dark realities of the moment," they knew whereof he spoke: their banks were closed, their farms were going on the block for the benefit of mortgage holders, their city streets rumbled with the footfalls of the unemployed, their business was at a virtual standstill. Many Nebraskans, as they listened to the inaugural address, could see in it remnants of the old Populist tradition, of William Jennings Bryan, of Theodore Roosevelt, of Woodrow Wilson; many others, too young to remember the old days, could sense that the sort of thing Senator Norris had been fighting for was now being advocated rather than opposed by the President.

In Lincoln, the state legislature—like the Congress, preponderantly Democratic—had been wrestling with the problem of depression for almost two months, and on the whole not in such a way as to inspire much confidence on the part of the people. Although that body and succeeding legislatures did take a number of significant steps designed to improve both state government and the condition of the people, it was clear that the great crisis of the early Thirties, in which financial distress was aggravated by prolonged drouth, was beyond the power of the state government. Nebraskans looked to Washington for the solution to their basic problems.

And from Washington a solution came. To be sure, it was not all that many people hoped; it brought anguished cries from certain segments of the population; it even disappointed some of its advocates. But it was a solution, a conscious effort to pull the nation out of the morass into which it had fallen since the end of World War I.

THE NEW DEAL IN AGRICULTURE

In agriculture, as in other segments of the economy, the immediate need was relief—not the soup kitchen variety, but relief from the oppressive burden of debt which threatened to wipe away the individual's equity in the land. Auctioneers and sheriffs, cooperating voluntarily or otherwise with grim-faced farmers who attended foreclosure sales to see to it that bids were made by the proper persons and by them only, restored a few farms to their foreclosed owners; but this was no solution to the farm credit problem and everyone knew it.

Since before the war the federal government had been making efforts to alleviate the age-old problem of agricultural credit, a problem complicated by the fact that the farmer required both long-term and short-term credit in addition to some means of protection against the vicissitudes of nature and the price system. By 1933 credit facilities existed in a reasonable degree, but their administration was so encumbered by the operation of a complicated bureaucracy that many farmers were unwilling or unable to make full use of them. On March 27, President Roosevelt, by executive order, consolidated all agricultural credit agencies under the Farm Credit Administration. Nebraska, Wyoming, South Dakota, and Iowa constituted the Eighth Farm Credit District with headquarters in Omaha. From May 1, 1933, to January 1, 1940, the institutions under the supervision of the Farm Credit Administration had advanced $185,000,000 to Nebraska farmers, the largest portion of which was loaned by the Federal Land Bank of Omaha. Until 1935 most of the federal land bank loans were used to pay off old debts; after 1935 a considerably greater portion went for farm purchases. By the end of 1939, the fourteen production credit associations operating in the state had made 18,719 loans amounting to $33,391,374. Another type of debt relief for certain farm families was provided by the Farm

Security Administration, which extended supervised credit to certain destitute farm families, thus helping them to get back on their feet. By 1940 the FSA had aided 15,004 Nebraska farm families with rehabilitation loans amounting to $12,695,300. In the vicinity of North Platte and Scottsbluff FSA resettlement "homesteads" were established.

The crushing burden of debt was the result rather than the cause of agricultural depression. The cause, most farmers believed—as they had since the days of the Populists—was to be found in low farm prices. There were many explanations for low farm prices, but most observers agreed that the farmers' principal difficulty arose from the fact that they had no control either over their production or their marketing. After almost a decade of struggle against an unfriendly Administration, farm congressmen in 1929 had secured the creation of the Federal Farm Board to stabilize farm marketing through the use of government purchases. This effort failed largely because price stabilization served to increase production and thus aggravate the total situation. The Farm Board itself—of which former Governor Samuel R. McKelvie was the grain member—came to the conclusion that without control of production there could be no effective price stabilization.

The Agricultural Adjustment Act, passed on May 12, 1933, was designed to improve farm prices through production control. Its goal was to establish and maintain a purchasing power for agricultural commodities equivalent to that of the period from 1909 to 1914; and the technique was a system of crop reduction contracts under which the Secretary of Agriculture could pay farmers benefits for reducing production. The system was not compulsory, but the benefit payments were looked upon as sufficient inducement to insure general compliance. The cost was to be borne by a processing tax on commodities covered by the act, and the program was to be administered through state and local farm committees organized by the Secretary of Agriculture.

There was little that could be done regarding crops for 1933, but emergency livestock reductions were carried out in the fall of the year. Approximately 470,000 Nebraska cattle were purchased by the government, either for shipment outside the state or for slaughter at a total of slightly more than six million dollars. This was only about ten to twelve dollars per head, and there was much resentment as farmers saw their herds disappear at a fraction of their value, but there also was the realization that they could not have maintained them under existing drouth conditions. Similarly approximately 438,000 pigs and about 36,000 piggy sows were purchased and slaughtered. Likewise, wheat growers who agreed to participate in the 1934 and 1935 crop reduction programs were given benefits in 1933. Approximately thirty-five thousand wheat growers participated. The corn-hog program included crop adjustment, hog contracts, and corn loans. The corn loans gave farmers an opportunity to obtain loans of forty-five cents per bushel on corn properly stored on their farms. Under this program a total of fifty-three million bushels of corn were sealed, and loans amounting to $23,000,-000 were advanced farmers of the state. Participating farmers received cash for their corn at a rate ranging from thirty to fifty percent above the market price at the time the loans were made, and they benefited further by prices ranging from two to three times the initial market price when they sold their corn. In all, approximately forty-one thousand farmers, or about one-third of those in the state, took out corn loans.

The AAA, declared unconstitutional in 1936 because of its processing tax features, was promptly replaced by a soil conservation act which provided for direct subsidies to farmers conforming to soil conservation and crop control standards established by the federal government. The program was administered through soil conservation districts organized under state law. In 1938 a new Agricultural Adjustment Act reintroduced adjustment of crop production by direct allotment of acreage. The law also provided for parity payments and standardized the conditions under which commodity loans would be offered. Another feature of the 1938 act was crop insurance, applying to wheat.

Except during 1937 and 1938, participation in the soil conservation program greatly increased even over the relatively heavy 1936 participation, as the following table indicates:

Year	Number Farms Participating	Total Benefits
1936	98,593	$13,919,601.54
1937	78,449	9,743,398.41
1938	81,390	12,052,956.92
1939	129,295	20,054,233.80
1940	143,430	18,452,308.80

Likewise, participation in the new AAA was substantial. In 1939, 81.2 percent of all crop land was covered, and in 1940, 88.3 percent. By the end of 1940, 23,214,961 bushels of corn were under seal, including 14,395,342 bushels of 1938 and 1939 corn resealed. Relatively little wheat was resealed and the total of 16,974,252 bushels of wheat under loan on farms and in warehouses in 1940 included only 374,552 bushels of 1939 farm storage wheat resealed. Loans were made available on rye in 1939, and 44,000 bushels of this crop were sealed on the farms, of which 9,129 were resealed in 1940 along with 59,105 bushels of the new crop. In 1940, the first year loans were made available on barley, 335,280 bushels were sealed.

The commodity loans had marked price-stabilization features. If, for example, the price of corn had dropped thirty cents in 1940—as competent authority indicates it would have without the impetus of the loan rate of sixty-one cents per bushel—the loss to Nebraska farmers would have been about thirty million dollars. Similarly, a decline of forty cents in the 1940 wheat price would have lowered the income of Nebraska's wheat farmers by about fourteen million dollars. Altogether, Nebraska farmers received nearly two hundred million dollars during the years from 1933 to 1940 in government payments of one kind or another. The significance of this in the economic life of the depression-racked state can hardly be ignored, particularly when one observes the portion of the state's total farm income during those years received as government payments:

Year	Crops and Livestock	Government Payments
1933	$180,244,000	$ 3,472,000
1934	211,202,000	29,916,000
1935	206,373,000	33,355,000
1936	278,106,000	17,293,000
1937	249,475,000	17,468,000
1938	203,568,000	15,371,000
1939	228,174,000	28,078,000
1940	224,289,000	46,296,000

At no time during the Thirties did farm income—either in terms of dollars or purchasing power—attain the level it had maintained during the middle and late Twenties. A part of the reason may be found in prices; though they increased greatly from depression levels, they generally stayed a little under the level of the Twenties. More of the reason may be found in production. As has been indicated,[1] the years 1934 and 1936 saw the most severe drouths the state had experienced.

[1]See pp. 290–292.

The decade generally was dry, and low yields combined with crop reduction programs to reduce total production.

Despite this comparison, however, the condition of the farmers was so vastly improved over the depression years that in some respects the recovery of the middle and late Thirties seemed almost like prosperity. Moreover, through government guarantees, the specter of foreclosure had been removed. Then, too, expanded programs in electric power, conservation, and irrigation[2] were adding to the chances for the good life on the farm and were building the basis for what seemed like permanent farm prosperity.

IN THE CITIES AND TOWNS

Nebraskans—and Americans generally—were wholly unprepared to meet the heavy demands for relief which faced them in the early Thirties. Over the years the state had developed a group of institutions to care for the unfortunate, and in 1921 a Veterans Relief Fund had been established; but relief for the needy generally had been left to the counties. In some instances, the counties expanded their relief programs to meet the new situation, but it soon became clear that the problem was beyond the capabilities of county government, and in 1933 both the state and federal governments were forced to take cognizance of the destitute. The state legislature adopted an old-age pension act, to be administered by the counties, and authorized the counties to levy up to one mill for the relief of unemployed and indigent persons. The federal government entered the field through the Federal Emergency Relief Administration, the Civilian Conservation Corps, and the Civil Works Administration. These agencies were supplemented or replaced by other agencies, but the federal government continued to bear the greater part of the relief burden, and as late as January, 1935, the Federal Emergency Relief Administration was contributing eighty-seven percent of all public assistance. Under the impetus of the Social Security Act of 1935, the legislature, in a special session that year, enacted a series of measures which provided for old-age assistance, aid to dependent and crippled children, and blind assistance. The impact upon state government of this effort to meet the needs of the indigent was second only to that resulting from the assumption of responsibility for providing highways to meet the needs of the automobile. Prior to 1936 the item

[2]See pp. 307–320.

of public assistance did not appear in the state's regular expenditures; by 1938 it ranked second only to highways in amount of money expended, and in the biennium 1937–1939 the budget for assistance accounted for nearly one-fourth of the state's total appropriations.

The extent of the relief program may be shown by the following statistics:

PUBLIC ASSISTANCE IN NEBRASKA

Year	No. of Recipients	Expenditures
Jan. 1, 1936–June 30, 1936	74,390	$11,598,964
July 1, 1936–June 30, 1937	98,362	27,962,485
July 1, 1937–June 30, 1938	96,663	27,165,668
July 1, 1938–June 30, 1939	100,332	29,939,186
July 1, 1939–June 30, 1940	95,971	27,192,751
July 1, 1940–June 30, 1941	95,362	27,054,391
July 1, 1941–June 30, 1942	75,924	20,165,514

The foregoing includes all types of assistance, both direct and emergency work relief, and expenditures from both state and federal funds. As has been indicated above, however, the federal government bore the major portion of the expense.

These figures by no means describe the impact of the relief program upon the state. For example, the number of recipients falls far short of indicating the number of persons actually affected by relief payments of one kind or another. The Legislative Council estimated in November, 1938, that the number of ultimate recipients would almost certainly reach, or exceed, 250,000—more than eighteen percent of the inhabitants of the state. Moreover, these figures in no way tell the story of the social benefits derived from the relief program, and particularly the work relief aspects of that program. Projects of all sorts were carried forward—everything from resodding a courthouse lawn, constructing public buildings, improving highways and other facilities, to inventorying archives and indexing newspaper files; the skills and self-respect of many professional and subprofessional people were kept alive through an opportunity to earn a living along lines related to the fields in which they were trained. The figures do reveal, however, that prior to the onset of World War II, the state was able to achieve no appreciable reduction in the number of persons receiving relief or in the expenditures for relief.

Manufactures—still a relatively minor part of the state's economic activity—increased somewhat during the decade, but in 1939 still remained below the level of 1929:

NEBRASKA MANUFACTURES, 1929-1939

Year	No. of Establishments	No. of Employees	Wages	Value of Products	Value Added
1929	1,440	29,159	$42,566,205	$460,757,514	$108,912,878
1937	1,071	24,489	31,175,166	282,502,287	67,425,143
1939	1,161	22,449	28,123,351	273,524,581	69,087,373

The story is about the same for retail and wholesale trade. The number of retail trade establishments jumped from 16,682 in 1929 to 19,330 in 1939; the number of wholesale trade establishments, from 2,886 to 3,391. In other categories, however, figures for 1939 were considerably below those of 1929. This is accounted for, in part, by lower prices in the latter year.

No matter what figures one looks at, however, one must come to the conclusion that all in all, though the disastrous depression of the early Thirties had been turned back, Nebraska's economy throughout the decade was far from being prosperous—at least in terms of the prosperity of pre-1929 years.

DEPRESSION POLITICS

The Thirties brought the Democrats greater and more sustained success than any other period in Nebraska's history—and for the most part their control of state politics during this period was more complete than any the Republicans had enjoyed during their periods of supremacy since 1890.

Though the Republicans cut into their majorities and picked up a few more seats in the legislature, the Democrats in 1934 generally repeated their landslide performance of 1932. Edward R. Burke, Omaha congressman who had defeated Charles W. Bryan in a bitter primary fight, went to the Senate in an easy victory over Robert G. Simmons. For governor, Roy L. Cochran, former state engineer, who had got less than a third of the vote in the Democratic primary in besting a field of eight opponents (including Terry Carpenter and Eugene D. O'Sullivan), defeated Dwight Griswold, Gordon publisher and former member of the state legislature, by a much less substantial margin, 284,095 to 266,707. The Democrats won all state offices except that of Commissioner of Public Lands and Buildings, and a large majority in both houses of the legislature. They also won all congressional races except in the third district, where the venerable Edgar Howard was soundly defeated by Karl Stefan, Norfolk radio man, who was to remain in Congress until his death in 1951 and develop into as substantial—if not quite as picturesque—a figure in the Nebraska congressional delegation as his erstwhile opponent.

In 1936, though Roosevelt got only slightly more than fifty-six percent of the vote as compared with a little over sixty-two percent in 1932, the Democrats generally repeated their performance: Leo N. Swanson, Commissioner of Public Lands, and Congressman Karl Stefan were the only persons elected on the Republican ticket; and Cochran, seeking re-election, defeated Griswold by a considerably larger margin than he had in 1934. There were signs, however, that the Democratic party in the state, as an organization, was in serious trouble and that Democratic successes were based, to a degree at least, upon the votes of Norris Republicans who supported the basic principles of the New Deal. Those signs showed up in the senatorial election. Senator Norris, who had supported Democratic presidential candidates since 1928 and who was one of Roosevelt's major bulwarks in the Senate, probably could not have had the Republican nomination if he had wanted it. He makes it clear in his autobiography that he did not want it. He likewise indicates there that under no circumstance would he have accepted a Democratic nomination, although he probably could have had it. He appeared to be ready to retire at the expiration of his fourth term in 1937. He would be seventy-six.

At this juncture, James E. Lawrence, editor of the Lincoln *Star*—which, as the Omaha *World-Herald* drifted away from the New Deal, became the state's leading Democratic newspaper—began a circulation of petitions to nominate Senator Norris as an Independent. This drive was successful, and Norris accepted the nomination. Meanwhile, Terry Carpenter, easily the state's most flamboyant politician, who had been elected to Congress in 1932 and had campaigned unsuccessfully for the Democratic nomination for governor in 1934, won the nomination for senator in the Democratic primary. The state convention, however, refused to recognize the action of the Democratic primary and instead endorsed Norris for the post. From the beginning, President Roosevelt had made it clear that he favored Norris' re-election, and during the campaign he came into the state to impress upon Nebraskans the fact that they owed a duty to the nation to return Norris to the Senate. With this support, Norris was re-elected and Carpenter ran a poor third, although his vote and that of Republican candidate Robert G. Simmons together totalled 72,967 more than that given Senator Norris.

By 1938, the pendulum had begun to swing toward the Republicans. Cochran won a third term as governor, defeating Republican Charles J. Warner (who had bested Griswold in the primary) and Charles W. Bryan, running by petition. He was able to carry the Secretary of State and Treasurer with him, but William E. Johnson, Ray C. Johnson, Walter R. Johnson, and Duane T. Swanson were elected Lieutenant Governor, Auditor, Attorney General, and Railway Commissioner, respectively. Indeed, it seemed that anyone whose name ended in a Scandinavian suffix could get elected to office in Nebraska no matter what ticket he ran on—the two Democratic victors on the state ticket were Harry R. Swanson and Walter H. Jensen. In the congressional races Republicans George Heinke, Karl Stefan, and Carl T. Curtis won in the first, third, and fourth districts; Democrats Charles F. McLaughlin and Harry B. Coffee won re-election in the second and fifth districts.

By 1940, the political pendulum had swung almost completely to the Republican side of its arc. Willkie took the state's electoral votes away from Roosevelt; Hugh A. Butler, Omaha grain dealer, defeated Governor Cochran for the Senate; and Dwight Griswold finally reached the executive office by defeating Terry Carpenter. Griswold took the whole state ticket in with him, and the only Democrat elected was Harry B. Coffee, who was returned to Congress from the fifth district.

World War II

During the Thirties, Nebraskans, in common with most of their fellow Americans, were preoccupied with the problem of recovery from the depression and generally oblivious to events transpiring elsewhere in the world. Their reaction to the growing menace of European dictatorships seems generally to have been the hope that America could remain free from Europe's troubles. The debate, though not as bitter as that preceding America's entry into World War I, was heated, and isolationist sentiment, at least in the newspapers, was strong. The fear of foreign entanglement was a factor in the Republican victory of 1940, although its importance is difficult to assess. Opposition to a third term for the President was strong, and there had been a general defection from the New Deal in much of the state. The debate over foreign policy continued, although after Pearl Harbor there was none of the type of opposition that had occurred during 1917–18. Likewise, there was none of the home-front hysteria which had marred the state's history during World War I.

At home, the war years were characterized by unprecedented prosperity, both on the farms and in the towns, as heavy yields and high prices strengthened the state's agricultural economy. This prosperity continued and increased after the war, to give the state by 1954 almost a decade and a half of the most prosperous years in its history.

The federalization of the armed services accomplished during World War I was continued and extended during World War II with the result that there was virtually no participation by state units as such, although Nebraska's National Guard, the 134th Infantry Regiment, was called to active duty in December, 1940, and under the command of General Butler B. Miltonberger of North Platte, fought with great distinction in France and Germany, playing a vital role in the break-through at St. Lo, one of the turning points in the war. Most of the 120,000 Nebraska men and women who served in the armed forces, however, were scattered throughout the Army, Navy, Marines, and Air Forces. A total of 3,839 Nebraskans lost their lives in the service.

Primarily an agricultural state, Nebraska did not attract the great war industries, although many of the state's small enterprises sub-contracted a wide variety of equipment, and heavy bombers were assembled in Omaha. Ordnance plants were located at Mead, Grand Island, and Sidney, and the Navy located one of its large ammunition depots at Hastings. The Army Air Forces found that the broad prairies and sunny skies of Nebraska provided excellent training facilities, and large air bases were located at Alliance, Ainsworth, Bruning, Fairmont, Grand Island, Harvard, Kearney, Lincoln, McCook, Scottsbluff, and Scribner. At Atlanta, near Holdrege, there was a prisoner-of-war camp, and historic Fort Robinson was pressed into service as a training center for the war dogs of the K-9 corps. After the war, Offutt Field, near Omaha, became headquarters for the Strategic Air Command.

But Nebraska's basic contribution during World War II, as in World War I, was the production of food, and the account of the contribution adds another chapter to the story of Nebraska's basic economic activity, agriculture. Unlike so many of the earlier chapters, this one can be captioned "Prosperity."

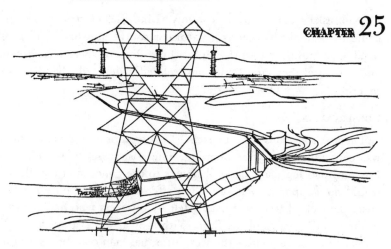

CHAPTER 25

Conservation, Irrigation, Public Power

ONCE THE SEARCH FOR COAL, salt, and other minerals had proved fruitless, Nebraskans came to content themselves with the fact that the state's principal resource was its generally fertile soil, which, given enough water, would support a thriving agriculture. Nebraskans soon realized that the key to a thriving agriculture—aside from prices—was water. For a while, they comforted themselves with the theory that agriculture would provide its own solution to the problem of moisture—the theory that "rainfall follows the plow."[1] They also busied themselves with efforts to increase the moisture supply, and much of the early interest in tree planting was based upon the theory that trees would improve moisture conditions. Further, in the Nineties, there was some interest in "rain making" through concussion and other artificial means. Finally, however, Nebraskans came to realize that the only satisfactory solution to the problem of moisture was the proper use and conservation of the relatively limited amount available. A little later they began to realize that their soil, too, needed to be conserved if it would continue to support the state's principal economic activity. Thus, in the twentieth century, soil conservation and irrigation have become an integral part

[1]See pp. 166–167.

of Nebraska's agricultural economy. Likewise, electric power has come to be looked upon as a natural resource and has been developed as a public enterprise. The three deserve special treatment, and because they are somewhat related, they will be discussed together.

CONSERVATION

The first conscious effort by Nebraskans to improve their environment was centered around tree planting. The absence of trees west of the Missouri had led many early observers to the conclusion that the area would not support agriculture. Even after this assumption was proved false, the lack of trees was keenly felt by pioneers who had grown up in the wooded states of the East. With typical western optimism, Nebraska's pioneer agriculturists were sure that man could do something about this natural shortcoming. When early fruit growing efforts proved successful in southeastern Nebraska, men like Robert W. Furnas and J. Sterling Morton began to promote the growing of fruit trees not only as an important economic activity but as a means to the good life. J. Sterling Morton told the State Horticultural Society in 1871:

> There is beauty in a well ordered orchard which is a "joy forever." It is a blessing to him who plants it, and it perpetuates his name and memory, keeping it fresh as the fruit it bears long after he has ceased to live. There is comfort in a good orchard, in that it makes the new home more like the "old home in the East," and with its thrifty growth and large luscious fruits, sows contentment in the mind of a family as the clouds scatter the rain. Orchards are missionaries of culture and refinement. They make the people among whom they grow a better and more thoughtful people. If every farmer in Nebraska will plant out and cultivate an orchard and a flower garden, together with a few forest trees, this will become mentally and morally the best agricultural State, the grandest community of producers in the American Union. Children reared among trees and flowers growing up with them will be better in mind and in heart, than children reared among hogs and cattle. The occupations and surroundings of boys and girls make them, to a great extent, either bad and coarse, or good and gentle.
>
> If I had the power I would compel every man in the State who had a home of his own, to plant out and cultivate fruit trees.

As a means of encouraging Nebraskans to plant trees, the State Board of Agriculture in 1872 adopted a resolution introduced by Morton desig-

Gilbert M. Hitchcock

John H. Morehead

Charles W. Bryan

James Dahlman

SOME DEMOCRATIC LEADERS

GEORGE W. NORRIS (*Photo by Harris & Ewing, Washington, D. C.*)

Farmers March on State Capitol, 1933

Modern Farm with Shelter Belt

DEPRESSION—AND PROSPERITY

Arbor Lodge

Halsey Forest

"THE TREE PLANTERS' STATE"

Medicine Creek Dam

Irrigating a Corn Field

HARNESSING THE WATERS—POWER AND IRRIGATION

OMAHA STOCKYARDS

Hugh Butler

Karl Stefan

Kenneth S. Wherry

Dwight Griswold

WAR AND POSTWAR LEADERS

WILLA CATHER

nating April 10 as Arbor Day and providing a prize for the person who should plant properly on that day the greatest number of trees. The Arbor Day idea spread rapidly. In 1874 Governor Furnas issued a proclamation calling upon Nebraskans to celebrate Arbor Day. In 1885 the legislature designated Morton's birthday—April 22—as Arbor Day and made it a legal holiday. Further efforts to encourage tree planting may be found in the provision of the Constitution of 1875 providing that improvements resulting from tree planting should not be included in assessments for tax purposes, in state legislation requiring towns and villages to plant trees along their streets, and in the efforts of Senator Phineas W. Hitchcock resulting in the Timber Culture Act of 1873.[2] In the same pattern were successful attempts by Lawrence and Uriah Bruner to grow trees in the Sandhills, and Dr. Charles E. Bessey's fight for the establishment of a man-made national forest in the Sandhills—efforts which grew to fruition under the Administration of that great conservationist, Theodore Roosevelt. In the same tradition are the millions of trees set out each year on farms of the state through the Clark-McNary program and the windbreaks planted across the Plains as part of the New Deal shelter-belt program in the 1930's.

During the early years Nebraskans evinced little interest in conserving their soil. Although here and there a voice was raised to admonish them that the process of "mining the soil" would lead to undesirable results, most Nebraska farmers proceeded on the apparent assumption that the fertility of their soil was inexhaustible. The problem in the Seventies and Eighties was expansion, not conservation. The drouth and depression of the Nineties resulted in considerable rethinking of the agricultural problem, and agricultural leaders—both practical and academic—began to urge the importance of diversification and systematic crop rotation. The soil-building qualities of alfalfa particularly were stressed.

The problem of soil fertility was kept constantly before the farmers of the state during the early years of the twentieth century, and though many were slow to appreciate its importance, by 1930 systems of crop rotation best suited to the various sections were well recognized and were being practiced by a substantial number of farmers. Providing added impetus was the obvious economic need for diversifying crops to remove the hazards of one-crop agriculture and to try to find a com-

[2]See pp. 161–162.

bination of crops and livestock that would insure a profit under conditions of high costs of production and static or declining prices. Much of the pioneering work was carried on under the direction of Dr. George E. Condra, Director of the Conservation and Survey Division of the University of Nebraska, successor to the Conservation Commission, established by Governor Sheldon in 1908 and made permanent by act of the legislature in 1913.

Widespread soil conservation work dates from the 1930's when the federal government began to take a direct hand in conservation. The Federal Soil Conservation Service, in cooperation with the College of Agriculture and the Conservation and Survey Division, began a program of erosion control in 1934 with demonstration projects in Boone and Nance counties. By 1936 there were projects in Douglas and Otoe counties as well, and demonstration work in erosion control was being carried forward by sixteen Civilian Conservation Corps camps scattered throughout the central and eastern portions of the state.

Under the impetus of the Federal Soil Conservation Act, which replaced the AAA,[3] the legislature in 1937 provided for the establishment of soil conservation districts and created a State Soil Conservation Committee to represent the state in the organization and administration of the districts. By 1940 eight soil conservation districts had been organized; by 1944 more than one-half of the farms of the state were in soil conservation districts; and by 1950 one hundred percent of the acreage of all the farms and ranches in the state was included in eighty-seven soil conservation districts. Heavy rains in the late Forties which frequently sent small streams out of their banks resulted in considerable interest in the eastern part of the state in the development of an integrated conservation, flood and erosion control program within the various watersheds, and in 1953 the legislature passed an act authorizing the establishment of watershed districts.

From the beginning, the soil conservation movement has faced an uphill struggle. Everyone believes in conservation in principle, but conservation practices are expensive and frequently involve the deferring of immediate returns in favor of long-term gains. Many individual farmers have been unable or unwilling to make that deferment. In any event, successful widespread conservation has been accomplished only through the expenditure of vast sums of federal money, both in terms of tech-

[3] See pp. 298–299.

nical assistance and direct payments to farmers. From 1936 to 1950, those direct payments to farmers in Nebraska amounted to $194,040,000.

IRRIGATION

Though there had been sporadic interest in irrigation since the Sixties, and the Army at Fort Sidney in the Seventies had successfully diverted water from Lodgepole Creek to irrigate a line of trees, there was little general interest in irrigation in Nebraska prior to 1890. A few private ditches had been constructed in the 1880's, but the Twelfth Census reports a total of only 11,744 irrigated acres in Nebraska in 1889, with Cheyenne, Lincoln, Scotts Bluff, and Sioux counties leading in that order. In 1889, the legislature authorized the acquisition of water rights by appropriation, but initially only a few applications were filed. As M. A. Daugherty of Ogallala told the third annual convention of the Nebraska State Irrigation Association in 1895, "Through these early years to speak of irrigation as the solution for crop raising was to invite condemnation upon oneself."[4]

The drouth years of the early Nineties brought a marked change in the attitude of many farmers in western Nebraska. Those who had scoffed at irrigation as a solution to the agricultural problems of the arid West were now quick to join the ranks of irrigators. A state irrigation convention was held in 1891, and Robert W. Furnas, whose name had been associated with almost every agricultural advance since territorial times, was elected its first president. The Nebraska State Irrigation Association, which grew out of the convention, met annually and campaigned tirelessly in the interest of irrigation. Its first major victory was achieved in 1895, when the legislature created the State Board of Irrigation to supervise applications for water rights under the Law of 1889 and to provide for the organization of irrigation districts. The functions of the State Board of Irrigation were transferred to the new Department of Public Works in 1919, but remained basically the same.

As a result of drouth conditions and active promotion of irrigation as a solution to the problem of dry-land farming, the number of irrigated acres in the state increased from 11,744 in 1889 to 148,538 in 1899. The leading counties, in order of acreage, were: Scotts Bluff, Lincoln, Cheyenne, Dawson, Keith, and Deuel. Most of the irrigation works built in the Nineties were constructed by private companies, occa-

[4] *The Nebraska Irrigation Annual* (Lincoln, 1896), pp. 28–29.

sionally representing outside capital, but more frequently representing associations of farmers. Most of the state's irrigation was carried on in the Platte Valley. But a small project was opened in the North Loup Valley in 1895, there was some activity in the Republican Valley, and Holt County had 2,218 irrigated acres. The cost of construction per mile of ditch was high in comparison with other sections having a similar topography, largely because canals of great length were required to bring the water out of the valleys onto the fields. In any event, it was becoming increasingly clear that extensive irrigation works were beyond the capacity of private capital.

The federal government entered the field with the Reclamation Act of 1902, creating a reclamation fund from the proceeds of public land sales in sixteen western states. The fund was to be used in the construction and maintenance of irrigation works, with the costs repaid by settlers on irrigated land. This was supplemented in 1911 by the Warren Act, authorizing the sale of surplus water from federal projects to land already irrigated but in need of additional water.

Through the North Platte Project, constructed under the Act of 1902, approximately 150,000 acres of land were reclaimed in Morrill and Scotts Bluff counties. Water is stored in the Pathfinder Reservoir, completed in 1910, about forty miles southwest of Casper, Wyoming. From the Pathfinder Reservoir, the water is withdrawn through the channel of the North Platte for a distance of about two hundred miles, then is diverted into two canals, one on each side of the river, and conducted to crops needing water. A regulatory reservoir at Guernsey, Wyoming, was completed in 1928, with a net capacity of 61,000 acre-feet. Lake Alice and Lake Minatare, supplementary off-stream regulatory reservoirs, have a combined capacity of 72,000 acre-feet. Further regulatory storage is provided by the Sutherland Reservoir, constructed in the 1930's by the Platte Valley Public Power and Irrigation District, with funds supplied by the Public Works Administration. Other major projects constructed with federal funds during the Thirties were the Central Nebraska Public Power and Irrigation District (Tri-County) and the Public Power and Irrigation projects on the Loup River. These projects, involving the expenditure of millions of dollars, not only added to the agricultural resources of the state, but were a significant factor in the income of drouth- and depression-stricken Nebraskans during the decade.

Initially, virtually all irrigation was from streams, but beginning in the 1920's, pump irrigation from wells began to be used increasingly, particularly in the lower Platte Valley. During the Nineties an amazing variety of homemade windmills pumped water in the Platte Valley, some of it for irrigation.[5] In 1919 there were only 546 acres under pump irrigation; by 1929 the acreage thus irrigated had increased to 23,452, and by 1939 to 80,673. Since that time it has increased steadily. The state's vast ground-water resources provide excellent supplies for pump irrigation and furnish much of the state's surface supply of water.

Perhaps the most meaningful statistics in connection with irrigation —at least to the layman—are figures on the number of acres irrigated. The increase in irrigated acres from 1889 to 1899 has already been indicated. From 1910 to 1940 the Census of Irrigation showed acres irrigated in Nebraska as follows:

Year	Acres Irrigated	Year	Acres Irrigated
1910	255,950	1930	532,617
1920	442,690	1940	610,379

Approximately eighty-five percent of the total irrigated area in 1939 was in the following counties:

Scotts Bluff	200,468	Keith	16,690
Morrill	79,962	Dawes	14,301
Dawson	70,308	Garden	11,804
Lincoln	44,022	Hitchcock	11,366
Sioux	32,824	Hall	10,875
Buffalo	24,076		

The total irrigated area in the state in 1939 was 610,379 acres. This was only a little more than 1.2 percent of the total land area. Even in the counties referred to above, where more than 10,000 acres were irrigated, the total irrigated area was only a little more than five percent of the total area. Scotts Bluff, the state's banner irrigation county, had a little less than forty-three percent of its area irrigated in 1939. Despite these relatively insignificant percentages, however, the impact of irrigation upon the economy of the counties where it was practiced and upon the state as a whole has been highly significant.

Scotts Bluff County affords a good example. In 1890 it had a population of only 1,188; in 1900, only 2,552. By 1930, however, it had

[5] See Walter Prescott Webb, "The Story of Some Prairie Inventions," *Nebraska History*, XXXIV (December, 1953), 229-244.

become the fourth most populous county in the state, and in 1940 it ranked third and was first in density of rural farm population. By 1940 the city of Scottsbluff, which in 1900 had been only a little huddle of tar-paper shacks, ranked sixth in the state. In the value of crops produced, the county ran well ahead of every other county in the state, with the margin being greatly increased during the dry years. The county's agricultural economy was based to a large degree upon specialized cash crops—sugar beets, potatoes, beans, and canning crops—grown under irrigation. In each of these it ranked first in the state and produced a sizable portion of the state's entire production—from about one-half to three-fourths. Irrigation farmers also grew alfalfa, corn, barley, and oats for livestock feed, and the county ranked first in the number of sheep on feed. Other aspects of the economy reflected the high efficiency of the county's agriculture. In 1940 the county ranked third in manufacturing and third in retail sales. In freight shipments Scottsbluff was second only to Omaha.

Scotts Bluff County's relative prosperity was shared by the other irrigation counties, where dependable supplies of moisture combined with fertile soil to produce large yields even in dry years. Estimates indicated that irrigation could be expected to increase production as follows: alfalfa, 65 percent; barley, 116 percent; corn, 126 percent; oats, 96 percent; potatoes, 162 percent; and wheat, 131 percent. Irrigation made possible the transformation of the sugar beet industry from a problem to an important agricultural enterprise, and by the Thirties Nebraska was exceeded only by Colorado in the production of sugar beets. Dawson County, in the central Platte Valley, developed into the nation's leading alfalfa producer, and dehydration processes, developed by Nebraskans, greatly increased the crop's potential uses.

Irrigation thus made the Platte Valley from Grand Island west a veritable garden and greatly increased production elsewhere in the central and western portions of the state. Even so, interest in irrigation fluctuated considerably, even after its value had been demonstrated. Irrigation farming is expensive, and after a couple of wet years people's inclination to depend solely on rainfall grows very strong. Then, too, irrigation, involving as it does the use of water from streams flowing not only through many counties but across state lines, has been the subject of much legislation and litigation. From that early irrigation law of 1889, legislation on the subject has grown to the point where it occupies 446 pages in the *Revised Statutes of Nebraska* (1943; Reissue of

1960). The state has been involved in controversy and litigation with Colorado and Wyoming over the use of water from the Platte River, and within the state the question of diverting water from one valley to another has on occasion so rocked the legislature that all other issues tended to revolve around it. Moreover, as irrigation developed, it became increasingly more apparent that neither the surface nor ground-water resources of the state were inexhaustible—the North Platte Valley at times faced the prospect of serious water shortages—and that farming by irrigation required continuous study and planning for achieving the proper combination of land and water use.

But if one drives through the valley of the Platte, the Loup, or the Republican—and particularly if he stands on top of Scotts Bluff and looks eastward down the North Platte Valley—he cannot help but come to the conclusion that irrigation has supplied at least part of the answer to the problems involved in the occupation of the Plains by an agricultural population.

Public Power

Coincident with the large-scale irrigation development of the late Thirties and early Forties, Nebraska developed a state-wide public power system. The system is complicated and causes much confusion at home and abroad, both as to its operation and the motives behind its creation. Though in some quarters Nebraska's public power system is looked upon with horror as a monstrous example of socialism, most Nebraskans do not share this view. They realize that though bitterly fought over and opposed on ideological grounds, it was brought about not as the result of any particular political movement, but primarily as the result of an effort to harness the rivers of the state for their maximum beneficial use.

Prior to 1930 there was little public appreciation of the hydroelectric potential of Nebraska's rivers. The total installed power of all hydroelectric plants in the Platte River Basin in Nebraska was only 10,446 horsepower, and surveys by federal, state, and private engineers were not particularly optimistic over the possibility of installing much more. In 1925 Senator Norris and others, through the Bureau of Reclamation, had tried to promote federal financing of irrigation and hydroelectric projects in central Nebraska, but without success. To be sure, there were those who disagreed with the prevailing view—Norris, Phil

Hockenberger, Keith Neville, R. O. Canaday, C. W. McConaughy, and George Kingsley, to mention but a few—but, as has been indicated, there was little popular or effective interest.

The depression of the early Thirties and an amendment of the RFC Act in July, 1932, permitting the Reconstruction Finance Corporation to provide loans to public groups for irrigation and/or hydroelectric projects stimulated considerable interest in the state in the development of such projects, not only for their inherent benefits but also for the employment that would be provided in their construction. Groups organized in Columbus, North Platte, and Hastings raised over $200,-000 to promote such activity.

Before anything could be done, however, it was necessary for the legislature to authorize the organization of public corporations to undertake the work. Lawyers for the three groups drew up a bill, and the legislature in 1933, over heavy opposition from the private utilities, passed the necessary legislation. The Act as passed and signed by Governor Bryan authorized the formation of public power and/or irrigation districts as political subdivisions with authority to borrow money backed by revenue bonds. The districts could be formed upon approval by the Department of Roads and Irrigation of petitions bearing signatures of fifteen percent of the qualified electors of the area concerned.

The Columbus group was the first to comply with the legislative requirements, organizing on June 3, 1933, the Loup River Public Power District, with headquarters at Columbus. Charles B. Fricke was named president; Phil Hockenberger, vice-president; C. C. Sheldon, treasurer; and Harold Kramer, secretary and general manager. Retaining Arthur F. Mullen, Democratic National Committeeman from Nebraska, who had been Roosevelt's floor leader at the Chicago convention of 1932, as its Washington attorney, the district submitted its application for funds to the Reconstruction Finance Corporation. The request was transferred to the newly-created Public Works Administration, and by November 15, the Loup River plan was approved. Construction was started in October, 1934, and by March, 1937, the project started producing power. The cost of construction had been about $14,000,000.

Meanwhile, the North Platte Group was under way, and the Platte Valley Public Power and Irrigation District was formally organized, also in June, 1933. It, too, retained Mullen as its Washington attorney. Its plans were approved on November 3—a few days before those of the Loup River district—and construction, begun in August, 1934, was completed in December, 1936, at a cost of $11,000,000. Whereas the Loup River project produced only power, this district, known also as the Sutherland project, provided both power and irrigation, and the Sutherland Reservoir[6] has a capacity of about 175,000 acre-feet. The district embraces Keith, Lincoln, Dawson, Buffalo, and Hall counties.

The Tri-County Project, organized on November 1, 1933, as the Central Nebraska Public Power and Irrigation District, embracing Adams, Gosper, Phelps and Kearney counties, did not fare so well. Its plan, denounced by Mullen as "an engineering monstrosity," did not meet PWA approval and had to be resubmitted. Though Mullen fought the Tri-County project to the last, Senator Norris advocated it before both Secretary Ickes and the President, and finally on September 28, 1935, PWA approved a revised project. Though the first contracts were awarded December 14, 1935, construction did not get well under way until the spring of 1938. It did not begin furnishing power until January, 1941, and was not considered officially completed until December 31, 1943. Its principal feature is Kingsley Dam, near Ogallala, the second largest earthen dam in the world, which forms Lake C. W. McConaughy. Built at a cost of $38,000,000, it can provide 233,000,000 kilowatt-hours of firm power annually and irrigates land in four counties.

By the late Thirties, with the Loup River and Platte Valley projects completed and Tri-County abuilding, it became clear that the hydros were going to have trouble marketing their power in sufficient quantities to pay their costs of operation and service their debt to the federal government. To provide outlets and to secure extra generating plants to increase their capacity to produce power, the hydros tried to buy the privately-owned electric utilities serving Nebraska. When this failed —largely because of difficulties encountered in financing—the Consumers Public Power District was organized in 1939 to make the purchases. Consumers was organized as a separate legal entity, having no connection with the hydros other than agreements to purchase and market their power. The first private utility acquired was in Columbus, and headquarters of the district were established there. Initially, the members of its board of directors were all members of the Loup River board. In 1943, however, the legislature divided the entire state, except five eastern counties still served by a private utility, into seven districts

[6]See p. 312.

for the purpose of electing a seven-member board to govern Consumers. Altogether, Consumers purchased fourteen private utility properties at a total price of $40,750,556.68, financed by revenue bonds. A great deal of public controversy surrounded the acquisition of the private utilities by Consumers and the sale of its bonds. At the center of the controversy was Guy C. Meyers, New York broker, who handled all of Consumers' negotiations with the private utilities and the marketing of its bonds, and who collected from the district over a five-year period a total of $899,171.30 in commissions and expenses.

Meanwhile, in order to provide a degree of stability in their operations, to prevent ruinous competition among themselves, and to make possible a refinancing of their obligations to the federal government, the three hydros in 1940 entered into a joint operating agreement under the name of the Nebraska Public Power System, by which they agreed to pool their production and revenues, thus in effect securing the unification which Senator Norris had tried unsuccessfully to achieve through a "Little TVA" for Nebraska. In 1949, Tri-County, wishing to be relieved of its participation in the state's power development so that it could concentrate on irrigation in its own area, withdrew from the Nebraska Public Power System. It maintained a close relationship with the system, however, selling it the entire output of its hydros and the Canaday Steam Plant.

Electric power for the farms of the state was provided by Rural Public Power Districts, also organized under the Act of 1933. President Roosevelt had created a Rural Electrification Administration by executive order in 1936 and had provided it with $100,000,000 of work relief funds. Legislation sponsored by Senator Norris made it permanent and provided federal loans to rural electrification districts. In 1964 there were thirty-four rural public power districts in Nebraska. In addition, three electric cooperatives in South Dakota, two in Wyoming, and one in Colorado served areas of Nebraska bordering on those states. The twenty-seven rural systems east of North Platte purchased their power from the Nebraska Public Power System, and twenty-one of them belonged to the Nebraska Electric Generation and Transmission Cooperative which constructed a 230,000 volt line from the Bureau of Reclamation power site at Fort Randall to a point near Columbus where it connected with the Nebraska Public Power System. The rural systems west of North Platte, except for the

Southwest Public Power District, purchase their power from the Bureau of Reclamation through the Tri-State Generation and Transmission Cooperative which has headquarters in Denver. The Southwest Public Power District, a cooperative which became a public power district, produces part of its power and purchases the rest from the Nebraska Public Power System. As the state approached its centennial, the rural systems were supplying power to virtually all of the farms and ranches in the state. The impact of REA upon the rural life of Nebraska can perhaps best be understood by the realization that in 1929 only 5.8 percent of its farms enjoyed the benefits of electric power.

Completing the state's conversion to public power was the organization in 1945 of the Omaha Public Power District, embracing the counties of Douglas, Dodge, Sarpy, Saunders, and Washington, and its purchase in 1946 of the Nebraska Power Company, a subsidiary of American Power and Light and Electric Bond and Share. Although it generated most of its own power, the Omaha district established connections with the Nebraska Public Power System, utilities in Iowa and Kansas, the TVA area, and the Bureau of Reclamation.

Meanwhile, a significant number of municipalities continued to own and operate their power systems. Crete had established the first municipally-owned system in the state in 1886. By 1902 there were eleven, and by 1926 the total had climbed to 282. The number declined in the late Twenties and Thirties as many municipalities sold their plants to private utilities, which later were acquired by Consumers. In 1966, however, there were still fifty-six municipally-owned systems in the state. Approximately forty generated all, or nearly all, of their power. Others bought power from the Nebraska Public Power System or from the Bureau of Reclamation; some of the smaller communities secured their power from the rural districts.

The Fifties and early Sixties were years of growth and controversy—indeed, much of the controversy was related to the unprecedented demands placed upon a power system created during the depression when the available supply far exceeded the demand. To provide badly needed additional generating facilities, Tri-County constructed a 100,000 KW steam plant (Canaday) near Lexington; the districts combined to build the 90,000 KW Kramer Station at

Bellevue; and Consumers, in cooperation with the Atomic Energy Commission, tried unsuccessfully to develop a 100,000 KW thermonuclear plant at Hallam, south of Lincoln. High voltage transmission lines were built to tap Bureau of Reclamation power generated at dams on the Missouri River. The strains put on the state's depression-born power structure and the efforts to relieve them led to many differences of opinion, and the districts engaged in almost continuous, and at times acrimonious, controversy, which they aired in the press, in the legislature, and in the courts. As the years wore on, however, the need for cooperation became increasingly apparent, and as the state approached its centennial its citizens had some cause to hope that its unique public power system would somehow be able to overcome its difficulties and bring to ultimate fruition the dreams of its founders.

CHAPTER 26

The Unicameral Legislature

WHILE WRESTLING with the problems of drouth and depression, Nebraskans adopted a major innovation in state government—the unicameral legislature.

The unicameral idea was not new, either in Nebraska or the nation. Most of the colonial assemblies originated as one-house bodies, although they gradually shifted over to the two-house system, and when state constitutions were formed, only Pennsylvania and Georgia adopted the one-house legislature—and even in these cases a "Board of Censors" acted as a virtual second house. When Vermont set itself up as an independent republic in 1777 it had a one-house legislature, but in 1836 the unicameral idea gave way there to what had by then become the traditional two-house system. Interest in the unicameral idea slept until early in the twentieth century when an increasing number of progressives began to concern themselves with legislative reform. State legislatures over the years had been subject to a great deal of criticism. Progressives especially condemned their inefficient methods and their frequent subservience to special interests. They were particularly critical of the conference committee between the two houses, in which reform legislation either died or was emasculated. As Senator Norris put it:

It has been the stock argument that in a two house legislature one branch serves as a check upon the other in the ultimate molding of good and wholesome legislation. As a matter of practice, it has developed frequently that, through the Conference Committee, the politicians have the checks, and the special interests the balances.[1]

Nebraska's two-house legislature appears to have been no better or no worse than most other state legislative bodies. The Conference Committee played an important role in legislation. For example, from 1921 to 1933, 10.95 percent of all measures enacted by the legislature passed through the Conference Committee, and in one instance—a bill permitting municipally owned electric light plants to build lines beyond their corporate limits—the Conference Committee was able to frustrate for six years legislation which—as is evidenced by a heavy majority in a special election on the question— the people generally approved. Perhaps the principal difference between Nebraska and other states was that here those who wanted to reform legislative procedures, if not more numerous, had better and more persistent leadership.

As early as 1915 a joint committee of the legislature, in a strongly-worded statement which declared that, "one body can more directly represent the public will of a democratic people than two or more," recommended the submission of a single-chamber amendment to the people. The legislature, possibly because it was interested in broader constitutional reform—it authorized a vote on the question of holding a constitutional convention—refused to accept the recommendation of its joint committee. The proponents of unicameralism brought the issue up again in the 1917 session, and again without success. They came close to succeeding in the constitutional convention of 1919–20, when they were beaten only by the vote of the President breaking a tie. In 1923, after failing again in the legislature, they circulated an initiative petition, but were unable to obtain enough signatures to put the proposition on the ballot. They tried the legislative route again in 1925 and in 1933, but without success.

[1]George W. Norris, *Fighting Liberal* (New York: The Macmillan Company, 1945), pp. 351–352.

All of this served to keep the idea before the people. Then, early in 1934, Senator Norris took an active interest in the proposal. He attended a meeting in Lincoln on February 22, called by Colonel John G. Maher, and urged the submission of an amendment to the constitution providing for a unicameral legislature. Before adjourning, the conference decided to try the initiative route which had failed in 1923.

The amendment, as finally initiated, provided for the election of a one-house legislature, to consist of not less than thirty nor more than fifty members, for two-year terms, on a non-partisan basis. There had been some feeling that the non-partisan feature of the proposal might cause its defeat, but Norris insisted upon it as basic to the whole idea, and his will prevailed.

The non-partisan feature brought opposition from the leaders of both political parties. Some farm groups opposed the amendment on the grounds that the proposed legislature's membership was too restricted and farmers would not be adequately represented. Others opposed it on the grounds that it was dangerous to experiment with the tried and true American legislative formula. Most of the press, led by the Omaha *World-Herald*, opposed the amendment. The only daily papers supporting it were the Lincoln *Star* and the Hastings *Tribune*.

At first it seemed that the effort might meet the same fate that had befallen it in 1923, but by June 5, a month before the deadline, 75,000 persons had signed the initiative petition, and only 57,000 signatures were required to place the proposal on the ballot. Once this hurdle was over, the unicameral movement rapidly gained ground. Senator Norris visited every section of the state in its behalf. He was assisted by many civic leaders, academic people, and others who volunteered their services in the cause.

As the campaign wore on, it appeared that the Norris leadership would be decisive. His large following in Nebraska was proud of his national reputation in the field of governmental reform, and it was willing to go along on the unicameral idea if he favored it. Moreover, the proponents of the amendment pointed to the savings in expense that would result from the one-house legislature and this had a profound influence during the depths of the depression, when Nebraskans were casting about desperately for means of securing more efficient and more economical government in the hope that a reduction in taxes would follow. Then, too, the legislature of 1933, which had included in its membership many inexperienced men swept into office in the Roosevelt landslide, had not provided many examples of bicameral efficiency. Finally, there were two other amendments on the ballot—one repealing the state prohibition law, and another legalizing pari-mutuel betting at the race tracks—and those who favored these were inclined to vote for all three even though some of them may not have had any great interest in the science of government.

The voters approved the amendment by a vote of 286,086 to 193,152, a majority of almost sixty percent—larger than the majority given the pari-mutuel amendment but smaller than that repealing the state prohibition law.

The amendment provided that the one-house legislature should be convened in 1937. The legislature of 1935, therefore, had the problem of redistricting the state and establishing the number of members in the new body. The limitations set in the amendment were not less than thirty nor more than fifty, but there was a further limitation in a provision that the combined salaries of all members should be $37,500 per year. The number of districts, therefore, would determine the salary of each member. Finally, the legislature agreed upon forty-three districts as nearly equal in population as was feasible. The amendment prohibited the splitting of counties to form legislative districts. Douglas County was given seven members, and Lancaster, three; Gage and Scotts Bluff counties were single-county districts; all of the rest were composed of two or more counties, with District 39 in the Sand Hills consisting of ten counties.

Senator Norris—who had demonstrated his hold upon the people of Nebraska by being re-elected in 1936 as an Independent—was in Lincoln to address the first session of the unicameral on January 5, 1937. (Later in the month—on the twentieth—he witnessed the inauguration of the first President under what is generally known as the

Norris amendment to the Constitution abolishing "lame duck" sessions of Congress.)

The first unicameral contained twenty-two Democrats and twenty-one Republicans. They had been elected on non-partisan tickets, however, and to demonstrate their non-partisan characteristics chose Republican Charles J. Warner as speaker. Later legislatures, dominated by Republicans, exhibited similar non-partisanship in the selection of their leaders, with Democrat Walter Raecke being chosen speaker in 1947, and Democrat John Callan being selected to head the powerful Budget Committee in 1941, 1947, and 1949. The first session also took a long step toward eliminating one of the most criticized evils of the old system—though not necessarily inherent in it—when it provided for a public hearing on every bill while it was in committee, even though votes were still taken in executive session to which reporters were invited under a "gentleman's agreement" whereby they would disclose neither discussion nor the vote of any member. The first session also created a Legislative Council to replace the old legislative reference service. At first the Legislative Council consisted of sixteen members, but in 1949 the legislature provided that the Legislative Council should consist of all members of the legislature, thus creating a vehicle through which the legislature could function as a committee of the whole in the interim between sessions. The council was provided with a professional staff headed by a political scientist as director of research. In 1961, the office of fiscal analyst was created within the Legislative Council.

Adoption of the unicameral system by no means cut off debate on its merits. Political leaders, who had opposed the non-partisan aspect of the new arrangement during the campaign for the amendment, continued to press their opposition to this particular feature of the unicameral. They argued that the lack of partisanship in the legislature created both a power and a leadership vacuum in the legislature and made it difficult, if not impossible, for the governor to achieve effective liaison with the legislative branch of government. They received little encouragement from either the governors or the legislators, and the people to date have evinced

little interest in returning to a partisan system. As A. C. Breckenridge suggests,

One reason for this may be that for the majority of the people of the state,
and for a majority of the legislators past and present (possibly for some
future ones too), the differences between Democrats and Republicans on
most state questions are difficult to ascertain. Indeed, the bases for party
distinctions may be difficult for most of them much of the time.[2]

More effective was the argument that the legislature was too small
—an argument which was bolstered by pressure from the urban
centers for redistricting to recognize the shift in population from
the farms to the cities. The 1961 session wrestled with the problem
of representation and finally submitted a compromise amendment
to the voters which provided that in redistricting the state, lines
other than county lines could be followed, and while primary emphasis should be given to population, a certain amount of weight
must be given to area. The voters approved the amendment in
1962, and also one which provided four-year terms of office for
legislators, with half of the membership bei.ͺ elected each two
years. Under this authority, the 1963 session re-districted the state
to provide for forty-nine legislators, to be elected from one-member
districts, with those from the odd-numbered districts to be elected
for four years in 1964 and those from the even-numbered districts
to be elected for two years.

In July of 1964, a three-judge federal court panel held invalid the
area amendment to the state constitution, but agreed to permit
legislators to be elected in 1964 under the re-apportionment law of
1963 which had been enacted pursuant to the provisions of the
amendment. The federal judges also held that while the legislature
elected in 1964 would have de facto status in 1965 it would have
to create a constitutionally valid legislative apportionment.

The legislature's first attempt to meet the court's demand was
struck down by the same three judges (Harvey M. Johnsen, Robert
Van Pelt, and Richard E. Robinson) on the grounds that the 48.4
percent disparity in the populations of the smallest and the largest

[2]A. C. Breckenridge, *One House for Two* (Washington: Public Affairs Press,
1957), p. 46.

districts provided in the apportionment was too great. At the same time, the judges warned the senators either to produce an acceptable law or run at large in 1966. A substitute measure, passed just before adjournment, reduced the disparity to 19.65 percent, but there was no assurance that this would be satisfactory, and the legislature adjourned with its members facing the gloomy prospect that they might have to run at large in 1966—a circumstance which would have wiped out the four-year terms to which half of them had been elected in 1964. In February, 1966, however, the three judges who had over-thrown the two previous efforts at reapportionment expressed satisfaction with the new arrangement, and the cloud of uncertainty which had hung over the legislature for two years was cleared away. The new apportionment breached seven county lines, and Hall County was sliced into three districts. Douglas County was given twelve of the forty-nine districts and Lancaster County, six. At the other end of the scale, District 44 in the southwest corner of the state, included six counties.

The apportionment crisis tended to deflect the debate on the merits of the unicameral legislature, and the successful weathering of that crisis seemed to have further entrenched the idea of unicameralism in Nebraska. Dr. Roger V. Shumate, director of research for the Legislative Council from its establishment until his death in 1954, observed in 1952: "The unicameral legislature is now beginning to enjoy the support of the very force which once constituted its greatest enemy—that is tradition."[3]

With each passing year, the force of tradition increased.

[3]Roger V. Shumate, "The Nebraska Unicameral Legislature," *The Western Political Quarterly*, V (September, 1952), 512.

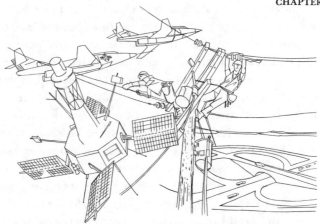

CHAPTER 27

A Quarter-Century of Prosperity

THE WAR YEARS ushered in a period of prosperity that was unprecedented in Nebraska's history, and as the state approached its centennial, its citizens could reflect that the last quarter of the century since statehood had been almost completely outside the drouth-and-depression stereotype which had characterized so much of the state's earlier history.

There had been recession years in the middle Fifties, oldsters still harked back to the grim years of the Thirties, and much of the state's political discussion seemed to be conducted in the context of the desperation of the 1890's rather than the promise of the 1960's, but the fact remained that by 1965 a whole generation of Nebraskans had been born and reared to maturity without having experienced the trials that at some time or other had beset every previous generation in the history of the state.

An important factor in the state's prolonged prosperity was continued rainfall. In 1941, the ten-year drouth which had shriveled crops and blighted hopes was broken, and with the exception of three years (1943, 1955, and 1956) annual precipitation through 1965 was at or near the normal mean of 22.84 inches, and in some years was considerably above the mean.

Crop production reflected the favorable moisture conditions. Although yields varied considerably from year to year, crops generally were good, and in some instances production records were attained. The average yield of corn in the years 1959–1963 was 53.6 bushels per acre, and of wheat, 23.2 bushels per acre. By way of comparison, corn yielded an average of 14.9 bushels per acre during the Thirties, and wheat, 12.3 bushels; during the Twenties the average yield of corn was 25.7, and of wheat, 15.3. The Twenties were fairly good years, too, so the marked increase in yields in the Sixties cannot be attributed solely to rainfall; rather, much of it resulted from spectacularly improved methods, seed, and fertilizer. Corn and wheat remained the state's leading crops, but the Fifties and Sixties saw an increased interest in soybeans and sorghum, which were relatively unimportant before World War II.

Likewise, there was a marked increase in the production of livestock, particularly cattle. The number of cattle on farms near the end of the war exceeded four million. There was some falling off in the immediate postwar years, but in the Fifties the number of cattle on farms again exceeded four million, and in the Sixties it went above five million. Hogs recovered markedly during the war from the sharp decline of the Thirties, but hog production continued to remain below what it had been in the Twenties and early Thirties. Sheep production, which was higher during the war than it had been, after the war generally declined to a position somewhat under that of the Thirties. Poultry production went into a steady decline after the war, and in 1964 was less than half what it had been in 1945. There was, of course, a steady and continued decline in horses and mules as mechanized power replaced horsepower, and "Old Dobbin" disappeared altogether from many Nebraska farms. (The downward trend in the number of horses in the state was reversed in the early Sixties as steadily increasing numbers of city dwellers took to riding as a hobby.)

Prices, although uneven, soared to unprecedented heights, and this, combined with increased production, brought Nebraska farm income to new record highs. Whereas in the Twenties total farm income never reached the half billion dollar mark, the year 1947

saw farm income go over a billion dollars, and in subsequent years
the billion dollar figure was either exceeded or so closely approached
that it came to be looked upon as the standard. Indeed, in the
Sixties, farm income began to edge up toward a billion and a half
dollars.

During the war years, Nebraska's farmers were beset with many
difficulties. Farm labor was siphoned off to war industry and to the
armed forces. Many farmers, entering the war with worn-out and
inadequate machinery, found it difficult to obtain repairs and
almost impossible to secure replacements. Nevertheless, they went
ahead to produce record amounts of food for the war effort; and,
after the war, as labor became more plentiful and new and improved farm machinery became available, their general position
greatly improved.

The countryside reflects that improved position. As one drives
around Nebraska today, he observes that farm buildings are generally painted and in good repair. Handsome new houses are frequently seen, and they are as well furnished as those in the towns.
The farmstead of the 1960's reflected its role as the headquarters
of a wide-spread business and production activity.

Nebraska's mid-century agricultural prosperity was not encumbered by the speculation which shackled the apparent prosperity
during and immediately after World War I. The number of mortgaged farms decreased from 54,246 in 1940 to 29,509 in 1950, or
from 44.8 to 27.5 percent. The ratio of debt to value on the mortgaged farms decreased from 54.7 to 23.1 percent. Taken as a percentage of total farm value, mortgage debt decreased from 27.2
percent in 1940 to 5.9 percent in 1950. Farms have continued to
decrease in number and increase in size. There were 133,616 farms
in 1935, 102,000 in 1955, and 82,000 in 1965; the average size during
the thirty-year period increased from 348.9 to 587 acres. This both
reflected and was a cause of the continued loss of farm population,
which between 1940 and 1960 decreased by almost 38 percent.

Although there was only a slight increase in the state's total population during the Forties and Fifties, the decline in farm population, brought about, in part, by the fact that a man could farm

larger acreages, was more than offset by the increase in urban population. Between 1940 and 1960, total urban population increased by almost 50 percent. Omaha's population increased by 30.3 percent, Lincoln's by 56.7 percent. The smaller cities scored gains, too, and the number of cities, in addition to Omaha and Lincoln, with ten thousand or more persons increased from eight to nine.

Manufacturing, though still relatively unimportant in the state's economy, increased considerably, as the following statistics will show.

Year	No. of Establishments	No. of Employees	Wages	Value added by Manufacture
1939	1,093	26,183	$ 34,133,000	$ 68,139,000
1947	1,344	47,031	119,923,000	260,658,000
1958	1,536	59,000	265,000,000	536,000,000

All available indicators pointed to continuing growth in the early Sixties. Preliminary estimates for 1963 showed 66,000 employees engaged in manufacturing, earning wages totalling $352,000,000, and adding value amounting to $757,000,000. As one would expect, Omaha was the dominant manufacturing center. Of the 1,536 establishments reported in 1958, approximately 31 percent, or 490, were located in Douglas County; Lancaster County reported a total of 155. Most of the establishments were small: 1,124 had fewer than twenty employees, and only 114 had more than one hundred employees, including five—all in Omaha—with a thousand or more employees. As in the past, food and kindred products were the most important, accounting for more than half of the total manufactures of the state. Other important industries were printing and publishing, machinery, electrical equipment, chemicals, fabricated metal products, transportation equipment, stone and clay products, furniture and fixtures, and lumber products.

Wages and salaries increased markedly after the war—106.36 percent between 1950 and 1962. The annual rate of growth for these years in all areas was 6.22 percent, ranging from 2.40 percent in farming to 20.82 in wholesale and retail trade.

In response to high wages and farm prosperity, business flourished as it never had before. Retail sales, a pervasive indicator of general business health, spiralled upward:

Year	Sales
1939	$ 397,196,000
1948	1,317,813,000
1958	1,730,000,000
1963	2,096,000,000

At the same time, the number of retail establishments steadily declined—from 19,330 in 1939 to 16,057 in 1963—as the small businessman, operating a family enterprise, found himself facing increasingly heavy competition from the large operators.

As on the farms, signs of prosperity were everywhere in the towns and cities. Shabby, rundown buildings were repaired and remodelled or replaced with new, modern structures. The characters as well as the faces of many cities were altered as bright new shopping centers developed for the convenience of a population which was becoming increasingly dependent upon the automobile.

THE POLITICS OF PROSPERITY

Since admission to the Union, Nebraska normally has been a Republican state. Its Republicanism, however, has been tempered by a considerable degree of independent voting, and in times of economic stress or uncertainty, Nebraskans have exhibited a tendency to react against the Republican party. In the 1890's the Democrats, through the magic personality of William Jennings Bryan and an uneasy alliance with the Populists, were able to establish themselves as a force to be reckoned with in each contest, and they won elections frequently enough, particularly outside the realm of state offices, to make Nebraska a rather close battleground in most years. As the Populists drifted back into the Republican party, and as new voters, unimpressed by the issues of the Civil War, made their appearance, the Republicans, under the impetus of national leadership furnished by Theodore Roosevelt, came under the control of the progressive element of the party. Hence, during the early years of the twentieth century, the dominant spirit in Nebraska politics, Democratic and Republican, was liberal and progressive, as those terms were defined at that time. By the close of World War I, however, the

Bryan influence had quite largely disappeared from the Democratic party, and the Republicans were generally under the control of the conservative wing of the party in Nebraska as in the nation.

The old Populist-Progressive spirit was still strong in Nebraska, however, and it centered around Senator George W. Norris. As the rift between Senator Norris and the Republican administrations in Washington widened, that influence tended to gravitate toward the Democratic party, a movement which culminated in the Roosevelt landslide of 1932. The Democrats, however, were unable to maintain their alliance with the progressive Republicans and, hence, their domination of state politics. The Democratic dilemma came sharply into focus in 1936. Terry Carpenter won the senatorial nomination in the Democratic primary, but the state convention, under prodding from Roosevelt, endorsed the independent candidacy of Senator Norris, and Roosevelt came into the state to urge Norris' re-election.

The Norris-Roosevelt victory of 1936 was the last one achieved by the coalition between progressive Republicans and liberal Democrats. Norris, running again as an independent in 1942, was defeated by Kenneth S. Wherry, Pawnee City merchant, former legislator, and former chairman of the Republican State Central Committee. This campaign, which brought to an end Senator Norris' long and distinguished legislative career, still awaits analysis. Norris was closely identified with the New Deal, and by 1942 that was a liability in Nebraska politics. Moreover, he did not have the official blessing of the Democratic party in the state as he had in 1936, although he was strongly supported by the Lincoln *Star*. Failure to get official support of the Democratic party, however, was not a major factor in the outcome—Terry Carpenter had secured approximately 17 percent of the total vote without it in 1936, and Foster May got only a little more than 21 percent of the vote with it in 1942. Senator Norris' advanced age—he was eighty-one—was used against him, but age has not always been a bar to success in Nebraska politics. The major factor in his defeat, it would appear, was simply resurgent Republicanism, spearheaded by an extremely energetic and effective campaigner. For one reason or another, Norris by 1942 had lost the active, energetic support of many Republicans on whom he had been able to count in the past.

During the Forties, the Republicans completely dominated politics in Nebraska. The only time the Democrats tasted victory in a major contest was in 1948 when Eugene D. O'Sullivan unseated Howard

Buffett in the second congressional district. Dwight Griswold, who gave the state a calm, careful wartime administration, served three terms as governor, to be succeeded for three terms by Val Peterson, of Elgin. Peterson's administrations stirred up considerably more controversy than did Griswold's, and, in 1950, seeking his third term, he had a comparatively difficult time defeating Walter R. Raecke, former speaker of the legislature. Hugh Butler easily won re-election to the Senate in 1946 and 1952, as did Kenneth S. Wherry in 1948.

For the most part, the major contests occurred in the Republican primaries. In 1948, a group led by Raymond A. McConnell, Jr., editor of the Lincoln *Journal,* took advantage of a provision in the election laws which permitted the placing of candidates' names on the ballot in the presidential primary without their consent, to provide voters with a wide choice of candidates; of the seven Republican candidates, including Thomas E. Dewey and Robert A. Taft, Harold Stassen received the largest vote. By 1952 the legislature had changed the election laws so that a man could not be entered in the presidential primaries without his consent. In this contest supporters of Senator Taft and General Eisenhower conducted vigorous "write-in" campaigns, with Taft receiving the largest number of votes and Eisenhower running second. Stassen, whose name was on the ballot, was third. The presidential primaries, while attracting wide attention, did not bind the delegates to the national conventions.

In the nominating primaries the most heated contests occurred in connection with unsuccessful efforts by Republican governors to unseat Senator Butler: Dwight Griswold in 1946, and Val Peterson in 1952. Indeed, it appeared almost impossible for a man to move directly from the governor's office to the United States Senate. Governor R. L. Cochran won the Democratic nomination in 1940 but was defeated by Butler. Governor Robert B. Crosby ran unsuccessfully for the Republican senatorial nomination in 1954, being defeated by Carl T. Curtis, congressman from the first district. The Republicans continued their hold on Nebraska's politics by electing their candidates to all state and national offices in the general election of 1954. Victor Anderson was elected governor; Carl T. Curtis, United States senator for the full term; Roman Hruska, senator for the remainder of the late Hugh Butler's term; and Mrs. George P. Abel, senator for the "short-short" term. The deaths of Senators Griswold and Butler in 1954 had complicated the senatorial situation. Mrs. Eve Bowring and Sam Reynolds, appointed to fill the vacancies, did not seek election.

The 1956 presidential year saw the Republicans sweep Nebraska again, although there were some signs that their hold on the electorate was beginning to weaken—President Eisenhower's margin over Adlai Stevenson was down almost one-fourth from 1952, and in the Third Congressional District, Robert D. Harrison had great difficulty in defeating Lawrence Brock. The trend away from the Republicans continued, and in 1958 the Democrats elected a governor for the first time in two decades as Ralph Brooks, superintendent of schools at McCook who was making his first try for a state-wide public office, defeated Governor Victor Anderson, who was seeking his third term. The Democrats also elected two congressmen, with Brock eking out a victory over Harrison and Donald F. McGinley defeating A. L. Miller who was seeking his ninth term as representative from the Fourth District. Although stunned by these reverses, the Republicans were by no means routed. Senator Roman Hruska was re-elected as were Congressmen Phil Weaver and Glenn Cunningham; also, the Republicans elected all state officers except the treasurer.

After giving the state a colorful, controversial term, Governor Brooks died on September 9, 1960. He had received the Democratic nomination for United States Senator. Indeed, his death came on the last day on which he could have withdrawn from the race and only four hours after he had announced that he would not withdraw. The Democratic State Central Committee named Governor Brooks' administrative assistant, Robert B. Conrad, to make the race against Senator Carl T. Curtis, seeking his second term. The veteran Minden lawmaker easily won re-election in a Republican landslide which brought defeat to Congressmen Brock and McGinley, and victory to all Republican candidates except John R. Cooper of Humboldt, who was defeated in the race for Governor by Frank B. Morrison, a McCook and Lincoln lawyer who had made five unsuccessful races for major offices.

In 1962, Governor Morrison again demonstrated his personal vote-getting abilities when he defeated Fred A. Seaton, Hastings publisher and former Secretary of the Interior, while Republicans were winning all other state and national offices. In 1964, Morrison won a third term by defeating Lieutenant-Governor Dwight W.

Burney, one of the most consistently successful campaigners in the history of the Republican party. This time, however, Morrison was not bucking as strong a Republican tide as he had in his two earlier victories: The Democrats won the state's electoral votes for the first time since 1936; Philip C. Sorensen was elected lieutenant governor over Charles Thone; and in the First District, Clair Callan unseated Ralph Beerman.

PROBLEMS AND PROMISE

Despite the prosperity of its people, Nebraska, in common with every other state, was hard pressed to find the money necessary to provide the services its citizens demanded. Particularly difficult were the problems connected with providing adequate highway and school facilities.

The state's highway system came out of the war in critical condition, wholly unsuited to meet the growing needs of automobile transportation. Both maintenance and construction had lagged during the war, resulting in an accumulated deficiency which was aggravated by the existence of many lightly-built bituminous roads unable to withstand heavy traffic, and by the excessive maintenance required on a considerable portion of relatively new pavement. Some areas, particularly in the Sandhills, had no hard-surfaced roads whatever, and many rural sections were without even adequate gravel roads. Adding to the overall burden were many miles of streets in the cities and towns in serious need of repair. There was simply not sufficient money to do all that was needed, and the basic problem was allocating funds available. The problem of fund allocation was not new. There had long been a conflict between those who insisted that local, rural "farm to market" roads should have first priority and those who insisted that the state trunk system should be favored. The conflict centered around the allocation of motor vehicle revenues (gasoline taxes and registration fees), the largest single source of highway funds. The legislature revised the allocation of gasoline tax revenue during each session from 1939 to 1943. In 1947, the cent of gasoline tax going to the assistance fund was allocated to the counties for mail route gravelling. In 1949 the legislature made an effort to increase the amount of money available for highways by increasing the gasoline tax and motor vehicle registration fees, but these measures were repealed by popular vote, through the referendum, in the election of 1950.

An entirely new dimension was added to highway financing and construction with the passage of the Federal-Aid Highway Act of 1956 which provided federal aid to the states at a 90–10 ratio for the construction of the Interstate Highway System. Nebraska's principal segment of the Interstate was to be an east-west road connecting Omaha with Denver and Cheyenne. From the beginning there was concern—and some little controversy—over the precise location of the Interstate. As finally approved, the Interstate ran southwest from Omaha to just north of Lincoln, and then headed west to Grand Island; from Grand Island it followed the north bank of the Platte River to Brady Island, where it crossed to the south bank whence it headed west past North Platte, Ogallala, and Sidney to the Wyoming state line near Pine Bluffs. Controversy over the route was accompanied by controversy over the rate of construction on various segments, particularly between urban and rural interests.

The first contract under the Act of 1956 was let in June, 1957. By 1965, 127 miles of Interstate Highway had been built, and it was expected that by 1972, the scheduled completion date, all of Nebraska's 478 miles of Interstate highway would have been completed.

Even with massive federal aid, Nebraska's highway problem remained complicated by the fact that the relatively small population of the state was required to provide a proportionately very extensive highway system.

Another serious problem was the provision of adequate school facilities. Although state, and particularly federal, aid increased markedly, the primary source of school support remained the local property tax. This resulted inevitably in considerable variation from district to district in the support given the public schools, and increasingly school people came to favor equalizing school support through a broader program of state aid. However, a constitutional amendment providing for state aid was defeated in 1946 by a margin of more than two to one. As a means of strengthening the public school system by reducing the number of districts, the legislature in 1949 passed an act providing for the permissive reorganization of school districts. By 1965 the number of school districts had been reduced from 7,200 to 2,332.

Markedly increased governmental costs brought the tax problem into sharp relief, and efforts to find a solution to the problem resulted in heated controversy between those who favored and those who intransigently opposed broadening the tax base to reduce reliance on the property tax. Generally speaking, politicians of both parties tried to avoid the issue. A notable exception was Dwight Burney, who called for a broadened tax base in his unsuccessful attempt to unseat Governor Morrison in 1964. Increasingly, the legislature, struggling to find funds to meet the mounting costs of state government, became involved with the tax issue, and bills providing for a state income or sales tax received mounting support. Finally, in 1965, the legislature enacted an income tax law. Immediately, however, referendum proceedings were started with the result that the measure was to be put on the ballot in the 1966 general election.

The postwar years brought an increased interest, both public and private, in the diversification of the state's primarily agricultural economy and in the conservation of its resources. The state benefited somewhat from the national trend toward decentralization of industry and from the inventiveness and ingenuity of its citizens. Outstate manufacturers established branch plants in the state's cities, notably Omaha and Lincoln; and numerous small "home grown" industries developed in various parts of the state. Oil and gas fields in southwest Nebraska, notably in the Sidney area, added greatly to the economy of the region and of the state.

There was a growing realization that conservation of the state's water resources is essential to its prosperity. The development of irrigation to 1940 has been discussed.[1] Subsequent to 1940, there was a steady growth in irrigation. In 1945, 873,960 acres were irrigated; in 1955, 1,700,000 acres; and in 1965, 2,900,000 acres. The most spectacular increases occurred in the Tri-County area and in the central Platte Valley. Most of the land in the Tri-County area is irrigated from reservoirs, but elsewhere in the central Platte Valley most of the water comes from wells. Indeed, the vast increase in pump irrigation was the major factor in the increase in the state's

[1] See pp. 311–315.

total irrigated acreage. Acreage under pump irrigation increased from 80,673 in 1939 to 2,100,000 in 1965. Expressed another way, wells accounted for approximately 13 percent of the total irrigated acreage in 1939, and for approximately 72 percent of the total in 1965. Despite the great increase in pump irrigation, the water table was largely maintained through recharge of ground water, a most significant natural resource and one which distinguishes Nebraska from the states surrounding it.

Nebraskans have benefited and will benefit from federal projects built and to be built under the comprehensive plan for Missouri River Basin development commonly known as the Pick-Sloan plan. This plan, which grew out of the Flood Control Act of 1944, envisions multiple-purpose projects to provide for irrigation, flood control, power, navigation, conservation, and recreation throughout the basin. Nebraska is the only state completely within the basin, and it stands to benefit as much as or more than any other state. Major projects completed include Lewis and Clark Lake on the Missouri River, Merritt Reservoir on the Snake River, and a series of reservoirs on the Republican River and its tributaries: Harlan County and Enders reservoirs, Harry Strunk, Swanson, and Hugh Butler lakes. In the Lincoln area significant flood control and recreational facilities are provided by a system of twelve reservoirs in the Salt Creek Watershed. Omaha and many smaller communities have benefited greatly from flood control projects.

The Pick-Sloan plan is primarily an engineering plan. To coordinate activities under it, the states of the Missouri River Basin and the various federal agencies concerned are represented on the Missouri Basin Inter-Agency Committee, organized in 1945. There has been much discussion regarding both the engineering plan and the operation of the projects. Discussion relative to the engineering plan has centered around a controversy over the merits of big dams on the principal streams and small dams designed to impound the water where it falls. Discussion relative to the operation of the projects has centered around a controversy over the merits of an over-all authority for the basin and an approach such as has been worked out under the Inter-Agency Committee, involving a compact among the states concerned. A majority of the Missouri Basin Survey Commission, appointed by President Truman and headed by James E. Lawrence of Lincoln, recommended the establishment of a Missouri Basin Commission as a federal instrumentality; a minority proposed an organization created by interstate compact to which the states and the federal government would be parties. Neither plan was adopted and the Inter-Agency Committee continues to function. In 1964 it established a Standing Committee on Comprehensive Basin Planning to undertake a coordinated study of water and related resource development. The study is scheduled for completion in 1969.

As Nebraska approached its centennial of statehood, it was clear that continued development of the state's resources contained the key to future progress in all fields. It was equally clear, however, that Nebraskans, who during their first century transformed the area from a part of the Great American Desert into a significant food-producing state, entered their second century keenly aware of the importance of such development. On the basis of the first century's experience, the prospects for the future were bright indeed.

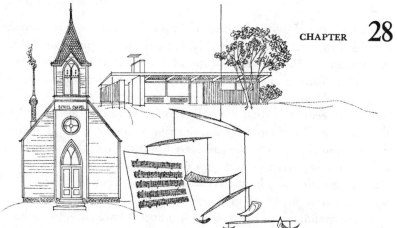

CHAPTER 28

Cultural Factors in Nebraska Life

ALL OF LIFE in Nebraska is conditioned by the fact that the state is primarily agricultural in its economy and in its outlook. Though the trend toward the cities, begun early in the twentieth century, has continued, Nebraska has only two places, Omaha and Lincoln, classified as metropolitan areas. Only eleven places, including Omaha and Lincoln, have a population greater than 10,000. The population of Grand Island, the third city, was only 25,472 in 1960. Even in the cities, the point of view remains agricultural—hardly surprising when one considers that the state's most important industry is the processing of farm products.

Further conditioning life in Nebraska is the fact that the state's agriculture over the years has been subject to violent fluctuations, resulting from both man-made and natural causes, with the result that at no time, save for the past fifteen years, has the state's basic industry enjoyed uninterrupted prosperity for as much as a decade. This, of course, has had its effect upon the support Nebraskans could give schools, churches, and other cultural agencies, and upon the energy they could devote to pursuits not directly related to making a living.

A further conditioning factor has been the nature of the state's population. A considerable portion of Nebraska's pioneer settlers were European immigrants—Germans, Swedes, Irish, Bohemians, English, Danes, Russians, Austrians, Scotch, Norwegians, Swiss, Poles, French, Italians, and others. Many of them came in groups to establish separate

341

colonies; many of those who came individually sought out areas already occupied by their countrymen. Many, particularly those who did not speak English, tended to live withdrawn from their fellow men, nursing their Old World prejudices and customs in isolated colonies. Most of them were desperately poor, and had come to America primarily to improve their economic condition. All of their efforts, therefore, were bent toward paying for their farms and securing a competence, and nothing was allowed to interfere with progress toward those goals. Gradually, some of the immigrants—and most of their children—abandoned their clannish isolation and began to participate in the cultural and political life of the state, and both they and the state have benefited greatly, as sons and grandsons of the immigrant pioneers have risen to positions of leadership in all aspects of Nebraska life. Though virtually all have been amalgamated into an indigenous whole, many communities retain traces of Old World culture which add variety and interest to the life of the state.

Finally, in considering the cultural aspects of Nebraska life, one must not lose sight of the fact that it is a young state, even in American terms. The oldest settlements were established only a century ago, and in some parts of the west, the first settlers arrived less than half a century ago. As Willa Cather expressed it:

Even as late as 1885 the central part of the State, and everything to the westward, was, in the main, raw prairie. The cultivated fields and broken land seemed mere scratches in the brown, running steppe that never stopped until it broke against the foothills of the rockies. The dugouts and sod farm houses were three or four miles apart, and the only means of communication was the heavy farm wagon, drawn by heavy work horses.[1]

CHURCHES

Though the Reverend George W. Barnes could complain that in early Omaha "there were but few Christians . . . and religion met only a left-handed favor,"[2] there were almost always a few persons in the new settlements interested in holding church services, and churches have played a conspicuous role in most Nebraska communities. The early territorial churches have been described.[3] The territorial experience was repeated in virtually every community as settlement moved west, except that the sod house replaced the log cabin as the structure in which the

[1]"Nebraska," *op. cit.*, p. 4.   [2]See pp. 99–100.   [3]See pp. 99–101.

first worship services were held. The Methodists, with their itinerant ministry and their strong emotional gospel, continued to lead the way, although they were by no means the only group active on the frontier. The United Brethren had an itinerant ministry and also held camp meetings, always popular in frontier communities. The Seventh Day Adventists likewise were active on the frontier, moving their gospel tents from place to place. The Congregational church, although not particularly organized for frontier work, was established early in many communities, and became an influential body. The Baptist church found many adherents in all parts of the state. The Catholic and Episcopal churches actively engaged in missionary work, and Episcopal Bishop George Allen Beecher was particularly effective in western Nebraska. The American Sunday School Union also was an active force in carrying religion to western Nebraska.

Many immigrants brought their religion with them from Europe, and this accounts in large measure for the state's substantial Catholic and Lutheran groups. Frequently colonies were established under the auspices of these groups, although other church groups, notably the Congregationalists, also were active in the establishment of colonies. In communities thus established the voice of the founding religious group was apt to be a dominant one for many years.

In 1906, when the first census of religious bodies in the United States was taken, there were 363,585 Nebraskans who were members of some church. This represents approximately 34 percent of the state's population of 1900. In 1936, the year of the last church census for which figures are available, there were 566,806 persons, or approximately 41 percent of the 1930 population, who were church members. The leading groups were:

	1906	1936
Baptist	17,386	19,119
Congregational & Christian	16,798	21,378
Disciples of Christ	19,121	23,359
Evangelical & Reformed	5,498	8,761
Evangelical	6,192	6,728
Lutheran	39,375	209,250
Methodist	62,586	85,124
Presbyterian	20,926	32,350
Protestant Episcopal	6,903	10,256
Roman Catholic	118,545	154,136
United Brethren	6,045	7,846

Membership statistics provide a guide to the influence of the churches upon the life of the state, but by no means the only one. They do not reveal, for example, the impact of certain evangelical Protestant groups upon various social questions, notably the prohibition controversies of the late nineteenth and early twentieth centuries, and upon the customs prevailing in many communities. Likewise, they do not indicate the importance of the church as a center for social intercourse, particularly in the days before the automobile and widespread commercial entertainment, when the church provided people with one of their most important opportunities to enjoy the company of their fellows. Finally, membership statistics do not show that a number of the churches, particularly those which conducted their services in foreign languages, were an important factor in maintaining European patterns of thought and life. The churches, in short, have influenced Nebraska life in far greater measure than is apparent from the importance of the less than half of the population they have claimed as members.

Further illustrating the importance of religion in the life of the state is the fact that religious issues provided grounds for much high controversy, particularly in the early years. The constitution clearly and firmly separates church and state by prohibiting sectarian instruction in any school or institution supported in whole or in part by public funds, by prohibiting the use of any public funds to assist any denominational or sectarian institution, and by prohibiting any religious test or qualification for teachers or students in public schools or educational institutions supported in whole or in part by public funds.

SCHOOLS

As has been indicated, the first territorial legislature provided for a system of free public schools.[4] The territorial system, involving a large measure of both local support and local control, was carried over into the statehood period. Naturally, the quality of the schools varied greatly from community to community, depending upon the district's ability— actual or assumed—to support education, and the interest in it. Most of the pioneers seem to have believed that education, at least in the "fundamentals," was a good thing and a proper object of public support. Beyond that, however, there was wide divergence of opinion as to the extent of the public's responsibility. Much work needs to be

[4]See pp. 98–99.

done on the history of education in Nebraska, but there is little reason to assume that the generality of pioneer Nebraskans differed markedly from other frontier people, busy with the physical subjugation of their environment, in the relatively unimportant place they assigned education in their scale of values. Teaching may have been an honored profession, but it was not a rewarding one, and teachers escaped into matrimony or other professions as soon as possible. The constitution of 1875 provided for a complete system of public schools, from the elementary level to the university, but the implementation of that provision was left quite largely to the local districts, and as late as 1890 there were only 260 graded schools in the state. In 1889, approximately sixteen percent of all children between the ages of eight and fourteen did not attend school at all.

Compulsory education was rejected by a resounding majority in 1871,[5] and as late as 1883 it was referred to in the press as "a case of legislative delirium tremens," but the Populist legislature of 1891 enacted a compulsory school law which guaranteed the opportunity for a common school education to all young Nebraskans. The one-room, single-teacher rural school remained—as it does even today—the most numerous of all types of schools. The State Department of Public Instruction is making strenuous efforts today to reduce the number of districts, and hence the number of rural schools, but in the day before the automobile and the development of an all-weather rural road system, the little sod and frame schools which dotted the countryside not only provided education for farm children but also served as social centers for the rural communities. Frequently on winter evenings, the stoves were fired and the lamps lighted for a debate, a meeting of the literary society, a spelling bee, a sing, a box social, a meeting of the Grange or the Farmers Alliance. Frequently the school served, too, for church services.[6]

There was considerable interest in higher education. Some of it, to be sure, was motivated by commercial considerations—it was a good thing if a town could boast of a "college" or "university"—but much of it seems to have been prompted by a genuine desire to provide opportunities for higher learning. The flurry of activity during territorial

[5]See p. 181.

[6]See Edward Everett Dale, "The Frontier Literary Society," *Nebraska History*, XXXI (September, 1950), 167–182.

times has been noted.[7] Much of this had been prompted by various church groups, which continued to interest themselves in higher education. Many of the early efforts failed for lack of support, and a substantial number of the twelve church colleges existing today are the result of numerous consolidations and reorganizations. The Catholics, Lutherans, and Seventh Day Adventists have included preparatory schools in their educational systems. Omaha maintains a municipal university; Fairbury, McCook, Norfolk, and Scottsbluff have junior colleges. In 1965, three new colleges were founded: John F. Kennedy at Wahoo, John J. Pershing at Beatrice, and Hiram Scott at Scottsbluff.

The University of Nebraska, chartered on February 15, 1869, and opened in the fall of 1871, has from the time of its establishment dominated higher education in the state. Organized as a land-grant institution under the Morrill Act of 1862, the University initially was provided for in the legislation passed in 1867, which resulted in the creation of Lincoln as the state capital. The decision made at that time to concentrate the University and the Agricultural College in one institution has had a profound effect upon the development of the University and must stand as one of the most significant actions ever taken by a Nebraska legislature. Had Nebraska followed the practice of other Plains states and created two schools instead of one, the University of Nebraska could hardly have developed into the great institution it is today.

Founded in the years of distress and doubt,[8] the University in its early years suffered not only financial vicissitudes but harassment from various forces across the state. There were those who felt that the state was wasting its money in trying to establish and operate a university when so few opportunities existed for secondary education, and the preponderance of students in the preparatory department caused the University to be dubbed derisively as "the Lincoln high school." Others opposed the establishment of professional schools and colleges as an unwarranted extension of publicly supported education. Still others looked with skepticism upon the activities of the professors, doubting, for example, that the theoreticians at the Agricultural College (or "state farm" as it was universally called) had much to offer the practical farmers of the state. Various religious groups opposed the University as a "godless institution," and, indeed, the religious problem vexed the school

[7]See pp. 98–99.
[8]See pp. 148–149.

for many years. Initially, there was fear that the University would fall under the domination of one particular sect, and to allay that fear the Regents, in selecting the first faculty, were careful to employ not more than one person from any denomination. In the early days the faculty occasionally was torn by religious controversies. In later years University administrations so rigidly interpreted the constitutional provision separating church and state as to give offense to certain groups, and the institution which developed into Cotner College originally was established to provide a Christian university in the capital city to counteract the influence of the state university.

Through vicissitude and controversy, however, the University of Nebraska continued to develop both the teaching and research aspects of its mission as understood by the faculty, and by the turn of the century was recognized as one of the great institutions in the West. Various of its faculty members had won wide renown,[9] and the products of its laboratories were finding acceptance among an ever-growing group of the state's citizens.[10] The Thirties were hard years for the University, and there was even some talk of closing the institution altogether. It weathered that storm, however, as it had others, and in the postwar years, under the distinguished leadership of Reuben G. Gustavson and Clifford M. Hardin, it strengthened its position and increased its services to the people of the state and to mankind, particularly in the fields of basic and applied science. By 1965 it had an enrollment of more than 15,000 students, and included among its highly diversified programs the activities of the Nebraska Center for Continuing Education, the Eppley Cancer Research Institute, assistance in the establishment and operation of Ataturk University in Turkey, and the development of the National College of Agriculture in Colombia.

One of the primary missions of the University and the denominational colleges was to provide teachers for the public and parochial schools. The lure of these schools was so weak, however, that many college graduates disdained to accept it, preferring instead business and the professions. Even if all of them had gone into teaching, they could hardly have filled the demand created by the ever-expanding number of schools. In 1867 the state acquired Mount Vernon Seminary and

[9]See pp. 256–257.
[10]See pp. 253–254.

College, a Methodist institution at Peru, and established it as the Nebraska State Normal School. This helped to provide teachers, but most of those who taught in the rural schools did so without the benefit of college training. An effort was made to remedy the deficiency by holding "teachers' institutes," short-courses conducted under the auspices of the State Superintendent of Public Instruction and the county superintendents. Occasionally private normal schools developed, and one—that owned by J. M. Pile at Wayne—was secured by the state and established as Wayne State Teachers College. Kearney State Teachers College was established in 1903, and Chadron, in 1911. In 1963 all institutions became state colleges.

THE ARTS

It is a truism that the arts, aside perhaps from the practical variety, seldom flourish in a new country, and pioneer Nebraska offered no exception. During the last half of its first century, however, Nebraska, for a young and sparsely populated state, has made a substantial contribution to the cultural arts, and no discussion of the history of its people would be complete without at least a mention of that contribution. "The Arts," as used here, will embrace literature, music, painting, and architecture. Though this is not a completely satisfactory use of the term, perhaps it may be condoned on the grounds of convenience.

The first, and for many years only, outlet for literary expression was that provided by the press. A number of the early editors were conscious of the literary aspects of their calling, and some of their work may properly be considered as a contribution to the literature of the region. Their primary interests were progress and politics. They were a vigorous breed of men, never at a loss for words, and never without an opinion. They described political opponents in terms that would bring libel suits today. They had an inexhaustible store of adjectives with which to describe the present condition and future prospects of their state and community. One of the first and most vigorous editors was Joseph E. Johnson, a Mormon who had taken the trek to Utah, but who turned up in Council Bluffs, Iowa, in 1852, as publisher of the *Bugle.* An ardent advocate of the organization of Nebraska territory, he began publishing a paper in Omaha, the *Arrow,* a few weeks after the Kansas-Nebraska bill was signed. In 1859, he moved out to Wood River to start one of the earliest papers in central Nebraska, the *Hunts-*

man's Echo, "Independent in Everything—Neutral in Nothing." In 1855, J. Sterling Morton began to impress his vigorous personality upon the Nebraska City *News;* the next year, Robert W. Furnas started the *Nebraska Advertiser* at Brownville, a folksy, influential paper which played a significant role in developing the influence of the Republican party in the territory; in 1865, Dr. George L. Miller began the quarter-century of editorial service which transformed the Omaha *Herald* from a struggling frontier paper to a journal of national importance. Others who were influential during the early years of statehood, and later, were C. H. Gere, who established the *Nebraska State Journal* at Lincoln in 1869; and Edward Rosewater, who founded the Omaha *Bee* in 1871. These papers, in many ways diametrically opposed to each other, were to become the principal editorial spokesmen for the Republican party in the state.

William Jennings Bryan usually is thought of as an orator and politician, but his career as a writer and as an editor cannot be ignored. A bibliography of his works would run to many titles. He became editor of the Omaha *World-Herald* in 1894, and in 1921 started *The Commoner,* in Lincoln, a national weekly devoted primarily to political and religious subjects. Prototype of *The Commoner* was *The Conservative,* edited by J. Sterling Morton from 1898 to 1902.

The early newspapers frequently gave space in their columns to poems and essays written by their readers. During the Populist period particularly, there was a spate of both poetry and prose giving voice to the grievances, the demands, and the aspirations of the embattled farmers. The verse frequently was set to old and familiar tunes, usually those of well-known hymns, and sung at political rallies. The *Nebraska State Journal* had two special writers who achieved more than ordinary popularity: A. L. "Doc" Bixby, whose comments on life, death, and politics were couched in doggerel always ending in "BIX"; and Walt Mason, practitioner of a doubtful verse form known as the prose poem.

Other aspects of pioneer literary activity were promotional and historical writing, at times difficult to separate. The work of Samuel Aughey and C. D. Wilber has been mentioned.[11] Harrison Johnson wrote the state's first extended history, *Johnson's History of Nebraska* (1880), a work which has much in common with contemporary promotional literature. Two years later, Alfred T. Andreas published his monumental *History of the State of Nebraska,* containing a general sketch of the state, followed by an extended account of the history of each county, heavily

[11]See pp. 166–167.

laden with biographical sketches of prominent pioneers. It remains an invaluable source of local history. The well-known Morton-Watkins *Illustrated History of Nebraska* was a subscription history originally projected by J. Sterling Morton and completed by Albert Watkins with the assistance of Clarence S. Paine. Carrying forward the tradition of the voluminous subscription history was Addison E. Sheldon's *Nebraska: The Land and the People.*

The newspapermen, the promoters, and even the early historians made little effort to interpret the life of the state. For the most part, they were simply chroniclers. Some of the obscure poets were trying to interpret the region, but their audiences were limited and their impact small. The first substantial effort to interpret Nebraska life through the medium of literature is probably Orsamus C. Dake's *Nebraska Legends and Other Poems* (1871). In this volume Dake, who was the first professor of English literature at the University of Nebraska, developed the Indian legends of Weeping Water and the Raw Hide. Ethnologists can find no Indian equivalent for these legends, and Professor Dake reduced their validity by trying to interpret them in language and form that were but a reflection of schoolboy instruction in the literature of southern Europe. Yet he must be recognized as the first serious poet in Nebraska, and for almost a generation he was the only one.

The state's participation in the production of the significant regional literature of the twentieth century began in 1913 when Willa Cather published *O Pioneers!,* a memorable regional story told simply and spontaneously. The next few years brought an intensive literary outpouring in Nebraska. Willa Cather published *The Song of the Lark* in 1915 and *My Antonia* in 1917. John G. Neihardt published the first of his epic cycle, *The Song of Hugh Glass,* in 1915. The same year brought also *Barbed Wire and Other Poems* by Edwin Ford Piper, and Louise Pound's *Folk-Song of Nebraska and the Central West.* Hartley Burr Alexander's *The Pageant of Lincoln* was presented in 1917.

Much of this literary activity centered around the University of Nebraska, and its products frequently were in poetic or dramatic form. Neihardt, who became poet laureate of Nebraska in 1921 and a professor of poetry at the University in 1923, continued his epic poems with *The Song of Three Friends* (1919), *The Song of the Indian Wars* (1925), and *The Song of the Messiah* (1935). Alexander, professor of philosophy at the University from 1908 to 1927, was a poet as well as the author of studies in philosophy, literature, and Indian art. Characteristic of his work are *Manito Masks* (1925), *Taiwa* (1934), and the inscriptions on the Nebraska State Capitol. Young poets have been greatly encouraged by the *Prairie Schooner*, the University's literary magazine, established in 1927 and edited by Lowry C. Wimberly, Karl Shapiro, and Bernice Slote. Frederick Ballard, Virgil Geddes, and E. P. Conkle have drawn upon Nebraska life for their highly successful plays.

After her Pulitzer-Prize winning novel, *One of Ours* (1922), and *A Lost Lady* (1923), a novelette dealing with the disintegration of pioneer values, Willa Cather did not return to the Nebraska scene until the Thirties with *Obscure Destinies* (1932) and *Lucy Gayheart* (1935). Significant interpretations of Nebraska life have been provided since then by Mari Sandoz, Sophus Keith Winther, Dorothy Thomas, Ivan Beede, Wright Morris, and Bess Streeter Aldrich. Mari Sandoz' *Old Jules* (1935), a biography of her father and a memorable account of life in the Sandhills, won the Atlantic Prize for its author. This was followed by *Slogum House* (1937), a rough, searing novel of the frontier; *Capital City* (1939), a devastating portrayal of life in a midwestern city, unmistakably Lincoln; and two sympathetic and moving interpretations of the Plains Indians, *Crazy Horse* (1942) and *Cheyenne Autumn* (1953). *The Buffalo Hunters* (1954) describes the destruction of the vast buffalo herds and its impact upon the Plains. *The Cattlemen* (1958) and *The Beaver Men* (1964) are the remaining volumes of her Trans-Missouri series. Sophus Keith Winther's trilogy, *Take All to Nebraska* (1936), *Mortgage Your Heart* (1937), and *This Passion Never Dies* (1938) interprets Danish immigrant life in Nebraska. Ivan Beede's *Prairie Woman* (1930) is a realistic portrayal of Nebraska life in the period after World War I. Dorothy Thomas' novels—*Ma Jeeter's Girls* (1933) and *The Home Place* (1936)—are humorous, sympathetic portrayals of farm people. The novels of Wright Morris, and particularly his photographic studies—*The Inhabitants* (1946), and *The Home Place* (1948)—offer starkly realistic interpretations of prairie life. Bess Streeter Aldrich's stories of the pioneers are sympathetic and understanding.

Nebraska's artists also have provided interpretations of life in the state. Among them are Robert Gilder, Elizabeth Dolan, Kady Faulkner, Dwight Kirsch, Terence Duren, and Eugene Kingman. The state has a lively interest in art, centering around the Joslyn Memorial in Omaha and the University of Nebraska Art Galleries in Lincoln. The state's musical tradition includes, of course, the songs of the Indians, the campfire songs of the overland emigrants and the cowboys, and the songs of the immigrant pioneers. Among Nebraska composers who have made significant contributions to American music are Howard Hanson and Thurlow Lieurance. Omaha and Lincoln support symphony orchestras, and during the Twenties and Thirties, the Lincoln Cathedral Choir, under the direction of John Rosborough, achieved national renown. Under the leadership of the University of Nebraska, a lively state-wide interest in both vocal and instrumental music has developed.

Architecturally, the state's builders usually have drawn upon precedents established elsewhere. The characteristic dwelling of the earliest pioneers was the log cabin, although as settlement moved west it became the sod house, a unique adaptation to the treeless Plains.[12] During the late nineteenth century large, square frame structures, with gable roofs and tall, narrow windows became common. The gable ends and window frames frequently were ornamented with elaborate scrolls of carved wood. County courthouses exhibit a wide variety of styles, from square, inexpensive frame buildings to elaborate stone and brick structures in the Victorian Gothic style. More recent public buildings tend to exhibit the simplicity of classic forms. A notable church structure is the First-Plymouth Congregational Church in Lincoln, designed by H. Van Buren Magonigle. Some of the recently built churches, particularly the Lutheran, show a radical departure from traditional design. Joslyn Memorial in Omaha, the work of John and Alan MacDonald, is an interesting example of monumental architecture. Recent structures of more than ordinary interest are Philip Johnson's Sheldon Memorial Art Gallery on the campus of the University of Nebraska, and Edward Durrell Stone's Stuhr Museum of the Prairie Pioneer in Grand Island.

The state's most notable architectural feature is the capitol, designed by Bertram G. Goodhue, with sculpture and other decoration by Lee Lawrie, Hildreth Meiere, Augustus Tack, and Elizabeth Dolan. Under the direction of the Capitol Mural Commission, created by the legislature in 1951, murals by Kenneth Evett, Reinhold Marxhausen, F. John Miller, James Penney, and Jeanne Reynal have been installed in the rotunda and Great Hall. A statue of William

[12]See pp. 204–206.

Jennings Bryan by Rudulph Evans stands at the front entrance, and one of Abraham Lincoln by Daniel French, at the west entrance. The capitol, generally acclaimed as one of the most significant public buildings in America, is dominated by a great central tower rising four hundred feet and crowned with a gold-glazed, tiled dome upon which stands Lee Lawrie's twenty-seven-foot bronze statue, *The Sower*. This monumental structure rising out of the prairie is an enduring symbol of the state's heritage and its hope for the future.

Appendix I

OFFICIALS OF THE TERRITORY OF NEBRASKA, 1854–1867

GOVERNORS

Francis Burt, October 16, 1854, to October 18, 1854. Died October 18, 1854, and vacancy filled by Thomas B. Cuming to February 20, 1855.

Mark W. Izard, February 20, 1855, to October 25, 1857. Resigned and vacancy filled by Thomas B. Cuming to January 12, 1858.

William A. Richardson, January 12, 1858, to December 5, 1858. Resigned and vacancy filled by J. Sterling Morton to May 2, 1859.

Samuel W. Black, May 2, 1859, to February 24, 1861. Resigned and vacancy filled by J. Sterling Morton to May 6, 1861.

Alvin Saunders, May 15, 1861, to March 27, 1867.

SECRETARIES

Thomas B. Cuming, August 13, 1854, to March 12, 1858.

John B. Motley, March 23, 1858, to July 12, 1858.

J. Sterling Morton, July 12, 1858, to May 6, 1861.

Algernon S. Paddock, May 6, 1861, to February 21, 1867.

Appendix II

GOVERNORS OF THE STATE OF NEBRASKA

David Butler (R)	1867–1871
William H. James (R), Acting	1871–1873
Robert W. Furnas (R)	1873–1875
Silas Garber (R)	1875–1879
Albinus Nance (R)	1879–1883
James W. Dawes (R)	1883–1887
John M. Thayer (R)	1887–1891
	1891–1892
James E. Boyd (D)	1891
	1892–1893
Lorenzo Crounse (R)	1893–1895
Silas A. Holcomb (Fusion)	1895–1899
William A. Poynter (Fusion)	1899–1901
Charles H. Dietrich (R)	1901
Ezra P. Savage (R)	1901–1903
John H. Mickey (R)	1903–1907
George L. Sheldon (R)	1907–1909
Ashton C. Shallenberger (D)	1909–1911
Chester H. Aldrich (R)	1911–1913
John H. Morehead (D)	1913–1917
Keith Neville (D)	1917–1919
Samuel R. McKelvie (R)	1919–1923
Charles W. Bryan (D)	1923–1925
	1931–1935
Adam McMullen (R)	1925–1929
Arthur J. Weaver (R)	1929–1931
Robert Leroy Cochran (D)	1935–1941
Dwight Griswold (R)	1941–1947
Val Peterson (R)	1947–1953
Robert B. Crosby (R)	1953–1955
Victor E. Anderson (R)	1955–1959
Ralph G. Brooks (D)	1959–1960
Dwight W. Burney (R), Acting	1960–1961
Frank B. Morrison (D)	1961–1967
Norbert T. Tiemann (R)	1967–1971
J. James Exon (D)	1971–

For Further Reading

Although many aspects of Nebraska's history have been imperfectly studied, there is a wealth of material relating to the state's past. This bibliography is not intended to be exhaustive, but it does make an effort to call attention to those works which should be generally useful and available.

GENERAL SUGGESTIONS

Many works dealing with general American history and especially with the Trans-Mississippi West have importance for the history of Nebraska. Two which will be found to be particularly useful are Ray Allen Billington, *Westward Expansion* (1960), and LeRoy R. Hafen and Carl Coke Rister, *Western America* (1960). Both contain extensive bibliographies. A useful guide and bibliography is Nelson Klose, *A Concise Study Guide to the American Frontier* (1964).

The earliest extended history of Nebraska is Harrison Johnson, *Johnson's History of Nebraska* (1880). This work by a Nebraska pioneer active in public affairs is largely promotional. Much more valuable is Alfred T. Andreas, *History of the State of Nebraska* (1882), a mine of information regarding the local history of communities which had been established by 1882. Particularly useful for its treatment of the political history of the territorial period is J. Sterling Morton and Albert Watkins, *Illustrated History of Nebraska* (3 vols., 1905–1913). Published contemporaneously with the Morton-Watkins history was Addison E. Sheldon, *Semi-Centennial History of Nebraska* (1904). In 1931 Sheldon published *Nebraska: The Land and the People* (3 vols.), which is particularly good on the settlement and Populist periods.

Virginia Faulkner, ed., *Roundup: A Nebraska Reader* (1957) is an interesting compilation of short pieces about Nebraska, including Willa Cather's significant essay, "Nebraska: The End of the First Cycle."

For younger readers there are: Ken R. Keller and Bruce Nicoll, *Know Nebraska* (1951); James C. Olson and Vera Farrington Olson, *Nebraska is My Home* (1958); and *This is Nebraska* (1960).

Nebraska History, the quarterly journal of the Nebraska State Historical Society, publishes valuable and interesting articles on all aspects of the state's history.

THE LAND
(CHAPTER 1)

Basic to an understanding of the history of the Plains is Walter Prescott Webb, *The Great Plains* (1931). Also essential are James C. Malin, *The Grassland of North America* (1947), and Henry Nash Smith, *Virgin Land* (1951). A useful guide to the work of James C. Malin is Thomas H. LeDuc,

356

"An Ecological Interpretation of Grasslands History," *Nebraska History*, 31 (September, 1950), 226–233. A convenient summary of early attitudes regarding the Plains will be found in Ralph C. Morris, "The Notion of a Great American Desert East of the Rockies," *Mississippi Valley Historical Review*, 13 (September, 1926), 190–200. Carl F. Kraenzel, *The Great Plains in Transition* (1955) vividly portrays the problems of the plains and suggests solutions; Robert G. Athearn, *High Country Empire* (1960) discusses the history of the plains and mountains with particular emphasis on the influence of environment. Although George E. Condra, *Geography, Agriculture, Industries of Nebraska* (1946) is a somewhat dated elementary text, it will be found useful. John Wesley Powell, *Report on the Lands of the Arid Region of the United States* (reprinted 1962) is an important pioneer study; Wallace Stegner, *Beyond the Hundredth Meridian* (1954) is an interesting discussion of the work of John Wesley Powell.

Although not for the general reader, J. E. Weaver, *North American Prairie* (1954), which summarizes the life work of the noted plant ecologist, contains much of significance, as does his *Native Vegetation of Nebraska* (1965).

The destruction of the buffalo is described dramatically in Mari Sandoz, *The Buffalo Hunters* (1954). The files of *Outdoor Nebraskaland*, published by the Nebraska Game, Forestation and Parks Commission, contain a great deal of interesting material on the wildlife of the state, and other descriptive information.

THE INDIANS
(Chapters 2 and 11)

The Indians of Nebraska and the West have been of interest to anthropologists, historians, and journalists. In recent years, anthropologists, aided by the Smithsonian Institution and the National Park Service, have been active in the interpretation of the prehistory of the Plains. Unfortunately, most anthropological studies are written for rather restricted professional audiences; notable exceptions are Ruth M. Underhill, *Red Man's America: A History of Indians in the United States* (1953), and Waldo R. Wedel, *Prehistoric Man on the Great Plains* (1961). Valuable reports on archeological work in Nebraska will be found in the files of *Nebraska History* and *Publications in Anthropology* of the Nebraska State Historical Society.

An indispensable guide to the Indians is Frederick Webb Hodge, ed., *Handbook of American Indians North of Mexico* (2 vols., 1907–1910). General studies of value are William T. Hagan, *American Indians* (1962), and Clark Wissler, *The American Indian: An Introduction to the Anthropology of the New World* (1931; reprinted 1950).

On the Pawnees, see Wedel, *An Introduction to Pawnee Archeology* (1936); George E. Hyde, *Pawnee Indians* (1951); and Gene Weltfish, *The*

Lost Universe (1965). The Pawnee Scouts are treated in George B. Grinnell, *Two Great Scouts and Their Pawnee Battalion* (1928), and Donald F. Danker, "The North Brothers and the Pawnee Scouts," *Nebraska History*, 42 (September, 1961), 161–180. Berlin B. Chapman, *The Otoes and Missourias* (1965) is a detailed study of the two tribes with particular emphasis on their lands. No satisfactory account of the reservation period in the history of the Omahas and the Poncas exists, but for information on the Omahas see Robert C. Farb, "Robert W. Furnas as Omaha Indian Agent, 1864–1866," *Nebraska History*, 32 (September, December, 1951), 186–203, 268–283; for the Poncas, Thomas Henry Tibbles, *Buckskin and Blanket Days* (1957).

Indian problems constituted an important aspect of the Civil War in in the West. For a general survey see Robert Huhn Jones, *The Civil War in the Northwest: Nebraska, Wisconsin, Iowa, Minnesota, and the Dakotas* (1960). Nebraska's military participation in the Civil War is treated specifically in Earl G. Curtis, "John Milton Thayer," *Nebraska History*, 28 (October–December, 1947), 225–238; and Farb, "The Military Career of Robert W. Furnas," *Ibid.*, 32 (March, 1951), 18–41. The Indian difficulties of 1864 are covered in Jennings C. Haggerty, "Indian Raids Along the Platte and Little Blue Rivers, 1864–1865," *Ibid.*, 28 (July–September, October–December, 1947), 176–186, 239–260; and Eugene F. Ware, *The Indian War of 1864* (1911; reprinted 1960). Ware also discusses the establishment of Fort McPherson, which is treated definitively in Louis A. Holmes, *Fort McPherson, Nebraska, Fort Cottonwood, N. T.* (1963).

There is a voluminous literature on the subjugation of the plains Indians and the establishment of the reservation system in the West. Paul I. Wellman, *Death on Horseback* (1947), and Ralph K. Andrist, *The Long Death* (1964), are popular general accounts. The Cheyennes are treated in George B. Grinnell, *The Fighting Cheyennes* (1915; reprinted 1956), and Mari Sandoz, *Cheyenne Autumn* (1953). Three volumes by George E. Hyde deal with the Sioux: *Red Cloud's Folk* (1937, 1957), *A Sioux Chronicle* (1956), and *Spotted Tail's Folk* (1961); see also, James C. Olson, *Red Cloud and the Sioux Problem* (1965), and Mari Sandoz, *Crazy Horse* (1942, 1958). Military studies of particular interest to Nebraskans are Robert G. Athearn, *William Tecumseh Sherman and the Settlement of the West* (1956); James T. King, *War Eagle: A Life of General Eugene A. Carr* (1963); and Merrill J. Mattes, *Indians, Infants and Infantry: The Story of Andrew and Elizabeth Burt* (1960). The best of numerous accounts of the ghost-dance troubles and the Battle of Wounded Knee is Robert M. Utley, *The Last Days of the Sioux Nation* (1963).

THE EARLY EXPLORERS
(Chapter 3)

For a general account of Spanish exploration in North America, see H. E. Bolton and T. M. Marshall, *Colonization of North America, 1492–1783* (1920). Documents relating to the Coronado Expedition will be found in George P. Winship, *The Coronado Expedition, 1540–1542* (1896), *The Journey of Francisco Vasquez Coronado, 1540–1542* (1933); and George P. Hammond and Agapito Rey, eds., *Narratives of the Coronado Expedition* (2 vols., 1940). The best and most recent work on the career of Coronado, with a careful discussion of the route of his exploration, is Herbert E. Bolton, *Coronado, Knight of Pueblos and Plains* (1950). For Spanish activity subsequent to Coronado, and particularly the Villasur expedition, see A. B. Thomas, *After Coronado: Spanish Exploration Northeast of New Mexico, 1696–1727* (1935). The best account of French and Spanish activity in the Missouri Valley will be found in the Introduction to A. P. Nasatir, ed., *Before Lewis and Clark* (1952).

Bernard De Voto, *The Course of Empire* (1952) covers in sweeping style the exploration of North America through the time of Lewis and Clark and is particularly good on the Lewis and Clark expedition. The best source for the Lewis and Clark expedition, however, remains the Journals, most easily available, in abbreviated form, in Bernard De Voto, ed., *The Journals of Lewis and Clark* (1953); and, in complete form, in R. G. Thwaites, ed., *Original Journals of the Lewis and Clark Expedition, 1804–1806, Printed from the Original Manuscripts* (7 vols. and an atlas, 1904–05). The 1814 edition of *The Lewis and Clark Expedition*, has been reprinted, with an Introduction by Archibald Hanna (3 vols., 1961). Another basic source is Elliott Coues, ed., *History of the Expedition Under the Command of Lewis and Clark* (4 vols., 1893; reprinted in 3 vols., 1965). Biographical studies include John Bakeless, *Lewis and Clark, Partners in Discovery* (1947); and Richard H. Dillon, *Meriwether Lewis, A Biography* (1965). See also, *The Field Notes of William Clark* (1964); Raymond D. Burrgoush, ed., *The Natural History of the Lewis and Clark Expedition* (1961); Donald Jackson, ed., *Letters of the Lewis and Clark Expedition, With Related Documents, 1783–1854* (1962); "Lewis and Clark Among the Oto," *Nebraska History*, 41 (September, 1960), 237–248.

FUR TRADERS AND MISSIONARIES
(CHAPTER 4)

For the expeditions of Pike and Long, the best sources remain the journals: Elliott Coues, ed., *The Expeditions of Zebulon Montgomery Pike* . . . (3 vols., 1895); and Edwin James, *Account of an Expedition from Pittsburgh to the Rocky Mountains* . . . (1823; reprinted in R. G. Thwaites, ed., *Early Western Travels*, 1905, Vols. XIV–XVI). W. Eugene Hollon, *The Lost Pathfinder: Zebulon Montgomery Pike* (1949) is also useful.

The classic work on the fur trade is Hiram M. Chittenden, *The American Fur Trade of the Far West* (3 vols., 1902), also available in an edition ed. by Stallo Vinton (2 vols., 1935), and in a reprint edition, with an introduction by Grace Lee Nute (2 vols., 1954). See also, Clarence L. Vandiveer, *The Fur Trade and Early Western Exploration* (1929); William J. Ghent, *The Early Far West* (1931); Paul C. Phillips, *The Fur Trade* (2 vols., 1961); Mari Sandoz, *The Beaver Men* (1964); John E. Sunder, *The Fur Trade on the Upper Missouri, 1840–1865* (1965); Lewis O. Saum, *The Fur Trader and the Indian* (1965); and Ray H. Mattison, "The Upper Missouri Fur Trade: Its Methods of Operation," *Nebraska History*, 42 (March, 1961), 1–28. For the career of Manuel Lisa, see Richard E. Oglesby, *Manuel Lisa and the Opening of the Missouri Fur Trade* (1963); and Walter B. Douglas, *Manuel Lisa, with Hitherto Unpublished Material, Annotated and Edited by Abraham P. Nasatir* (1964).

For a general treatment of the Yellowstone Expedition and Fort Atkinson, see Edgar Bruce Wesley, *Guarding the Frontier* (1935). See also Cardinal Goodwin, "A Larger View of the Yellowstone Expedition, 1819–1820," *Mississippi Valley Historical Review*, 4 (December, 1917), 299–313. Over the years, *Nebraska History* has contained a number of valuable articles on Fort Atkinson: Marvin F. Kivett, "Excavations at Fort Atkinson, Nebraska: A Preliminary Report," 40 (March, 1959), 39–66; Sally A. Johnson, "Cantonment Missouri, 1819–1820," 37 (June, 1956), 121–134; "Fort Atkinson at Council Bluffs," 38 (September, 1957), 229–236; "The Sixth's Elysian Fields: Fort Atkinson on the Council Bluffs," 40 (March, 1959), 1–38; Roger L. Nichols, ed., "General Henry Atkinson's Report of the Yellowstone Expedition of 1825," 44 (June, 1963), 65–82; Edgar B. Wesley, "Life at Fort Atkinson, 30 (December, 1949), 348–358.

No satisfactory general account of missionary activity in the region exists, although the general study of the missionary movement, Colin B. Goodykoontz, *Home Missions on the American Frontier* (1939) will be found useful. Father DeSmet's life is exhaustively treated in H. M. Chittenden and Alfred T. Richardson, *Life, Letters, and Travels of Father Pierre Jean DeSmet, S.J.* (4 vols., 1905); and more briefly in Helene Magaret, *Father DeSmet, Pioneer Priest of the Rockies* (1940). Nebraska State Historical Society, *Transactions and Reports*, contain some documentary material relating to the work of Missionaries in Nebraska: Samuel Allis, "Forty Years Among the Indians and on the Eastern Borders of Nebraska," II, 133–166; Elvira Gaston Platt, "Reminiscences of a Teacher Among the Nebraska Indians, 1843–1885," III, 125–143; "Extracts from the Diary of Rev. Moses Merrill, A Missionary to the Otoe Indians from 1832 to 1840," IV, 160–191.

Useful on the period and subjects treated in Chapter 4 is Everett Dick, *Vanguards of the Frontier* (1941).

THE GREAT ROAD WEST
(CHAPTER 5)

Dick, *Vanguards of the Frontier*, is useful here, too. A good general account of overland emigration to the Pacific is Jay Monaghan, *The Overland Trail* (1947); for the Oregon Trail specifically consult W. J. Ghent, *The Road to Oregon: A Chronicle of the Great Emigrant Trail* (1929), which though old is still useful. Irene D. Paden, *The Wake of the Prairie Schooner* (1944) retraces the overland routes in an interesting fashion. Bernard De Voto, *The Year of Decision: 1846* (1943) is particularly good on "manifest destiny" and the Mormons. For Fremont's expedition, the best source is the report, J. C. Fremont, *Report of the Exploring Expedition to the Rocky Mountains in the Year 1842* . . . (1845); a good biographical account is Allan Nevins, *Fremont: the West's Greatest Adventurer* (2 vols., 1928), which should be read in conjunction with De Voto's *Year of Decision*.

The Mormons have been the subject of a voluminous literature, much of it controversial. For their experiences in Nebraska a number of articles in *Nebraska History* will be useful: Jay Monaghan, "Handcarts on the Overland Trail," 30 (March, 1949), 3–18; A. R. Mortensen, "Mormons, Nebraska and the Way West," 46 (December, 1965), 259–272; E. Widtsoe Shumway, "Winter Quarters, 1846–1848," 35 (June, 1954), 115–125; 36 (March, 1955), 43–53.

On Fort Kearny see, Albert Watkins, "History of Fort Kearny," Nebraska State Historical Society, *Collections*, XVI, 227–267; Lillian M. Willman, "The History of Fort Kearny," Nebraska State Historical Society, *Publications*, XXI, 211–268; Lyle E. Mantor, "Fort Kearny and the Westward Movement," *Nebraska History*, 29 (September, 1948), 175–207; "Stage Coach and Freighter Days at Fort Kearny," *ibid.*, (December, 1948), 324–338. The definitive study of Fort Laramie is LeRoy Hafen and Francis M. Young, *Fort Laramie and the Pageant of the West* (1938).

Landmarks and facilities along the trail have been of considerable interest to historians. For those in Nebraska see particularly Merrill J. Mattes, *Scotts Bluff* (1958), and the same author's articles in *Nebraska History:* "Robidoux's Trading Post at 'Scott's Bluffs,' and the California Gold

Rush," 30 (June, 1949), 95–138; "Fort Mitchell, Scotts Bluff, Nebraska Territory," 33 (March, 1952), 1–34; "Chimney Rock on the Oregon Trail," 36 (March, 1955), 1–26. See also in *Nebraska History*: Earl R. Harris, "Courthouse and Jail Rocks: Landmarks on the Oregon Trail," 43 (March, 1962), 29–52; Robert W. Richmond, "Developments Along the Overland Trail from the Missouri River to Fort Laramie, Before 1854," 33 (September, 1952), 154–179; (December, 1952), 237–248.

Of the countless journals and reminiscences of the overland trail, only a few can be cited here. Jesse Applegate, "A Day with the Cow Column in 1843," *The Quarterly of the Oregon Historical Society*, 1 (December, 1900), 372–373, and frequently reprinted, is a classic account of life on the trail by one who participated in the "great migration" of 1843. For the Mormon Trail perhaps the most useful is *William Clayton's Journal* (1921). The best journal of the California gold rush is Georgia Willis Read and Ruth Gaines, eds., *Gold Rush: The Journals, Drawings and Other Papers of J. Goldsborough Bruff* (2 vols., 1944). An interesting composite journal of the Gold Rush is Archer B. Hulbert, *Forty-Niners* (1931; reprinted 1949).

THE KANSAS-NEBRASKA ACT

(CHAPTER 6)

The Kansas-Nebraska Act has been the subject of much controversial writing by American historians. The student should begin with Roy F. Nichols, "The Kansas-Nebraska Act: a Century of Historiography," *Mississippi Valley Historical Review*, 43 (September, 1956), 187–212. For general treatments of the failure of statesmanship in the 1850's of which the Kansas-Nebraska Act was a part, see Nichols, *The Disruption of American Democracy* (1948; reprinted 1962); and Allan Nevins, *Ordeal of the Union* (2 vols., 1947). Frank H. Hodder, "Genesis of the Kansas-Nebraska Act," *Proceedings of the State Historical Society of Wisconsin*, 1912, 69–86, and "The Railroad Background of the Kansas-Nebraska Act," *Mississippi Valley Historical Review*, 12 (June, 1925), 3–22 are useful older summaries. P. Orman Ray, *The Repeal of the Missouri Compromise* (1909), argues the question from the point of view expressed in the title and as a projection of Missouri politics.

Of particular importance are the works of James C. Malin: *Indian Policy and Westward Expansion* (1921); *The Nebraska Question* (1953); "Thomas Jefferson Sutherland, Nebraska Boomer," *Nebraska History*, 34 (September, 1953), 181–214; "The Nebraska Question: A Ten Year Record, 1844–1854," *ibid.*, 35 (March, 1954), 1–16; "The Motives of Stephen A. Douglas in the Organization of Nebraska Territory: A Letter Dated December 17, 1853," *Kansas Historical Quarterly*, 19 (November, 1951), 321–353; "Aspects of the Nebraska Question, 1852–1854," *ibid.*, 21 (May, 1953), 385–391.

Many of the foregoing are concerned, in part at least, with an analysis of the motives of Stephen A. Douglas. Throwing additional light on the subject are the biographies of Douglas, of which the best is George Fort Milton, *The Eve of Conflict: Stephen A. Douglas and the Needless War* (1934).

Documents relating to the provisional government of Nebraska territory are published in William E. Connelley, ed., *The Provisional Government of Nebraska Territory* . . . (1899). Hadley D. Johnson, "How the Kansas-Nebraska Line Was Established," Nebraska State Historical Society, *Transactions and Reports*, II, 80–92, is a discussion of the division of the territory by one who was a participant.

TERRITORIAL HISTORY
(CHAPTERS 7 AND 8)

The best and most detailed account of the establishment of territorial government will be found in Morton and Watkins, *Illustrated History of Nebraska*, I, 194–255. A briefer treatment is provided by Sheldon, *Nebraska: The Land and the People*, I, 238–263. These studies concentrate on the political history of the territory; on territorial politics, see also James C. Olson, *J. Sterling Morton* (1942), and the reminiscences of the early territorial pioneers published in Nebraska State Historical Society, *Transactions and Reports*.

Norman A. Graebner, "Nebraska's Missouri River Frontier, 1854–1860," *Nebraska History*, 42 (December, 1961), 213–236, is an excellent brief discussion of the urban aspects of Nebraska's territorial development. Donald F. Danker has a number of important articles on territorial town building in *Nebraska History*: "C. W. Giddings and the Founding of Table Rock," 34 (March, 1953), 33–54; "Columbus, A Territorial Town in the Platte Valley," 34 (December, 1953), 275–288; "The Nebraska Winter Quarters Company and Florence," 34 (March, 1956), 27–50. For early Omaha see Walker D. Wyman, "Omaha: Frontier Depot and Prodigy of Council Bluffs," *Nebraska History*, 27 (July–September, 1936), 143–155; for Bellevue see J. Q. Goss, "Bellevue, Its Past and Present," Nebraska State Historical Society, *Transactions and Reports*, II, 80–92, and William J. Shallcross, *Romance of a Village* (1954).

Everett Dick, *The Sod House Frontier* (1937; reprinted 1954), the standard work on the social and economic history of the plains, is particularly valuable for the territorial period. Also important are Morton-Watkins and Sheldon, cited above; volume II of the former contains much information on territorial banking, territorial products, the press, and various church groups. Nebraska's standard land history is Sheldon, *Land Systems and Land Policies in Nebraska* (1936), of which pp. 25–79 are useful for the territorial period. A brief summary of the educational history of the territory will be found in Helen Siampos, "Early Education in Nebraska," *Nebraska History*, 29 (June, 1948), 113–133.

Personal documents of importance are: Donald F. Danker, ed., *Mollie: The Journal of Mollie Dorsey Sanford in Nebraska and Colorado Territories, 1857–1866* (1959); Ruth K. Nuermberger, "Letters from Pioneer Nebraska by Edward R. Harden," *Nebraska History*, 27 (January–March, 1946), 18–47; George W. Barnes, "Pioneer Preacher," *ibid.* (April–June, 1946), 71–91. In addition, the publications of the Nebraska State Historical Society contain many reminiscences of territorial pioneers which are useful for social and economic as well as political history.

TRANSPORTATION
(CHAPTER 9)

The best summary of the history of transportation in the West is Oscar O. Winther, *The Transportation Frontier* (1964). Dick, *Vanguards of the Frontier* also contains much that is useful.

The standard work on Missouri River steamboating is H. M. Chittenden, *History of Early Steamboat Navigation on the Missouri River* (2 vols., 1903). See also: Joseph Mills Hanson, *The Conquest of the Missouri* (1946); William E. Lass, *A History of Steamboating on the Upper Missouri* (1962); Phil E. Chappell, "A History of the Missouri River," *Transactions of the Kansas State Historical Society*, IX, 237–316; Walker D. Wyman, "Missouri River Steamboatin'," *Nebraska History*, 27 (April–June, 1946), 92–103; William J. Petersen, "Steamboating on the Missouri River," *ibid.*, 35 (December, 1954), 255–275.

No satisfactory history of overland freighting exists. Raymond W. Settle and Mary Lund Settle, *Empire on Wheels* (1949) is an excellent study of the firm of Russell, Majors and Waddell. Alexander Majors, *Seventy Years on the Frontier* (1893) is a valuable reminiscence. For the stage coach and Pony Express, see LeRoy R. Hafen, *The Overland Mail* (1926). Also useful are: Frank E. Root and William E. Connelley, *The Overland Stage to California* (1901); Settle and Settle, *Saddles and Spurs: The Pony Express Saga* (1955); Merrill J. Mattes and Paul C. Henderson, "The Pony Express: Across Nebraska From St. Joseph to Fort Laramie," *Nebraska History*, 41 (June, 1960), 83–122; Norbert R. Mahnken, "The Sidney-Black Hills Trail," *ibid.*, 30 (September, 1949), 203–225. W. Turrentine Jackson, *Wagon Roads West* (1952) contains much of value, and Chap. 8 is particularly useful for the history of Nebraska.

Definitive histories of the Western Union Company and the Union Pacific Railroad Company remain to be written. The most recent and generally most satisfactory account of the building of the transcontinental railroad is Wesley S. Griswold, *A Work of Giants* (1962). Older works of value are Edwin L. Sabin, *Building the Pacific Railway* (1919) and Nelson

Trottman, *History of the Union Pacific* (1923). A popular biography of the man who built the Union Pacific is J. R. Perkins, *Trails, Rails, and War: The Life of General G. M. Dodge* (1929); Grenville M. Dodge, *How We Built the Union Pacific Railway, and Other Railway Papers and Addresses* (1910) is of interest and value. Of great importance is Wallace D. Farnham, "The Pacific Railroad Act of 1862," *Nebraska History*, 43 (September, 1962), 141–168.

ESTABLISHING THE STATE GOVERNMENT
(CHAPTERS 10 AND 12)

The best and most detailed source on the political history of Nebraska during the period of admission to the Union and establishment of the state government is Morton and Watkins, *Illustrated History of Nebraska*; a briefer and less useful account will be found in Sheldon, *Nebraska: The Land and the People*. For the struggle over statehood, see Albert Watkins, "How Nebraska Was Brought Into the Union," Nebraska State Historical Society, *Publications*, XVIII, 375–434; and Wallace Brown, "George L. Miller and the Struggle Over Nebraska Statehood," *Nebraska History*, 41 (December, 1960), 299–318.

The old standard history of Lincoln is Andrew J. Sawyer, ed., *Lincoln and Lancaster County* (1916), which discusses the founding and early development of the capital city in great detail and reproduces the Report of the Capital Commissioners on the location of the capital. More recent and more readable is Neale Copple, *Tower on the Plains* (1954). See also, Louise Pound, "The Legend of the Lincoln Salt Basin," *Western Folklore*, 10 (April, 1951), 109–116.

For the location and disposition of the state lands see Sheldon, *Land Systems and Land Policies in Nebraska*, pp. 219–285; Agnes Horton, "Nebraska's Agricultural College Land Grant," *Nebraska History*, 30 (March, 1949), 19–49; "The History of Nebraska's Saline Land Grant," *ibid.*, 40 (June, 1959), 89–104.

SETTLEMENT
(CHAPTERS 13 AND 14)

The standard work on Nebraska's land history is Sheldon, *Land Systems and Land Policies in Nebraska*. For a briefer statement, see Fred A. Shannon, *The Farmer's Last Frontier* (1945). Howard W. Ottoson, ed., *Land Use Policy and Problems in the United States* (1963) consists of the papers presented at the Homestead Centennial Symposium at the University of Nebraska in 1962; of particular value for the settlement period is Paul W. Gates, "The Homestead Act Free Land Policy in Operation, 1862–1935," which modifies his earlier article, "The Homestead Law in an Incongruous Land System," *American Historical Review*, 41 (July, 1936), 652–681. A useful compilation of source material will be found in Thomas Donaldson, *The Public Domain* (1884). For a general survey, see Roy M. Robbins, *Our Landed Heritage* (1942; reprinted 1962).

Essential to an understanding of the settlement of Nebraska is Richard C. Overton, *Burlington West: A Colonization History of the Burlington Railroad* (1941); also of importance is his *Burlington Route* (1965). Olson, *J. Sterling Morton* discusses railroad promotional activity. See also a number of articles in *Nebraska History*: James J. Blake, "The Brownville, Fort Kearney and Pacific Railroad," 29 (September, 1948), 238–272; Thomas M. Davis, "Building the Burlington Through Nebraska—A Summary View," 30 (December, 1949), 317–347; "Lines West!—The Story of George W. Holdrege," 31 (March, 1950), 25–47; (June, 1950), 107–125; (September, 1950), 204–225; C. Clyde Jones, "A Survey of the Agricultural Development Program of the Chicago, Quincy and Burlington Railroad," 30 (September, 1949), 226–256; Ray H. Mattison, "Burlington Tax Controversy in Nebraska Over the Federal Land Grants," 28 (April–June, 1947), 110–131; Overton, "Why Did the C. B. & Q. Build to Denver?" 40 (September, 1959), 177–206; and John D. Unruh, Jr., "The Burlington and Missouri River Railroad Brings the Mennonites to Nebraska, 1873–1878," 45 (June, 1964), 177–206.

James I. Dowie, *Prairie Grass Dividing* (1959) is a useful study of certain aspects of the Swedish immigration to Nebraska. See also, Dowie, "Sven Gustaf Larson, Pioneer Pastor to the Swedes of Nebraska," *Nebraska History*, 40 (September, 1959), 207–222; Louise Pound, "Olaf Bergstrom: Swedish Pioneer," *ibid.*, 31 (March, 1950), 64–74; and Joseph Alexis, "Swedes in Nebraska," Nebraska State Historical Society, *Proceedings and Collections*, XIX, 78–85. For the Bohemians see Sarka B. Hrbkova, "Bohemians in Nebraska," Nebraska State Historical Society, *Publications*, XIX, 140–158. Much work remains to be done on immigrant groups in Nebraska.

Dick, *The Sod House Frontier* is the standard treatment of the social and economic history of homesteading. See also, Martha Ferguson McKeown, *Them Was the Days* (1950; reprinted 1961), and the following articles in *Nebraska History*: Edward Everett Dale, "Wood and Water: Twin Problems of the Prairie Plains," 29 (June, 1948), 87–106; Dick, "Free Homes for the Millions," 43 (December, 1962), 211–228; Robert N. Manley, "In the Wake of the Grasshoppers: Public Relief in Nebraska, 1874–1875," 44 (December, 1963), 255–276; Homer E. Socolofsky, "Why Settle in Nebraska—The Case of John Rogers Maltby," 44 (June, 1963), 123–131; Walter Prescott Webb, "The Story of Some Prairie Inventions," 34 (December, 1953), 229–244; and Walker D. Wyman, ed., "Reminiscences of a Nebraska Pioneer of the '70's," 28 (July–September, 1947), 187–195.

A discussion of the "desert theory" will be found in Ralph C. Morris, "The Notion of a Great American Desert East of the Rockies," *Mississippi*

Valley Historical Review, 13 (September, 1926), 190–200. There is no published history of the Granger movement in Nebraska, but for a survey of the movement generally, see Solon J. Buck, *The Granger Movement* (1913; reprinted 1963).

THE RANGE CATTLE INDUSTRY

(CHAPTER 15)

General histories of the range cattle industry include: Edward Everett Dale, *The Range Cattle Industry* (1930); Ernest S. Osgood, *The Day of the Cattleman* (1929; reprinted 1957); Louis Pelzer, *The Cattlemen's Frontier* (1926); and Mari Sandoz, *The Cattlemen* (1958). On the destruction of the bison, see Sandoz, *The Buffalo Hunters* (1954); and Wayne Gard, *The Great Buffalo Hunt* (1959).

Everett N. Dick, "The Long Drive," Kansas State Historical Society, *Collections*, XVII, 27–97, is a convenient summary of the history of trail driving north from Texas. Other accounts of the long drive north are James H. Cook, "Driving Texas Long-Horn Cattle Through Nebraska," Nebraska State Historical Society, *Publications*, XVIII, 260–268; and the following articles in *Nebraska History*: Cook, "Trailing Texas Longhorn Cattle Through Nebraska," 10 (October–December, 1927), 339–443; "Early Days in Ogallala," 14 (April–June, 1933), 86–99; "The Texas Trail," 16 (October–December, 1935), 229–240; Marshall M. Davis, "Last Trail Herd of Texas Longhorns," 19 (October–December, 1938), 374–376; Norbert R. Mahnken, "Early Nebraska Markets for Texas Cattle," 26 (January–March, 1945), 3–25; "Ogallala—Nebraska's Cowboy Capital," 28 (April–June, 1947), 85–109.

The development of the cattle industry in the Sandhills is treated in William D. Aeschbacher, "Development of the Sandhill Lake Country," *Nebraska History*, 27 (July–September, 1946), 205–221; "Development of Cattle Raising in the Sandhills," 28 (January–March, 1947), 41–64; and H. E. Wolf, "Taming the Sandhills," *The Westerners, New York Posse Brand Book*, 1959.

Accounts of individual cattlemen include A. B. Snyder and Nellie Snyder Yost, *Pinnacle Jake* (1951, reprinted 1962); and the following articles from *Nebraska History*: Robert H. Burns, "The Newman Ranches: Pioneer Cattle Ranches of the West," 34 (March, 1953), 22–32; James C. Dahlman, "Recollections of Cowboy Life in Western Nebraska," X (October–December, 1927), 335–339; and A. B. Wood, "The Coad Brothers: Panhandle Cattle Kings," 19 (January–March, 1938), 28–43.

THE EIGHTIES
(Chapters 16 and 17)

Many of the references cited for Chapters 13 and 14 will also be found useful for the Eighties, as will those cited below for Chapter 18.

Sawyer, *Lincoln and Lancaster County* and Copple, *Tower on the Plains* are useful for the development of Lincoln, as is Everett N. Dick, "Problems of the Post-Frontier Prairie City as Portrayed by Lincoln, Nebraska, 1880–1890," *Nebraska History*, 27 (April–June, 1947), 132–143. For Omaha see Alfred Sorenson, *The Story of Omaha* (1923). The development of urban and interurban transportation is treated in three articles by E. Bryant Phillips in *Nebraska History*: "Horsecar Days and Ways in Nebraska," 29 (March, 1948), 16–32; "Interurban Projects in Nebraska," 30 (June, 1949), 163–182; "Interurban Projects in and Around Omaha," 30 (September, 1949), 257–285. See also, Charles Jenkins, "The Kearney Cotton Mill—A Bubble That Burst," *Nebraska History*, 38 (September, 1957), 207–220.

Donald L. McMurray, *The Great Burlington Strike of 1888* (1956) has some significance for Nebraska. A specific treatment of labor unrest in Nebraska is Roland M. Gephart, "Politicians, Soldiers and Strikes: The Reorganization of the Nebraska Militia and the Omaha Strike of 1882," *Nebraska History*, 46 (June, 1965), 89–120.

Mari Sandoz, *Old Jules* (1937; reprinted 1962) is a moving story of life in northwest Nebraska during the last two decades of the nineteenth century and the first two decades of the twentieth; Ora A. Clement and W. H. O'Gara, *In All Its Fury: A History of the Blizzard of January 12, 1888* (1947) is a detailed account of the most celebrated natural disaster in the history of the state.

POPULISM
(Chapter 18)

There is a growing literature on Populism, much of it controversial. The standard work is John D. Hicks, *The Populist Revolt* (1931; reprinted 1961). Hicks' treatment of the Populists is generally sympathetic. More recent work is highly critical; see especially Richard Hofstadter, *The Age of Reform: From Bryan to F.D.R.* (1955; reprinted 1960). Rejecting many of Hofstadter's interpretations are Norman Pollack, *The Populist Response to Industrial America, Midwestern Populist Thought* (1962); and Walter T. K. Nugent, *The Tolerant Populists* (1963). David F. Trask, "A Note on the Politics of Populism," *Nebraska History*, 46 (June, 1965), 157–161, is suggestive of possible new interpretations; Stanley B. Parsons, "Who Were the Nebraska Populists?" *ibid.*, 44 (June, 1963), 83–100 suggests, on the basis of an intensive study of seven Nebraska counties, that the conflict between farmer and villager was of particular significance during the Populist period.

An older study of the conditions that produced Populism is Arthur F. Bentley, "The Condition of the Western Farmer as Illustrated by the Economic History of a Nebraska Township," *Johns Hopkins University Studies in Historical and Political Science* (1893). See also John D. Barnhart, "Rainfall and the Populist Party in Nebraska," *American Political Science Review*, 19 (1925), 527–540; Hallie Farmer, "The Economic Background of Frontier Populism," *Mississippi Valley Historical Review*, 10 (March, 1924), 406–427; and "The Railroads and Frontier Populism," *ibid.*, 13 (December, 1926), 387–397. Alan G. Bogue, "Farmer Debtors in Pioneer Pebble," *Nebraska History*, 35 (June, 1954), 81–114, uses Pebble Township, Dodge County, to modify the standard Populist view of the moneylender, a position which is discussed definitively in his *Money at Interest: The Farm Mortgage on the Middle Border* (1955).

Biographical sketches of important Nebraska Populists include the following in *Nebraska History*: Marie U. Harmer and James L. Sellers, "Charles H. Van Wyck—Soldier and Statesman," 12 (1929, printed 1931), 81–128, 190–246, 322–373; 13 (1932), 3–36; N. C. Abbott, "Silas A. Holcomb," 26 (October–December, 1945), 187–200; 27 (January–March, 1946), 3–17; Addison E. Sheldon, William Vincent Allen," 19 (July–September, 1938), 191–206; and "John Holbrook Powers," (October–December, 1938), 331–339. Works on William Jennings Bryan are cited below.

POLITICAL REALIGNMENT
(CHAPTER 19)

A good general survey of American history in the period is George E. Mowry, *The Era of Theodore Roosevelt* (1958). Sheldon, *Nebraska: The Land and the People*, I, 732–868, provides a good general review for Nebraska.

Of the numerous biographies of William Jennings Bryan, the most satisfactory promises to be Paolo E. Coletta, *William Jennings Bryan*, a projected two-volume work, of which Volume I, *Political Evangelist, 1860–1908*, was published in 1964; this incorporates many of Coletta's articles in *Nebraska History*. Limited in scope, but essential, are two books by Paul W. Glad: *The Trumpet Soundeth: William Jennings Bryan and His Democracy* (1960), and *McKinley, Bryan, and the People* (1964). Lawrence W. Levine, *Defender of the Faith, William Jennings Bryan: The Last Decade, 1915–1925* (1965) is useful on the later years of the Great Commoner's life. Richard Hofstadter, *The American Political Tradition and the Men Who Made It* (1960) includes a highly critical essay, "William Jennings Bryan: The Democrat as Revivalist." Among the older biographies which might be mentioned are: Paxton Hibben, *The Peerless Leader, William Jennings Bryan* (1929); and M. R. Werner, *Bryan* (1925). Bryan,

Memoirs (1925) is valuable, as is Bryan, *The First Battle, A Story of the Campaign of 1896* (1897).

For the early career of George W. Norris, the definitive study is Richard Lowitt, *George W. Norris: The Making of a Progressive, 1861–1912* (1963), the first of a projected two-volume biography. Compare this with Norris' autobiography, *Fighting Liberal* (1945).

Arthur F. Mullen, *Western Democrat* (1940) is a lively and valuable reminiscence. Victor Rosewater, *Back Stage in 1912* (1932) is the personal account of the Nebraskan who served as chairman of the Republican National Committee in that year; Donald F. Danker, "The Election of 1912 in Nebraska," *Nebraska History*, 37 (December, 1956), 283–310 is a useful summary. Russel B. Nye, *Midwestern Progressive Politics* (1951) has much of value for an understanding of Nebraska. Fred Carey, *Mayor Jim: The Life of James Dahlman* (1930) is an account of Omaha's colorful cowboy-mayor.

THE FADING FRONTIER
(CHAPTER 20)

Sandoz, *Old Jules*, cited earlier, is a classic account of life in northwest Nebraska during the late years of the nineteenth century. H. C. Filley, *Every Day Was New* (1950), provides an interesting portrait of life in southeastern Nebraska and in Lincoln. Also of value for Lincoln is Annie L. Miller, "The Social Life of Pioneer Lincoln," *Nebraska History*, 27 (January–March, 1946), 47–57. Mary Wilma M. Hargreaves, *Dry Farming in the Northern Great Plains, 1900–1925* (1957) has much that is of value for Nebraska. Other sources for the agricultural history of the state during the period are: Arthur R. Reynolds, "The Kinkaid Act and Its Effects on Western Nebraska," *Agricultural History*, 23 (January, 1949), 20–29; Gilbert C. Fite, "Flight From the Farm," *Nebraska History*, 40 (September, 1959), 159–176; A. Bower Sageser, "Attempted Economic Adjustments in Holt County During the 1890's," *ibid.* (June, 1959), 105–118. The bulletins issued by the Experiment Station, College of Agriculture, University of Nebraska, contain much that is helpful. Nebraska's role in the Spanish-American War is well covered in four articles by J. R. Johnson in *Nebraska History*: "Nebraska's 'Rough Riders' in the Spanish-American War," 29 (June, 1948), 105–112; "The Saga of the First Nebraska in the Philippines," 30 (June, 1949), 139–162; "The Second Nebraska's 'Battle' of Chickamauga," 32 (June, 1951), 77–93; "Imperialism in Nebraska," 44 (September, 1963), 141–166.

NEBRASKA AND WORLD WAR I
(CHAPTER 21)

Relatively little has been written on Nebraska's military participation in World War I. For General Pershing, see Frederick Palmer, *John J.*

Pershing, General of the Armies (1948); Donald L. Smythe, "John J. Pershing at the University of Nebraska, 1891–1895," *Nebraska History*, 43 (September, 1962); "The Early Years of John J. Pershing," *Missouri Historical Review*, 48 (October, 1963), 1–20. Bascom N. Timmons, *Portrait of an American: Charles G. Dawes* (1953) devotes some attention to Dawes' military career. *A Military History of Nebraska* (mimeographed, 1939) contains much useful information. The "home front" is ably treated in Robert N. Manley, "The Nebraska State Council of Defense and the Non-Partisan League," *Nebraska History*, 43 (December, 1962), 229–252; for the foreign language problem which grew out of the war, see Jack W. Rodgers, "The Foreign Language Issue in Nebraska, 1918–1923," *ibid.*, 39 (March, 1958), 1–22. Theodore Saloutos and John D. Hicks, *Agricultural Discontent in the Middle West, 1900–1939* (1951; reprinted 1964) is valuable on agriculture and the Non-Partisan League. H. C. Filley, *Effects of Inflation and Deflation Upon Nebraska Agriculture, 1914–1932* (1934) and Eleanor Hinman, *History of Farm Land Prices in Eleven Nebraska Counties* (1934) are useful.

ADAPTING GOVERNMENT TO THE MACHINE AGE
(Chapter 22)

Sheldon, *Nebraska: The Land and the People*, I, 961–1097, discusses in some detail the constitutional convention and the decade of the Twenties. A number of relatively recent articles in *Nebraska History* deal with various aspects of the Twenties: Robert E. Bader, "The Curtailment of Railroad Service in Nebraska, 1920–1941," 36 (March, 1955), 27–42; R. E. Dale, "Back to Normal," 38 (September, 1957), 179–206; C. Clyde Jones, "Purebred Dairy Sire Development in Nebraska," 42 (September, 1961), 191–200; Maurice C. Latta, "The Economic Development of Custer County Through World War I and the New Era, 1914–1929," 33 (September, 1952), 139–153; Clinton Warne, "The Acceptance of the Automobile in Nebraska," 37 (September, 1956), 221–236; "Some Effects of the Introduction of the Automobile on Highways and Land Values in Nebraska," 38 (March, 1957), 43–58; Floyd W. Rodine, "The County Agent and the Nebraska Farm Bureau," 36 (September, 1955), 205–212; Kurt Wimer, "Senator Hitchcock and the League of Nations," 44 (September, 1963), 189–204. The career of Governor McKelvie is treated in Bruce Nicoll and Ken R. Keller, *Sam McKelvie: Son of the Soil* (1954).

DEPRESSION AND WAR
(Chapters 23 and 24)

Sheldon, *Nebraska: The Land and the People*, I, 961–1097, discusses the politics of the period in some detail. Gilbert C. Fite, *George N. Peek and the Fight for Farm Parity* (1954), and John R. Crampton, *The National*

Farmers Union (1965), while dealing with the national situation, are of value for the understanding of the local problem. Useful articles in *Nebraska History* include: Walter Johnson, "Politics in the Midwest," 32 (March, 1951), 1–19; Maurice C. Latta, "The Economic Effects of Drouth and Depression Upon Custer County, 1929–1942," 33 (December, 1952), 221–236; John L. Shover, "The Farm Holiday Movement in Nebraska," 43 (March, 1962), 53–78.

No comprehensive story of Nebraska's participation in World War II is available, but much of interest will be found in James A. Huston, *Biography of a Battalion* (1950), a detailed history of the Third Battalion, 134th Infantry Regiment, during World War II.

Many books and articles cited for Chapters 21, 22, and 25 are also of value here.

CONSERVATION, IRRIGATION, PUBLIC POWER
(CHAPTER 25)

Robert E. Firth, *Public Power in Nebraska: A Report on State Ownership* (1962) is a good general survey. No comparable work exists for the history of either irrigation or conservation, although Gene E. Hamaker, *Irrigation Pioneers: A History of the Tri-County Project to 1935* is a careful study of both irrigation and power in the Tri-County Area. Marquis Childs, *The Farmer Takes a Hand: The Electric Power Revolution in Rural America* (1952) is general but useful; more specific on rural electrification is H. S. Person, "The Rural Electrification Administration in Perspective," *Agricultural History*, 24 (April, 1950), 70–88. Supplementing Firth on municipal power is C. G. Wallace and Harold O. Johnson, "Municipally Owned Power Plants in Nebraska," *Nebraska History*, 43 (September, 1962), 197–202. Mullen, *Western Democrat*, and Norris, *Fighting Liberal*, are valuable on the controversy over irrigation and public power. The *Nebraska Blue Book*, the reports of the Nebraska Department of Water Resources, the proceedings of the Nebraska Irrigation Association, and various reports issued by the State Department of Agriculture and Inspection and the State-Federal Division of Agricultural Statistics provide much useful information. Olson, *J. Sterling Morton* is useful on the establishment and growth of Arbor Day; Raymond J. Pool, "Fifty Years on the Nebraska National Forest," *Nebraska History*, 34 (September, 1953), 139–180, is an excellent account of the development of Nebraska's man-made national forest.

THE UNICAMERAL LEGISLATURE
(CHAPTER 26)

The standard work is John P. Senning, *The One-House Legislature* (1937). A newer work, which provides a careful analysis of the operation of the Nebraska legislature, is Adam C. Breckenridge, *One House for Two* (1957). Roger V. Shumate, "The Nebraska Unicameral Legislature," *The Western Political Quarterly*, 5 (September, 1952), 504–512, is a thoughtful discussion by one who both observed and participated in the deliberations of the unicameral legislature. Norris, *Fighting Liberal,* is valuable on the struggle surrounding the adoption of the unicameral system.

RECENT HISTORY
(CHAPTER 27)

Many of the works cited for Chapters 23–26 are also of value here. A general study of considerable significance is Kraenzel, *The Great Plains in Transition* (1955). Much has been written on the problems of the Missouri River Basin. Of particular interest are: *Missouri: Land and Water,* Report of the Missouri Basin Survey Commission (1953); Rufus Terral, *The Missouri Valley, Land of Drouth, Flood, and Promise* (1947); Henry C. Hart, *The Dark Missouri* (1957); and Thomas H. Langevin, "Development of Multiple-Purpose Water Planning by the Federal Government in the Missouri Basin," *Nebraska History,* 34 (March, 1953), 1–21. The *Nebraska Blue Book,* published in even-numbered years, will be found very useful. Much interesting information will be found in the publications of various state agencies, particularly the reports of the Department of Agriculture and Economic Development, the State-Federal Division of Agricultural Statistics, the Department of Roads, and the State Department of Education. *Outdoor Nebraskaland,* published monthly by the Game, Forestation and Parks Commission, contains many articles of interest.

CULTURAL FACTORS
(CHAPTER 28)

Perhaps the best brief interpretation of the cultural factors in Nebraska life is Willa Cather's essay, "Nebraska: The End of the First Cycle," most easily available in Virginia Faulkner, ed., *Roundup: A Nebraska Reader* (1957), which also contains many other pieces of value. The works cited in the text are useful in connection with this chapter.

Histories of various church groups will be found in Morton and Watkins, *Illustrated History of Nebraska,* Vol. II. The Catholics are treated in Henry W. Casper, *History of the Catholic Church in Nebraska,* a projected three-volume work, of which Volume I, *The Church on the Northern Plains,* appeared in 1960; the Congregationalists in Motier A. Bullock, *Congregational Nebraska* (1905); the Methodists, in David Marquette, *A History of Methodism, First Half Century* (1904); and in Everett E. Jackman, *The Nebraska Methodist Story* (1954). Generally useful is Orville H. Zabel, *God and Caesar in Nebraska: A Study of the Legal Relationship of*

Church and State (1955). An interesting account of missionary work in western Nebraska is C. H. Frady, "First Years Gospel Giving on the Frontier," *Nebraska History*, 10 (October–December, 1927), 269–325. George W. Barnes, "Pioneer Preacher," *ibid.*, 27 (April–June, 1946), 71–91, throws light on the early churches of Nebraska.

A good brief account of education will be found in Helen Siampos, "Early Education in Nebraska," *ibid.*, 29 (June, 1948), 113–133. Howard W. Caldwell, *Education in Nebraska* (1902), is invaluable on the early history of education. Robert P. Crawford, *These Fifty Years* (1925), discusses the early history of agricultural education. Alvin Johnson, *Pioneer's Progress* (1952; reprinted 1960), provides an interesting account of both student and faculty life at the new University of Nebraska. Frank E. Weyer, *Presbyterian Colleges and Academies in Nebraska* (1940), is useful on one group of denominational colleges. Among histories of individual colleges are: William E. Christensen, *Saga of the Tower: A History of Dana College and Trinity Seminary* (1959); James Iverne Dowie, *Prairie Grass Dividing* (1959), a history of Luther College; and *History of Doane College* (1957).

For the arts, the best general survey is that found in the Federal Writers' Project's *Nebraska: A Guide to the Cornhusker State* (1939). Clarissa Bucklin, *Nebraska Art and Artists* (1932) is a useful compilation. Part of this discussion of literature is based on James C. Olson, "The Literary Tradition in Pioneer Nebraska," *Prairie Schooner*, 24 (Summer, 1950), 161–167; Dick, *The Sod House Frontier*, is generally useful; of value for newspaper history is Benjamin Pfeiffer, "The Role of Joseph E. Johnson and His Pioneer Newspapers in the Development of Territorial Nebraska," *Nebraska History*, 40 (June, 1959), 119–136. On Willa Cather, see: Mildred R. Bennett, *The World of Willa Cather* (1951; revised ed. 1961); Introduction, *Willa Cather's Collected Short Fiction, 1892–1912* (1965); E. K. Brown, completed by Leon Edel, *Willa Cather: A Critical Biography* (1953); Robert L. Gale, "Willa Cather and the Usable Past," *Nebraska History*, 42 (September, 1961), 181–190; Maxwell Geismar, "Willa Cather: Lady in the Wilderness," in *Last of the Provincials: The American Novel, 1925–1940* (1949; reprinted 1959); Edith Lewis, *Willa Cather Living: A Memoir* (1953); Elizabeth Shepley Sergeant, *Willa Cather: A Memoir* (1953; reprinted 1963); Bernice Slote, "Willa Cather and Her First Book," in Willa Cather, *April Twilights (1903)* (1962); and "Writer in Nebraska" and "The Kingdom of Art," in *The Kingdom of Art: Willa Cather's First Principles and Critical Theories, 1893–1896* (1966). For autobiographical sketches by Mari Sandoz, see "Recollections," in *Hostiles and Friendlies: Selected Short Writings of Mari Sandoz* (1959), "Outpost in New York," *Prairie Schooner*, 37 (Summer, 1963), 95–106; and *The Christmas of the Phonograph Records* (1966).

Index